THE AMERICAN FAMILY: Past, Present, and Future

THE AMERICAN FAMILY: Past, Present, and Future

MICHAEL GORDON
University of Connecticut

RANDOM HOUSE New York

To The Memory of Michael Serber

First Edition
987654321
 All inquiries should be addressed to Random House, Inc., 201 East 50th Street, New York, N.Y. 10022. Published in the United States by Random House, Inc., and simultaneously in Canada by Random House of Canada Limited, Toronto.

Library of Congress Cataloging in Publication Data

Gordon, Michael.
The American family.

Bibliography: p.
Includes index.
1. Family—United States—History. I. Title.
HQ535.G662 301.42'0973 77-22689
ISBN 0-394-31722-X

Manufactured in the United States of America. Composed by Datagraphics, Phoenix, Arizona. Printed and bound by R. R. Donnelley & Sons Co., Crawfordsville, Indiana.

Picture Editor: R. Lynn Goldberg
Picture Researcher: Roberta Guerette
Designed by Brenda Kamen

ACKNOWLEDGMENTS

Excerpts from Michael Gordon, *The American Family in Social Historical Perspective* (New York: St. Martin's Press, 1973), pp. 1–5.

Excerpts from Nelson M. Blake, *The Road to Reno* (New York: Macmillan, 1962), pp. 61–62, 119–120, and 158. Reprinted with permission of Macmillan Publishing Co., Inc. © Nelson M. Blake 1962.

Excerpts from John Scanzoni, *Opportunity and the Family* (New York: The Free Press, 1970) pp. 21, 22, and 187. Reprinted with permission of Macmillan Publishing Co., Inc. Copyright © 1970 by the Free Press, a Division of Macmillan Publishing Co., Inc.

Excerpts from Daniel R. Miller and Guy E. Swanson, *The Changing American Parent* (New York: Wiley, 1958), pp. 40, 44, 56, and 97.

Excerpts from William J. Goode, *World Revolution and Family Patterns* (New York: The Free Press, 1963), pp. 56, 81, and 590–591.

Excerpts from John Demos, *Little Commonwealth* (New York: Oxford University Press, 1970), pp. 73–75, 124, 134–135, 140, 152, and 154.

Excerpts from Robert Smuts, *Women and Work in America* (New York: Schochen Books, 1971), pp. 6, 11, and 38. Copyright © 1959, Columbia University Press (Schochen edition 1971).

Tabular material from Daniel Yankelovich, *The New Morality* (New York: McGraw-Hill, 1974), Chapters 2 and 3. Copyright © 1974 by the JDR 3rd Fund. Used with permission of the McGraw-Hill Book Company.

Excerpts from Robert W. Fogel and Stanley L. Engerman, *Time on the Cross* (Boston: Little, Brown, 1974), pp. 49, 134, and 141. Copyright © 1974 by Little, Brown and Company, Inc.

Table from Michael Young and Peter Willmott, *Family and Kinship in East London* (London: Penguin, 1962), p. 36. Reprinted by permission of Routledge & Kegan Paul and by permission of Humanities Press, Inc.

Figure 8, from T. H. Hollingsworth, *Historical Demography,* p. 381. Reprinted by permission of Cambridge University Press, publisher.

Tables from Michael Anderson, "Household Structure and the Industrial Revolution" in Peter Laslett (ed.), *Household and Family in Past Time* (New York: Cambridge University Press, 1972), pp. 219 and 220.

Francis Place's Contraceptive Handbill. Reprinted by permission of the British Library Board.

Excerpts from Ira L. Reiss, "The Universality of the Family: A Conceptual Analysis" in *Journal of Marriage and the Family,* Volume 27 (November 1965), p. 441.

Table from Herbert G. Gutman, "Persistent Myths About the Afro-American Family" in *Journal of Interdisciplinary History,* Volume VI (Autumn 1975), p. 196. Reprinted by permission of the *Journal of Interdisciplinary History* and The M.I.T. Press, Cambridge, Massachusetts.

Table from Charles F. Westoff, "Trends in Contraceptive Practice: 1965–1973" in *Family Planning Perspectives,* Volume 8 (March/April 1976), p. 56.

Table from Cynthia F. Epstein, *Woman's Place* (University of California Press, 1971), p. 7. Copyright © 1970 by the Regents of the University of California; reprinted by permission of the University of California Press.

Table from Daniel S. Smith, "The Dating of the American Sexual Revolution" in M. Gordon (ed.), *The American Family in Social Historical Perspective* (New York: St. Martin's Press, 1973), p. 327.

Table from Ethel Shanas and Philip M. Hauser, "Zero Population Growth and the Family Life of Old People" in *Journal of Social Issues,* Volume 30, No. 4 (1974), p. 85.

Excerpts from Eleanor Macklin, "Heterosexual Cohabitation Among Unmarried College Students" in *Family Coordinator,* Volume 21 (October 1972), pp. 465, 466, and 467.

Tables from Melvin Zelnick and John F. Kantner, "Sexual and Contraceptive Experience of Young Unmarried Women in the United States, 1976 and 1971," *Family Planning Perspectives,* Volume 9 (March/April 1977), pp. 56 and 61. © John Kantner May 25, 1977.

Excerpts from Philip Larkin, "Annus Mirabilis" from his collection *High Windows* (New York: Farrar, Straus, and Giroux, 1974), p. 34. Copyright © 1974 by Philip Larkin.

PREFACE

This book was written because, as someone who regularly taught and did research in the sociology of the family, I found myself dissatisfied with all currently available texts. While many were comprehensive and well-written, they lacked the perspective I felt was needed to integrate the subject matter that is normally covered in such texts. More specifically, none of these books conveyed to students a sense of how the present relates to the past—where there was continuity, discontinuity, and why. With this in mind, I decided to write a text that would show the links between the body of literature familiar to most family sociologists and the findings being generated by those working in the new social history of the family.

Among the more provocative and significant developments in the social sciences since World War II has been the application of new techniques to the study of historical phenomena that were previously neglected. Historians who previously limited their research to monumental events and pivotal people began to investigate the form and quality of everyday life in past time. Sociologists who had narrowly focused on contemporary American society broadened their scope to include comparative material drawn from other cultures and from other eras in their own culture. An area in which the interests of historians and sociologists converged was the family. By using techniques initially developed by demographers and by developing others of their own, they explored historical aspects of domestic life that had previously appeared to be inaccessible, and in the process they offered us new insights and demolished some long cherished beliefs.

It is probably fair to say that a great deal of sociological thinking on the family, and other areas as well for that matter, has until recently been based on linear models of change. For example, we have been presented with a picture of increasingly permissive premarital sexual behavior. As we shall see in the chapter on courtship, there is growing evidence to suggest that a cyclical rather than a linear model is appropriate here. That is to say, patterns of premarital intercourse seem to have been relatively low in the nineteenth century compared not only with the twentieth century but with the eighteenth as well. Moreover, we find that we can no longer talk about the nineteenth century as though it were of one piece; rates of premarital intercourse appear to have been on the rise in this country during the second half of that century. Sexual behavior is not the only area in which such divergence with linear models of change has been discovered. Household composition also shows ups and downs over time that were previously unrecognized. For example, three-generation households seem, contrary to what was once thought, to be more common in early industrial cities than in rural areas before the industrial revolution. Findings such as these force us to rethink our assumptions about the family and develop new theories that take into account the kinds of change that do not move in a direct line toward greater simplicity or complexity.

Apart from trying to show the relevance of history for a complete understanding of family phenomena, I have also attempted to select areas which are sometimes neglected or given short shrift in other texts. Thus, I have included chapters on households; the work of women inside and outside of the home; and the family life of the elderly. Each of these areas has in recent years emerged as a subject of developing scholarly concern and each represents new emphasis and interests in the sociology of the family. By adding a discussion of them to the more frequently encountered areas such as courtship and socialization, I feel that the student will leave this book not only with a more complete picture of the American family, but also with a better appreciation of the field of family sociology.

A number of people at Random House have assisted me during the period between initial concept and publication of this book. While a special note of thanks is owed to David Bartlett, now with Temple University Press, I should also like to express my appreciation to Glenn Cowley, Barry Fetterolf, and Fred Burns. Since some recognition of one's family is almost obligatory in this context, I would like to say that my own, nuclear and extended, has probably without realizing it kept me humble by continually making me aware of the limitations of my own expertise.

M.G.

CONTENTS

TABLES

FIGURES

THE AMERICAN FAMILY: Past, Present, and Future

"The Talcott Family" by Deborah Goldsmith. *(Abby Aldrich Rockefeller Collection, Colonial Williamsburg)*

INTRODUCTION

1

Textbooks are usually written by specialists in the field covered by the book. My own special area in sociology is the family. There are few things, if any, that I am more concerned with than the family and phenomena that relate to it. I read books about the family, I do formal research about the family, I teach about the family, I go to movies about the family, and when I am doing none of the above, I am often thinking, "What are the implications for the family of what I am doing or observing?" This preoccupation with familial matters is not the sort of thing I expect most of my readers to bring to the book, nor, for that matter, do I expect them to leave the book with such a preoccupation. Still, I do hope to be able to convey to the reader what it is about the family that makes it for me and for many of my colleagues the most interesting area of that most interesting discipline, sociology.

In the eyes of many, the family is an embattled institution holding off assault after assault from the forces of darkness. Michael Novak, a professor of philosophy and a well-known author, made the following statement in *Harper's* not long ago:

> Choosing to have a family used to be uninteresting. It is, today, an act of intelligence and courage. To love family life, to see in family life the most potent moral, intellectual, and political cell in the body politic is to be marked today as a heretic [1976:37].

This sort of family fundamentalism in a magazine known for the sophistication and liberalism of its readers is noteworthy, if only because it gives the lie to the claim that such views are only held by scripture-quoting, down-home types in the more remote reaches of the country. In fact, concern over the safety, sanctity and, most importantly, the viability of the family is a theme that can be discerned in popular and professional literature throughout this century, and considerably earlier as well. Why, we must ask, is the family felt to be so threatened when most social indicators, as we shall show later, give little cause for alarm? This book was in part written to answer that very question.

Some inkling of the kind of alarm about the family that is evident today can be found in the Novak article quoted above, in which the author sets forth what he apparently feels are two key social maxims:

1. *What strengthens the family strengthens society.*
2. *If things go well with the family, life is worth living, when the family falters, life falls apart* [emphasis Novak, 1976:38].

For Novak, and for many others as well, the future of the family and the future of civilized life go hand in hand. Such thinkers hold that "What was, should be." But as we shall see, what is causing Professor Novak so much distress is really the behavior of a small minority.

When anyone does anything that sets himself or herself apart from the straight and narrow, it often calls forth considerably more attention than it deserves, and when there is a group of people involved in the unconventional, their behavior is often seen as having more wide-ranging implications than it in fact has. For example, we have recently witnessed a growth in voluntary childlessness among married couples. Some interpreters of the social scene feel that this means that the decision to have a child is becoming a statement of unusual commitment to family life (see the first Novak quote above). However, when we look at the statistics on this phenomenon we see that while since 1940 there has been a growth in voluntary childlessness, the proportion of the population involved is quite small. For example, in the early 1970s a survey of 1,600 married women in Toronto found that only 1.1 percent *planned* never to become parents (Balakrishnan et al. quoted in Veevers, 1974:312). Yet, given the tendency of people to make too much of the behavior they observe without checking national trends (a particular problem for writers and academics, whose circle of friends is hardly representative of America), we find a minority phenomenon such as this being made into an ominous trend. The same kind of exaggeration takes place in regard to group marriages, cohabitation, and certainly divorce—topics which will be discussed in depth later on.

The "what was, should be" syndrome involves the assumption that since things now are not what they were a generation or two ago, they have somehow gotten worse. In our discussion of household size in Chapter 3, we shall have occasion to refer to what William Goode (1956) characterized as "the classical family of Western nostalgia." Goode uses this phrase to make the point that the image of ma, pa, the kids, the married kids with their kids, and other relatives living together in the old rambling farm house 150 years ago is more real in the minds of people today than it is in any demographic record. But the problem involves more than people recreating a past that never was; it also involves their placing an interpretation on the qualitative aspects of that past that is difficult to reconcile with the growing body of historical information. For example, we are often subject to invidious comparisons between the relations between husband and wife and parent and child at the turn of the century and the same relationships today. Think of a movie such as "Life with Father," which turns up on television from time to time. Here we have affectionate and positive portraits of a blustering, but good-natured, tyrant of a father, his deferential, but by no means powerless wife, his brood of respectful, but hardly subdued children, and their brow-beaten, but loved servants. Life seemed so orderly and comfortable then! Wives knew their place, children knew their place, and servants, of course, knew *their* place. But those who would have us hark back to such times forget to tell us that the woman in such a family seldom entertained the idea of being anything but wife and mother; her relations with her husband in and out of the bedroom probably lacked the warmth, spontaneity and, yes, sensuality that we today value so much; the children, who were supposed to be seen and not heard, might not have developed the sense of self and personhood today's childrearing experts tell us is desirable; and the servants, well, the less said about their working conditions the better.

Certainly, much of the above description is merely caricature meant to point out the dangers inherent in longing for a past that either never was or which, when carefully analyzed, comes up smelling more of fertilizer than flowers. The reason commentators often succumb to such nostalgia —apart from their exaggerating minority phenomena and seeing the past through rose-tinted lenses—is that they fail to employ a much-needed sociological perspective.

THE SOCIOLOGICAL PERSPECTIVE

The goal of the family sociologist is to understand the relationship between the familial institution and the society in which it is being studied. Most sociologists today would not accept Novak's notion about the relationship between familial strength and societal strength. Yet, Charles Horton Cooley's (1909) discussion of the primary group, of which the family is a key example, is the source of much of this thinking. As Bottomore has pointed out:

> Cooley and some recent sociologists seem to imply that it is possible to move directly from the study of small groups to the study of inclusive societies. *This is associated with the view that small groups have a determining influence upon social life. Yet all the evidence points to the opposite conclusion.* Histori-

> cally considered, small groups have been shaped by society much more than they have shaped it [emphasis added, 1962:96].

As a family sociologist, I hope to be able to convey to the reader how the family has changed and continues to change as a result of developments in Western societies during the last few centuries.

When one assumes a sociological perspective it becomes possible to understand change without immediately hitting the panic button every time some beloved behavior pattern seems to be on the verge of extinction. We begin to develop an appreciation of how change in any institution (familial, governmental, or economic) is not a piecemeal process, but rather is the result of pressures and cross-pressures within a society which bring various structures into line with its emerging organization. This perspective enables us to make sense out of such things as the declining role played by parents in the selection of their children's mates, the smaller number of children married couples are choosing to have, and the greater frequency with which marriages end in the divorce court. We also begin to appreciate how much of the talk about declining morality and the imminent resurrection of Sodom and Gomorrah is based on fixed notions of morality. This is not to say that "everything is relative" and thus within a given societal context all phenomena from nudity to genocide must be justified in terms of "the values of that particular culture." Such extreme cultural relativism is sophomoric. Rather, the point is that a society's notions of what is good and proper in interpersonal matters often reflects the structural conditions that prevail in it. Premarital sex, for example, is no longer seen as the dark secret and shameful act it once was. In part, this is because women can drive a better "role bargain" (Goode, 1963) as a result of their bringing more to marriage than a hymen or dowry. Not surprisingly, we find an increasingly sympathetic and uncritical view of such behavior being offered everywhere from the White House to Hollywood.

Having denounced the prophets of doom and gloom and having affirmed the viability of the family, it is now incumbent upon me to provide the evidence to support my case. But before I go on to present a discussion of the various aspects of family life that make up this, as well as most other texts on the sociology of the family, it is necessary to set forth the book's organizing theme and the perspective I bring to it. Sociologists of the family are unified by their interest in the same phenomenon, but differ in terms of what aspect of that unit they study and what sort of theory and methodology they employ in their studies. Some look at fertility, others at childrearing, still others at kinship, and so on. To some extent what the sociologist studies is influenced by the theoretical perspective that he or she is committed to, since one's theory generally determines what aspects of social life are deemed important and worthy of investigation. In order to understand this, it is worth stopping here to enter into a very relevant digression on the sorts of theoretical approaches that have characterized and continue to characterize sociology.

THEORY IN FAMILY SOCIOLOGY

If five family sociologists were asked about the number and type of approaches that characterize their field we might very well get five different lists in response. In fact, when Ivan Nye and Felix Berardo (1966) wrote their *Emerging Conceptual Frameworks in Family Analysis* and initially sent it out for editorial review they found that:

> The several prominent scholars who have read this volume in typescript have all proposed a total number of frameworks both different from each other and ours. We anticipate, therefore, a continued lively debate concerning the number and identity of the most significant frameworks for viewing the family [1966:iii].

This diversity of opinion is both a strength and weakness of family sociology. It is a strength because it reveals the field's vitality; it is a weakness because it reveals how far we have to go in developing anything resembling solid theory. It is not without significance that Nye and Berardo titled their book *Emerging Conceptual Frameworks* . . . rather than *Emerging Theoretical Frameworks.* Sociologists are developing conceptual frameworks, but we are still a long way from theory.

While this is not the place to get into a philosophical discussion of what is theory, a few words on this topic are in order. Braithwaite defines theory as a

> set of hypotheses which form a deductive system; that is, which is arranged in such a way that from some of the hypotheses as premises all other hypotheses logically follow. The propositions in a deductive system may be considered as being arranged in an order of levels, the hypotheses at the highest level being those which occur only as premises in the system, those at the lowest level being those which occur only as conclusions in the system, and those at intermediate levels being those which occur as conclusions of deductions from higher-level hypotheses and which serve as premises for deductions to lower-level hypotheses [quoted in Selltiz et al., 1962:480].

This is certainly a difficult bill to fill and few, if any, sub-areas of sociology would achieve high marks here. At present, most sociological work involves little more than the development of concepts and their use in research is informed by theory of a much less ambitious kind than that set forth by Braithwaite. Hence, Nye and Berardo's title.

Concepts are shorthand for ideas that normally would take many words to describe. Thus concepts facilitate communication. For example, in the sociology of the family we use the terms "kinship" or "socialization" or "courtship" to refer to complexes of behavior oriented around different aspects of family life. Later on in the book we shall discuss these concepts at length, but for now the point to be made is that these are the most basic elements of any attempt to construct scientific theory. They are our building blocks. However, in sociology we cannot look upon a concept as a fixed entity whose meaning, once established, endures unchanged. Quite the contrary. For the sociologist, concepts are dynamic elements that may undergo change as knowledge of a field grows (Stinchcombe, 1968:38–40, quoted in Burr, 1973:6). We use concepts in order to establish relationships between different aspects of a society for the purpose of trying to explain how these aspects of society change over time and how they vary among members of a society at the same point in time. The specification of such relationships is where theory enters the picture. The form of this theory is illustrated by a recent article in the *American Sociological Review* by Linda Waite and Ross Stolzenberg (1976). The authors attempt to discover if there is a relationship between whether or not a woman plans to be working when she is thirty-five and the number of children she plans to have, as well as the converse. Using a large national sample of American women and some rather sophisticated analytic techniques, they find a strong relationship between work plans and fertility, but a weak one for fertility and work plans.

The relationships they initially posit are *hypotheses* not theories, though some might argue that hypotheses *are* simple theories. Still, the hypotheses that Waite and Stolzenberg use are embedded in theory dealing with the relationship between the employment of women outside the home and its impact on family change, one aspect of which is fertility. The roles an individual plays may make harmonious, conflicting, or complementary demands. In the case of the infant-mother relationship and the career-woman role, there is sufficient tension to affect fertility patterns. To be sure this "theory" would warrant considerable specification and elaboration to meet Braithwaite's criteria, but as I have already indicated, it is typical of the level of theorizing that exists in much of sociology in general and family sociology in particular.

Despite the low level of most of what passes as theory in family sociology, there are different schools of family sociology based on their members' "theoretical" allegiances. If theory is so rudimentary how can this be? As indicated earlier, part of the answer lies in the fact that much of what passes for theory should really be thought of as "conceptual frameworks" (following Nye and Berardo). But the matter goes even deeper, and has its roots in what Alvin Gouldner has aptly labeled "domain assumptions."

> Domain assumptions are the background assumptions applied only to members of a single domain; they are, in effect, the metaphysics of a domain. Domain assumptions about man and society might include, for example, dispositions to believe that men are rational or irrational; that society is precarious or fundamentally stable; that social problems will correct themselves without planned intervention. . . . I say that these "might" be examples of domain assumptions made about man and society, because whether they are or not is a matter that can be decided finally only by determining what people, including sociologists, believe about a given domain [1970:31].

It is Gouldner's belief that while domain assumptions generally go unrecognized, they are at the heart of sociological theory. At the beginning of this chapter we quoted Michael Novak on the societal significance of the family. We can now see his ideas as a set of domain assumptions that might be used to construct theory. Perhaps a better way to convey how domain assumptions operate and how they lead to different theoretical formulations would be to contrast what some would call a Marxist family sociology with a structural-functional one.

THE MARXIST PERSPECTIVE

It is instructive to compare a Marxist perspective on the family with a structural-functional one because the domain assumptions are so readily discernible. Fundamentally, the Marxists see the family largely as a malignant institution, while the functionalists see it as largely benign. Listen to Friedrich Engels:

> The first class antagonism which appears in history coincides with the development of the antagonism between man and woman in monogamiam marriage, and the first class oppression with that of the female sex by the male. Monogamy was a great historical advance, but at the same time it inaugurated, along with slavery and private wealth, that epoch, lasting until today, in which every advance is likewise a relative regression, in which the well-being and development of the one group are attained by the misery and repression of the other. It is the cellular form of civilized society, in which we can already study the nature of the antagonisms and contradictions which develop fully in the latter [quoted in Skolnick and Skolnick, 1971:280].

Thus, according to Engels, the family, and especially monogamous marriage, is a microcosm of the economic relations that prevail in capitalist society. Engels maintains that with the coming of the revolution and the overthrow of capitalism, that is, under a more benign socialist economic structure, the family will undergo change in a more positive direction.

> What will most definitely disappear from monogamy, however, is all the characteristics stamped on it in consequence of its having arisen out of property relationships. These are, first, the dominance of the man, and secondly, the indissolubility of marriage [quoted in Skolnick and Skolnick, 1971:282].

Some readers may feel that I have misinterpreted Engels, that he really did not see the family as inherently malignant, but rather what is made of it in societies with capitalist forms of economic organization. What must be kept in mind, however, is that at the time that Engels was writing about the family, the only example of monogamy he felt to be significant was the one then existing in Europe. Thus his discussion of the family of the future was speculative and, ironically enough (see Dotson, 1974), not at all borne out by realities of life in the socialist world today. The point here is that despite the anticipated change, Marxian theory assumes that capitalist society's institutional structures, familial or otherwise, are reflective of the conflict, coercion, and exploitation that are held to be their very essence. The kinds of questions that Marxist sociologists ask, the kinds of hypotheses they formulate, and the kind of theory they ultimately arrive at are therefore rooted in this kind of domain assumption (Zaretsky, 1976).

THE STRUCTURAL-FUNCTIONAL PERSPECTIVE

A structural-functional perspective is rooted in a set of domain assumptions very different from the Marxian ones. To begin with, society is seen as an integrated set of elements, each of which exists in a relationship of interdependence to the other, with each element making a contribution to the maintenance of the whole system. Moreover, and most directly in contrast to the Marxian perspective, relations between members of the society are felt to be governed by consensus and cooperation. Some might also add that structural-functional theorists generally put a greater emphasis on stability than do Marxists, who see change as a constant element.

No figure has loomed larger in his influence on functionalist theory in the twentieth century than has Talcott Parsons. In the eyes of many he symbolizes this theoretical approach. Therefore his views on the family provide us with an important illustration of the functionalists' thinking in this area. While Parsons has written on the family in a number of places, his major work on this topic is the one published with Robert F. Bales, *Family, Socialization and Interaction Process* (1955). Commenting on the reduced function of the family in industrial societies (what functions have been lost, and why, is something we shall be discussing at length later) he remarks:

> We therefore suggest that the basic and irreducible functions of the family are two: first, the primary socialization of children so that they can truly become members of the society into which they have been born; second, the stabilization of the adult personalities of the population of the society. It is the combination of these two functional imperatives, which explains why, in the "normal" case it is both true that *every adult* is a member of a nuclear family and that every child must begin his process of socialization in a nuclear family [Parsons and Bales, 1955:16–17]

According to Parsons, the family is an effective part of society, providing the socialization necessary to transform amorphous neonates into functioning members of the society. At the same time, it provides adults with the intimacy and psychological reinvigoration necessary for them to maintain their places in an impersonal and demanding extrafamilial world.

MARXIST AND STRUCTURAL-FUNCTIONAL RESEARCH

When one starts out with domain assumptions as fundamentally different as those of Marxism and structural-functionalism, it is not surprising when the end result turns out to be rather different. Let us look at some examples of work informed by both perspectives. Al Szymanski (1976) has attempted to empirically reappraise Engels' thesis that the economic domination of women by men in capitalist societies is rooted in women being kept at home as housewives while men have been the primary breadwinners. Szymanski's thesis is that since women have, during the course of the twentieth century, increased their participation in the work force as regular rather than as marginal workers, they are manifesting the "proletarianization of women" that Engels predicted would result in the decline of sexist domestic oppression even before the revolution. He maintains, however, that sexism is now rampant in the marketplace.

Szymanski draws heavily and effectively on federal statistics to show how female employment patterns have changed. He even cites an often overlooked Department of Labor study (Hedges and Barnett, 1972) which shows that married women spent 71.4 hours on work, commuting to work, and domestic tasks, while married men spent 66.5 hours on the same tasks. The importance of this study is that women may not be carrying as heavy a domestic load as some have argued, or alternatively, that the male domestic tasks (yard work, repairs, etc.) may be more demanding than previously thought. The data Szymanski offers to show that sexism may be migrating from the home to the office and factory again derive from government sources and reveal that despite the enormous growth of female participation in the labor force since 1900, most of the growth has been in the low-prestige and low-paying jobs. Moreover, he maintains that women are concentrated in jobs that are very much sex-role stereotyped, not only in the sense that women are seen as the most "appropriate" people to fill them, but also in the sense that "feminine traits" (e.g., meekness) are desired and encouraged. It should be noted that Szymanski does not see such traits as inherently feminine, but rather views them as the result of sexist socialization. The upshot of this is that sexism is becoming less of an important issue for women than "class oppression," since women are increasingly subject to economic exploitation outside of the home. He holds that, "The lot of working class women, although sexism persists, is becoming more and more like that of working class men" (Szymanski, 1976:50). Certainly, this is a most provocative thesis.

Szymanski's article neatly illustrates the way in which a scholar's domain assumptions influence his or her research and theory. From the student's point of view what is important to keep in mind with regard to Szymanski and Engels is that their domain assumptions focus on the nature of the economic system; they agree that its basically oppressive character creates a society in which exploitation is rife. Their conception of the family and the way in which the economy impinges upon its structure is also fundamentally similar. This is not surprising, since Szymanski sees himself as Engels' heir and views his own role as that of attempting to refine Engels' theory in light of historical change rather than rejecting it out of ideological discomfort.

Having considered a study informed by the domain assumptions of the Marxian perspective, let us do the same for Parsonian functionalism. We could ask for no better example than Morris Zelditch's "Role Differentiation in the Nuclear Family: A Comparative Study" (1955). Zelditch attempts to test two hypotheses in this study:

1. If the nuclear family constitutes a social system stable over time, it will differentiate roles such that instrumental leadership and expressive leadership of the system are discriminated.
2. If the nuclear family consists in a defined "normal" complement of the male adult, female adult and their immediate children, the male adult will play the role of instrumental leader and the female adult will play the role of expressive leader [1955:314–315].

Translated from Parsonese into more conventional English, what Zelditch is saying is that where you find husband, wife, and dependent children (nuclear families) existing as stable units, there will be certain tasks allocated among them in terms of leadership in the areas of economics and decision making (the key provider and authority figure) and leadership in the area of socioemotional expression (the key provider of affection, support, and conciliation). Zelditch also predicts that men are more likely than women to be found in the "instrumental leader's" role, and women in the "expressive leader's" role.

In order to test these hypotheses he selected a sample of cultures from various ethnographic sources and developed measures of instrumental and expressive leadership. For the most part his findings confirm his hypotheses, but a good deal of the paper is devoted to an interpretation of why the negative cases fail to conform to his hypothesis. Generally, these are to the point, and not merely attempts to explain away unruly findings, but my intention here is not to critique Zelditch's piece; rather it is to point out how fundamentally different his domain assumptions are from those that inform the Szymanski piece.

Zelditch begins with the implicit assumption that the nuclear family is a unit that contributes to the stability of the society. Remember that Parsons sees the family as providing the functions of the socialization of children and the "stabilization of adult personalities." What Zelditch is doing is looking at an aspect of the division of labor relevant to those functions and attempting to establish certain universals in role allocation. He is concerned with universals in the task allocation necessary for the functioning of the familial unit. To some extent he appears to attribute this sex-role differentiation to biology. In contrast, Szymanski sees the position of women being largely the result of learning. For Zelditch the conception of the family unit as an important aspect of the sexist oppression of capitalist society is an alien one. As far as he is concerned, the system is basically benign and really does not require reorganization. For Szymanski it is fundamentally malignant and change is necessary, if not inevitable. Thus, while Zelditch tries to establish familial universals in sex-role allocation without raising questions about the meaning of this divison of labor, Szymanski explores the way in which sexism has migrated from the home to the marketplace and condemns capitalism in the process.

The comparison we have just provided between research rooted in Marxist theory and that rooted in Parsonian theory represents the most basic and thoroughgoing difference in a set of assumptions about the nature of society and the role of the family in it as one could imagine. Interestingly enough, Nye and Berardo (1966) do not even include a section on the Marxist approach in their book, while they do have one on the structural-functional approach. This is probably testimonial to the fact that in the mid-1960s (and even today), a relatively small but growing group of American family sociologists were working in the Marxist tradition. This is not to say, however, that the remaining majority of American sociologists are all cut from the same theoretical cloth. What they do have in common, however, despite their theoretical differences, and what sets them apart from the Marxists, is their acceptance of the legitimacy of the society, even if they feel that the familial institution is in need of change. Let us look at some of the differences that exist between mainstream American family sociologists.

Without too much damage being done to anyone's sensibilities, American family sociologists can be divided into those whose approach is social psychological and those whose approach is more institutional or macrosocial. Those inclined toward the social-psychological approach tend to focus on questions dealing with such issues as the dynamics of marital adjustment and the way in which personality type affects various forms of social behavior and in turn is affected by it. On the other hand, the macrosocial sociologists tend to look at questions such as variations in rates of intermarriage and divorce, and try to account for such variations in structural terms. To make matters even more complex, within each of these broad approaches there also exist numerous "schools." So among those inclined toward social psychology we have symbolic interactionists, needs theorists, small group analysts, etc., each representing a particular viewpoint on a similar level of analysis.

The existence of what some might see as a morass of theories and perspectives is certainly a commentary on the current status of the field of family sociology. We have a long way to go before we achieve the level of axiomatic theoretical rigor that Hans Zetterberg (1963) would have us aspire to. Nonetheless, this theoretical diversity can also be interpreted as evidence of progress and the movement away from the sort of bald empiricism that characterizes some areas of sociological investigation. This in itself, while hardly evidence of scientific maturity, is evidence of positive growth and development.

A SOCIAL-HISTORICAL PERSPECTIVE ON THE FAMILY

Having discussed at length other sociologists' perspectives, I must now define my own approach. The predominant perspective of this book—and the one which I hope will give it a unique place among texts on the sociology of the family—is a historical one. Over the last decade there has been a growing interest among sociologists in the new research being done by family historians and historically oriented social scientists. Nevertheless, for the most part, the fruits of this research and its implications for sociological thinking on the family have not been communicated to many professionals in the field, much less to students. Therefore, it is my intention to convey how the new historical research forces us to consider many of our pet beliefs about the family in a new light. For example, we shall see that popular notions about extended familialism in premodern Europe and America are not easily reconciled with the data that has been generated on this topic.

Our primary purpose, however, is not to debunk, but rather to convey to students how an appreciation of long-term change in family-related phenomena enables us to better understand current manifestations. One might say that our motto is that the present is only understandable if we have knowledge of the past.

Recent developments in the field of history offer a wealth of material that is relevant and important to sociologists. This is especially evident in the area of the social history of the family. The new concern on the part of historians with questions of family and kinship can, in part, be interpreted as the product of two shifts of emphasis: first, an emerging interest in common people and everyday life, and second, the diffusion into the discipline of quantitative techniques. These are interrelated phenomena. Farmers and laborers generally do not keep diaries or write family histories. Their role in "great" events often goes unrecorded, or at best, is set down by the hardly objective hand of their social "betters." Thus when an interest in history's inarticulate actors began to develop, it became necessary to look for new sources of data. These were often found in such places as church and civic records, government reports and surveys, and other similar aggregations of material. Such material lent itself to enumeration and statistical manipulation, and, not surprisingly, computer tapes have appeared where previously only index cards were to be found.

Another factor that has contributed to the development of historical investigation of the family is the blurring of lines between the disciplines of sociology and history that has occurred during the 1960s and 1970s. This blurring has been particularly evident to those who study such topics as social mobility, urban growth, politics, and violence (e.g., Thernstrom and Sennett, 1969). The writings of historians now include such concepts as reference group, extended family, and total institution, as well as theoretical frameworks derived from the writings of Talcott Parsons and Robert Merton, among others. In fact, the debt of history to sociology resides more in the realm of concepts and theory than in the adoption of quantitative techniques, most of which were developed by statisticians. Conversely, a growing number of sociologists now see the importance of long-term trend analysis and the relevance of historical data for their understanding of contemporary events. Furthermore, they have gained from historians an awareness of data sources that they previously ignored.

The social-historical study of the family lends itself well to the further merging of these disciplines, and a fair amount of progress has already been made in this direction. Still, differences between the disciplines persist. For example, sociologists exhibit a much greater concern for generalization than for details of specific events, a proclivity that has often caused them to neglect the temporal limitations of their data while pursuing social laws (Kai Erikson, 1970).

Until the 1960s, if one wanted to know anything about the history of the American family he or she had very few places to turn. The only major work available was Arthur Calhoun's (1917) three-volume study tracing the development of the American family from the colonial era to World War I. While this was a pioneering, comprehensive, and influential piece of work, it suffered from many of the defects we generally associate with traditional historiography, for example, a reliance on limited and often problematic sources that permitted only highly qualified generalizations. Between the time of the publication of Calhoun's study and World War II, there was virtually no work of any scope done in this field, with the exception perhaps of Levin Schücking's *The Puritan Family* (1929).

The development of a technique that was to provide an important vehicle for the growth of family history occurred in France. Historical demographers have traditionally relied on censuses, which have only been taken in Europe and England during the last two centuries. This created a wall that was breached only after World War II, when a group of demographers interested in the historical study of fertility, under the leadership of Louis Henry, began to elaborate a method of data analysis that has since come to be known as family reconstitution.

> Family reconstitution is the bringing together of scattered information about the members of a family to enable its chief demographic characteristics to be described as fully as possible. The family reconstitution method is not new. Genealogists have for generations searched out the dates of birth and death of the partners to marriages of the rich, the wellborn, and famous, and have listed the dates of birth of their offspring and the dates of the marriages and deaths to establish lineages and relationships. The tracing of family histories and the

> recording of family histories of these sorts is actively prosecuted to this day. But it is only very recently that attempts have been made to apply this method to a sample of the families of a whole community by making use of parish registers as a source of information. Where this is possible the community's demographic history can be examined in greater detail and with greater precision than with any other method [Wrigley, 1966:96].

Through the use of this technique, parish records in Western Europe and other areas have been made to yield quantities of data crucial to our understanding of trends not only in births and deaths, but also in age at marriage, bridal pregnancy, patterns of remarriage, and so on.

While it is generally agreed that the reconstitution or nominal method, as it is sometimes called, is quite accurate, it is nonetheless a time-consuming and expensive procedure that is not suited to solving all problems in demographic or family history. An alternative methodology is aggregate data analysis, a technique that involves analyzing records at different points in time in order to develop a picture of trends. This method examines numbers of events, for example, births as they are distributed over time in particular populations, rather than events as they occur in individual families as in the reconstitution method. However, the reader should not conclude that these are mutually exclusive techniques.

> Aggregation, in fact, can often be a prelude to reconstitution, for with this comparatively rapid system of analysis, it is possible to pinpoint those areas and periods of population history which saw the most striking changes [Eversley, 1966:44].

In some respects, the impact of these new methods of data analysis transcends the study of population trends. Indeed, it may be said that with some ingenuity and a great deal of hard work various bodies of existing data can offer new and relevant data to the historical study of the family (Wrigley, 1972). Wills, city registers, and other diverse sources help recreate past family life.

We must recognize, however, that historians working with traditional sources and using traditional historiography have also made very important contributions to the social history of the family (Morgan, 1944; Bailyn, 1966). As often happens when new paradigms are discovered, there are some who criticize those who do not adopt new techniques and points of view. These "data snobs" look down their noses at those whose findings are not quantifiable. Given the newness of this research area and the attacks that these quantitatively oriented historians have come under from their more humanistically oriented colleagues, this sort of snobbery is perhaps understandable, although hardly desirable. Ideally, the methodology that a scholar employs should reflect the kinds of questions he or she is asking. Thus varied approaches should not be thought of as mutually exclusive.

The 1970s have witnessed the new family history move from the esoteric into a major concern of social scientists interested in the general area of family. In 1976, for example, the National Council on Family Relations began the *Journal of Family History,* a publication devoted solely to this topic. People in this field have gone from asking simple, though groundbreaking, questions (such as who lived with whom and who married when) to a consideration of broader phenomena (such as changes in life stages [Modell et al., 1976] and the impact of family values on architecture [Clark, 1976]). There is good reason to believe that we shall see a number of important studies published in the next few years as sociologists and historians of the family cast their nets wider and wider in search of a better understanding of the way things were.

THIS BOOK'S PERSPECTIVE

An appreciation of the contribution made by historians and historically minded sociologists does not constitute a theoretical perspective. One could adopt a variety of theoretical perspectives and still be sensitive to the importance of historical data. The theoretical perspective I will assume might be characterized by some as a functionalist one in its emphasis, if not in all its assumptions. I am indeed committed to most of those emphases that gave functionalism its distinctiveness when it was introduced at the beginning of the century.

> Explanations for social behavior must be found in the social structure.
> More emphasis on the interconnections between different areas of social action in this society, even when participants do not recognize those connections: a greater attempt to analyze social behavior by taking the point of view of the participant and thus a greater emphasis on informal social behavior and structures [Goode, 1971:xiii].

Where I differ with functionalism is in the assumptions that began to characterize it—especially its Parsonian variety—in the years after World War II, that is, its emphasis on consensus and cooperation, and the failure to give sufficient attention to conflict and coercion as key elements in societies such as our own. Moreover, I see change as more omnipresent than stability, but unlike the Marxists, I do not see the basic integrity of society threatened by such change. This approach could be characterized as a dynamic functionalism informed by a strong sense of history.

This is not the end of our self-revelations, however. One important theme that will run through this book warrants some discussion. (Too often such themes are dealt with implicitly with the result that readers are never sure just what the author means by certain ideas and concepts that crop up repeatedly in the book.) It is my belief that a good textbook has a unifying theme. Many texts suffer from the pressure their authors feel to cover everything in the field, with the result that they often produce encyclopedias rather than coherent books. In this book the unifying theme will be provided by the concept of modernization.

MODERNIZATION

At the outset it is important to note that we are using modernization as a concept rather than as a theory. A number of articles have appeared in the last few years attacking modernization "theory" because of its inability to account for patterns of development in the Third World (Tipps, 1973; Lasch, 1975). This text will use the term modernization to encompass the aspects of change in the Western world during the post-Renaissance period. I do not subscribe to the view that the experience of England, the United States, and other Western nations is going to be replayed verbatim in Colombia and Bangladesh, though I do expect to see some similarities. When we look at the last few centuries of Western European and North American history, however, definite and coherent trends do emerge; I think that these trends are best characterized by the concept of "modernization."

In discussing the concept of modernization as it applies to the history of Western societies we must keep in mind that this is a process rather than an event. Such a warning would not be necessary were it not for the fact that some of the most influential books on modernization create the opposite impression. E. J. Hobsbawm's *The Age of Revolution, 1749–1848* (1962) and Robert A. Nisbet's *The Sociological Tradition* (1966) both treat the Industrial Revolution and the French Revolution of the eighteenth century as the catalytic events that pushed Europe into the throes of modernization. Both of these authors realize that the factory system of production and the overthrow of traditional monarchies by more representative governments were not overnight events, but they nonetheless give undue emphasis to the "revolutionary" quality of these developments. While it is important for us to recognize the significance of the separation of work and home and the decline in traditional authority, we must always focus on the sociological significance of such events, because ultimately this is what modernization is all about. In trying to come to grips with the question of modernization, it becomes apparent that the "dual revolutions" of the eighteenth century, while important events, did more to contribute to changes that were already at work than to initiate them.

There are a number of different approaches to the topics of modernization, but a good way to start is by examining social stability and change. Premodern or traditional societies were not stagnant entities, but the rate at which change occurred was dramatically slower than that of today. Therefore there was much greater continuity between generations. Parents had a sense of the kind of future for which they were preparing their children. Since agriculture was the predominant form of economic activity, most sons followed their fathers into the field and most women followed their mothers into the field and farmhouse. Even the minority of families that were engaged in nonagricultural pursuits, whether artisans (e.g., tailors or cabinetmakers) or professionals (e.g., physicians and ministers), did so in shops and offices that were part of their homes. Thus work and family were not separate spheres, and parents exerted considerable influence over the economic future of their children, either through the control of access to land or by contracting for the apprenticeships necessary to engage in nonagricultural pursuits. This continuity between generations provided an element of stability and tradition that was an important force in peoples' lives.

Long before the industrial revolution we see the seeds of economic change being sown in European society (Wrigley, 1972c). The development of capitalism preceded industrialism and it could be argued that it is of equal importance for the sociologist trying to comprehend the essence of modernization. The factory system of production did not just happen. It was called forth by the increased demand for manufactured products and by changes in technology which allowed manufacturing to be centralized and at the same time freed a segment of the population from agriculture. The textile industry was the first to undergo the change we associate with modernization. But well before factories began to dot the English landscape, thread was being spun and cloth was being woven in homes under the so-called "putting out" system whereby a middleman supplied individuals with the raw materials and then paid them on a piecework basis for the finished goods (Smelser, 1959). Work of this kind, while still set in the home and involving the family as a production unit, nonetheless reflected a degree of specialization that was midway between the textile production for home consumption that many preindustrial families engaged in, and the factory system of today.

As the demand from abroad grew, the capacities of the putting out system were exceeded, and with the development of machinery, such as the spinning jenny and power loom, it became possible to centralize work. Initially this did not mean that the father left home while the mother stayed with the children. In the early factories families worked as families. It was some time before the inefficiency of this arrangement, in addition to child labor legislation, brought about the separation of work and family (Smelser, 1959).

Specialization grew rapidly throughout the nineteenth century and continues at a high rate to this very day. Just stop and think for a moment what has happened to the medical profession. The general practitioner is rarer and rarer while the specialist is more and more common. Obviously, the more knowledge we have, the more difficult it is for any one person to master it. Specialization becomes a necessity. As an illustration of this, the U.S. Department of Labor's *Dictionary of Occupational Titles* (1965) lists 35,550 separate job titles! While there may not be 35,550 distinct types of jobs in this country, the actual number is probably not much less. This large number represents a far cry from the small number of jobs the preindustrial world was familiar with.

Specialization and education go hand in hand. While the skills needed to become a functioning adult member of a premodern society could be transmitted within the home—especially for families engaged in agriculture, but also for artisans and merchants—more and more economic activity began to require specialized training that had to be acquired outside the home. Even among the growing group of what we would today call blue-collar workers, certain minimal educational skills were needed. Formal education was becoming more and more widespread during the nineteenth century. No longer was school something one attended irregularly for a few years to pick up some basic skills. Legislation made attendance mandatory and the school leaving age was prolonged. In addition, during the twentieth century, we have seen an enormous explosion first in the high school and later in the college population. Thus the family has lost most of its function as an educational and economic institution.

The fact that Hobsbawm, Nisbet, and others placed such emphasis on the French Revolution in the process of modernization must be understood as reflecting more than a shift from a monarchy to a parliamentary democracy. They see this as a shift which had much wider implications, implications associated with both rationality and authority. No longer was the weight of tradition sufficient to bring about obedience and conformity. Those in power had to account to the people they governed. The principle of universal adult participation in the election of officials, while begrudgingly extended to the masses and minorities, affected the way people thought about their place in society.

Moreover, changes in authority went beyond the governmental sphere. Changes can be seen in the family as well. To some extent, sons and daughters were freed from parental control as a result of the proliferation of economic opportunities that were not directly controlled by parents. To be sure, parents continue to be the gatekeepers to certain kinds of opportunities. They pay tuition bills and in general support young people while they are acquiring the often lengthy education necessary to pursue many of today's complex jobs. But their control is more limited and their authority attenuated.

During the nineteenth century not only was the authority of governments and parents called into question, but also religion experienced a similar fate. It was not so much a matter of falling church attendance, but rather of increasing secularization, that is, the declining influence of religion on everyday behavior. Many people attended church regularly, but few gave regular thought to the question of salvation. And everyday acts were no longer seen as having religious significance. Viewed on a macrosocial level, religious leaders played less of a role in national and community affairs. This change, too, reflected the growth of secularism. As religion became less of an important force in people's lives, the question of what was to provide moral guidelines became an issue. While this added to people's sense of autonomy, it also added to their anomie.

In order to obtain work and education, people left the land during the nineteenth century in increasing numbers to make their way to the rapidly growing cities. The attendant shift in population from rural to urban settings also had an effect on the character of social life (Warner, 1968). It was not just a matter of having to adjust to the crowding and unsanitary conditions that produced high rates of disease and premature death in the cities; it was also an adjustment to variety and change. Growing up on a farm or in a small village, a person was able to maintain stable relationships with people whose backgrounds were similar to his or her own. (As we shall discuss later, however, we must be careful not to exaggerate the degree of stability in premodern rural populations.) While many newcomers to the industrial cities had friends or relations already there who eased their acculturation process, they still had to adjust to the vastness, anonymity, and impersonality of the cities. At the same time that this posed acculturation problems, it also freed people from the restraints of more traditional communities and was probably viewed by many as a liberating experience. As an old German expression, loosely translated, put it, "City air makes one free."

For many people the kinds of occupational opportunities that industrialism provided were not to be coveted. The work was hard, the hours were long, the pay poor, the fringe benefits nonexistent, and the tasks not very stimulating or satisfying. On a farm or in a preindustrial workshop, people were able to identify with their work. They got a sense of completing a job and observing the fruits of their labor, even if the work was as rigorous as that in the factories. What set factory work apart from the industrial work of the previous period was its fragmentation and regimentation. The whole point of factory production, especially as this form became more advanced, was that it allowed work to be broken down into constituent parts and thus an individual could not feel any identification with the product of his or her labor. Moreover, one had to report to work at a fixed time and leave at a fixed time. The more natural rhythms of rural work, geared to both time and season were broken. The famous philosopher-economist, Karl Marx, writing in the middle of the nineteenth century maintained that work as it existed in capitalist societies was alienating. This term was later picked up by other scholars who applied it to more general aspects of life and spoke of people being alienated from themselves as well as from society (Ollman, 1971).

What many nineteenth-century writers (and even writers today) did not seem to realize was that alienation and freedom are really different sides of the same coin. The freedom produced by the decline of traditional work, traditional authority, and traditional community in association with the rising level of education gave people a new sense of their own individuality and a feeling of control over their destinies. Of course, it was the more educated and less burdened middle classes who experienced this first, but what we are seeing today is the filtering down of this feeling to a broad segment of society—one of many phenomena that should make us aware of the evolutionary nature of modernization. When a person develops a sense of individuality and personal freedom, and in the process throws off the fatalism of the past, he or she is likely to raise questions about the meaning of life and the quality of relationships between people.

One final point needs to be made with regard to modernization. While modernization is most frequently identified in the professional mind with the concept of industrialization, another critical variable that figures importantly in this concept is that of rationalization. Our discussion of authority, religion, and alienation touched this variable to some extent. In the simplest possible terms, rationalization refers to the sense that human beings are capable of dominating their environment through the use of reason; it is the converse of fatalism. But there is more to it than just this. Rationalization means that personal criteria, such as those of kinship, are replaced by more universal ones, especially in the economic realm. For example, bosses start hiring the best qualified person for a job rather than their nephews. In general, planning, objective criteria, and the attempt to bend nature to human will are the key themes in rationalization. The theme of rationality should not be confused with the theme of progress, though the two sometimes do go hand in hand (Bury, 1932). The idea of progress, as it took form in the eighteenth century, meant that, historically, human society was improving both morally and materially, that life was better now than it had ever been. Rationalization, as we have learned in the twentieth century, has not always worked to improve the lot of humankind. Its application does seem to insure efficiency, but not necessarily morality.

I have shown my hand so to speak, and revealed the intellectual preconceptions, or as some might say "biases," that inform this text. Yet, I would like to think that I have avoided being dogmatic and that sociologists whose orientations are somewhat different from my own will nonetheless find this book useful.

SUMMARY

In this chapter it has been argued that much of the alarm generated over the question of the viability of the family rests on unsupported claims and a lack of sociological perspective.

In order to help students develop an appreciation of the need for such a perspective, a discussion of the current status of theory in the sociology of the family was offered. The point was made that much of what passes for theory in this field really should be thought of as conceptual frameworks associated with specific sets of domain assumptions. As an illustration of the latter we contrasted the Marxist and structural-functional perspectives and presented examples of research informed by each method.

The perspective of this book is a multiple one. While the general theoretical approach is structural-functional, it is a dynamic structural-functionalism that recognizes the role of societal dissension. Given the emphasis that will be placed upon change, a strong reliance on social-historical material has been adopted in order to convey the nature and direction of family variation over time. The book will not, however, "begin at the beginning." Instead it will focus on the change brought about in the Western, and especially the American, family system as a result of modernization.

While this is a sociology of the family textbook and discusses the areas traditionally covered in such a book, it is not meant as an encyclopedia. Rather, it is a book with a point of view about where the American family has come from and where it is going.

Library of Congress

KINSHIP: The Meaning of Family 2

THE FAMILY

This book was written for students taking courses in the sociology of the family. Most students sign up for such courses with certain expectations about the subject matter. Primary among these expectations, I assume, is the notion that the course will deal with "the family." Yet, in my own courses in this area, I have found that when students are asked to write a brief definition of the family, they have trouble articulating what this concept means to them. I usually reassure them by pointing out that they are not alone; people who claim to be experts on the family also have problems defining their subject matter. Despite the thousands of books and articles that have been written on the family, not to mention the multitude of courses in college catalogs, there is still no agreement on what is meant by the term "the family." Unfortunately, many professionals either ignore this question and act as if no problem exists, or refer to George P. Murdock's classic definition:

> The family is a social group characterized by common residence, economic cooperation, and reproduction. It includes adults of both sexes, at least two of whom maintain a socially approved sexual relationship, and one or more children, own or adopted, of the sexually cohabiting adults. The family is to be distinguished from marriage, which is a complex of customs centering upon the relationship between a sexually associating pair of adults within the family [1965:1, first published, 1949].

Despite the frequency with which this definition is quoted and the important role it has played in molding the outlook of a generation of family sociologists and their students, it is seriously flawed.

In order to comprehend the shortcomings of Murdock's definition, we must first realize that he has put the *nuclear family,* the unit consisting of husband, wife, and dependent offspring, at the heart of his conception of the family. He considers this to be a universal and fundamental unit, and the one upon which all other familial units are built. For example, polygamous families are families in which two or more women or men share a spouse in common. But according to Murdock, each marriage creates a nuclear family. Most of the family's functions, then, are the nuclear family's functions:

> In the nuclear family or its constituent relationships we thus see assembled four functions fundamental to human social life—the sexual, the economic, the reproductive, and the educational. Without provision for the first and third, society would be extinct; for the second, life itself would cease; for the fourth, culture would come to an end. The immense social utility of the nuclear family and the basic reason for its universality thus begin to emerge in strong relief [Murdock, 1965:10].

The criticism that Murdock's definition has called forth falls into three categories: (1) some social scientists question the universality of the nuclear family (Spiro, 1954; Gough, 1968, first published 1959); (2) others question the universality of the functions Murdock assigns to it (Levy and Fallers, 1959; Reiss, 1965); and (3) others question his methodology (Hendrix, 1975).

It is worth treating the last criticism on methodology first. Murdock's data were taken from the Cross Cultural Survey (CCS) which now exists in an expanded and more comprehensively coded form as the Human Relations Area File (HRAF). The CCS was originally developed by Murdock and a group of associates at Yale because they felt that there was a need to systematically collate the vast amount of ethnographic information contained in the hundreds of studies anthropologists had done since the nineteenth century. Thus a file was created in which information about particular aspects of a culture, including everything from the form of its economy to the form of its toilet training, were listed under headings that enabled the researcher to make a large number of cross-cultural comparisons without reading through a multitude of books. Today there are 296 cultures included in the HRAF and the data on them is more complete than it was in the CCS, but the basic organizational principle remains the same.

Using the HRAF to examine the same cultures as Murdock cites, Hendrix has argued that:

> Murdock may have had complete data for less than half of the 250 societies he examined. A total of 26 cultures, or 12% of the present sample, are contrary to Murdock's assertions in one way or another, and most of these have not previously been cited as contrary cases. Undoubtedly, more contrary cases exist, for which data were misinterpreted or overlooked during data collection [1975:133–134].

He also maintained that the reason so many sociologists were ready to accept Murdock's claims for the universality of the nuclear family was that the time was right for it:

> Murdock's notion of the nuclear family as the common denominator of family structure was the kind of idea that sociologists were looking for. It was a simple answer to the problem of cultural variation in general, and family variation, specifically [Hendrix, 1975:135].

Those who criticized Murdock's book soon after it was published were anthropologists rather than sociologists (Leach, 1950; Opler, 1950).

Spiro (1954), in an article entitled "Is the Family Universal?" pointed out that some problems become evident when one attempts to apply Murdock's definition of the nuclear family to the family as it exists on some Israeli kibbutzim (collective farms). There, men and women enter into marriage-type relationships and share a room together, but they work for the commune, not for themselves or their children. Moreover, the children are reared and educated by the commune and only see their parents for a few hours each day. Initially, Spiro's analysis led him to conclude that the Israeli kibbutz represented an instance of the absence of the nuclear family, but later (1968) in a revised version of his article he decided that despite the family's abdication of most of the functions that Murdock assigns to it, a definable nuclear family unit did exist (i.e., husband, wife, and children saw themselves as a distinct unit and manifested strong affective ties). Thus, Spiro began by questioning the universality of the nuclear family and wound up by raising questions about the universality of its functions.

Katherine Gough (1959) has similarly commented on the familial pattern of the Nayar, a warrior subcaste, during the precolonial era in India. Here women are initially "married" (tali-tied) to one man who has no economic responsibilities to them or any children they may subsequently bear. The women, in turn, are only obliged to engage in the ritual mourning ceremony for the husband upon his death. Women live with the maternal group and have a series of visiting lovers (among whom the tali-tied husband may be included), but the economic and educational functions reside with the women's maternal kin group. As Gough points out, the marriage ceremony puts women in the category of those who are entitled to bear children, but it does not, even in contrast to the kibbutz, create a definable nuclear family unit.

More recently, Ira Reiss (1965) developed a theme first voiced by Marion Levy and Lloyd Fallers (1959). Reiss argued that a careful review of the cross-cultural data makes it evident that of the four functions assigned to the nuclear family by Murdock—sex, reproduction, economic cooperation, and socialization (Murdock refers to the latter as education)—only socialization, and then only a specific aspect of it, appears to be the sole domain of the family, since negative cases (among them those cited by Spiro and Gough) have been found for the other three.

> As far as a universal structure of the family to fulfill the function of nurturant socialization (the giving of positive emotional response to infants and young children) is concerned, it seems possible to set only very broad limits, and even these involve some speculation. First, it may be said that the structure of the family will always be that of a primary group. Basically, this position rests on the assumption that nurturant socialization is a process which cannot be adequately carried out in an impersonal setting and thus which requires a primary type of relation. The author would not specify the biological mother as the socializer or even a female, or even more than one person or the age of the person. If one is trying to state what the family must be like in a minimal sense in any society—what its universally required structure and function is—one cannot be too specific. However, we can go one step farther in specifying the structure of the family group we are defining. The family here is viewed as an institution, as an integrated set of norms and relationships which are socially defined and internalized by the members of a society. In every society in the world, the institutional structure which contains the roles related to the nurturant function is a small kinship structured group. Kinship refers to descent—it involves rights of possession among those who are kin. It is a genealogical reckoning, and people with real or fictive biological connections are kin [Reiss, 1965:448].

One must keep in mind that while the definition implicit in Reiss' statement ("the family institution is a small kinship structured group with the key function of the nurturant socialization of the newborn," Reiss, 1965:449) is an inductive one, it has built into it certain assumptions about the biological needs of humans and the way in which these needs have to be met. The growth of single parenthood, although still very much a minority group phenomenon, along with other developments, may result in Reiss having to rethink his definition. However, he would not have to rethink his linkage of family and kinship, as we shall attempt to show.

One issue that has not been touched upon in our critique of Murdock so far is his insistence that common residence is also a crucial aspect of the family. This has resulted in a certain amount of confusion over what constitutes a household and what constitutes a family, since in many people's minds the two are one and the same. Yet, as Donald Bender has pointed out:

> There are two basic grounds for making an analytic distinction between families and households: first, they are logically distinct; and second, they are empirically different. As to the first point, the referent of the family is kinship, while the referent of the household is propinquity or residence [1967:493].

Certainly, not all people who live together are family, and not all people who are family live together. The importance of Bender's argument is that it moves us away from the questions of what functions constitute the family, always treacherous ground, and directs us toward what is really the key aspect of family, namely kinship.

KINSHIP

In virtually every society we know of individuals who see themselves standing in a special obligatory relationship to certain other members of that society. Most of the latter are referred to as "kin" or "relatives." A distinction is usually drawn, however, between *consanguineal* and *affinal* kin. Consanguineal kin are people such as your mother, father, siblings, grandparents, first cousins, etc., to whom you can trace your relationship by means of "shared biogenetic material," as David Schneider called it (1968:25). To put it somewhat differently, you can specify the procreative patterns that resulted in particular people being born and trace your relationship by means of them. For example, "Barbara Wilson is Aunt Betty's daughter and Aunt Betty is my mother's sister, therefore Barbara Wilson is my first cousin." By means of consanguineal links we are related, potentially, to a vast number of people. But, as we shall see, relatively few of these relationships have any sociological significance.

If and when you marry you will vastly enlarge your potential kin network. Your spouse's consanguineal kin will become your affinal kin and your consanguineal kin will become your spouse's affinal kin. In other words, affines are kin as a result of the legal relationshp established with your spouse, and thus it is not surprising that they are spoken of as "in-laws." In our own society we are able to observe some interesting variation in the extent to which in-laws are incorporated into people's kin group. In fact there are systematic legal and social differences in various parts of the country.

> One pattern (the Western American system) is found mainly in Midwestern and Western states; the other (the American-Biblical system) mostly in New England and Southern states. The Western American system prohibits first-cousin marriage but permits marriage between any affines. According to the kinship model implied in these statutes, marriage does not change an individual's obligations to his maternal or paternal kin, and affines are not admitted to his intimate-kin group. However, the Biblical system (described principally in Leviticus) prohibits certain affinal marriages, but permits first-cousin marriages. In the intimate-kin model of Biblical kinship, although initially an individual has membership in the intimate kin group of both parents, after marriage he also affiliates symbolically with his spouse's intimate-kin group [Farber, 1971:40]

In the Biblical system then, the spouse's parents and siblings are incorporated into one's kin group, but in the western American system they are not. These differences, Farber maintains, are also reflected in forms of address. For example, in the western American system we would expect parents-in-law to be referred to by the formal Mr. and Mrs. or by the informal use of first names. In the Biblical system, we would expect mother and father or mom and dad to be the accepted forms of address. Variation in the incorporation of affines is just one instance of how societies manipulate the definition of kinship and how vulnerable kinship is to such manipulation.

It may come as a shock for some students to learn that there are societies in which a person's father or mother may *not* be considered part of his or her kin group. While there are several ways that descent is reckoned, cross-culturally most methods fall into one of two classifications: *unilineal* or *bilateral* (sometimes called *omnilineal* for reasons that will soon become obvious). In the case of unilineal descent a person sees himself or herself as either being descended only from members of his or her father's father's line (patrilineal), or from his or her mother's line (matrilineal). Bilateral descent is traced through both (all four) parental lines. In both cases, however, the tie is one of blood.

> *Unilineal* rules or principles for the affiliation of descent unit members are those in which sex is systematically used as the distinguishing criterion, so that those kinsmen related through one sex are included and those related through the opposite sex are excluded. When male sex is the distinguishing criterion the descent principle or rule is called *patrilineal.* Ego is thus patrilineally related *to* females, but *not through* females for the purpose of constituting a particular descent unit. His initial relationship is of course through his father. From the point of view of the observer, either within the society or outside it, a patrilineal descent unit consists in consanguineal kinsmen related through males. When female sex is the distinguishing criterion the principle is called *matrilineal.* In the latter case the individual's initial relationship is to his mother and through her to other kinsmen, both male and female, but continuing only through females [Schneider, 1961:2–3].

In practice this means that if you lived in a matrilineal society, your mother, her sisters, her sisters' children (male and female), her mother, her grandmother, would be part of your descent group. But your father, his brothers, their children, his father and grandfather would not. The opposite would be the case if the society were patrilineal. Since we live in a bilateral society where members of all four parental lines are included, the exclusion of three of these lines in a unilineal society sounds odd, to say the least, especially when we learn that one parent is not included in the person's kin group.

This seeming denial of what we would view as a blood kin may become slightly more comprehensible when we realize that such rules of descent are often associated with rather special notions about the physiology of conception. Robin Fox (1967:34–35) points out that in some cultures the role played by the male's sperm in fertilizing the egg is not acknowledged, and thus he is *not* the consanguineous relation of those we would see as *his* offspring. In other societies the child is seen solely as the product of the father's sperm, and the mother is perceived as little more than an incubator. Not surprisingly, societies of the first type tend to be matrilineal and those of the second type tend to be patrilineal. There are societies in which the biological contribution of both parents is recognized, yet the mother or father is still excluded from the child's kin group.

However, this exclusion is more a matter of where a person's *primary social obligations* lie than it is a matter of affectionate ties between people. For example, in a matrilineal society, a man's primary social obligations are to his mother's line, but this does not mean that he does not have a special fondness for his own children and that they do not reciprocate this fondness. The problem is that discussions of unilineal societies often do not pay sufficient attention to the qualitative aspects of relations within the nuclear unit. To put it somewhat differently, they have failed to recognize that even where a society's rules of descent exclude one's father or mother from the descent group, a person's relationship with that parent still has a kinship quality.

We said earlier that kinship is founded on ties of blood or marriage. (There are instances of fictive kinship which we will discuss later.) Nevertheless, out of the vast number of potential kin one has, a relatively small number are singled out in most societies as actually being part of a person's kin group. We may recognize some people as being related to us and even be able to name them (Raymond Firth, 1969), but those who are singled out as kin in the sociologically meaningful sense are people with whom one shares certain reciprocal obligations. To illustrate this point ask yourself the question, "If you were a physician, to which of your relatives would you give your services without pay?" Based on classroom and field surveys (1977b), I have observed that people are almost unanimous in their willingness to render such service gratis to their parents, grandparents, and siblings. As we move from siblings' children to aunts and uncles and first cousins, we see a marked decline in this sense of obligation, so much so that by the time the categories of second and third cousin have been reached only a small minority answer "yes." This tells us something about the boundaries of our own bilateral kinship system. While potentially relating us to large numbers of people on both parents' sides, this system in fact only includes a small number in that group who are really significant sociologically, that is, those to whom we feel a sense of obligation. This group has been referred to as "kindred" in the kinship literature (Rivers, 1924; Freeman, 1961; Rosenberg and Anspach, 1973). While there is some question as to whether spouses, parents, and siblings are to be included among the kindred, there does seem to be agreement that this group is "ego centered," that is, each individual has his or her own kindred (shared by siblings if affines are excluded). Thus, in contrast to unilineal kinship groups, the kindred group has no enduring sociological existence when the individual dies.

Having emphasized earlier that kinship has a strong obligatory character, it might follow that those people who *assume* those obligations traditionally associated with kinship might be placed in that category even though they are related by ties neither of blood nor marriage. I would guess that at one time or another many of us have called certain of our parents' friends "aunt" or "uncle" even though they were not really blood relatives. The use of such honorary titles is known as *fictive* kinship.

Those who use these terms are fully aware of the fact that no ties of kinship exist, but they are responding to the quality of the relationship, which in all other respects resembles that of kinship. The same sort of thing holds for *discretionary* kin. For example, people tend to speak of the spouse of one's wife's or husband's sibling as "in-laws" when the quality of the relationship makes this appropriate even though strictly speaking they are not in-laws.

What does all this mean? The most important point here is that matters of family and matters of kinship go hand in hand. We must start with the idea that societies provide individuals with a special category of personnel called kin, though the rules may vary for deciding who falls into this category, and only a small number will be sociologically significant in terms of the existence of reciprocal obligations. Given the large number of potential kin one has, it is not possible for all kin in many societies to know each others' names, much less live together. In modern and post-modern societies the most prevalent form of familial residential unit is the nuclear family, both as an ideal and as a reality. We call this unit the nuclear family even though many such families may be incomplete because of a number of factors: either the children have not yet been born, or they have grown up and left, or one spouse has died or left. When most adults are asked to name those in their family, the nuclear family is the unit that comes to mind. Those questioned tend to name either their *family of orientation* (the family in which they were raised) if they are unmarried, or their *family of procreation* (the family formed by their marriage and parenthood) if they are married. Most also add that their grandparents, siblings, and aunts, uncles, and first cousins are also "family." Thus we distinguish our residential family from our nonresidential or extended family. The reason the residential unit is so salient in the minds of both professionals and lay-people alike in our society is that it is strongly tied to marriage, which continues to be the structure upon which parenthood is based. This is still true, even though some slight weakening of this link is now evident.

Thus the family is the unit made up of the individuals a person is related to by blood or marriage and to whom he or she feels ties of obligation, that is to say, the family includes a person's sociologically significant kin. Typically, only a small number of these will be found residing in the same household. In fact, some households have nonkin residing in them. As we shall see, there has been change over time in the West in the composition of the household. But differences in the personnel present are mostly a matter of which nonkin are residing there rather than which nonnuclear kin are present. Our definition of the family side-steps the issue of what functions a family must have. This has been consciously done both to avoid the problem of having to deal with negative cases in the anthropological literature, and also because modernization has resulted in so many of the family's functions being lost or at least strongly attenuated. Therefore, we feel that it is not possible to tie specific functions to the family, since at different points in history and at different times in its own life cycle the family will adopt and discard various functions.

KINSHIP AND SOCIAL CHANGE

In view of the emphasis we have placed upon kinship in our discussion of the family we must consider the kinds of changes that have occurred in kinship relations as a result of modernization. Until fairly recently, conventional sociological wisdom held that the family today is but a shrunken remnant of the extended family's past glory (Wirth, 1938; Parsons, 1943). In the old days people supposedly either lived in households with several generations present or lived near many kin. As a result of empirical work carried out since the 1950s, sociologists have come to reject the notion that people today live in isolated nuclear families cut off from kin contacts and kin services. Nevertheless, sociologists have yet to develop a clear image of the way in which kinship relations have changed in the West during the last few centuries as a result of the process of modernization.

The task of looking at kinship in historical perspective is especially problematic because it is very difficult to get data on the subject. Church and government records can give us information on births, household size and composition, age at marriage, death, and so on, but they do not give us information on the availability of relatives not residing in the household and what the nature and quality of relations between such relatives were. In our society today the boundaries of kinship appear to be defined in terms of a sense of mutual obligations, seldom go beyond first cousins, and are usually limited to one's parents and siblings. Was this different in colonial America? Writing on "wider kin connections" in Plymouth Colony, John Demos maintains:

> Direct bloodlines were accorded a special sort of precedence in the family feeling of the colonists; a man was involved, first of all, with his wife and children, and then with his grandchildren. Somewhat less intense was the relation to his own brothers and sisters, and to their children. Parent-child; grandparent-grandchild; brother (or sister)-brother (or sister); uncle (or aunt)-nephew (or niece): this was the general order of priority. But except for the will of John Hazell there is no evidence that notions of family and kin extend to a wider field of relationship. First cousins may have been recognized as such—but the fact implied no special feelings or responsibilities [1970:124].

It is interesting to compare this description of seventeenth-century kinship patterns with a description by Bert Adams of these patterns in the second half of the twentieth century in Greensboro, North Carolina, a middle-size industrial city.

> When attention turns from parents and siblings, the kin of orientation, to cousins and other secondary relatives, one is hard-pressed to find great significance in such relationships among young adult Greenboroites. A small minority, just slightly over 10 percent of the respondents, state that both objectively and subjectively their relations with certain secondary kin are valued. However, on the whole the young adults consider these relationships—to aunts, uncles, cousins, and so on—to be functionally irrelevant [1968:165].

The obvious similarities between these two descriptions, separated by three centuries, is most striking. At best, both studies only tell us that the people considered to be "family" may not have changed, but we cannot make comparable inferences for the uses to which these people were put. Moreover, recent research has shown us that we are treading on thin ice indeed when we make bipolar distinctions between life, in any sphere, as it existed in the premodern world and as it exists today. This before and after approach ignores the shifts that occur during periods of rapid change. For example, Michael Anderson's (1971) masterful study of family life in nineteenth-century Lancashire shows clearly that kinship and household structure during the early stages of industrialization were different from what preceded and followed them. What has led some people to expect important differences between current and premodern kinship patterns is the alleged increase in geographic mobility associated with modernization.

GEOGRAPHIC MOBILITY

An examination of geographic mobility shows that notions of stable preindustrial populations are being questioned by researchers working on both English and colonial American sources. In the absence of a national census, reliable data may be hard to obtain. Nevertheless, tax and landholder lists, as well as local censuses, do give the researcher some insight into the important problem of mobility, and other sources are available as well (Prest, 1976). English data referred to by Douglas Jones in his excellent review of this topic indicate that in sixteenth- and early seventeenth-century England, mobility was hardly a rarity.

> In early seventeenth century Bassetlaw Hundred, Nottinghamshire persistence levels of freeholders assessed for regular tax subsidies were well below fifty per cent. . . . Perhaps the more important point to be learned from the Nottinghamshire data is that families in the same village and tilling the same soil for more than one generation were relatively uncommon [1972:2–3].

For data on the seventeenth century we have Peter Laslett and John Harrison's (1963) detailed analysis of the population of two small parishes in Nottinghamshire—Clayworth and Cogenhoe. Over the twelve-year period between 1676 and 1688 roughly 61 percent of the total population of 401 had apparently left the village of Clayworth. Similarly, Cogenhoe lost

54 percent of its population of 185 between 1618 and 1628. We must however distinguish between those who "left" as a result of death and those who actually migrated. One way of doing this is to look at the persistence rates (the percent of a population remaining at a later point in time) of male household heads. In Clayworth such persons had a persistence rate of 51.0 percent. Jones points out that migration was responsible for 10.2 percent of this and death accounted for another 34.7 percent. At the same time, however, migration of new household heads into the village was 25.3 percent, more than double the outmigration figure of 10.2. Jones quite correctly draws our attention to the fact that, "the result was that at least one-fourth of the 91 household heads in 1688 were new to the village" (1972:6).

The situation in New England obviously had certain different components. First, the population was an emigrant one and therefore one which, we might assume, was already predisposed to mobility (Breen and Foster, 1973). Second, the opportunities to obtain land were greater and therefore the pressure on the existing land was much less than was the case in the mother country. The data Jones draws upon to explore this question are those found in taxpayer persistence lists.

Looking at the first generation New Englanders in seven seventeenth-century towns, Jones found rates which resemble those discovered by Laslett and Harrison in Clayworth for the period from 1676 to 1688. Dedham, Massachusetts, for example, shows a persistence rate of 52 percent in its first decade (1648–1660) and Rowley, Massachusetts shows one of 59 percent in its first decade (1643–1653). Jones points out that for a frontier area this was not a remarkably high rate of mobility, especially when compared with rates in the nineteenth century.

After 1660, persistence rates rise sharply, reaching as high as 83 percent in one of the towns for which data are available as the first generation began to settle in. However, in the eighteenth century, persistence rates again begin to resemble the pre-1660 levels. Jones maintains that this level was not a result of any influx of emigrants—as was the case in the early nineteenth century—but rather was a result of actual movement in the resident population. He concluded that crowding was created in large part by the high rates of fertility that characterized New England at the time. Philip Greven's study of Andover (1970) is especially revealing on this point, since it shows a pattern of increasing outmigration of sons, as we move from the sons of the first generation to the sons of the second and third generations. This pattern was hardly idiosyncratic to Andover. In fact, it was characteristic of the New England population center, though there were differences in migration patterns that grew out of differences in the economic base of various communities as well as other factors, such as town size (Rutman, 1975).

The point of this brief voyage into the world of prenineteenth-century American migration is to provide ourselves with some information on the availability of kin at different points in history. If, as Demos (1970) holds, kinship priorities in Plymouth colony were not significantly different from what they are today, can we make any statements about the differences in availability of kin in preindustrial and postindustrial America? The data that Jones has brought together from seven New England towns in the period before 1800 seem to indicate that our colonial forebears were not people adverse to moving on, either because of the "push" of crowding or the "pull" of rich land and opportunity elsewhere. This is not to say that they were as mobile as subsequent populations in the nineteenth and twentieth centuries, when factors such as large-scale immigration from abroad, the growth of cities as industry exploded, and the ever-expanding frontier kept the American people moving at a rate well above that during the eighteenth century.

Peter R. Knights's (1969) investigation of residential mobility in Boston during the period between 1830 and 1860 indicates a very fluid population indeed. In his sample the *annual* turnover of population between 1830 and 1840 was roughly 30 percent, and between 1850 and 1860 it rose to about 40 percent. If we are interested in residential mobility rather than movement in and out of the city, we see annual rates that Knights estimates to be as high as 40 or 50 percent. This means that about every other family moved each year. If we consider the crude estimate often bandied about that among Americans today about one family in five moves every year we can understand how Knights can claim "that ante-bellum Bostonians were at least twice as mobile residentially as are Americans of today" (1969:261). Did such dynamic population movement preclude the maintenance of kin ties?

Like most such questions of a historical nature, direct answers are not immediately forthcoming; however, we do have some data from Anderson's (1971) Lancashire study which do shed light on this question. Mid-nineteenth-century Lancashire was a place where industrialization was writ large, in growing factories and cities. The magnitude of this growth is evident from the following:

> The population of Preston in 1851 was 5.7 times what it had been in 1801 and Burnely, Ashton, Blackburn, Stockport, Rochdale, Bolton and Bury had all grown by more than three times. The population of Preston, and also of Burnely, more than doubled between 1831 and 1851 [Anderson 1971:33].

Those who accounted for this fantastic growth came largely from the rural areas that surrounded the cities. What kinship ties, if any, were these rural migrants able to maintain in the growing urban-industrial centers?

Anderson (1971) deals with the question of propinquity between married adults and their parents. His research seems to cast doubt on assertions concerning the "isolated nuclear family" in industrial societies. While his data are hardly conclusive, they do seem to show that residential patterns show much more congregating of relatives, especially married adults, near their parents than would be expected by his own estimate of random dispersion—in the case of married sons two and one-half to three times as great. However, Anderson does issue a warning regarding the fact that we might expect a bias to be operating here, to the extent that young married men would look for homes near where they worked and where their friends lived. Moreover, they would be more apt to know about housing vacancies in the area where they were brought up than in other areas. Still the fact that we do find such patterns of propinquity cannot be readily dismissed.

In addition to the propinquity between married adults and their parents, we must consider the quality of the kin relationships. Here again Anderson has insights to offer.

> There is a mass of cases in the literature where people are noted as interacting with and engaging in activities in company and co-operation with relatives, both with their current nuclear family and with wider kin. Among types of interactions noted are shared leisure activities (trips to the beer shop or to the country, or just a chat over tea), visiting and dropping in, at holiday times outings and family gatherings, parties for birthdays and weddings and mothers' day. Families attended funerals and church and night school together. They are recorded as begging together and as criminals together, and as minding each others' children and helping in sickness and unemployment and death and old age and every other crisis and contingency. Knowledge seems often to have been widespread about relationships and where relatives lived or were last heard of as living and about their jobs and sizes of their families [1971:62].

Anderson also offers data derived from the content analysis of a report of a cholera epidemic in 1832 which shows that kin provided assistance to the ill and to the immediate families of the dead. His data on the household, which we will discuss later, also serve to confirm that kin were hardly peripheral to the lives of working people in England's industrial centers during the middle of the nineteenth century.

KINSHIP IN THE TWENTIETH CENTURY

The point has already been made that it is very dangerous to assume a bipolar model of social change—putting the modern world on one side and the premodern world on the other. Doing this forecloses a consideration of change within periods. Therefore, having shown the vitality of extended kinship in the early days of industrialization, it is important for us to consider kinship in a contemporary working class section of an English city. We are fortunate in having available an excellent book on this topic by Michael Young and Peter Willmott, *Family and Kinship in East London* (1962). This classic study offers us considerable insight into family life in a working-class borough of London, Bethnal Green, during the mid-1950s. Written approximately 100 years later than Anderson's Lancashire study, this study gives us some sense of the continuity and change in urban kinship.

The most startling fact to emerge from this engaging piece of research is the extent to which married children, but especially daughters, maintained close ties with their mothers. Fifty percent of the married men and 59 percent of the married women still lived in Bethnal Green where their parents resided; another 18 percent of the men and 16 percent of the women lived in an adjacent borough. So we can see that a healthy majority of men and women in the Young and Willmott sample did not live very far from their parents. The extent to which this is true is evident from Table 2-1, which is adopted from the Young and Willmott study.

Another aspect of the matrifocal tendency of the London sample is not revealed in Table 2-1. According to the study, women are more than twice as likely to be living in the same home as their parents as are men, and more than one and one-half times as likely to be living on the same block. This tendency of women to live near their mothers is not explainable simply in terms of housing being more likely to be available in the wife's parent's rather than in the husband's parent's neighborhood. It reflects what appears to be a very definite residential preference that has consequences for the quality of kinship relations as well.

Although it is not the *preferred* pattern for a newly married couple to take up residence with her or his parents, there appears to be a marked desire to live near them, in particular near the parents of the wife. This has been found in other studies as well. Young and Willmott, quoting Geoffrey Gorer, point out that there is "a marked tendency towards matrilocality in the English working class" (in Young and Willmott, 1962:37). Similar findings have been reported for the United States (Komarovsky, 1962:242). Part of the same general residential pattern, but of even greater significance, is the nature of interaction with the wife's kin among working-class people, both in England and in the United States.

The households of married women and those of their mothers seem almost intertwined, as is evident from the following description of an average day by one of Young and Willmott's married female informants, a mother of three children, two of whom are preschoolers.

Table 2-1. PROXIMITY OF MARRIED CHILDREN TO PARENTS (General sample—369 married people with at least one parent alive)

Parents' residence	Married men (%)	Married women (%)
Bethnal Green	50	59
Adjacent borough	18	16
Elsewhere	32	25
Total %	100	100
Number	195	174

SOURCE: Michael Young and Peter Willmott, *Family and Kinship in East London* (Baltimore: Penguin Books, 1962), p. 36.

> After breakfast I bathe the baby and sweep the kitchen, and wash up. Then I go up the road shopping with Mum, Greta (one of the wife's married sisters who also has a child), and the three children. After dinner I clean up and then round about 2 o'clock I go out for a walk if it's fine with Mum and Greta and the children. I come back at about a quarter to four to be in time for Janice when she gets back from school. She calls in at Mum's on her way home just to see if I'm there. This is an ordinary day. If anything goes wrong and I'm in trouble I always go running round to Mum's [1962:47].

Evenings tend to be devoted more to one's husband, though there is no shortage of evidence to indicate that socializing is also pretty much limited to family circles. Not surprisingly, the wife's family tends to be the arena for more of these get-togethers than the husband's.

From the above the reader may have been led to believe that blue-collar English and American families are matriarchies. However, the suffix "archy" means rule, or ruling, and working-class women, especially if they are not employed, do not exercise much power in the family, no matter how central a role they may play in the lives of their daughters and, to a lesser extent, in the lives of their sons. Such families are better described as "matrifocal," that is, families in which the mother is at the heart of the social-emotional life of the family. To be sure, this provides mothers of married daughters with considerable influence vis-à-vis the female offspring, but it is influence, not power in the traditional sense.

The strong relationship between working-class women and their mothers is a phenomenon that a number of social scientists have commented upon. David Schneider and Raymond Smith (1973) maintain that middle-class and working-class kinship priorities are fundamentally different. Within the working class, the primary link is between married women and their mothers, while in the middle class the primary link is between married women and their husbands. Of course, this is an assertion rather than an explanation. Young and Willmott (1973) in a recent book do attempt to offer an explanation. They trace the origins of this pattern to the working-class slums of nineteenth-century Britain, where relations between husband and wife were marked by poverty, alcoholism, and brutality.

> When a man was treated at work with callous disregard of his humanity he could always turn on the troop of scapegoats at home, headed by the person to whom he had promised—'With this Ring I thee wed, with my body I thee worship, and with all my worldly goods I thee endow" [1973:77].

The strong relationships between working-class married women and their mothers are seen by the authors as a defensive reaction against husbands who drank away their earnings in a pub and then came home and beat their wives and children. Thus, in Young and Willmott's words:

> They created an informal women's trade union. There was only one out of the many kin relationships they could stress, between the mother and her daughter.... Ever since the father had to move out of the home to work, it has been

> easier for daughters to build upon this tie because they have in their mothers a model whom they can copy. This bond was accentuated well into adult life. Daughters lived near their mothers, or with them, even after they were married [1973:91–92].

It is Young and Willmott's belief, however, that the tie between working-class mothers and daughters has been weakened in the twentieth century as a result of the increasingly benign character of husband-wife relations.

To return to Bethnal Green, the services kin provide for each other are many and diverse. These include taking care of children, looking after a woman who has recently given birth, or just being available when needed. Kin also help out in a broader sense, for example by helping others to find housing and job opportunities. Here again the similarities between Bethnal Green, London, in 1955 and Preston in the 1850s are very striking.

> Since relatives often have the same kind of work, they can sometimes help each other to get jobs. They do this in the same way as they get houses for each other —by putting in a good word at the right quarter—and reputation counts for one as much as for the other. A mother with a record of always being prompt with the rent has a good chance of getting a house for a daughter; a father with a record of being a good workman has a good chance of getting a job for his son, or indeed for any other relative he may recommend [Young and Willmott, 1962:94].

While the matrifocal family may be disappearing, mother-daughter relationships continue to be important. *(George W. Gardner)*

Michael Anderson describes the counterpart of this situation 100 years earlier.

> Even where employers did not follow a deliberate policy of recruiting family members, workers, particularly if they were reliable, could often obtain places for children and other kin in the firm on a preferential basis [1971:118].

If there are so many similarities over the span of 100 years between the preferential ordering of kin, among other things, in premodern and modern societies, then where are the differences between kinship as it appeared in preindustrial, early industrial, and contemporary urban societies?

Our discussion so far has focused on continuities in kin interaction and the services working-class kin provide each other in two industrial settings separated by a century. Now let us look at the question of overall differences and class differences in kinship between the premodern and modern settings; perhaps here the differences between kinship in the two periods will emerge.

As we saw earlier in the chapter, the social and geographic mobility that was attendant upon industrialization may have initially created considerable distances between kin. Yet there is no current evidence to suggest that people were cut off from kin either metaphorically or literally. An English study, for example, found that 74 percent of the married persons with living mothers in a working-class section of London and 66 percent in a middle-class London suburb had seen their mothers either in the previous week or in the preceding twenty-four hours (Willmott and Young, 1960:33). In the United States, a national sample of married men revealed that 46 percent lived in the same community as their fathers (Klatsky, n.d.:8). Komarovsky, in her research on a group of American working-class families, found that:

> While the great majority of the couples live apart from their parents, they do live close by. Sixty-eight per cent of all husbands and wives reside in the same community as their parents. The parents of others reside in nearby communities, easily reached by car or bus. In only 7 per cent of the cases do parents live farther than "two hours away by car" [1962:241–242].

The words contained in quotes above are particularly important because they get at an aspect of current life that is very relevant to the understanding of modern kinship, namely the role of technology in reducing distances between kin. In 1800 it was about a two-day trip by stage coach between Hartford, Connecticut and Boston, Massachusetts. Today the same trip can be made by car in about two hours. Moreover, air travel has made it possible to cross the continent in considerably less time than it took to go between adjacent major cities in the eighteenth century. The tremendous significance of this development for the maintenance of kin ties needs little elaboration. Kin no longer need to live in the same community to interact regularly with each other. Furthermore, the telephone and a reasonably efficient postal service are available today, so that over distances that are either too expensive or too far to quickly traverse, contact can be maintained in a meaningful and regular way. Our point here is not that distance cannot be an obstacle to interaction—a number of studies have shown it to be the key variable affecting kin contact (for example, Hammel and Yarbrough, 1973)—but rather that it is not an insurmountable one. The upshot of this is that in terms of measures of distance between kin, more valid than mere miles, people today may have just as many kin available to them as was true in the past. How, then, have kinship patterns changed in other respects?

In the 1950s and early 1960s a number of studies appeared which were to have an important influence on kinship researchers (Dotson, 1951; Sussman, 1953; Axelrod, 1956; Litwak, 1960). This research supposedly dispelled the myth of "the isolated nuclear family," which Talcott Parsons (1943), among others, is alleged to have perpetuated. Parsons was seen as having presented a picture of life in advanced industrial societies that portrayed the nuclear family as cut off from contact with any larger kin group. While a careful rereading of Parsons suggests that some of his critics may have exaggerated the extent to which he saw this isolation as a reality rather than as a tendency, it is not our purpose to set the record straight here. The empirical research that came out in the 1950s and later revealed that not only were people in contact with kin, but for some segments of the population, contact with kin represented the most important form of leisure activity (Dotson, 1951). Later, Litwak's (1960) work showed that kin involvement was not an impediment to upward social mobility, another bugbear that Parsons is accused of perpetuating, but rather in certain instances actually contributed to it.

The problem with much of the kinship research of the 1950s and 1960s is that apart from establishing the existence of meaningful interaction between physically separate but related households, it did not tell us much about the nature of the American kinship system. However, it did touch upon the question of class differences in kinship patterns, a topic that certainly warrants our consideration.

SOCIAL CLASS AND KINSHIP

The paucity of historical material on family and class often makes it necessary for the researcher to brush aside intrasocietal variations in the past and talk as though no differences existed between various groups at any one time in history (Berkner, 1973). While such a strategy is understandable given limited sources, it is, nonetheless, problematic in that it may provide us with false comparisons, that is, we may wind up comparing middle-class people in one period with working-class people in another. Research dealing with contemporary kinship does offer evidence which indicates that class differences do exist. For example, what is characteristic of poor families on New York's Lower East Side is not necessarily characteristic of wealthy families on the Upper East Side.

In our discussions of the proximity of kin we have already noted that there is some evidence to suggest that working-class people in our society live closer to their kin than do middle-class people. However, when it comes to the question of the role kin play in the lives of members of these classes there is considerable ambiguity and confusion. This is well illustrated by the following two passages, both written by sociologists who have done important research on the contemporary American family.

> The data . . . suggest that the higher social strata maintain a more vigorous kin network than do lower strata. Naturally, the contacts of upper strata families with their kin form a smaller proportion of their total social interactions, since the higher strata belong to more voluntary organizations, clubs and formal groups than the lower strata. On the other hand, they have more resources with which to maintain their ties with kin, and because of these means, mutual exchanges are also more frequent than in the lower strata [Goode, 1963:76].

> In general, research of the '60's has found the working classes to express a stronger kin orientation, live closer to their kin and interact with them more regularly than the middle classes [Adams, 1970:585].

While at first glance these two statements might appear to be contradictory, I feel that they are really reconcilable.

To begin with, we must recognize that it is possible to interact with kin in a variety of ways, including phone calls, letters, and periodic visits, not to mention sharing a residence or visiting on a daily basis. I have been engaged in a study of these types of interaction (Gordon and Noll, 1975). What Goode speaks of as "maintaining ties" we would describe as *overall* kin contact (all types of contact from letter writing to face-to-face interaction). It was our hypothesis that as one moves up the socioeconomic status hierarchy (hence referred to as SES), there is more overall contact with kin. We also hypothesized that there would be a negative relationship between SES and *regular* (frequent) face-to-face contact, that is, as SES goes up, the amount of such visiting goes down, in part for the reasons Goode cites, such as membership in voluntary organizations, but also because of broader friendship networks and alternative resources that can be called upon in place of kin. If we make this distinction between regular face-to-face and overall kin contact the statements of Goode and Adams become less contradictory.

Our hypotheses in the study were not without theoretical underpinnings. These underpinnings were rooted largely in the work of Bernard Farber, who has set forth a rather interesting and important theory of class differences in kinship.

> At the higher socioeconomic levels, kinship sustains social differentiation in society, whereas among lower-class populations, it keeps a *lumpenproletariat* within the system [Farber, 1971:6].

What Farber implies is that high SES is associated with a conception of kin as a "lineage" in the sense that some anthropologists use the word. That is to say, there is a "symbolic family estate" involving a sense of line, a feeling of continuity, and a recognition of past achievement. Such families are not only wealthier in terms of material possessions such as land and access to various opportunity structures, but they are also richer in the status or prestige that kin bring to them. For example, being a Jones in a particular town may mean being part of a family that for several generations has played an important role in community affairs. The family's position in the community reflects favorably upon all its members, calling forth considerable deference; doors may be opened for family members irrespective of their own accomplishments. In contrast, being a Smith in the same community may bring few benefits, despite the fact that the Smiths have also lived there for many years. But this family may not be able to provide its members with much in the way of wealth, prestige, influence, or reflected glory. Obviously, then, we are dealing with the essence of social class, which any good sociologist knows is privilege—privilege that is stable and transmitted from one generation to the next. The effect that such differences in "family estates" has upon kin contact has been neatly summarized by Charles Mindel:

> Kinship relations then, take on a different character depending on the presence of symbolic estates. For the lower class where these estates might be expected to be of low value, kinship relations take on a character that has been described in much of the previous literature on urban kinship, namely, visiting and mutual exchanges of aid and service. . . . In the upper and middle classes where symbolic estates are of greater value, they function to provide a tradition, guidelines, and a style of life for the family. *The kin group becomes not a friendship group but a reference group.* Valuable kin become family role models, they provide guidelines for appropriate behavior, in particular achievement oriented behavior [emphasis added, forthcoming:5].

This statement supports the two hypotheses raised in the study done by this author and Noll, where it was maintained that higher the SES of an individual the more overall kin contact there would be, since kin represent a symbolic estate and a reference group. This sort of contact is easy to maintain because they have the resources and the skills necessary to call, write, or even fly across the country if necessary. However, we expected persons with lower SES to have more regular contact (face-to-face) with kin because of greater dependence on kin for help on a frequent basis and because kin are an important part of a more restricted friendship circle.

There is a third hypothesis implicit in the other two, that is, we would expect there to be a positive relationship (as one goes up, so does the other) between SES and contact with friends, both in terms of the number of friends contacted and the frequency of contact. Our reasoning here was that the nature of middle- and upper-class life is such that it affords many more opportunities to meet friends. Furthermore, higher SES individuals are not limited to friends who can be used in patterns of mutual help; friends can be enjoyed purely for recreation, with little or no concern for the effect that mutual demands would make on the relationship.

The data that we used to test these hypotheses came from a study of health-related behavior and attitudes conducted by the National Opinion Research Center in 1963. The interviews were conducted in five areas: (1) in each of the ten largest metropolitan areas; (2) in an ethnic white community in Chicago; (3) in an inner-city Black community; (4) in an automobile-work suburban community of Detroit; and (5) in a suburban county around Washington, D.C.

Our findings only partially confirmed our hypotheses. SES was found to be positively related to overall contact with kin and for the total number of friends seen and the frequency with which they were seen. However, regular kin interaction, instead of showing a negative relationship with class, manifested somewhat of a curvilinear one, that is, the middle SES group showed the greatest amount of regular kin contact followed by the low SES group and then the high SES group. We were then faced with the problem of explaining why our hypothesis concerning regular kin contact was apparently wrong.

In reconsidering our initial theorizing we felt that we might have overlooked or underestimated the importance of the resources that are necessary to sustain regular kin interaction. That is to say, while we were still in agreement with Mindel that the lower SES group were more likely to use kin as friends and as a resource for basic security, rather than as a reference group, the direct interaction with and visiting of kin requires economic means. Thus we are suggesting that the middle SES group exceeds the lower group in kin contact because they have the kinds of homes in which kin can be entertained and the cars to get them there. Certainly the high SES group resembles the middle group in this respect, but as we have documented, they are also faced with competing demands from friends as well as from work and community. Thus they have less time to directly interact with kin. However, this may not be the whole story.

The reader will recall that earlier in this chapter we talked about the phenomenon of "working-class matricentricity." If, as several studies have indicated, working-class husbands and wives spend a disproportionate amount of time with the wife's family, this could result in a narrowing of the overall interactive kin network and in part contribute to the lower regular kin contact among this group.

There are, of course, alternative explanations to our findings and a consideration of these explanations will serve as a good vehicle for looking at some of the literature on differential kin interaction. Robert Winch and his associates at Northwestern University have placed a great deal of stock in religion and/or ethnicity (there is some confusion here) in explaining variations in kin contact (Winch, Greer, and Blumberg, 1967). In one study of a Chicago suburb, they showed that Jews had more kin present, these kin were closer, they interacted more regularly with these kin, and their relationships with them were more functional than among either Catholics or Protestants, though the Catholics ranked higher than the Protestants in these respects. Later studies carried out by Winch and Greer (1968) suggest that ethnicity may also be a factor, since when they separated Protestants in a Wisconsin sample into Lutherans and "other Protestants" they found that the Lutherans (who were largely of German extraction) had more extended families than the other group. Some research has also suggested that there may be ethnic and religious differences with regard to involvement and interaction with kin. In view of this, it was important for us to consider if the apparent class differences we observed were really the results of ethnicity and religion.

When faced with the problem of possible spurious relationships between two variables (in our case SES and kin interaction), the researcher must hold constant what might be the spurious variable and then observe the effects of the new variable.

While we did find differences between Catholics and Protestants (there were too few Jews in the sample to put much weight on their patterns), the direction of the relationship between SES and kinship interaction was unaltered. That is, as SES went up, so did overall contact, and the most regular contact was shown by the middle SES group irrespective of religion. This indicates that the effects of SES are stronger than the effects of religion. As was noted earlier, there is some confusion in the literature over the relative effects of ethnicity and religion on relations between kin. If, as our findings showed, religion is not as significant a factor as SES, what about ethnicity?

When we looked at ethnic differences in overall and regular kin contact (with SES controlled), we saw that with a few exceptions the original SES patterning continues to be evident. Italians and South Americans do manifest some divergent patterns. Nonetheless, we must recognize that the other groups, which account for the great majority of ethnic groups in this country, show no basic divergence from the general SES patterning revealed in the study. Socioeconomic status, then, does appear to be a factor in determining differential involvement with kin, much more so than either religion or ethnicity. But what is it about SES that creates this effect?

In a study I did in Ireland (Gordon, 1977a) I found that people's preference for kin over neighbors or friends in a series of hypothetical situations (e.g., "Who would you leave your children with if you had to go downtown for an hour, if you had to go into the hospital for two days of tests?" etc.) was related to SES. The higher SES people were more likely to choose neighbors or friends than kin. In trying to explain this phenomenon, I found that they had fewer siblings in their families of orientation than those in the lower SES group. In addition, the higher SES group tended to be more geographically mobile, and therefore were more apt to be living in a city other than the one they were born in. Thus they were more separated from their kin and had fewer primary kin (one's own and one's spouse's parents and siblings) available to them. However, high SES people were more likely to choose friends than their lower SES counterparts even if both had an equal number of relatives available in the city. We might interpret this by saying that SES operates both structurally (creating differential fertility and mobility) and normatively (creating different values) in relation to kinship. Both of these factors should figure in any overall explanation of SES differences in kinship patterns.

One last word on the topic of SES and kinship. There are those (Firth et al., 1969; Klatsky, n.d.) who feel that SES does not have an effect on kinship. Given my own Irish findings (1977), where SES differences in geographic mobility and fertility seemed to account for a good portion of the variation in the differential usage of kin, one could argue that as such differences decline, as they have already with regard to fertility in the United States and England (see Chapter 5), we should observe less and less SES variation. However, at present SES differences continue and therefore we should not dismiss hastily its significance as an explanatory variable.

Kin, then, continue to play an important role in the lives of people today. In most respects we see more continuity than discontinuity when we compare modern kinship with premodern kinship, despite claims to the contrary by a number of commentators (Richard Sennet, 1970; Edward Shorter, 1975). From my own perspective, the only area in which significant discontinuity is apparent is in the economic sphere. Extended families now play a less significant role in job choice and employment as economic activity has become less of a family endeavor. Farber (1972) portrayed how importantly kinship figured in the recruitment patterns of Salem's merchant families in 1800. Today nepotism is less evident, formal criteria such as test performance and the possession of diplomas having become the rule. This is not to say that it doesn't help to be the nephew of the chairman of the board, but rather that it doesn't help anywhere near as much as it did a couple of centuries ago.

SUMMARY

I began this chapter by critically appraising Murdock's definition of the family and by showing how his assumptions about the universality of the nuclear family and its basic functions do more to cloud the issue than shed light. In its place, I offered a kinship-based definition, "The family is the unit made up of the individuals a person is related to by blood or marriage and to whom she or he feels ties of social obligation." By using a definition that makes the family and kinship parallel, we avoid the problems encountered by those definitions that attempt to specify family functions. However, we did recognize that for most people in the West today, the nuclear family is the most prevalent residential family unit.

Turning more directly to kinship, it was noted that kinship rules show considerable variability, not merely in terms of the descent reckoning systems that are tied to them (e.g., bilateral and unilineal), but also in terms of differences in the incorporation of kin within systems. In our own society, while we are potentially related to a vast number of kin derived from all four of our parental lines, only a relatively small number —what some social scientists refer to as the "kindred"—are sociologically meaningful.

The next question that was considered was the way in which kinship had been altered as a result of the impact of modernization. In general, considerable continuity was revealed. While people *may* now live further from their kin than was true in the eighteenth century, advances in communication and transportation technology have offset these distances. Thus, we continue to see frequent interaction and exchange of services. The only area in which important change has probably occurred is the economic one, with kin now playing a less significant role than previously.

The topic of current class differences in kinship patterns was also explored. After having shown that working-class kinship patterns during the early stages of industrialization (midnineteenth-century Lancashire) and during the later stage of industrialization (midtwentieth-century London) show more similarity than dissimilarity, we went on to look at class differences today. Drawing upon studies carried out by the author here and in Ireland, a number of points were made about normative and structural factors that enter into the relationship between SES and kinship. We concluded that while SES continues to affect kinship patterns, its impact could be weakening as, for example, SES variation in fertility declines.

When all is said and done, kinship, both within and outside of the nuclear family, continues to be a robust aspect of social life, even in those countries that have undergone modernization.

NYPL Picture Collection

HOUSEHOLDS: Who Lives with Whom 3

Who lives with whom is a question of some consequence to sociologists in general, and family sociologists in particular. In Chapter 2 we noted that households and families are not the same thing, because members of the same family, even the same nuclear family, often don't live together, and people who are not members of a family often do live together. This chapter is concerned with the question of change over time in the size and composition of the household. We will discover that while there has been an extraordinary amount of consistency in household size over the last four centuries, there has also been considerable variability in household composition.

One aspect of what Goode characterized as "the classical family of Western nostalgia" is the notion that "there are lots of happy children, and many kinfolk live together in a large rambling house" (1963:6). It has been the belief of some sociologists that modernization rang the death knell for this extended family form as it ushered in the age of the nuclear family. This new family unit was sometimes characterized as the "isolated nuclear family" to emphasize the absence of any sort of meaningful involvement with other kin, though there is little evidence to substantiate this picture. We shall also soon see that there is little evidence to substantiate popular views concerning changes in the size and composition of the household unit, though this issue is more complicated than some would have us believe.

Peter Laslett, who has played and continues to play a major role in the new social history of the family, recently attempted to reduce some of the confusion and ambiguity that has surrounded the terminology used by students of the family in describing various units of analysis. While he himself sometimes confuses the reader by speaking of "the household" and then "the domestic group," nonetheless he has tried to explain an aspect of "family" that is vital to our understanding of change over time. According to the definition he offers us:

> The domestic group is the family which the suburban worker leaves when he catches his bus in the morning, and returns to in the evening; it was the family which the English husbandman or petty farmer of our preindustrial past sat with at table and organized for work in the fields. It consists and consisted of those who share the same physical space for the purposes of eating, sleeping, taking rest and leisure, growing up, childrearing and procreating (those of them belonging to the class of person whom society permits to procreate). In earlier times, and nowadays in undeveloped societies, this same space was also where the domestic group worked at those tasks which could not be done in the open air, and these were not a few, even in agriculture. In the households of craftsmen, the industrial producers and service workers of that era, and in those engaged in commerce, everything went forward within this living space; such households made up fully a third of all domestic groups in pre-industrial England. Since the insistence is on residence, the full term to be defined is the *coresident domestic group,* and our interest is in changes in the structure and size of that group over time [1972:24].

Laslett recognizes that this definition cannot be applied at all times and in all places. Nevertheless, it goes a long way toward helping us deal with the question of what constitutes the domestic group—a question that is of vital importance to students of family sociology.

If we are to understand the question of change in the domestic group over time, it might be wise for us to adopt a broader perspective than we have up to this point. We are fortunate in having at our disposal a very important study by Blumberg and Winch (1972), which specifically deals with this issue. Their work takes issue with the notion, frequently encountered in anthropological and sociological literature, that there is a negative relationship between societal complexity and household complexity, that is, the more complex the society, the less complex the household. Meyer Nimkoff and Russell Middleton (1960), drawing upon data from 549 societies in the *World Ethnographic Sample,* observed that as societies developed from hunting and gathering to those engaged in agriculture and the raising of animals, the percentage of the population living in extended families went from 17 to 89. Yet a few years later Goode (1963), looking at modernizing societies, argued that this process was associated with the appearance of a family form that he characterized as a conjugal one and which is in part characterized by its deemphasis on extended family ties.

Blumberg and Winch see no basic contradiction in these two studies. They maintain that neither Nimkoff and Middleton nor Goode looked at the whole spectrum of societal differentiation, but only looked at half of the spectrum—the 1960 study looking at the transition from hunting and gathering to pastoral and animal husbandry societies, and the 1963 study looking at the transition from the latter to industrial societies. Blumberg and Winch hypothesized that when one looks at the total picture, what emerges is a curvilinear relationship. That is, as societies become more complex there is a movement toward extended familism, but a point of inflection is reached and the opposite begins to develop. This is why modernized and modernizing societies have smaller family units. In order to put this hypothesis to the test the authors looked at data derived from 962 societies that were listed in the *World Ethnographic Atlas.* As independent variables they looked at technology, size of the local community, permanence of settlement (nomadic versus sedentary), degree of stratification, and political complexity. Their dependent variable, family complexity, was conceived of in terms of familial structure, function, and influence, but measured only in terms of structure. A society was considered to show low family complexity if it had independent nuclear families as its household units. The point should be made that constraints on their data forced the authors to consider household unit only. While this is problematic in terms of their larger theoretical considerations, it provides us with just the data we want in this chapter.

The findings do support the hypothesis of curvilinearity. Blumberg and Winch summarize them as follows:

> The point of intermediate societal complexity, where large familiar systems are most frequent, is characterized by "extensive agriculture" and "intensive agriculture with irrigation" . . . largest towns in the range 200–5000 . . . hereditary aristocracy . . . and one or two levels of political hierarchy beyond the local community [1972:912].

In appraising their conclusions, we should keep in mind that none of the 962 studies in the *World Ethnographic Atlas* are of modern nations. This is important on two levels: (1) movement in the direction of small family size occurs, or at least pressure in that direction occurs, before modernization; and (2) a full test of the hypotheses requires data on more modern nations in addition to the *World Ethnographic Atlas* data. The authors recognized this shortcoming and attempted to introduce additional data. They used Adelman and Morris's (1967) study of seventy-four countries (all of which are beyond the point of inflection, but which are not yet modern industrial nations) and they find that within this group the more complex the society, the lower the level of family complexity.

The findings of Blumberg and Winch are more suggestive than conclusive, but they are very important for our understanding of the question of change in both household size and kinship. On one level they vividly illustrate the danger of taking too narrow a perspective on social change, that is, looking only at the premodern and modern periods provides a narrow perspective when seen in terms of the larger sweep of history.

One point that is central to our understanding of the question of the impact of societal complexity upon family complexity is the nature of the personnel involved in this shift. When we look at a study which reports that at two different points in time, for example England in 1650 and in 1850, household size remained the same, can we assume that the personnel were the same, or might there have been more children, fewer grandparents, servants, boarders, lodgers, etc.? Thus we have two questions to consider when we examine shifts in household size in the premodern and modern eras: we must consider both the numbers as well as the categories of kin and nonkin who make up these numbers.

In an essay written over a decade ago, Marion J. Levy, Jr. argued:

> The general outlines and nature of the actual family structures have been virtually identical in certain strategic respects in all known societies in world history for over 50 percent of the members of those societies [1965:41–2].

The "strategic respects," according to Levy, refer to:

1. size of membership,
2. age composition and relationship of the membership through time,
3. composition by sex,
4. generational composition,
5. number of marital pairs, and
6. number of siblings [1965:41n].

In part, what Levy is getting at is that we must differentiate between cultural ideals and statistical regularities. For example, some societies permit and encourage men to take more than one wife; however, given the fact that it requires wealth to obtain and maintain several wives, only a small portion of the population can, in fact, live in polygamy. However, the thrust of Levy's argument goes deeper than this, especially when we realize that all of "world history" is encompassed in his statement. He distinguishes between three types of societies: type I, in which the absence of modern medical technology results in a high mortality rate; type II, where mortality is minimal but family limitation is also at work; and type III, "transitional" societies, where some modern medical technology exists and mortality is reduced, but where birth control may not as yet be practiced (1965:44–45). It is in the transitional societies that we can expect to see the most variation and deviation from Levy's general description quoted above.

Thomas K. Burch (1967) has taken Levy's thesis to task on a number of grounds. First, he notes that Levy is only speaking of the residential family; second, Levy ignores nonkin who may be present in the household; third, he points out that Levy fails to specify the size from which little variation is observable. The importance of Burch's work rests not so much in his critique of Levy as in the data he himself presents on variation in household size.

Using current United Nations data on countries at various stages of development, Burch discovered a number of things that are relevant to Levy's thesis. To begin with, there was considerably less variation in the average size of households than one might have anticipated. The overwhelming majority had a range of from three to six persons. However, the distribution was a bimodal one, with most nations clustering either at the three to four range or at the five or more range. The overwhelming majority of households with more than five people were in societies that would be classified as "transitional" or type III by Levy. Moreover, these modes are associated with fertility differentials suggesting that the variation in household size may be more attributable to the number of children present than to members of the extended kin group.

When Burch looks at the percentage of the population living in households of three to six (his operationalization of Levy's notion of same size households), he finds that roughly 40 percent of the nations do not conform to this expectancy, but these are the developing nations that Levy would expect to show variation. What makes Burch's data so significant is that he also has information on the components of average household size, thus giving us a window into what factors may be at work here.

Focusing on nations showing a mean household size over 4.5, which include Brazil, Chile, Cuba, Mexico, Thailand, and Panama, Burch finds:

> In every case except India, the nuclear family comprises 80 per cent or more of the total family group (all related persons living in the household). Looked at differently, less than one-quarter of the members of families are persons other than the head, his spouse, and own children, that is, other relatives [1967:358].

The remaining 20 percent or less are not all relatives, however. While Burch's data do not allow us to distinguish between persons in his "other" category, there is evidence to show that developing nations are more likely to have such persons present in the household than are the United States and the Netherlands, the two nations used for comparative purposes.

Three very important points emerge from Burch's study: (1) the range in variation of household size is smaller than one might have expected; (2) large families, in conformity with Levy's thesis, are found in those nations currently undergoing development; and (3) most of the variation in household size is not explainable in terms of the number of extended kin in residence, but rather in terms of the number of children.

While the Burch study does provide us with much useful material bearing on the question of changes wrought by modernization on household size and what the components of these changes may be, we cannot forget that his data are all taken from contemporary sources, even though they do apply to nations at various stages of development. Nations undergoing modernization, or those that have already undergone this process, share certain basic things, but there are still differences between what Levy referred to as the "latecomer" and the "survivor" nations, for example, in the speed with which modernization occurred (Levy, 1972:2). In order to get a comprehensive picture of the effects of modernization on household size, we must also consider historical data.

We are fortunate in having available a volume published by the Cambridge Group for the History of Population and Social Structure and edited by Peter Laslett, entitled *Household and Family in Past Time* (1972). This book contains a series of papers dealing with questions of changes over the last three centuries in the size and structure of the domestic group in several nations including England, the United States, Japan, and France. The cross-cultural nature of the data allows us to make some rather revealing comparisons, but in what follows we will be most interested in looking at trends and patterns in the United States and England.

It is the contention of Laslett and his associates that a *mean household size* of 4.75 was characteristic of England from the sixteenth through at least the end of the nineteenth century. Moreover, with the exception of servants, the structure of the English household remained relatively constant, that is, the basic nuclear unit of husband, wife, and dependent offspring. Where the family did differ was in terms of the number of servants present, since in preindustrial England it was common for children and adults (though more likely the children) to live as unmarried members of another household. Often they were apprenticed to a master but sometimes they were simply domestics in the household. This practice did not affect average household size since it simply meant that children of one family were shifted to another. But not all families had servants. Therefore, much of the differential in household size was caused by the presence of servants in those households that could afford them rather than by the presence of extended kin. To be sure, there were some three-generation families in preindustrial England, but Laslett maintains that they were no more common in 1660 than they were in 1960.

Not all scholars share Laslett's views on this point (Berkner, 1972; Plakans, 1975; Wheaton, 1975). In his research on eighteenth-century Austrian peasants, Berkner discovered that many such families were extended in the stem form (where one son marries and remains in the paternal household) for at least a brief period in their life cycle—the period when the father retired and allowed his son to marry and take over the farm (see also Wheaton, 1975; Plakans, 1975). Berkner makes the point that Laslett may not have discovered this pattern in England because he used aggregate data analysis techniques rather than family reconstitution techniques. To state it differently, since Laslett and his associates were looking at their parish samples at one point in time, they would be expected to find only a small number of households containing three-generation extended families, despite the fact that this may have been characteristic of many families at one point in their life cycle. However, Berkner also notes that in England, well before industrialization, there had been a movement away from peasant-owned farms. Therefore there would have been less transmittable land, and consequently fewer extended families. This again makes evident the importance of considering and specifying what *point* in the premodern past of a nation we are talking about. It is relevant to note here that stem families of the type described by Berkner have been characteristic of sections of nineteenth-century France (Parish and Schwartz, 1972) and twentieth-century Ireland (Arensberg and Kimball, 1940), to name only two modern examples.

Keeping Berkner's work in mind, let us look more carefully at Laslett's research on mean household size. In arguing that mean household size has maintained itself more or less at 4.75, Laslett is not making the assumption (as Levy did) that constancy in size also reflects constancy in composition; yet, with the already noted exception of servants, his data do seem to lend themselves to the interpretation that Burch casts on his contemporary cross-cultural data; most of the variation is attributable to the presence of many or few children and not to the presence of extended kin. The same is apparently the case for this country. In 1790 the average size of American households was 5.8, while in 1973 it was 3.0 (Kobrin, 1976a:127). The importance of children to this figure is evident when we realize that in 1790 there were an average of 2.8 children under 16 per private household, while in 1970 the average was 1.0. To look at it slightly differently, in 1790, 35.0 percent of households in the United States had 7 or more people, while in 1970 this was true of only 5.1 percent (U.S. Bureau of the Census, 1975:42). The figures for the seventeenth-century are quite similar, though they are based on censuses for individual colonies. Mean household size was 5.4 and the mean number of children was 3.2 in New York in 1698 (Wells, 1975a:306).

SERVANTS IN THE HOME

As we have already indicated, size and composition of the household are not parallel phenomena. Turning first to the category of servants, it seems clear that they were much more prevalent in preindustrial households than they are today. We must recognize, however, that the concept of a servant was very different then from what it is now. Today most people conceive of a servant as a person who performs burdensome tasks for the well-to-do, such as cleaning, cooking, and childcare—in the manner depicted in the popular television show, "Upstairs, Downstairs" (Davidoff, 1974). In our society there are important status differences between servants and their employers. Moreover, the occupation of servant today is something which a person may pursue as a life's vocation, although not all servants do this. In contrast, the position and social background of the servant in the preindustrial world was very different. Servants were frequently young people who came from the same class as the families they served, though there is some evidence to suggest that the wealthy were more apt to have young servants than were the poor (Macfarlane, 1970). Commenting on colonial New England, Edmund Morgan remarked:

> Most of the inhabitants of seventeenth century New England either were or had been "servants." Today the word "servant" usually means a domestic; the cook, the butler, the chambermaid. In the seventeenth century it meant anyone who worked for another in whatever capacity, in industry, commerce, or agriculture, as well as in what we now call domestic economy [1966:109].

It should be noted that those who were paying off indentures incurred in obtaining passage to the colonies probably held lower status than children who were placed outside the parental home to learn a trade to improve their character, or for some other reason.

How a decision was made regarding the home in which a child would be placed is something we do not know much about. In the case of a young man, we might assume that his choice of a trade would be a factor; beyond this, kin ties seemed to have been the primary determinant. Consequently, it is not surprising that Demos, in his study of Plymouth Colony states: "Scholars have not appreciated how frequently such arrangements followed lines of family connection, yet for Plymouth the point seems indisputable" (1970:120). Sometimes the kin was an older married sister or brother, in other instances an uncle, aunt, or grandparent.

How common was this practice? Again, turning to Demos (1970:74) we find evidence from the census of Bristol, Rhode Island, which was taken in 1689. This data lead Demos to estimate that as many as 90 percent of the children in the community were living with their own parents. As he is careful to point out, however, this is taken at one point in time, rather than throughout the life cycle, and includes all the children rather than just the older children. If we look at other societies and observe the pattern for older children, a somewhat different picture emerges. In the seventeenth century, in an English parish studied by Macfarlane, two-thirds of the boys and three-quarters of the girls between puberty and marriage were living away from home, and some began leaving at age ten. Roger Schofield (1971), in studying another English parish in the eighteenth century, found evidence to indicate continuation of this trend. Still, just at what age and in what number children moved out temporarily or permanently from the parental home in premodern societies are questions that the currently available research cannot answer for us with any certainty; nonetheless, it does seem clear that the practice of children leaving home was by no means uncommon in seventeenth- and eighteenth-century England and America.

In the nineteenth century, servants do not disappear from the household; instead, their distribution and social status change markedly. Domestic service becomes a popular form of employment for rural and foreign immigrants to the burgeoning cities of the United States, England, and the Continent, especially for women (Branca, 1975a). The growing middle classes begin to regard a large domestic staff as an important symbol of their new-found and often insecure status (Banks, 1954). Accordingly, we see marked class differences emerging between servants and their masters, a pattern which previously was characteristic only of the servants of nobility. (But even the nobility often drew their staff from the well born, for example, the Queen's "lady's maid" might herself be a "lady.")

The demographic consequences of the decline of the more general patterns of placing children outside of the home for a period and its replacement by what we might call "a professional domestic service" did result in a general decline in the number of homes having servants. Laslett's samples of rural English communities for the period 1564–1821 reveals that 29 percent had servants, while Michael Anderson's figure for Preston in 1850 is 10 percent, and the percentage has continued to decline (Anderson, 1971:85). With the growing attractiveness of wages in industry, offices, and stores at the end of the nineteenth and the beginning of the twentieth century, domestic service lost its attractiveness and live-in servants are now only to be found in the homes of the very rich. Thus, the massive houses built by the middle class in the nineteenth century to house their large families of children and servants are now used by institutions rather than families, that is if they are not torn down. The servant, who was once commonplace in American households, is now a rarity.

BOARDING AND LODGING

Another category of household personnel, as distinguished from servants, are boarders (nonkin residing in a household) and lodgers (boarders who take meals). Such personnel deserve more than a passing glance here because of the lesson their presence teaches us about the dangers of discussing modern societies as though they were all alike. In certain respects boarding and lodging can be seen as an extension of the earlier pattern of

Table 3-1. MEAN HOUSEHOLD SIZE AND PERCENTAGE OF HOUSEHOLDS WITH KIN, LODGERS, AND SERVANTS FOR VARIOUS COMMUNITIES

	$\bar{X}$ Household Size	Lodgers	Servants[a]	Kin
England and Wales, 1966 (approx.)	3.0	N.A.[b]	0	10
Swansea, 1960 (approx.)	N.A.[b]	<3	<3	10–13
Preston, 1851	5.4	23	10	23
Rural, 1851	5.5	10	28	27
Laslett, 1564–1821	4.8	<1	29	10

SOURCE: Michael Anderson, "Household Structure and the Industrial Revolution," in *Household and Family in Past Time*, ed., Peter Laslett (Cambridge: Cambridge University Press, 1972), pp. 219 and 220.

[a] Servants include apprentices in Preston and Rural sample.

[b] N.A.: Not available.

sending children away from home to work as servants (Katz, 1975), but in other respects it is a new phenomenon. Boarding and lodging represented an adaptation to the fantastic growth of urban-industrial centers in the first half of nineteenth-century England and the second half of nineteenth-century America. What both nations experienced during these periods was a tremendous influx of workers into manufacturing cities that did not have the housing needed to provide the people with single residences; moreover, these individuals could not have afforded such residences even if they were available (Glasco, 1975). Where kin were present, residence could be taken up with them, but where such kin were absent, alternative arrangements had to be made, and these alternative arrangements were found in boarding houses and with families that took in a person or two. In midnineteenth-century England, lodgers (this includes boarders as well) were found in 23 percent of the households, and as a group made up 12 percent of the population (Anderson, 1971). Similar rates have been found for a Canadian city during the same period (Katz, 1975:221). John Modell and Tamara Hareven (1973) estimate that during the height of the boarding and lodging phenomenon in the United States (the last decades of the nineteenth and the first decade of the twentieth centuries), the proportion of urban households with such people in residence was between 15 and 20 percent. Furthermore, Modell and Hareven's data, derived from an intensive study of Rhode Island communities, indicate:

> strong and significant positive correlations between the lodging ratio and such characteristic aspects of industrial urbanization as five-year population gain, proportion of manufacturing employees in the local labor force, and proportion of the local population born in foreign countries [1973:470].

Despite the fact that the last variable (foreign-born population) accounts for almost half of the variation between towns in the boarder and lodger population at the end of the century, Modell and Hareven felt that this may have been the result of an ecological correlation.

> The correlation observed in the Rhode Island materials can and should be explained quite simply: the kind of town the foreign-born came to was the same kind of town potential lodgers both foreign-born and native came to [1973:470].

Clearly, the authors are elaborating upon the theme of population growth in industrial centers where adequate housing was not available.

What about the families that took in lodgers? Were they in any way atypical? In brief, the answer is yes, but obviously some elaboration on this response is required. We must recognize that by taking in lodgers a family could add to its income. Furthermore, it added to the family income without forcing the wife to leave the home to work. This was a factor of no small importance to many families, not merely because of the need for childcare, but also because of the basic definitions of feminine roles prevalent at the time. Virginia Yans McLaughlin has shown that such considerations were particularly salient among Buffalo's Italian-American population at the beginning of this century.

> Most women who contributed to the family budget in this year [1905] did so by providing housekeeping services to roomers and boarders residing with their families [1971:306].

Furthermore, boarding and lodging provided a form of family income not affected by the work status of the male breadwinner, that is, even if he were sick or laid off, the boarders' money would still come in.

It appears that boarding and lodging were not equally distributed over the life cycle of the household, both from the point of view of those who boarded and those who let the rooms. Turning first to those who provided this service, we see that whether or not a family engaged in this "occupation" appeared to be a function both of financial need and available space, two things which often were not positively correlated. While families earlier on in the family life cycle, for example, those with nonworking children, were more likely to show a gap between income and expenses, in Modell and Hareven's Rhode Island group, it is the older couples who show the greatest propensity to take in boarders. The explanation for this may be found in the simple consideration of space. Older families were

The boarding house was a common sight in late-nineteenth- and early-twentieth-century America. *(Culver Pictures, Inc.)*

more likely than younger families to own their own home, and thus have the space to take in another person. We must also realize that apart from considerations of space, it was the older couples who were most likely to have lost the income of their older children, who had probably left the home to start independent lives of their own. Thus, from the point of view of a society undergoing industrial urbanization we might see boarding and lodging in terms of:

> a social equalization of the family which operated *directly* by the exchange of a young-adult person and a portion of his young-adult income from his family of orientation to what might be called his family of re-orientation—re-orientation to the city, to a job, to a new neighborhood, to independence. It was a transfer from a family (often rural, whether domestic or foreign) with excess sons (or insufficient economic base) to one (usually urban) with excess rooms (or present or anticipated economic need). And often both the excess room and the present or anticipated economic need can have come from the departure from the household of a newly independent son [Modell and Hareven, 1973:475].

The typical lodger, if such a creature existed, was a young unmarried worker; however, young couples also lodged with other families, as did widows with children. Returning to Anderson's (1971) data on Preston we find that while almost half of the lodgers in this sample were unmarried (48 percent), the other half were made up almost equally of married couples, some with children and some without, and widowed people with or without children. Comparable figures are not available at present for American cities, but at the comparable stage in industrial growth they probably were not very different. Lodging, then, was an experience that many young people, especially migrants both from foreign countries and rural centers, experienced at a particular stage in industrial growth. The question remains, why did boarding and lodging finally decline?

This question can in part be answered by referring to statistics. A more complete answer requires that we consider certain intangibles, but first let us look at the "facts." We commented earlier that the phenomenon of boarding and lodging was partially a response to the crowding created by large-scale migrations to cities from both the countryside and abroad. Modell and Hareven's figures (quoted earlier) estimate that during the second half of the nineteenth century the extent of boarding and lodging was somewhere between 15 and 20 percent. These figures maintain themselves during the first decades of the twentieth century. However, we do begin to see a decline by the beginning of the 1930s. Census Bureau figures for large American cities in 1930 show 11.4 percent of families with lodgers. The Depression, not surprisingly, resulted in some temporary rises in the frequency of boarding, as families accommodated to the financial problems so common during this bleak decade. Nonetheless, by 1940 the figure for households with boarders was down to 9.0 percent. The continuation of this trend is evident in very recent statistics, which show that national figures are less than half of what they were thirty years ago

(Modell and Hareven, 1973:6). Clearly, in the last generation, boarding has gone from something most urbanites were familiar with to something which only a few even know exists.

SINGLE-PERSON HOUSEHOLDS

At the same time that boarding and lodging were declining, another related phenomenon was on the increase—single-person households. Young people today, especially those who attend college, take it for granted that during or after college (finances allowing), they will have their own apartments. More often than not, financial limitations force young people to share apartments rather than have their own. This is probably equally true of both sexes during college, but it is more true of women after college, since their lower salaries make sharing more of a necessity. In 1790, single-person households accounted for only 3.7 percent of the households nationally; in 1890, the figure was 3.6 percent; in 1940, it was 13.3 percent; and by 1974 this figure had risen to 19.1 percent (Modell and Hareven, 1973; U.S. Bureau of the Census, 1975a). It is interesting to note that a 1774 census of Rhode Island shows that only 1.4 percent of the households at that time were single-person households (Wells, 1975a:107). Other data show that along with the rise in single-person households there has been a concomitant decline in couples without their own household. Although this decline is not as linear as the rate of increase for single-person households, by 1972 the figure for couples without their own households was down to 1.5 percent (U.S. Bureau of the Census, 1973:53) from 6.8 percent in 1940 (Modell, 1972:29). Similarly, the number of widowed and elderly people who live alone has also grown (Chevan and Korson, 1972). For example, just before World War II, 58 percent of American women 65 and over who were not married and residing with husbands lived with kin, but as of 1970 this was only true of 29 percent (Kobrin, 1976a:136). These trends are so marked that Frances Kobrin has concluded, "If one is neither a spouse nor a child, one is unlikely to live with other types of relatives" (1976b:233).

The importance of these phenomena are greater than one might conclude from first glance. The fact that more and more young and elderly people live alone now than ever before has some interesting implications:

> The continued decline in household size, then, is a result of a general redefinition of the family toward invariable and perhaps uncompromising nuclearity. While there may never have been an extended family pattern in U.S. history, the evidence so far is that norms have changed to make it less likely, despite demographic pressures, that there will ever be such a pattern in the foreseeable future [Kobrin 1976a:136].

The point Dr. Kobrin is making is that while, as we have stressed in this chapter, the fundamental household unit in this country has been the nuclear family, the percentage of variant families (that is, those with servants, lodgers, and non-nuclear kin) is at an all-time low.

The development of such residence patterns is partly explainable in economic terms. It is considerably more expensive for a single person to maintain a residence than it is to room with someone else. The same is of course true for married couples, but other factors explain the decline in the number of couples without their own residence. The growth in per capita income since World War II is one factor here. In constant 1958 dollars, personal income, on a per capita basis, rose from $1,810 in 1958 to $3,341 in 1974. This is no small increase, despite inflationary pressure (Department of Commerce, 1975:383). Income, however, is never the only answer when it comes to discretionary behavior such as choice of housing; values are at work as well. More specifically, there is the desire for privacy.

PRIVACY

A number of students of the family (Ariès, 1962; Sennett, 1970; Shorter, 1975) argue that the modern family is an institution in retreat from society. Philippe Ariès maintains that the modern family and the concept of childhood go hand in hand, and that the nuclear family as a private entity arose in response to the extended period of dependence to which young people were subjected as a result of prolonged formal education. While Ariès does not seem to place much stock in the role of industrial capitalism in this whole matter, it seems to us that it certainly was a key factor. Be that as it may, it is his view that the path of development taken by the family can be characterized in terms of a retreat from a society, a shutting off of contacts as the domestic unit draws in upon itself. Richard Sennett is largely in agreement with Ariès, but carries his work further into the modern realm, comparing American middle-class families of today with those of working-class emigrants at the beginning of the century. For the working-class emigrants he feels many "contact points" existed between themselves and the urban world around them, not merely in terms of the boarders and lodgers they were more likely to have in their midst, but also in terms of the varied settings that forced them into interaction with different kinds of people—the work world of a man, the school world of a child, and the domestic life of a nonworking woman all brought them into contact with people different from themselves. While Sennett does not attempt to glamorize the lives of these people, he nonetheless states:

> This life . . . required an urbanity of outlook, and multiple, often conflicting points of social contact, for these desperately poor people to survive. They *had* to make this diversity in their lives, for no one or two or three institutions in which they lived could provide for all of their needs . . . It is the mark of a sophisticated life style that loyalties become crossed in conflicting forms, and this sophistication was the essence of these poor people's lives [1970:31].

The prosperity achieved by the grandchildren of these immigrants has been paid for, Sennett feels, by the loss of this diversity. In their suburban homes families have fashioned a life of great privacy and intensity, but at the expense of extrafamilial diversity. Sennett maintains that this loss of diversity and the insularity of the nuclear family has created an atmosphere that has a "brutalizing" quality. We will not debate the validity of Sennett's view of modern family life here, though we will return to it later. What is of importance to us at this point is that Sennett has directed our attention to a crucial theme of current family life—the theme of privacy.

Barbara Laslett (1973) is one of a few scholars who have focused specifically on familial privacy and in the discussion that follows we shall draw upon her work to a great extent. It must be recognized that the separation of work and home which was brought about by industrialization had a profound impact on privacy. Before work and home were separated, the economic aspect of domestic life was open to public view. To be sure, the significance of this for the farm family was minimal in the sense that agricultural work often took place away from the eyes of others. This was not the case for families engaged in craft work, which was usually open to observation—work space and domestic space often being one and the same. The waning of domestic industry was associated with a dramatic decline in categories of household personnel who were fundamental to the premodern world, namely, the apprentice, and ultimately the servant

Part of the American dream: privately owned suburban houses. *(George W. Gardner)*

as well. This increased the possibility of privacy, though the growth of boarding and lodging during the first stages of industrialization reintroduced "strangers" into some households.

We must also recognize that architecture was to have an effect on family privacy, though it is sometimes difficult to separate cause from effect in looking at this variable. Many people in the United States live in homes that are described as "colonials." Some in the East actually own houses that were built before the American revolution. But what most people (irrespective of their residence) do *not* realize is that the term "colonial" refers to a very specific and basic architectural form—that is, the center chimney form rather than the central hallway construction. Throughout the seventeenth century and during the first half of the eighteenth century most colonists lived in houses with the center chimney plan and had one and one-half or two stories. In the middle of the eighteenth century the center hallway style appeared. This is important here because the latter style afforded greater privacy, since it was not necessary to walk through one or more rooms to get to another. Still, the absence of soundproofing and the large number of people residing in such houses made privacy a rarity (Flaherty, 1972:39–43). The sharing of rooms continued to be a common phenomenon.

There is some evidence to suggest that it was not really until the nineteenth century that people began to think of the detached house, with a room for each child, as the ideal setting for the family, an ideal, not surprisingly, which took shape at a time when cities were beginning to grow rapidly (Clark, 1976). It may be difficult for us to gain enough distance to realize that this is not the way things have always been, that the suburban ideal of a house with some land around it is something to which people have not always aspired, that in fact it is a symptom not only of our affluence, but also of our family ideology. Perhaps no one has put it as well as Kirk Jeffrey, who wrote:

> During the years from about 1800 to 1870, and particularly after 1825, the values and expectations about family life which many Americans share today became implanted in middle-class culture for the first time. These included beliefs . . . about the private world of the family and the larger society. The last assumption pervaded the writings of the popular moralists and advisors of that age—the physicians, phrenologists, clergymen, "scribbling women," and others who instructed middle-class Americans about their "duties and conduct in life." In the sermons and novels, the magazines and hortatory literature of the mid-nineteenth century, they asserted over and over that *home was a distinct sphere,* an enclave emphatically set apart from the activities and priorities of "the world," as they usually called the non-domestic part of their society. Associated with this idea was a second one which could be stated in a good many ways but which amounted to an affirmation that, ultimately, *the individual found meaning and satisfaction in his life at home and nowhere else* [emphasis added, 1972:21–22].

The development of the idea that the home was "a distinct sphere" was given further impetus in the twentieth century by the fact that the home was becoming increasingly a self-contained entity. While the family previously had to leave home to seek entertainment in the theater, moviehouse, or sports arena, now television brings such events into the living room. That great nineteenth century discovery—ice cream—consumed in giant quantities by Americans, was initially obtained at the soda fountain; now freezers allow us to have sundaes at home. Religion is now *brought* to the family on Sunday mornings, and even vacations are now taken by the family enclosed in a sleep-in trailer. The family has never before had such opportunities for self-encapsulation. . . .

The reader may have discerned a paradox in what has been discussed above. On the one hand, we have argued that the notion of the isolated and atomized nuclear family of modern Western society is more a myth than a reality; on the other hand, we have argued that the familial privacy has become an increasingly important theme. Perhaps the seeming paradox will be resolved if we recognize that because work is now for the most part done outside of the home and much recreational activity takes place in it, the family is less and less under community surveillance and perhaps less involved in community-based recreational activity. Robert Malcolmson's research, *Popular Recreations in English Society 1750–1850* (1973) certainly suggests that the latter, at least, is the case. This does not mean, however, that the family has been cut off from kin, as the data cited in the last chapter make clear. While today the family may be "in retreat from society" in the sense that Ariès (1962) speaks of it in contrast to the more communal quality of family life that characterized medieval Europe, where the boundaries between family and the rest of society may have been vague, the family has by no means severed its ties with extended kin; this is why sociologists speak of the "*myth* of the isolated nuclear family."

SUMMARY

If this chapter contains a general lesson for students of the family, it is that questions must be phrased in terms of the life cycle of the family, since most family-related phenomena, and the household in particular, show considerable variability during a person's lifetime. Still, there appears to be little doubt that household size has diminished since the colonial era and that the major factor responsible for this has been declining fertility (see Chapter 5). However, there have also been changes in the categories of personnel making up the household. The custom of newly married young people starting their own households is apparently as old as this country's history, and thus three-generation households were probably not much more common in 1670 than in 1970.

However, we have also seen that at different times in our history there were persons in the household who have become either increasingly rare or whose position has changed dramatically. For example, resident servants are now only seen in the homes of the very wealthy, and in contrast to 200 years ago, they are now drawn largely from strata dramatically below those of their employers. In the case of boarders and lodgers, not only has the boarding house almost disappeared, but also the practice of individual families taking in a "roomer" has declined significantly since the fifty-year period (toward the end of the last and the beginning of the present century) when this was very much part of the American urban family scene. While the number of people in the household was decreasing and the personnel was changing, the number of families and single people with their own residences was increasing. Yet when all is said and done, it is clear that we began as a nation in which the nuclear family was the primary residential unit, and this continues to be the pattern, even though there have been interesting and important size and compositional shifts along the way.

ALWA

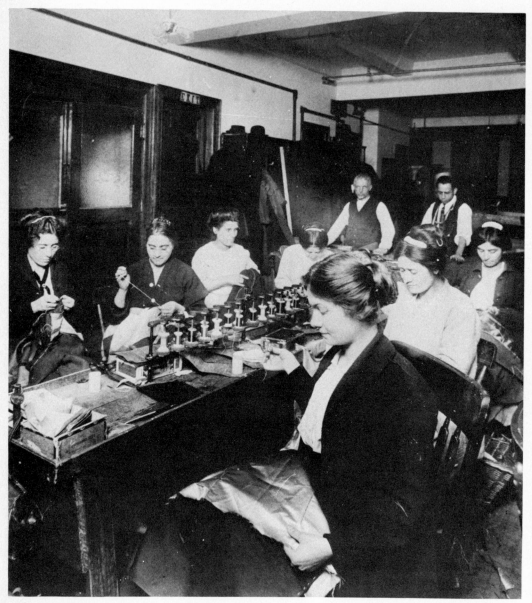

WOMEN AND WORK: Family Implications 4

Among the many events of the twentieth century that have been characterized as "revolutions," the changing pattern of female participation in the labor force has to be included. In 1890, married women made up less than 3 percent of the labor force; now they make up 42 percent of it. This monumental rise must be understood in terms of its historical antecedents, but we must also understand the impact it has had on the family. In order to accomplish this we have devoted two chapters to the question of women and work. In this chapter we shall explore the changing pattern of female economic activity during the last few centuries; Chapter 8 will look directly at how this pattern has affected marriage.

One of the fundamental features of premodern societies, whether historically or in the Third World today, is the link between home and work, and the functioning of the family as an economically productive unit. What modernization has meant, or more specifically capitalism and industrialization as important dimensions of this larger process, is both the separation of work and home and the emergence of the family as a unit of *consumption* rather than *production.*

While premodern families in the West were economically productive units, they were not generally self-sufficient; this is more of a myth than a reality, at least in those societies that show any degree of stability. To be sure, in some settings we may see an approximation of self-sufficiency.

> The people on the frontier from Maine to Georgia were driven by necessity during the years of the Revolution to supply themselves in their homes with practically every necessity of life. Mills for grinding grain, tanneries for making leather, smiths for making and repairing their farming utensils, carpenters, tailors, cabinetmakers, shoemakers, brewers and weavers did not generally

> exist. Professional tradesmen as such were almost unknown. Because of such primitive conditions, each family tanned its own leather and made shoes, shoepacks, hunting-shirts, and leggings for its own use; spun, wove, and tailored its textile clothing from wool, flax, or cotton; and supplied itself with farming implements, household furniture, harnesses, wagons, sleds, cooperware, etc. . . . This independence was one of the home rather than the town or community, as was the case in the older settlements [Tryon, 1917:119–120].

This is a very revealing statement because it points to the atypicality of the situation it describes and at the same time conveys that more settled communities had specialists who were engaged in the various manufacturing activities. Thus if we were to look at a town like Andover or Hingham, Massachusetts during the American Revolution or even a century earlier we would see millers, blacksmiths, tanners, coopers, etc., indicating that almost from the start of the settlement families went outside of the home to obtain certain durable goods. Some of those engaged in these activities did not do so on a fulltime basis; many farmed as well as practiced their craft. But the important point for us is that there existed external suppliers of goods necessary for household use.

Despite this dependence on certain community specialists, there was an extraordinary amount of manufacturing going on within each individual household. While there was a considerable dependence upon England for manufactured goods in New England's early stages (Tryon, 1917:62), the irregularity of shipments and restrictive legislation made it necessary to encourage domestic production, especially in the manufacture of textiles. In any case, during the seventeenth and eighteenth centuries families not only produced much of the cloth for their clothing, but also raised and processed most of their food, built their own homes, made shoes, and did a host of other jobs as well.

It appears that a division of labor based on sex did exist with regard to domestic production. Edith Abbott remarks on the colonial period:

> But although daughters and wives often helped at home with what was rather rough work, cutting wood, milking and the like, and the girl in service did similar "chores," it was not customary to employ women to any large extent for regular farm work [Abbott, 1910:12].

Women did at least supervise the cooking and cleaning, and assumed major responsibility for spinning, weaving, and clothing production. They were also responsible for some tasks related to agriculture such as the care of certain animals and the tending of gardens. These contributions were of such importance that a man without a wife was seriously impaired if engaged in farming. As Clark (1968) has noted, such men did not regard marriage as an economic burden but rather as an economic asset. In addition, some women were employed outside the home.

As in the case with most historical research on the American family, there is no abundance of material on the external employment of women during this country's preindustrial era. There are a few classic works—

such as Abbott's *Women in Industry* (1910), Julia Spruill's *Women's Life and Work in the Southern Colonies* (1938), and parts of Tryon's *Household Manufactures in the United States 1640–1860* (1917)—which we must turn to if we are to develop some sense of the opportunities and realities of female employment before industrialization in order to be able to assess the importance of the changes wrought by the coming of the factory system of production. One is impressed by the diversity of occupations women found during the colonial era. They kept shops, worked as dressmakers, laundresses, and in such traditionally masculine establishments as gunsmith and blacksmith shops and tanneries. According to Spruill (1938:289), however, most of the women in these occupations were likely to have taken such establishments over after their husband's death, though according to Abbott (1910:17) many eighteenth-century American women were independently employed as printers (compositors and press operators) and several ran their own newspapers or publishing houses. Tavern keeping seemed to be one of the more traditional female enterprises, at least as common as the keeping of shops by women.

The professions were by no means closed to women during the colonial era or in the years immediately after. In part, this reflects the fact that this period preceded licensure, which prevented those without special qualifications from calling themselves by some title. As we shall see, the coming of industrialization was to close off the professions to widespread participation by women (Barker-Benfield, 1975). Only teaching held its place, from the seventeenth century on, as a job in which women could be found, though during that century most teachers were men; however, in the half century before the Revolution women increasingly made their numbers felt in the classroom (Spruill, 1938:255).

While it will come as no surprise to many readers to learn that women served as midwives, it may surprise some to learn that they were also engaged in the medical profession as it existed during the colonial period.

> One of the professions which nineteenth century women found it most difficult to enter was that of medicine. Yet in the period before the Revolution, they were apparently allowed unlimited freedom in practicing "physick" and "chirurgery." The reason for this difference of attitude lies, of course, in the fact that in the early days no special training was required, and women were regarded as having as great natural ability for the healing arts as men. Amateur doctors did not always attend the sick gratuitously, and women as well as men were paid for their treatments [Spruill, 1938:267].

Early newspapers also show women advertising remedies of their own concoction for various ailments from cancer to piles; others advertised their services as nurses. The practice of medicine and nursing were, according to Spruill, carried on as sidelines. Midwifery was a fulltime occupation and the exclusive domain of women until the eighteenth century, when male physicians began to emerge in obstetrical work (Spruill, 1938:272).

As we noted above, many of the women engaged in so-called masculine work were widows. This is because almost all the colonial women who engaged in business were partners of their husbands. Together the couple would advertise their services, which were often complementary activities, such as an umbrella maker and a milliner or a stay maker and mantua maker in the same shop (Spruill, 1938:290). Similarly, widows would run their own farms. But generally this was the sort of activity that single women did not enter into, and the early custom of apportioning some land to an unmarried daughter ("maid's lots") was discontinued because it was felt to set a bad precedent (Abbott: 1910:12). The great majority of women during this country's preindustrial period were wives, who acted as their husband's partners, whether he was engaged in agriculture or some form of business activity.

We can see from this discussion of the woman's place during the colonial period and the general attitudes toward women in society how very difficult the situation of a single woman was; however, we would be wrong to assume that the early settlers disapproved of women working. The Puritans, for example, held strongly to their belief that work was good in itself and idleness a dangerous evil. Abbott quotes the Province Laws of the Massachusetts Bay for the session of 1692–1693:

> The law ordered that every single person under twenty-one must live "under some orderly family government," but added the proviso that "this act shall not be construed to extend to hinder any single woman of good repute from the exercise of any lawful trade or employment for a livelihood [1910:33].

TOWARD A UNIT OF CONSUMPTION

If we are to appreciate the changes in the economic position of women that were wrought by industrialization, we must first consider the nature of this transformation in the social organization of production. Tryon offers a rather clear-cut discussion of the shift from domestic to factory production in the United States, though he is careful to point out that this occurred at different rates in various sections of the country. The first stage is referred to as "the family stage," since here the lion's share of the family's needs are met by its own household members. Even when this was the predominant mode, and Tryon (1917:244) maintains that at the beginning of the nineteenth century this mode was still common in many parts of the country, there was some supplementary manufacturing being carried out by such specialists as blacksmiths and potters. There were also shopkeepers who provided goods such as cloth, sugar, etc. The important point about the first stage in the development of factory production is that in general the family was still largely self-reliant. The second stage, referred to as the "itinerant-supplementary" stage, is characterized by the presence of such specialists as dyers, fullers, tanners, weavers, and so on, who either took over part of the processes of certain aspects of domestic manufacture, particularly in the case of textile production (the most important family industry) or who did the whole task. The important point about this stage is that there is complementarity between the home and craftsman—with cloth being brought to a dressmaker, hides to a shoemaker, or yarn to a weaver—who in return provided finished goods. It is this blending of home and external production that is of significance. The reason that this is referred to as the itinerant-supplementary stage is that many of the craftsmen involved were in fact itinerants, traveling from place to place with the tools of their trade on their back or in their wagon. These craftsmen might stop with a family for a few days—for example, in the case of a weaver, to weave a coverlet from the yarn the women of the family had spun—and then move on.

The third or "shop stage," Tryon tells us, "both followed and paralleled the itinerant-supplementary" one (1917:244). The chief characteristic of this stage is that *all* of the work was done in a shop and the finished goods either sold or traded to people in the surrounding area. This stage represented an important intrusion on the economic autonomy of the family, and while eighteenth- and early nineteenth-century Americans gladly relinquished some of the more onerous manufacturing tasks, the effect on the family economy was great. We should point out here that in urban centers such as New York, Philadelphia, and Boston, which had concentrated nonagricultural populations early, we see the shop stage appear long before its emergence in frontier or in more rural settings. This development reflects the variability in the chronology of these three stages.

The next stage is referred to as the "mill-small-factory-stage." Here we see the growth of mills, which supplied finished products such as lumber, flour, and cloth in return for raw goods. This stage was also characterized by the growth of factories, which are really large shops producing goods for distribution in areas that often extend beyond their immediate location. The transition from this stage to the one of large factory production was brought about, for the most part, through technical innovations that made it impractical to engage in manufacturing on a domestic or small factory basis. Nonetheless, the appearance of the spinning jenny and the power loom (the textile industry was the first to move into the factory stage) did not mark the immediate demise of the domestic production of cloth (Smelser, 1959). While in 1790 a mill was established in Pawtucket, Rhode Island using English-type machinery, and in 1814 a spinning and weaving mill was established in Waltham, Massachusetts, domestic production hung on well into the middle of the nineteenth century, when the growth in population created pressures that resulted in an increase of textile factories.

It is Tryon's contention that by 1830 Americans were relying predominantly on factory-made goods. What we observe between the middle of the seventeenth and the first quarter of the nineteenth century is the slow but definite movement of manufacturing outside of the home. (This may have been erratic because of restrictive legislation and war.) When we realize that the population of New England in 1650 is estimated to have been around 22,000 and in 1830 it was over 2 million, about one-seventh of which was urban, we see the kinds of population pressures placed upon the domestic economy. We must also recognize that the growth of factories in this country was also impeded by Britain's understandable reluctance to allow innovations such as Hargreave's spinning jenny and Cartwright's power loom to be used here. Nevertheless, American inventors were quick to jump into the breach and come up with counterparts of the English inventions.

The growth of the factory as the predominant mode of manufacturing had a notable effect on the family. As we have already pointed out several times, it moved the family from a unit producing the goods needed for its own consumption to one engaged in the consumption of goods. The basic economic partnership that existed between husband and wife and, to a somewhat more variable extent, between parents and children, could not survive in a factory setting. Although in the early stages of factory work in England and the United States families worked as families in the mills under paternal supervision, just as they had done under the putting-out cottage industry system, this represented a brief transitional phase that was soon discarded because of its impracticality (Smelser, 1959). Moreover, the apprentice-type relationships between father and son that existed in prefactory crafts and agriculture also underwent change, though the situation here is complicated by the growth of schools and ultimate restrictions on child labor.

Before going on to discuss the role of women in early American industry, we should note that some historians have recently begun to question the view that industrialization resulted in the family moving from a unit of production to a unit of consumption (Pleck, 1976). Based on research dealing with French-Canadian families in a New England mill town during the early decades of the twentieth century, Tamara Hareven has argued:

> Despite the sophisticated structures of industrial capitalism, families continued to function as production units, even though the workplace shifted from the home to the industrial plant. Within the limited flexibility of a corporation-controlled factory town, the family could continue to make its own labor force decisions and to maintain controls over the careers of its members, as long as the market was open. Migration to an urban setting and industrial work did not challenge paternal authority and traditional sex roles [1975:384].

This is an interesting argument and it is not without merit. What we see in this community, Manchester, New Hampshire, is a situation that resembles Young and Willmott's (1962) picture of working-class families in East End London in the middle of this century, but—and this is a crucial point—in both situations married women with children were not generally employed outside the home. In Hareven's words, "For family reasons as well as corporation needs, they found themselves in the reserve labor force rather than as regular workers (1975:379)." Thus, despite the protestations of the revisionists, industrialism did, until recently, for the most part exclude married women in the childbearing and childrearing years from *direct* participation in the work force.

WOMEN IN EARLY AMERICAN INDUSTRY

The establishment of the first mill at Waltham, Massachusetts in 1814, which contained machinery for the conversion of cotton into cloth, was soon followed by the establishment of similar mills in the same area and in neighboring towns. Cities such as Lowell, Massachusetts and Manchester, New Hampshire soon emerged as major manufacturing centers, the former gaining the title of "City of Spindles." The employees of this burgeoning industry were to come largely from farm families. The industry drew mainly upon young women and children of both sexes, and to a lesser extent upon mothers. By 1816 it was estimated that almost twice as many females (adults and children) as males (most of the latter being children under 17) had found employment in the cotton industry (Baker, 1964:10). By 1836, 74 percent of those working for one of Lowell's largest employers, the Hamilton Manufacturing Company, were women and 96 percent were native-born (Dublin, 1975b:30). This large-scale employment of the daughters of farmers was eagerly anticipated before it even came about. In 1791 Alexander Hamilton, then Secretary of the Treasury, speaking of the English experience said:

> The husband-man himself experiences a new source of profit and support, from the increased industry of his wife and daughters; invited and stimulated by the demands of the neighboring manufactories. . . .
>
> It is worthy of particular remark, that, in general, women and children are rendered more useful, and the latter more early useful, by manufacturing establishments, than they would otherwise be [quoted in Baker, 1964:6].

What is interesting here is that Hamilton did not see any threat to the family posed by the external employment of children and women. Obviously, he eagerly anticipated the coming of factories to this country. Women would help the new nation deal with its economic growing pains.

> Woman's place was thus not in the home, according to our founders, but wherever her "more important" work was. She was not unschooled for her new duties [textile production long having been her purview] in either temperament or discipline, and society would somehow have to make the necessary adjustments [Baker, 1964:7]

The manner in which these adjustments were made is of great interest, because it was done in a way which was to prove minimally disruptive to existing family structure, at least in the first half of the nineteenth century.

Our current image of a young woman who works in what we might call a blue-collar job is that such a person probably did not go beyond high school and would be classified by sociologists as "working class." At the beginning of the twentieth century it might have been assumed that she was a member of an ethnic minority. Interestingly enough, this was not the case in the early days of the textile mills. In fact, mill workers were likely to be the daughters of old Yankee families (Dublin, 1975b). Moreover, as Abbott points out:

> Before 1850 this line [between middle class and working class women's work] was scarcely discernible in New England, and work in the mills involved no social degradation. There was, indeed, no "field of employment" for educated women, and opportunities for training practically did not exist. A few months' term as a schoolmistress was a very unremunerative occupation, and . . . this was frequently combined with mill work as a sort of by-employment [Abbott, 1910:110–111].

Abbott even feels that for some the mills were a stopping place on the way to the academy and seminary. One contemporary was later to write, "For twenty years or more Lowell might have been looked upon as a rather selected industrial school for young people" (quoted in Abbott, 1910:112). There is also evidence that some young women worked in the mills half the year and went to schools such as Branford Academy and Mt. Holyoke Seminary during the other half.

In certain respects the relationships between the mills and the young women they employed was not unlike what some women encountered at the boarding schools they attended, though with several very important differences. While the Lowell mills were not typical of all New England mills, they are extremely important to study because of their large-scale employment of single women. Employees there had to live in company-run boarding houses, which had a strict 10:00 p.m. curfew. The women who ran these houses were generally widows, frequently with children of their own employed in the mills, who were supposedly chosen because of their exemplary character. This allowed the mill operators to exercise an extraordinary amount of control not only over the eating and sleeping patterns of their employees, but also over their social life as well (Dublin, 1975a). When hired, girls had to sign a document which was a written promise to attend church regularly, and in some mills it was demanded that a fee be paid for the support of a company-run church, even if it happened to be one that many of the operatives did not belong to.

There also appears to have been opportunity provided for self-improvement at Lowell. Classes in foreign languages were held in the boarding houses and a periodical was put out by the young women workers known as the *Lowell Offering.* Also in the town of Lowell itself the workers could hear lectures by such notables as John Quincy Adams and Ralph Waldo Emerson. Lending libraries also existed. In fact it appears that the literary interest of these young women was such that the mill owners passed regulations forbidding the bringing of books to work (Abbott, 1910:118).

One could easily get carried away with this image of the early mills as genteel boarding schools through which the daughters of New England's hearty agriculturalists briefly passed on their way to marriage or some other equally desirable outcome, and which in the process left them better educated, more worldly, and in general improved. The fact that most women employed during this period fell into the 16–25 age bracket with a very small minority married or widowed, might tend to support such notions. Yet, there is the other side of the coin, which is most vividly seen in the terrible working conditions of the mills.

It was not uncommon for employees to work as long as fourteen hours a day in the summer and twelve hours in the winter, though in general somewhere between twelve and thirteen hours was probably an average working day for Lowell before the middle of the century (Abbott, 1910:126). Not only were the hours long, but also the buildings were badly lit and poorly ventilated. Poor ventilation was especially problematic because of the omnipresence of cotton dust, which caused many respiratory ailments. It should also be noted that the boarding houses, much lauded by the mill owners, were crowded and poorly ventilated as well.

> On the whole then, it seems fair to say that conditions in early Lowell . . . as it appeared to many girls at that time were far from being idyllic as those prone to idealise the past would have us believe. Long hours, unsanitary mills, crowded boarding houses, compulsory supported corporation churches, all of these things are forgotten, and the young factory seems to us, as it seems to Dickens and other early visitors, sufficiently justified because of the remarkable intelligence and refinement of its operatives. *But their presence there was not symptomatic of ideal conditions in the mills, but rather of the lack of alternative occupations for women of education or superior abilities at that time* [emphasis added, Abbott, 1910:133–134].

Protests and strikes were not uncommon in the pre–1850 period. These women were apparently liberated by their economic independence and thus capable of militantly defending their interests when exploitation became intolerable (Dublin, 1975a).

In order to place the situation of the early New England cotton mills in the proper social-historical perspective, we must recognize that the period roughly between 1815 and 1850 was one of rapid national growth, a growth which, given available technology, required that a considerable portion of the work force be engaged in agriculture. Thus, labor was scarce and people had to be attracted to the mills. Mill owners recruited women out of necessity; the women in turn welcomed the jobs because there were few alternative employment opportunities. We know very little about these women after they left the mill. Did they return to rural regions as farmers' wives? Did they stay in the mill towns as wives of operatives? Or was neither their fate? These are questions that remain to be answered, but one cannot help but think that their experience in the mills and their earning of wages, however meager, gave them a sense of independence and autonomy that must have had some effect on how they thought of themselves as women, wives, and mothers (Lerner, 1969).

It is useful to take a careful look at the employment opportunities women had at the beginning of the nineteenth century to see what changes, if any, occurred as the century progressed. Abbott (1910:70) has very carefully reviewed existing documents, which include industrial censuses for the second quarter of the nineteenth century, and she concludes that women were employed in more than 100 different industries at the time, though some of these industries were still in the more or less domestic manufacturing category. In 1850, a census of manufacturers revealed that 24 percent of employees were women (Abbott, 1910:81). Yet there were during this time and well into the second half of the nineteenth century very few women in professional and clerical positions. Moreover, the technological advances resulting in the formalization of training and the institution of licensure served to push women out of professions such as medicine, where they had at least a toehold, and midwifery, where women were dominant. As Lerner has so aptly remarked:

> In seventeenth-century Maine the attempt of a man to act as midwife was considered outrageous and illegal: in mid-nineteenth-century America the suggestion that women should train as midwives and physicians was considered equally outrageous and improper [1969:9].

Nursing and teaching were perhaps the only professional fields from which women were not excluded as a result of upgrading, though nursing did not become an organized profession until the Civil War. On the other hand, teaching opportunities expanded because of the explosive growth of public education during the first half of the nineteenth century, combined with the aforementioned shortage of labor. So women filled the breach and did so at wages that were generally much lower than those obtained by their male counterparts.

Patricia Branca (1975b) has pointed out that scholarly discussions of female employment in the nineteenth century often overlook the fact that the Anglo-American and European experiences were far from identical. Women in France, Germany, and Italy were far less likely than their English or American sisters to seek employment in the factory. They were more apt to be found working in agriculture, domestic service, and home industry. In fact, Branca argues that much too much emphasis has been placed upon factory experience even in England and America, and notes that for a woman, working as a servant was the most popular form of employment from 1830 to the end of the century in these countries as well as on the Continent. From our perspective, where women worked is less important than the fact that they did work and their work took them out of the home and often out of the countryside into the city.

What manifests itself as the century progresses is the emergence of clear-cut, class-based patterns of female employment associated with what Barbara Welter (1966) speaks of as "the cult of true womanhood," while Lerner (1969) speaks of it in terms of the image of "the lady." We noted earlier that at the beginning of the nineteenth century employment in a mill did not define a woman as working class. The explanation for this is not merely that many of the mill workers were daughters of successful farmers working for a brief period to pay for their own or a brother's education or for some other less noble reason, but rather because it is difficult to speak of clear-cut class distinction before industrialization took place on a national scale.

As we have noted, the generally favorable images of the Lowell-type mills probably had more to do with the background of the women working in them than with the conditions of life and work that prevailed there. The upright, educated, and seemingly moral daughters of "good New England" stock were seen as the flowers of the nation at work in the nation's rapidly expanding industrial sector. But these were very special times, times when the attraction of the ever-growing frontier for men made mill owners seek out women and children as employees. And even these people were not easy to attract, as is indicated by the strategies and tactics employed by mill owners in both the boarding house and family-type systems. Agents were even sent out to rural communities and paid a fee for every employee they brought back (Ware, 1931: chapter 8). However, this situation was to change during the second half of the nineteenth century.

If we look at demographic aspects of the industrial work force, especially in the cotton industry, we see two important shifts: (1) men replacing women; and (2) immigrants replacing native-born workers (Dublin, 1975b). In 1831 women formed 68 percent of the cotton industry work force nationally. By 1900 this was down to 49 percent. In Massachusetts in the period from 1831 to 1895, the drop was from 80 to 50 percent (Abbott, 1910:102–103). At the same time, by 1900, 95 percent of the operatives at work in the Massachusetts cotton industry—men and women alike—were either foreign born or of foreign parentage, and 72 percent of the men and 68 percent of the women were in fact foreign born themselves. How did this transformation come about?

THE DEPARTURE OF WOMEN FROM THE FACTORY

The changes in the composition of the textile industry work force were the result of a number of factors. Regarding the shift in sex ratio, it is claimed that as the work grew more physically demanding, both in terms of heavy machinery and speed, women were pushed out because of a lack of strength and stamina (Abbott, 1910:107–108). Perhaps of greater significance was the tremendous influx of immigrants at a time when the sources from which the early mill operatives were drawn were drying up. Many of the New England families that had sent their daughters into the mills during the first half of the century were leaving New England for the West, where agriculture appeared to be a more viable enterprise. (The Great Plains offered a much higher yield with much less effort than the rocky soil of Maine and New Hampshire.) Even for those Yankees who remained, the expansion of fields such as teaching and other white-collar trades made the mills increasingly unattractive. At the same time this was happening, the mills themselves were undergoing a crisis. Business downturns created by recurrent fires and depressions, which required the laying off of the work force, forced mill owners to look for new sources when the time came to rehire. In addition, the growing number of Irish immigrants dramatically changed the ethnic character of a town like Lowell between 1840 and 1870. These immigrants, who increasingly entered the mills during the second half of the century, were not generally seen as pushing native Americans out of their jobs, because, as we have already indicated, the latter had more often than not moved west or moved up the occupational ladder. Hence *these* "foreigners" were initially welcomed rather than damned. The preponderance of men among the Irish helped tilt the scale in the direction of male laborers in the textile mills.

An important and related development is the change that took place during the last decades of the nineteenth century in the marital status of female textile operatives (Dublin 1975b). Earlier in this chapter we pointed out that the overwhelming majority of women in the Lowell-type mills appear to have been single. Given their concentration in the 16–25 age group, this is hardly surprising. However, by the turn of the century this situation had changed so that married women made up about one-sixth of the women in the cotton mills, and over half of the married women were foreign born (Abbott, 1910:123). These figures reflect the beginning of change in female employment patterns and the presence of an urban working class in which female employment, even after marriage, is becoming increasingly common. Yet the whole question of women, work, and marriage in the nineteenth century requires considerable untangling.

The prevailing image, both among professionals and laymen, is that the nineteenth century was the heyday of "traditional" husband-wife relations. This image is strongly associated with feminine idealization, and like much conventional wisdom, there is an element of truth to it. Barbara Welter has neatly summarized what she speaks of as the mid nineteenth-century "cult of True Womanhood."

> The attributes of True Womanhood, by which a woman judged herself and was judged by her husband, her neighbors and society could be divided into four cardinal virtues—piety, purity, submissiveness and domesticity. Put them all together and they spelled mother, daughter, sister, wife—woman. Without them, no matter whether there was fame, achievement or wealth, all was ashes. With them she was promised happiness and power [Welter, 1966:151].

To be sure, this description appears to be the ideal presented in the hortatory literature of the period. To the sociologist this marks the appearance of an essentially leisured group of married females, something which was really unknown on a large scale previously and which had been made possible only by the growth of an urban middle class (Branca, 1975a). Moreover, we should recognize that while the feminine ideal of the lady might have been only nascent in the working classes, the extent of female employment in all classes during the nineteenth century was in general insignificant. In 1890 only 4.6 percent of married American women were in the labor force (U.S. Bureau of the Census, 1975b:133). In a broader perspective, both in the United States and England, the employment rate of married women—which includes home industry as well as domestic service, factory work, and all other remunerative economic activity—never exceeded 10 percent during the nineteenth century (Branca, 1975b:135). To be sure, economic necessity drove more working-class women into the labor force than their middle-class counterparts. But while figures showing class differences are not available, it is obvious from the strikingly low national rate that the rates of employment for working-class women were not terribly high.

The period from 1890 to the present represents a very important era in the history of women, work, and marriage, for it is during this period that some significant changes occur in the educational and vocational opportunities available to women. Table 4-1 contains data on female participation in the work force by marital status. While the figures presented in Table 4-1 are not strictly comparable over time, because of slight monthly vari-

Table 4-1. PARTICIPATION OF WOMEN IN THE LABOR FORCE BY MARITAL STATUS FOR THE YEARS 1890–1970[a]

Year	Percentage of Total Work Force	Single[b]	Married[b]	Widowed/ Divorced[b]
1890	18.2	68.2	13.9	17.9
1900	20.1	66.2	15.4	18.4
1910	N.A.[c]	60.2	24.7	15.0
1920	22.7	77.0	23.0	N.A.[c]
1930	23.6	53.9	28.9	17.2
1940	25.8	49.0	35.9	15.0
1950	29.9	31.9	52.2	16.0
1960	35.7	23.6	60.7	15.7
1970	41.4	22.5	62.3	15.0

SOURCE: *Historical Statistics of the United States* (Bureau of the Census, 1975), pp. 132–133.

[a]These figures are based on monthly enumerations and thus reflect seasonal variation.

[b]As a percentage of the female labor force.

[c]N.A.: Not Available.

ation, they nonetheless make evident that the broad trend over the past eighty years has been toward a greater participation of women in the labor force in general, with married women manifesting the greatest increases.

THE RETURN OF WOMEN TO THE WORK FORCE

In general, while female participation in the labor force has been increasing since the nineteenth century, only since World War II has it moved ahead rapidly. Let us look more carefully at this development. It is necessary for the reader to keep in mind that during the last decades of the nineteenth century women were faced with a situation where both ideology and opportunity (related, though separable) operated against their participation in the work force, especially for middle-class women. Furthermore, a good percentage of the population was still engaged in agricultural work that required economic partnership between husband and wife.

> Nearly half of all American women still lived on farms in 1890. Like farm women throughout history, they rose before sun and spent their days as active partners in the family's common work. Just what they did depended on the kind of farm, its income, what other members of the family were able to do, the customs of the locality, and many other circumstances [Robert Smuts, 1971:6].

While in 1890 the frontier was closed in the eyes of the government, conditions that prevailed in the Far West and even in parts of the Midwest resembled pioneer conditions at their most primitive. Women in such situations found no shortage of tasks to occupy their time; and this was even more the case for that sizable minority of widows and wives of disabled men who ran their own farms.

Even among those families that had become part of the industrial work force, agricultural activity was not always absent, and given the small amount of female work force participation outside of the home, it is probably safe to assume that women bore the lion's share of the responsibility for this sphere of family life (Kleinberg, 1976). Smuts cites such a situation:

> Especially in the coal and steel regions, the grounds around the urban and suburban houses sometimes looked much like a rural farmyard. Many families kept chickens or rabbits, sometimes pigs or goats and even a cow or two, and raised vegetables and fruits in their own garden plots. A study of 2,500 families living in the principal coal, iron and steel regions in 1890 suggests that about half of them had livestock, poultry, vegetable gardens, or all three. Nearly 30 percent purchased no vegetables other than potatoes during the course of the year [1971:11].

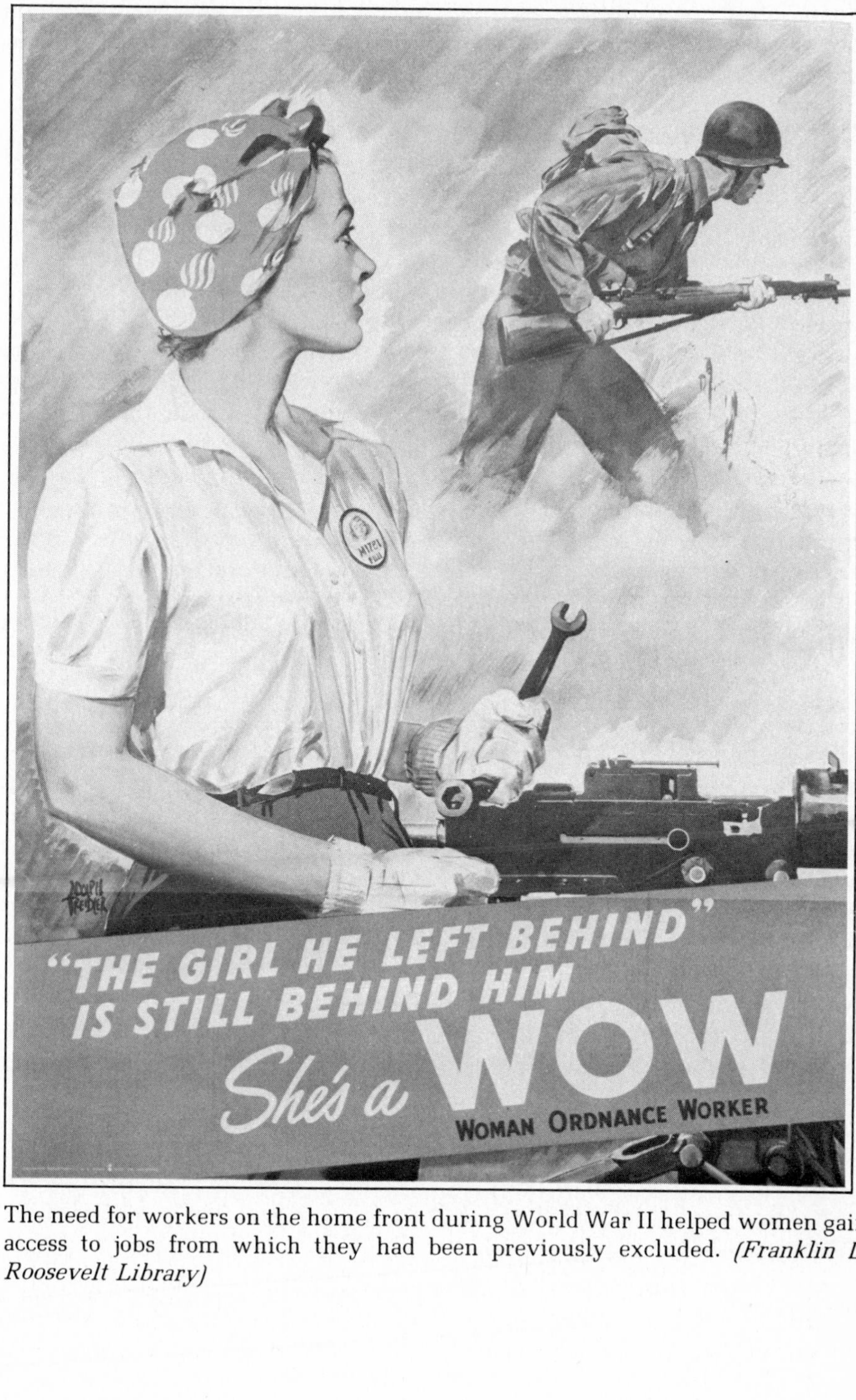

The need for workers on the home front during World War II helped women gain access to jobs from which they had been previously excluded. *(Franklin D. Roosevelt Library)*

Such marginal agricultural activity was important because it represented a way in which women could stay at home, honoring traditional patterns, and at the same time be economically productive.

There were other ways in which wives and mothers could contribute to the family's finances while remaining in the home. Among the more significant of these was the taking in of boarders, followed by sewing and laundry work (McLaughlin, 1971). Boarding and lodging, as we have already indicated in Chapter 1, was a phenomenon of considerable significance on the urban American scene from 1880 to 1940, and can be seen as a response to both the growing number of single people in industry and the economic need for many urban families. Sewing usually involved doing dressmaking and alterations for people in the community. In some towns it also involved doing piecework for nearby firms that were either still in transition between domestic and factory-type production, or were unable to find enough fulltime factory employees who could work at the wages they were offering (Neff, 1929). Taking in washing and ironing also provided income for women. Other occupations, such as cigar rolling, also lent themselves to "homework." While no figures are immediately available on the number of women engaged in home manufacturing at the turn of the present century, it does appear that this represented an important piece of female employment during what was apparently a transitional period in the employment of married women (Pleck, forthcoming).

For single women, growing industry did provide opportunities. We have already commented at length on the important role played by women in the early New England textile mills. However, as the nineteenth century progressed, their numbers diminished. In the cotton industry the trend from 1850 to 1900 was as follows: the proportion of women to the total number of men and women workers over 16 in 1850 was 64 percent; in 1860, 62 percent; 1870, 60 percent; 1880, 57 percent; 1890, 54 percent; 1900, 48 percent (Abbott, 1910:360). The general industrial trend was the same for all industries on which data were available: in 1850, 24 percent of the workers were women; in 1860, 21 percent; 1870, 18 percent; 1880, 22 percent; 1890, 20 percent; 1900, 21 percent (Abbott, 1910:360). While these figures are not completely accurate, their compiler considered them to be the best available estimate, correcting for known sources of error. However, at the same time that opportunities for women were declining in blue-collar industry, they were opening up in the white-collar sphere. Up until at least the middle of the nineteenth century, the office and the retail establishments were largely men's domains. During the second half of the century, however, this was to change, and by the last decades women were making their presence felt in increasing numbers in both types of establishments. The appearance of office machinery, beginning with the introduction of the typewriter in 1870, as well as growing demands for male labor in other areas, was to bring about important changes in the office. Table 4-2 contains some very revealing statistics drawn from the Women's Bureau of the Department of Labor. Perhaps the significance

Table 4-2. WOMEN OFFICE WORKERS[a]

Year	Number	Increase Over Preceding Census (%)
1940	1,863,154	25.6
1930	1,482,947	42.8
1920	1,038,390	168.5
1910	386,765	270.3
1900	104,450	129.3
1890	45,553	1,867.7
1880	2,315	148.9
1870	930	—

SOURCE: Janet M. Hooks, *Women's Occupations Through Seven Decades* (Washington, D.C.: Bureau Bulletin no. 218, 1947), p. 75.

[a] Includes stenographers, typists, and secretaries; shipping and receiving clerks; clerical and kindred workers (not elsewhere classified); and office machine operators.

of the figures in Table 4-2 will become more obvious when we add that in 1870 there were almost 29,000 men engaged in office work in contrast to the 930 women indicated in the table. Clearly this is an area of the work world in which opportunities for women have expanded rapidly during the last 100 years. It is important to note that while women made up only 3.1 percent of the office worker population in 1870, and 29.3 percent by 1900, in 1940 they made up 54.1 percent, and in the 1920s their numbers surpassed those of men (Hooks, 1947:76). Concomitantly, in the realm of sales personnel, women went from 0.5 percent of those so employed in 1870 to 4.1 percent in 1900 to 6.6 percent in 1940 (Hooks, 1947:85). Similar changes are seen in other white-collar occupations, such as medical and dental assistants (Hooks, 1947:81). The effect of such changes was to increase the percentage of women in the labor force, as is evident in Table 4-1.

Before we go on to discuss changes in the composition of the female work force, it will be instructive to look at some other areas of female employment, namely, the professions. As Table 4-3 clearly shows, the general growth in female work force participation since the beginning of the century has not been matched by concurrent rises in the representation of women in various professions, especially in the more prestigious and highly remunerative ones, such as medicine and law. Women show a predominance in areas such as nursing, social work, and librarianship. In a recent article Stricker has, however, pointed out that the representation of women in some nonprofessional but still prestigious fields did increase significantly since the beginning of the century. "For example, the proportion of real estate agents, managers and superintendents tripled from 1910 to 1920, from 2.3% to 6.1% of the total, doubled to 12.9% in 1930, and almost doubled again to 20.2% of the total in 1940 [Stricker, 1976:5]."

Table 4-3. WOMEN IN SELECTED PROFESSIONAL OCCUPATIONS IN THE UNITED STATES (percentage of all workers)

Occupation	1900	1910	1920	1930	1940	1950	1960	1970
Lawyers	—	1.0	1.4	2.1	2.4	3.5	3.5	4.7
Clergy	4.4	1.0	2.6	4.3	2.2	8.5	5.8	2.9
Doctors	—	6.0	5.0	4.0	4.6	6.1	6.8	9.2
Engineers	—	—	—	—	0.3	1.2	0.8	1.6
Dentists	—	3.1	3.2	1.8	1.5	2.7	2.1	3.4
Biologists	—	—	—	—	—	27.0	28.0	35.0
Chemists	—	—	—	—	—	10.0	8.6	11.9
Mathematicians	—	—	—	—	—	38.0	26.4	22.4
Physicists	—	—	—	—	—	6.5	4.2	4.0
Nurses	94.0	93.0	96.0	98.0	98.0	98.0	97.0	97.3
Social Workers	—	52.0	62.0	68.0	67.0	66.0	57.0	62.7
Librarians	—	79.0	88.0	91.0	89.0	89.0	85.0	81.9

SOURCES: Cynthia F. Epstein, *Woman's Place* (Berkeley: University of California Press, 1971), p. 7; and U.S. Bureau of the Census, *Characteristics of the Population*, vol. 1, part 1, table 222 (Washington, D.C.: Government Printing Office), pp. 725–727.

Robert W. Smuts in *Women and Work in America* (1971) offers us a useful benchmark for looking at the change in the composition of the female work force at the end of the last century.

> The typical 1890 working woman is easily sketched. She was young and single, the daughter of ambitious, hardworking immigrant or native farmers. With little education or training, she was spending the years between school and marriage in one of the many kinds of unskilled jobs available in the city. The main variations from this type can also be readily discerned: widows, wives whose husbands did not support them, Negro women in farm or domestic service jobs in the South, immigrant wives in the cotton mills of the North, and a few unconventional women who worked even though others in similar circumstances did not [1971:38].

Currently, single women make up slightly over one-fifth of the female work force and married women over three-fifths (U.S. Bureau of the Census, 1975a). Clearly, changes have occurred not only in the composition of the female work force, but also in the meaning of work for women. In contrast to her great grandmother, who worked only until she was married, a woman today is likely to spend a much greater part of her life employed outside the home. How are these shifts to be interpreted? By way of a general assessment, T. Aldrich Finegan has written:

> The rising labor force participation rate of married women is one of the most interesting long-run trends in the American economy. The more important reasons for this trend include the growth in the real wages of women, the development of labor-saving innovations in the home, shifts in the occupational and industrial composition of employment, the shorter workweek, the

> falling birthrate (since 1960), the earlier school enrollment of children, and the rising educational attainment of married women [1975:52].

Taking a sample of women from the 1960 census, Finegan found that the variables with the strongest effect on women's employment were the presence of preschool children, education, and husband's income. Preschool children appear to be an important deterrent to work, but as Figure 4-1 shows, this is becoming less and less the case. In fact, since World War II, and especially since the 1960s, the proportion of employed married women with children under six has grown fantastically. Between 1971 and 1977 alone the percentage of preschool children with working mothers rose 8 percent (*New York Times,* March 1, 1977:27). This development suggests that attitudinal changes may have occurred, but one would have to know more about the economic circumstances of these women before one could attribute it to attitudinal change alone rather than to economic pressure.

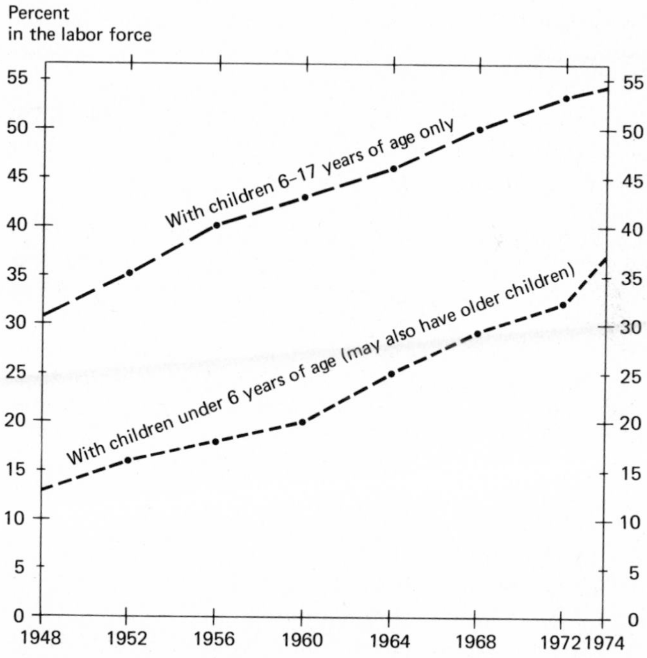

Figure 4-1 Civilian labor force participation rates of ever-married women, by age of children, selected years 1948–1974*

*Data cover March of each year except for April 1948 and 1952, and are for females 14 years of age and over except in 1963, 1972, and 1974, which are for 16 years and over.

SOURCE: *1975 Handbook on Women Workers* (Washington, D.C.: U.S. Department of Labor, 1975), p. 27.

Holding other things constant "a married woman is more likely to be in the labor force the lower her husband's income and the more formal schooling she has had" (Finegan, 1975:52). These findings illuminate some of the more subtle dynamics behind the employment of married women, especially the counterpressures. The reason education is positively associated with participation in the labor force is that it is not only associated with higher incomes and more pleasant work surroundings, but also because it is associated with the kinds of employment that are supportive of a "career" orientation, that is, work which is seen as an intrinsic part of a woman's life rather than merely as something a woman does as an adjunct to her roles as wife and mother (Degler, 1964). At the same time, however, we see that the higher a husband's income, the more it operates to depress his wife's labor force participation, something which can probably be interpreted as a reflection of the obeisance still being paid to the notion of the man's role as primary breadwinner. Such conservatism notwithstanding, the general trend is one of growing support for the working wife and mother. William Chafe (1972:148) cites a government study which shows that during the most economically harrowing days of the Depression 80 percent of the American public was opposed to a wife working, but by the early years of World War II, 60 percent were in favor of women being hired by defense industries. To be sure, this change in attitude came at a time of national crisis when all hands were needed on the home front; still, patterns of married women's employment in the postwar years indicate that the change in attitude persisted after the crisis passed. There have been other factors at work as well. As evidence of this, roughly 69 per cent of a national sample of Americans said in 1974 that they approved of a woman working when her husband's income alone could support her (N.O.R.C., 1974:49).

Valerie K. Oppenheimer (1973) offers us some demographic insights into these changes. She points out that a dramatic change in both numbers *and* composition of the female work force has taken place since 1940. After 1940 we see the reentry of older married women (those over thirty-five) into the work force, and in 1950 younger married women, including those with preschool children, start showing up in increasing numbers. Oppenheimer's explanation for these changes rests largely on the argument that demand for female labor has grown as a result of economic expansion. This has been augmented by demographic changes in the number of women available (Oppenheimer, 1972:948). The fact that the demand has been for *women* workers is a result, she maintains, of the sex stereotyping of certain jobs, for example, nurses, teachers, secretaries, librarians, etc., which have throughout the century had a disproportionate concentration of women. Thus, as the demand for workers in these categories expanded, the pressure on women to reenter or stay in the labor force continued. In addition, the kind of discrimination that had worked to keep older married women out of the work force was relaxed, since the low fertility of the Depression had created a shortage of younger women. Oppenheimer by no means feels that she has explained the whole question of women's increasing employment by her consideration of supply and demand factors, but she has touched upon an important aspect of this change and one which is often neglected by those who try to explain such phenomena.

SUMMARY

During this country's colonial era and continuing into the Federal period, most economic activity took place within or near the home. The family was an economically productive unit and the husband and wife were partners in this enterprise. With the coming of the industrial revolution and the increasing separation of home and work, we initially find few married women leaving their homes to enter the labor force, in contrast to young unmarried women who play an important, if not dominant, role in the early stages of the American textile industry, the first to undergo industrialization. Still, both in the United States as well as in England and Europe throughout the nineteenth century, more single women were to be found in domestic service and various kinds of home-based manufacturing than in the factory.

What we have seen in this century is a dramatic overall increase in female participation in the labor force, as well as a change in the marital status of those who participated. Instead of single women working for a

Occupations that were once the preserve of men are now opening to women. Here we see a woman reporter at work. *(George W. Gardner)*

brief period before marriage, we now have a situation in which most working women are married and a growing minority have young children. Women are, however, still concentrated in the less prestigious and less remunerative areas of the economy. Oppenheimer has shown us that the future does not look bright in terms of expansion of opportunity for women in the more desirable areas of employment, despite work increasingly assuming an important place in their lives as their educational achievements continue to rise. As she notes, "If this is considered undesirable, then policies promoting increased job opportunities for women are essential" (1972:325).

Marriage—a satiric nineteenth-century view. *(NYPL Picture Collection)*

FERTILITY: Toward the "Contraceptive Society" 5

During the 1970s, newspaper headlines began proclaiming that the birth rate in the United States had fallen below the "replacement level." While it will be some time before this reduction in fertility (if it continues) actually results in a declining population, it is a most interesting and important development. Some interpret this decline as evidence of the crumbling of pronatalism—the fall of what Ellen Peck and Judith Senderowitz call "The Myth of Mom and Apple Pie" (1974). Others see it as an aberration growing out of temporary economic circumstances (Easterlin, 1976b). Irrespective of one's own ideology, a glance at long-term American fertility statistics will reveal that the decline in the birth rate in fact represents the continuation of a trend that goes back to the eighteenth century.

In this chapter we shall examine the patterns of Western fertility since the eighteenth century, and in doing so attempt to explain the way in which these fertility patterns have been linked to broader social change. It is important to recognize that the study of fertility offers more than just a picture of the way in which people have handled their reproductive capacities; it also provides us with insights into attitudes towards parenthood as well as marriage.

LEGITIMACY

In our society a great deal of emphasis is put on the sexual aspects of marriage, since at present marriage is the only relationship in which coitus is supposed to occur—even if this is only a reflection of the mores, and does not reflect actual practice. Study of the ethnographic literature makes it evident that this attitude is not found in all cultures (Stephens, 1963). People in many cultures engage in sexual intercourse before marriage with persons other than their anticipated spouses. Even after marriage intercourse with someone other than the spouse is permissible in many cultures. This is done without calling forth either the covert or overt disapproval of other members of society, though there may be restrictions on the people with whom intercourse is permissible, that is, the partner must be from certain groups within the society and not from others. While our culture obviously differs from such societies in attitudes toward sexual freedom, virtually all societies do share the belief that children should be born into a relationship that has been sanctified by marriage; otherwise the children will not be considered "legitimate."

Many typewriter ribbons have been expended over the concept of legitimacy, if only because there appear to be so many exceptions to "the rule." Kingsley Davis provides us with a good place to start the discussion of this topic.

> The social definition of fatherhood we may call, following Malinowski, the "principle of legitimacy"—the universal social rule that "no child should be brought into the world without a man—and one man at that—assuming the role of sociological father, that is, guardian and protector, the male link between the child and the rest of the community." Without this general rule, to which many others are subsidiary, there would be no family; hence it is as universal and fundamental as the familial institution itself. It prevails no matter what other conditions prevail. Children may be an asset or a liability, prenuptial and extramarital intercourse may be forbidden or sanctioned, still the rule runs that a father is indispensable for the full social status of the child and its mother. Otherwise the child is illegitimate and the mother disesteemed [1949:400–401].

In other words, Davis (and Malinowski) hold that, sociologically speaking, a child is not supposed to enter the world without his or her mother being part of that category of women who are entitled to bear children. Any child born of a woman not in this category is seen as unlinked to the society, not only in the sense in which Davis has mentioned, but also in the sense of not having any tie to a larger family and kin unit within that society. Such a child lacks any location in significant social space.

This "classic" interpretation of legitimacy and the function of marriage in providing for the social placement of children has often been challenged in the sociological literature by examples that appear to call into question the universality of the marriage-legitimacy rule. The two most notable examples are the cases of the Nayar people and the people of the Caribbean area (Rodman, 1966). The anthropologist, Kathleen Gough (1968), offers us a very insightful discussion of marriage customs among the Nayar, a warrior subcaste, in her reconstruction of their life in precolonial India.

An annual ceremony was held by each of the Nayar lineages during which prepubescent girls ranging in age from roughly seven to twelve years old were married in a ritual fashion to men from lineages that were linked with their own. The men were chosen on the basis of astrological considerations. After a ceremony (tali-tying), each couple spent three days alone together. If the girl was close to menarche, she and her new bridegroom might engage in coitus during this time. At the end of the seclusion period the couple engaged in a purification ritual. Then the husband departed, unencumbered by any obligation to his wife; the wife, in turn, only owed him the implicit promise that when he died she and any children she might subsequently bear—though these were unlikely to be his biological children—would engage in the mourning ceremonies for him.

After going through this ritual marriage known as the tali-rite, the status of a young woman changed dramatically. From our point of view, the most notable change was that she was now permitted to receive "visiting husbands." These were men from her own subcaste but of different lineages, as well as others from higher subcastes. While a tali-rite husband might engage in sexual intercourse with his wife after she reached puberty, he had no particular claim to her over the other husbands she might have chosen to enter into liaisons with. During the sixteenth and seventeenth centuries, it was not unusual for a woman to have as many as eight such husbands. These husbands limited their visits to the time between the completion of the evening meal and the following sunrise. Their obligations were limited to providing the "wives" with luxuries such as betel nuts (a mild narcotic) and clothing in addition to the regular garments provided her by the matrilineal group to which she belonged. These gifts were only expected while the relationship lasted. Once a relationship was terminated, a man ceased to have any obligation to his former "wife." (The point should be made that this was *not* a case of what might be described as serial monogamy, where a woman usually had several "visiting husbands" at the same time.)

It is easy to see that under the Nayar system biological paternity might indeed be difficult to establish. But what is of interest and importance to us is that from the point of view of members of such a culture establishing biological paternity was unimportant, just so long as one of the husbands recognized the child as his own. This was done by the man making appropriate gifts to the midwife who assisted at the child's birth. Once having made these gifts, the man "had no economic, social, legal, or ritual rights in, nor obligations to his children" (Gough, 1968:87). All obligations fell on the woman's maternal kin group; the children in turn had no obligations to their "genitor," since only at the death of their mother's tali-rite husband would mourning be right and proper.

What makes the case of the Nayar of such importance to our discussion of legitimacy is that it has been the subject of a mild controversy in anthropological circles. Dr. Edmund Leach has argued that the legitimation of children is not universally associated with marriage, and he has cited the Nayar in support of this argument. He maintains that among the Nayar, "The notion of fatherhood is lacking" (quoted in Gough, 1968:81) and that children born of the marital liaisons, as described above, were "simply recruits to the woman's own matrilineage." Gough strongly takes issue with Leach on the grounds that:

> . . . unless his [the child's] mother was ritually married by a man of appropriate caste, and unless his biological paternity was vouched for by one or more men of appropriate caste, a child could never enter his caste or lineage at all [1968:92].

Thus, the Nayar represent a special case, but one which nonetheless puts legitimacy at the heart of marriage. In the absence of the tali-rite, a woman is not entitled to engage in those relationships that may produce a child. Thus, even in a situation resembling group marriage, there is a definite link between marriage and legitimacy.

Before leaving the Nayar, the point must be made that it is *not* Gough's claim that there are *no* societies in which children are born without an acknowledged father and where they must acquire their placement in society solely through the mother. Rather, the point is that where marriage is a recognized relationship, it is usually tied to the concept of legitimacy. However, in our own country we have recently seen the beginning of an important trend in regard to legitimacy, namely, the growing number of single parents, especially females. We are also witnessing an increase in the number of adoptions by single women and an increase in the number of single women who decide to have children of their own in the absence of a husband or any specific male (Francoeur, 1970). Moreover, Sweden has attempted to completely do away with the legal category of the bastard, and in the process has removed the notion of legitimacy from the statute books. While such developments are still in their early stages, they are important because of what they suggest concerning the changing relationship between marriage and the social placement of children *and* women. We shall return to this point later in the chapter.

Marriage, then, provides a vehicle through which a child may enter society. If marriage and childbirth are so importantly linked, then we must now consider the motives for having a child as they relate to the motives for marrying. Children enable a family to perpetuate itself, to maintain the family line, though today most of us do not think of offspring in such terms—or at least the less affluent members of our society do not. In peasant societies, however, wealth exists in the form of land. Therefore such wealth must be transmitted from generation to generation. Moreover, given the level of agricultural technology that prevailed in the premodern West and still prevails in premodern nations, children are an asset in terms of the economic assistance they provide the family. They are also a source of economic and emotional support in the parents' old age.

As family wealth has become more fluid, as work and home have become more separate, and retirement benefits more commonplace, we would expect motivation for childbearing to undergo change. Indeed, the available evidence suggests that it has. People now enter marriage for the personal satisfactions it provides. As a broad generalization it is probably safe to say that we also have children for the personal satisfactions they provide, though considerations of perpetuation—in a personal rather than in any familistic sense—may still be at work.

PREMODERN POPULATION DYNAMICS

The study of fertility in the modern world is complicated both by the paucity of reliable information and by the variety of patterns shown by the nations on which data do exist. Nonetheless, from the limited material we do have available, it appears that fertility, like preindustrial household size, cannot be discussed in terms of a "before and after" model. Rather, it requires that we consider changes *within* both the modern and premodern periods. For example, E. A. Wrigley's research on family limitation in Colyton, England reveals higher fertility rates in the seventeenth century than in the eighteenth century (in Wrigley, 1972b:64). The more we learn about premodern population patterns, the more we realize that totally uncontrolled fertility was the exception rather than the rule (Engerman, 1976).

Given our modern perspective, we tend to think of fertility control in terms of consciously employed contraception, but we must keep in mind that premodern populations had other ways of controlling population, most notably through varying the age of marriage and the number of people who married (van de Walle, 1968). Let us consider the first of these methods:

> In societies in which there is little control of contraception within marriage this is one of the most important variables bearing upon reproduction rates. Indeed, it is sometimes asserted that a lowering of the age of first marriage for women largely accounted for the rapid rise of population in England in the second half of the eighteenth century. The mean age at which women bore their last child in European communities with little or no control of contraception was usually about forty, and for some years before this their fecundity declined rapidly. It is clear therefore that a mean age of first marriage of 22 in these circumstances will give rise to twice as many births in completed families as a mean age of, say, 29 or 30 [Wrigley, 1972b:60–61].

The point of Wrigley's statement is that since the period in a woman's life when she can become pregnant is limited, the later she marries, the fewer children she is likely to bear, even when subject to maximum exposure from coitus without contraception.

In Colyton parish, for the 300 years that were covered by Wrigley's study, there was relatively little variation in the age of men at marriage, but this has not been the case in all premodern communities; moreover, we must recognize that while much of the emphasis has been placed on the woman's age at marriage in determining fertility—especially in communities not practicing contraception—insufficient attention has been paid to the men's marriage age. Daniel Scott Smith (1972a), in his research on the population of Hingham, Massachusetts, has suggested that the husband's age at marriage may work to alter marital fertility to the degree that increasing age among males is associated with a decline in marital coital frequency (Kinsey et al., 1948)—a factor that should obviously be associated with the likelihood of conception in any one menstrual cycle.

Thus we see that in any community, variation in age at marriage alone can account for some degree of variation in fertility. Yet age at marriage represents a somewhat unconscious way of regulating population size—it is almost like the instinctive practice of Tribolium beetles, which control their fertility in response to the amount of food available (Chapman, 1928). To the sociologist, the more direct and seemingly conscious steps people take to control their reproductive capacities are of more interest, though not necessarily of more significance.

Ariès provides us with a succinct history of contraceptive knowledge and practice in the West since the medieval period.

> Contraceptive techniques were either unknown or at least neglected during the Middle Ages, except in extramarital sexual relations and in prostitution. In the seventeenth century they were at least accepted, admitted or wished for among the bourgeoisie and the nobility, by lawfully married women who were tired out by too many pregnancies and concerned with the future of a large family. Lastly, entire families appear to have accepted them after the second half of the eighteenth century as an unavoidable means of social progress [1972:115].

It is important to note that the basic method of contraception during the eighteenth and nineteenth centuries was nothing more elaborate than withdrawal by the male prior to ejaculation (*coitus interruptus*). This did not represent any technological breakthrough as do, for example, oral contraceptives in our day. It merely represented a change in attitude, which enabled and motivated people to use a means of family limitation and planning that had always been available (Schnucker, 1975; Wells, 1975a). We might note in passing that demographic historians are debating whether contraception in the form of withdrawal was being used to limit fertility in English villages as early as the seventeenth century (Crafts and Ireland,1976).

Since the withdrawal method has always been available, the question is not so much why haven't people exercised control over their fecundity in the past, but rather, why do they choose to control it at present? We know relatively little about the marital sex lives of our ancestors, since sex is a phenomenon that does not lend itself to direct historical examination. Also, old customs often militated against its discussion in literary documents. Yet it seems apparent that little direct restraint was exercised on sexual impulses in the premodern and early modern West, given the high rates of marital fertility that can be observed for those periods. The question remains as to whether this propensity to push women to the limits of their reproductive capacities grew out of the desire for large families or other factors which made people unable to control sexual impulses or employ *coitus interruptus.*

Let us consider the general picture of population dynamics in the premodern world. Advocates of so-called "demographic transition theory" maintain that premodern rates of fertility and mortality offset each other, resulting in a situation of relatively little growth. Industrialization (they speak of industrialization rather than modernization) initially lowered the death rates more quickly than the birth rates, creating a transition period of high growth before the birth rates also declined, resulting in a return to relative population stability (Notestein, 1945). Demographic transition theory has been attacked from several points of view (Goldschneider, 1971; Caldwell, 1976) but from our perspective, one of its more important shortcomings is its failure to recognize the often volatile changes in premodern populations.

Looking at Figure 5-1, which charts England's population changes from 1234 to 1489, we see that the situation could hardly be described as stable. According to T. H. Hollingsworth (1969), most of the graph's valleys were the result of famines or disease. Thus we would expect the reason for the declining death rates in the eighteenth and nineteenth centuries to be found in factors which reduced the impact of both disease and famine.

Mortality

While it is true that bad harvests continue to occur in the modern world, and therefore famine is still possible, the nature of modern agricultural production is such that modern nations are now interdependent rather than independent in food production. This interdependence reflects two developments: (1) subsistence farming has declined and growing specialized cash crops has increased; and (2) advances in transportation allow food to be sent to those areas that are suffering from shortages created by natural disasters. (This exchange takes place between nations as well as within nations.) Furthermore, as technology began to have its effects on the agricultural sphere, land became more productive and more reliably so. New crops were introduced, as well as crop rotation and different techniques of fertilization. The lowly potato—because of its high yield per acre and its ability to thrive where other crops fail—may have played an important part in reducing mortality as it became the staple crop in many European countries during the nineteenth century. One could devote a whole chapter, if not several books, to the impact industrialization had upon the production and distribution of foodstuffs, as well as diet, but the brief remarks that have already been made should give the reader some

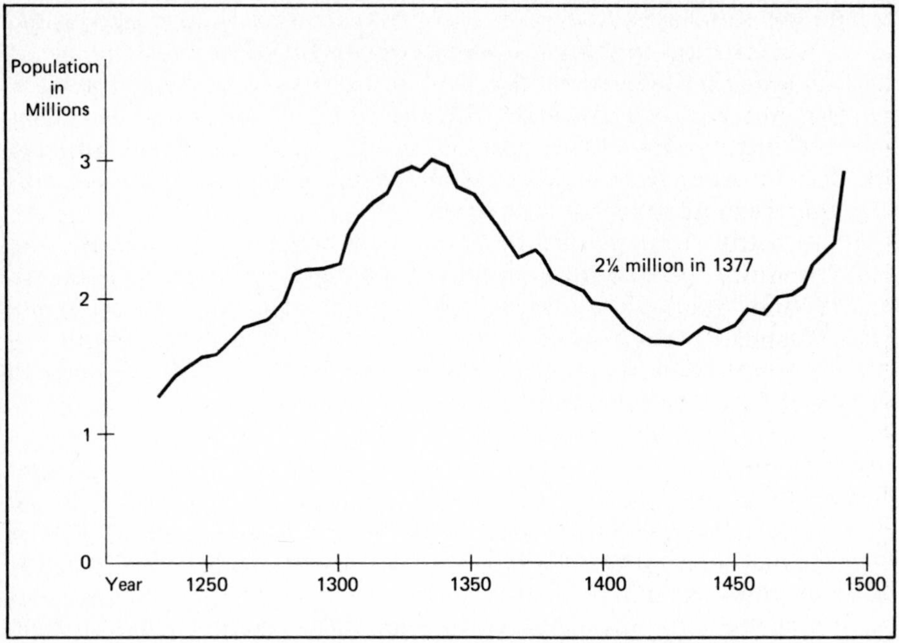

Figure 5-1 The Population of England, 1234–1489 (based on inquest generation survival rates)

SOURCE: Reprinted from T. H. Hollingsworth, *Historical Demography* (London: Hodder and Stoughton, 1969), p. 381.

idea of the effect that the agricultural innovations associated with industrialization had on mortality.

During the nineteenth century there was a reduction in mortality in those countries undergoing industrialization, particularly among children and adolescents. While there are some instances of decline in the eighteenth century (Shorter, 1975: chapter 5), it is not until the end of the nineteenth century that infant mortality declines substantially and consistently. Wrigley offers us an interesting interpretation of this:

> During the period of heaviest infant mortality in the first days and weeks of life a baby is dependent on his mother for food, so that the type and quality of his food does not alter much over a wide range of environmental conditions. Children at this age are, however, highly susceptible to infectious diseases of the stomach and chest. A radical improvement in infant mortality, therefore, is only likely when the nature of these infections is understood and effective countermeasures are available. Only at the end of the nineteenth century was the necessary knowledge attained [1969:169–171].

In addition, for the child who has already been weaned, the improvement in the supply of food may have had an effect on the ability both to resist ravaging diseases such as tuberculosis, scarlet fever, and whooping cough, and to survive once having contracted a disease.

In general, the slow but steady rise in life expectancy during the nineteenth century is probably attributable more to the robustness created by superior nutrition than to breakthroughs in the control and prevention of disease. However, we must recognize that these improvements were offset to some extent by new health problems arising as a result of population density in the growing urban centers. In the enlarging cities of nineteenth-century Europe the concentration of large numbers of people in squalid and crowded conditions, aggravated by a low level of public health standards, did much to keep mortality rates up. In the middle of the nineteenth century, when male life expectancy averaged 40.2 years in Britain, it was under 20 years in some sections of Manchester and Liverpool (Wrigley, 1969:173).

As the nineteenth century drew to a close, some headway was being made both in sanitary conditions such as sewage and water supply systems. In part, these improvements grew out of a new appreciation of how disease was communicated and spread. For example, following the installation of a municipal filtration plant in Pittsburgh in 1908, the number of cases of typhoid dropped from 593 in October 1907 to 96 in October 1908 (Kellogg, 1914:63–64). Previously the water supply had come from the Allegheny River, where both industrial and human waste freely mingled. At the same time, advances were being made in disease control through the pasteurization of milk (Beaver, 1973) and the development of various vaccines. The availability of such knowledge today accounts for the extraordinary rapidity with which high mortality rates have been reduced in developing nations.

To briefly summarize then, in the premodern world mortality was relatively high by comparison with modern standards. Moreover these levels were regularly aggravated by such natural catastrophes as famines and epidemics—not to mention such human-initiated holocausts as wars, which often contributed greatly to both crop destruction and the spread of disease. While new levels of agricultural, sanitary, and medical technology have not done away with these "natural" devastators, modern technology has brought their effects under control.

Fertility Patterns

In general, modernization is associated with declining birth rates. This should come as no surprise to readers, since we have already discussed the fact that changes over time in household size were largely the result of declining fertility. Yet, the study of fertility is quite complicated—as is the case with most things that sociologists discuss, the fabric is an elaborate one, and it is difficult to figure out the pattern, much less separate the threads.

If we look at fertility trends in England, France, and the United States during the past two centuries we observe three somewhat distinct patterns. In England fertility did not begin to decline nationally until 1870, a century after the beginning of industrialization. However, between 1870 and 1950, marital fertility fell by almost two-thirds, from 295.5 legitimate live births per 1,000 married women aged 15–44 to 105.0 (Wrigley, 1969:195). There is some evidence, however, of fertility control among certain segments of the middle class as early as 1850 (Branca, 1975a:117). France, on the other hand, has shown declining fertility since the last quarter of the eighteenth century (van de Walle, 1974). In the U.S. the pattern resembles that of France, with national fertility declining from about 1800, though in New England there is some indication that it declined earlier (Smith, 1972a).

No completely adequate explanation of why fertility fell in France and the United States before it fell in England, the first of the three to industrialize, is available. That is, there is no theory of fertility change that applies to all countries; nevertheless, we can look at some of the explanations that have been put forth in order to gain some insights into what population experts feel are the factors that enter into such shifts.

An important factor in the changing fertility rates was the new role assumed by the family. As was noted earlier, industrialization caused the family to change from being a unit of production to being a unit of consumption. We must recognize, however, that this was not an overnight process. It involved a long adjustive process during which old forms of social organization were stretched and pulled to adapt to emerging economic conditions. This can be seen vividly in the area of child and family labor. According to Smelser:

> Almost as a matter of definition we associate the factory system with a decline of the family and the onset of social anonymity. Certainly the steam-power mule created a new type of factory system. By virtue of an intricate set of controls based on kinship and community ties, and by virtue of the continuing authority of the spinner, however, the potential anonymity of factory life was postponed. The departure from the traditional working-class family was far from complete in 1820, even though the factory system has been prospering for four decades [1959:193].

Smelser's point is that at first the factory system was *not* antithetical to family labor. That is, in the early stage of industrialization families could to some extent work as units within the factory, or at least, sons could work under the supervision of their fathers, who in some instances received their pay. This is significant for two reasons: first, it meant that industrialization did not immediately alter role structures within the family (the family that engaged in cottage industry and the family that engaged in early factory work could be structurally similar); and second, children still represented an economic asset. These two factors may, in part, have accounted for the persistence of high fertility during the early period of industrialization in England.

On the other hand, some argue that changes in the standard of living brought about by industrialization caused fertility rates to go down. The basic thrust of this argument is concisely presented by J. A. Banks in his classic study *Prosperity and Parenthood.*

> With the development of large-scale industry and commerce men and women were presented with more and more objects of desire and greater opportunities for obtaining them. The levels of life once regarded as the prerogatives of the few became the aspirations of the many. But the financial resources are always limited in comparison with the possible wants that can be satisfied, and in the attempt to span the gap family limitation was called in to play the major role [1954:7].

While by no means conclusive, this pioneering piece of research allows us to look at fertility in terms of the standard of living aspired to by the English middle classes during the nineteenth century. This research gives us some sense of the pressures they were under to rise to and maintain what was deemed an acceptable way of life.

A sweatshop in a tenement apartment at the turn of the century. *(Library of Congress)*

In terms of household expenditure, Banks argues that between 1850 and 1870 prices only rose by 5 percent, yet new expectations concerning the proper manner in which middle-class life should be conducted resulted in the need for a 50 percent increase in outlay. More specifically, we see a greater percentage of family income being spent on food, wine, laundry, rent, and household help. More and more middle-class families took in domestic servants during this period, resulting in the latter's wages going up and the financial burden on the family growing accordingly.

> In order to maintain the level of expenditure required of them, especially if they aspired to rise in the social scale, middle-class men and women were obliged to employ more expensive forms of labour in larger quantities. At the same time they were being called upon to drink wine regularly with their meals, to give little dinners occasionally, and to spend far larger sums of money on their household needs [Banks, 1953:85].

The household was not the only area of growing expenditure. Increasingly, private secondary education became the ticket for entry into the occupations deemed appropriate for the scions of the middle class. This was reflected in an increase in the number of private boarding schools for boys during this period. Branca (1975a:46) has some statistical data which indicate that the extent of the middle-class usage of boarding schools at this time may have been exaggerated. But even if Eton or Rugby, much less Oxford or Cambridge, were out of the question, some form of education was deemed essential to gain entry into even the lower echelons of the middle-class world.

While Banks focuses on the middle class, we must realize that in the last third of the nineteenth century, the working class was also beginning to be burdened by the rise in fertility rates (Tilly et al., 1976). The economic depression of the 1870s affected all classes and while the working class did not face the situation of having to maintain inflated living standards, their lives were made more difficult by such laws as the Workshop Regulation Act of 1867, which prohibited the employment of children below the age of eight, and the Education Acts of 1870 and 1876, which made education between five and fourteen compulsory and raised the age of employment from eight to ten (Fryer, 1965:177–178). Moreover, there were school fees involved in compulsory education. While the fees were seldom more than ten shillings, they nonetheless placed a burden on poor families, whose children had suddenly been converted from economic assets to economic burdens.

Yet Banks, after carefully scrutinizing the available evidence, is not convinced that therein lies the answer. He knows that simply showing correlation is not proof of causality. Thus Banks hypothesizes:

> It might well be the case, indeed, that the key to the whole problem lies in the development of science and the spread of the scientific attitude of mind, sweeping away traditional values at the same time it made possible a greater produc-

> tion of wealth. This could conceivably be used to account for the changed attitude toward birth-control [1953:202].

The implication of this statement Banks is making is that one should not assume that the standard of living is the only variable affecting fertility; while it may have been an important contributing factor in the acceptance of family limitation by the middle classes, it has to be understood in terms of its interaction with other factors, such as the development of science.

We must remember that during the second half of the nineteenth century science was enjoying tremendous popularity. Through the employment of science, people had come to exert control over their environment in an unprecedented manner. Since the middle classes were most involved in the use of science, we might expect that its popularity would begin to affect their personal lives. If people could successfully alter and manipulate their environment, one would expect a reduction in the fatalism that characterized so much of premodern life. When you are no longer as subject to the will of nature in the extrafamilial sphere, why be subject to it in the familial one? This question, in slightly different form, was recently and eloquently posed by Robert Wells (1975). In addition, Patricia Branca (1975a:119–120) has shown, using British census data, that those in the newer professions who were in the vanguard of modernization (such as engineers) reduced their fertility before people engaged in the more traditional professions (such as clergy).

Although such factors as the separation of work from home, the rise in middle-class aspirations, the growth of a scientific frame of reference, and the new attitudes toward the family may not account for all of England's vital revolution (and we have no way of mathematically evaluating the relative impact of each), nevertheless these appear to be the key factors. Yet is the picture the same in all countries? Why do France and the United States show different profiles? Are different theories needed for different nations, or are the same variables at work, but in somewhat different order?

We have already indicated that fertility in France began to fall during the last decades of the eighteenth century, while English fertility was still maintaining itself at a high level. If we are to make any sense out of this we must recall that population increase is an outgrowth of the interaction of three factors: births, deaths, and migration. The last may hold the key to an understanding of British-French differences. During the first two-thirds of the nineteenth century England experienced both considerable emigration and simultaneously considerable internal migration—from the countryside to the cities, which were expanding at a staggering rate. France did not experience either of these two phenomena to anywhere near the same extent at that time.

Dov Friedlander (1969), using data from two European countries, has argued that a relationship exists between fertility and migration. We can profitably apply his theory to the elucidation of British-French differences in that the early decline in French fertility may have been the result of the pressure that was created by lowered mortality in a residentially stable rural area. Under the French landowning system, an unusually large amount of the arable land, about one-half, was in the hands of the peasants. Moreover, the French did not follow the English practice of primogeniture which entitled the eldest son to the entire estate. Even before the Revolution, the French employed a system of equal shares. Thus, with the absence of large-scale out-migration, more children meant a greater atomization of family holdings. This could have resulted in people being strongly motivated to limit the number of children they had. Furthermore, the Revolution of 1789, with its broad themes of anti-authoritarianism and individualism, might have worked to reorient thinking about the family and life goals in general.

Turning to the United States, we see a situation resembling that of France where fertility declined consistently throughout the nineteenth century. The economist Richard Easterlin, a pioneer in the movement to bring together economic and sociological theories of fertility, offers one of the more interesting attempts to explain this pattern. Easterlin points out that the fertility decline did not occur simultaneously in all portions of the United States. Birth rates fell first in the settled Northeast. As the population moved westward and as land there became scarce, fertility rates declined in the West, too. Fertility continued, however, to maintain itself at high levels on the frontier. Easterlin offers what he describes as a "bequest" model to explain this change. American farmers, he feels, were concerned that the economic standards that they had achieved be maintained by their children.

> Suppose one assumes that the farmer wishes to provide for each of his children at least as well as he himself was provided for. Then the number of children he can "afford" will depend on the outlook for multiplying his initial capital over the course of his lifetime. If, for example, he can anticipate a six-fold multiplication of his capital, he will be able to provide for six children; if he can only expect a doubling of his capital, he can "afford" no more than two children. Since the prospective growth of capital declines with the stage of settlement of an area, pressures for limiting fertility grew correspondingly [1976b:422].

While the data on capital growth that Easterlin brings to bear on this problem are not perfect, he is able to show not only that the decline in fertility followed the decline in the availability of land but also that land values were negatively associated with fertility (Easterlin, 1976a).

Given the similar factors at work in England, France, and the United States, one wonders whether developments in the three countries were really that distinct. In all of them it had become difficult for people to maintain existing life styles in the face of traditional fertility patterns, even though there were differences in the timing of responses to these difficulties. Therefore we see that the vital revolution in Europe cannot be explained merely in terms of industrialization—much more is at work.

This brings home the importance of the use of the concept of modernization in any analysis of fertility, for modernization involves not only economic change, but also change in the social organization of society and in the manner in which people think about themselves and their world (Wells, 1975b). These processes did not occur at once, but rather took place gradually and made their effects felt differently in each country. Thus modernization *is* associated with declining fertility and a smaller number of children per family.

THE "DEMOCRATIZATION" OF CONTRACEPTION

Another way of understanding what happened in the nineteenth century is to consider how fertility was actually reduced, both in the earlier and in the later stages of the vital revolution. Fertility control during the late eighteenth and nineteenth centuries—and well into the twentieth century for that matter—was probably achieved mainly through the use of *coitus interruptus* or withdrawal, a technique that has always been available. (Branca [1975a] has argued that female-controlled techniques, such as Carlile's sponge, douching, and pessaries, played a larger role in the nineteenth century than was previously believed.) Withdrawal was one of the first means of family limitation, apart from controlling age at marriage, abortion, and infanticide. The Old Testament mentions this practice in the story of Onan, Judah's son, who in accordance with the Hebrew custom of the Levirate was enjoined by his father to impregnate his dead brother's wife, Tamar, so that she would not be without offspring. He deceived his father by withdrawing or, in biblical terms "spilling his seed upon the ground," and for this mortal sin, God struck him down. There is also evidence of this technique being practiced in other ancient cultures, as is shown by Norman Himes in his masterful book, *Medical History of Contraception* (1936, reprinted 1963).

Given current concerns about the danger of this technique (i.e., sperm leakage during preseminal emission), it is surprising to learn how effective it appears to have been. Despite the very real danger that men in the throes of orgasm will not have the control or be willing to withdraw prior to ejaculation, it certainly appears that over the course of the past 200 years many males in the West have found it within their powers to do this. The nineteenth century also saw the emergence of other techniques. A consideration of them will allow us to get some sense of the spread of contraceptive techniques and ideology during the nineteenth century, and the effect it may have had on fertility control.

In 1789 the Reverend Thomas Malthus published his now famous *Essay on the Principle of Population, as it Affects the Future Improvement of Society.* His concern was to investigate those factors that impeded people from progressing toward "happiness." According to Malthus, primary among these impediments was the human tendency to reproduce beyond the capacity of the earth to provide sustenance for them. Population, he argued, grew geometrically, doubling itself every twenty years, while food production increased arithmetically resulting in either famine or a dramatic reduction in the quality of nourishment available. Two checks, Malthus felt, existed to prevent disaster from occurring: one was positive, the other preventive. The former involved such phenomena as starvation, war, etc., which checked the growth of population. The latter grew out of conscious attempts to control fertility in order to prevent population growth from getting out of hand. As a preventive check Malthus recommended delayed age at marriage; he did not recommend contraception within marriage.

Malthus's contribution is more to population theory than it is to the literature on contraception, and since the method he recommended was one which had limited potential he does not figure importantly in the nineteenth-century movement toward what Himes (1963) called "the democratization of birth control." Yet Malthus played an enormously important role in awakening people to the problem of unchecked population growth and in doing so laid the foundation for those writers such as Place, Carlile, Owen, and Knowlton who were to speak more directly to the issue of fertility control.

Francis Place (1771–1854) has been described as the father of the birth control movement (Himes, 1963:212). As a child Place was apprenticed to a breeches maker. This was his trade early in adult life, though he is remembered for his contributions to demography rather than to tailoring. He hoped to make enough money as a tailor to retire and go into politics. In 1816, when he was forty-six, he had a fabulously profitable year and left tailoring to achieve an important place in English politics (Fryer, 1965:53). In 1822 Place published *Illustrations and Proofs of the Principle of Population,* which, according to Himes, was "the first treatise in English to propose contraceptive measures as a substitute for Malthus's 'moral restraint' " (Himes, 1963:213). Place's impact was really made by the distribution of handbills to working-class men and women in London and in the north of England in the early 1820s. These handbills, one of which is reproduced in Figure 5-2, drew people's attention to the relationship between large families, low wages, and human suffering. He recommended two contraceptive techniques: (1) the use of a walnut-sized sponge tied to a ribbon and inserted into the vaginal canal before intercourse which would absorb the semen and prevent the sperm from reaching the egg; and (2) withdrawal, which was held to be less desirable, though useful when a sponge was not available.

Place took issue with Malthus both in terms of theory and method. For him, population control would improve the standard of living among the working classes and in the process reduce suffering—he argued, the fewer workers, the higher the wages. He also focused on the question of the supply of people and the supply of nourishment. Furthermore, he felt that the "moral restraint" proposed by Malthus was not realistic in that it

TO THE

MARRIED OF BOTH SEXES

OF THE

WORKING PEOPLE.

THIS paper is addressed to the reasonable and considerate among you, the most numerous and most useful class of society.

It is not intended to produce vice and debauchery, but to destroy vice, and put an end to debauchery.

It is a great truth, often told and never denied, that when there are too many working people in any trade or manufacture, they are worse paid than they ought to be paid, and are compelled to work more hours than they ought to work.

When the number of working people in any trade or manufacture, has for some years been too great, wages are reduced very low, and the working people become little better than slaves.

2

When wages have thus been reduced to a very small sum, working people can no longer maintain their children as all good and respectable people wish to maintain their children, but are compelled to neglect them;—to send them to different employments;—to Mills and Manufactories, at a very early age.

The misery of these poor children cannot be described, and need not be described to you, who witness them and deplore them every day of your lives.

Many indeed among you are compelled for a bare subsistence to labour incessantly from the moment you rise in the morning to the moment you lie down again at night, without even the hope of ever being better off.

The sickness of yourselves and your children, the privation and pain and premature death of those you love but cannot cherish as you wish, need only be alluded to. You know all these evils too well.

And, what, you will ask is the remedy?

How are we to avoid these miseries?

The answer is short and plain: the means are easy. Do as other people do, to avoid having more children than they wish to have, and can easily maintain.

What is done by other people is this. A piece of soft sponge is tied by a bobbin or penny ribbon, and inserted just before the sexual intercourse takes place, and is withdrawn again as soon as it has taken place. Many tie a piece of sponge to each end of the ribbon, and they take care not to use the same sponge again until it has been washed.

3

If the sponge be large enough, that is; as large as a green walnut, or a small apple, it will prevent conception, and thus, without diminishing the pleasures of married life, or doing the least injury to the health of the most delicate woman, both the woman and her husband will be saved from all the miseries which having too many children produces.

By limiting the number of children, the wages both of children and of grown up persons will rise; the hours of working will be no more than they ought to be; you will have some time for recreation, some means of enjoying yourselves rationally, some means as well as some time for your own and your childrens' moral and religious instruction.

At present every respectable mother trembles for the fate of her daughters as they grow up. Debauchery is always feared. This fear makes many good mothers unhappy. The evil when it comes makes them miserable.

And why is there so much debauchery? Why such sad consequences?

Why? But, because many young men, who fear the consequences which a large family produces, turn to debauchery, and destroy their own happiness as well as the happiness of the unfortunate girls with whom they connect themselves.

Other young men, whose moral and religious feelings deter them from this vicious course, marry early and produce large families, which they are utterly unable to maintain. These are the causes of the wretchedness which afflicts you.

4

But when it has become the custom here as elsewhere, to limit the number of children, so that none need have more that they wish to have, no man will fear to take a wife, all will be married while young—debauchery will diminish—while good morals, and religious duties will be promoted.

You cannot fail to see that this address is intended solely for your good. It is quite impossible that those who address you can receive any benefit from it, beyond the satisfaction which every benevolent person, every true christian, must feel, at seeing you comfortable, healthy, and happy.

Figure 5-2 Francis Place's Contraceptive Handbill

SOURCE: Place Collection, British Museum, vol. lxi, pt. II, p. 42.

placed too great a hardship upon men and women and promoted immorality, particularly prostitution. Obviously, Place was a much better prophet than the Reverend Malthus, since we have seen no trend among the working classes in this country or in England to delay marriage, as Malthus suggested. What we have seen is a marked decline in marital fertility.

Through the efforts of Place and his disciples Carlile, Hassell, and Campion, contraception became a controversial issue during the 1820s, as Place's handbills and Carlile's *Every Woman's Book* (1826) achieved wide circulation. However, it appears that this campaign was to have little direct impact on fertility in the first half of the nineteenth century. Himes nonetheless feels that these men set in motion a movement that ultimately made its presence felt in an important way. Their campaign represented the first organized attempt to propagandize for family limitation (Himes, 1963:223).

The next episode in the drama of the birth control movement was played out in the United States rather than England, though it was later to have a very crucial impact on the latter. In the opening years of the 1830s, two books appeared in this country that dealt with the issue of family planning: Robert Dale Owen's *Moral Physiology; or A Brief and Plain Treatise on the Population Question* (1831) and Charles Knowlton's *Fruits of Philosophy* (1832).

Owen was the son of Robert Owen, the utopian socialist who founded the New Harmony colony. The younger Owen argued that uncontrolled fertility created great economic hardship and thus pushed mothers toward early graves. In the pamphlet's various editions, a number of techniques of contraception are discussed, including Carlile's sponge, the condom, and withdrawal. Owen favored withdrawal both from the point of view of its efficacy and what he saw as the minimal loss of pleasure. While most American journalists responded to the publication of his tract with silence, those who did speak out seem to have been divided on its virtues and dangers. Nonetheless, the book is estimated to have sold somewhere between 20,000 and 25,000 copies in the United States and an even larger number in England between 1830 and 1875 (Fryer, 1965:94).

Charles Knowlton was a country doctor who practiced in various Massachusetts communities during the second quarter of the nineteenth century. He was a truly original thinker who had begun to lecture on evolution in a relatively informed manner twenty-six years before Darwin's theories appeared in print. He also published a book on birth control that has been described as "the first really important account of contraception after those of Soranos and Aetios" (Himes, 1963:227). Knowlton felt that the benefits to be derived from contraception were many and varied. Not only would it deal with the problem of excessive population, which Malthus raised, but it would also serve the moral purpose of reducing man's temptations to consort with prostitutes, since men could marry earlier and thus find a sexual outlet without incurring the financial burdens of a family. Moreover, contraception would improve the health of the general population by cutting down on maternal mortality (both from exhaustion and abortion), as well as reduce hereditary disease, crime, and other social ills. The means by which all of this would be achieved, according to Knowlton, was douching; he even offered recipes for several solutions that could achieve the desired effect, such as mixing alum and cold water, or bicarbonate of soda and water, among others. And if nothing else was available, he recommended a hearty dose of cold water.

> In Knowlton's opinion the above methods had the following advantages: they were sure, cheap, harmless, would not cause sterility, and involved no sacrifice during coitus. Moreover, control was thus placed in the hands of the woman where, for good reasons, it ought to be. Place and Knowlton seem to have been among the first to stress the desirability of placing control in the hands of the wife [Himes, 1963:229].

While the scientific merit and efficacy of Knowlton's recommendations may be open to question, the influence of his ideas was great.

Knowlton's *Fruits of Philosophy* was to find its greatest audience in England rather than in America. This is not to say that Knowlton was ignored here; quite the contrary. He was fined and spent three months in prison at hard labor for his views. It is estimated that by 1839, 10,000 copies of his book had been sold in the United States. Initially the book did not create much of a stir in England, although about 42,000 copies were sold between 1834 and 1876 by a variety of publishers. The initial calm which met the book was not to last, however.

In many respects the second and third quarters of the nineteenth century in England were a quiet period in the movement toward the democratization of birth control. The Reform Bill of 1832 and the New Poor Law of 1834 seemed to soothe public concern about social reform. Consequently, interest in birth control declined. This is not to say that the work of Knowlton and Owen went unattended. Obviously this was not the case, but contraception was not seen as an overriding public issue. However in 1854, Dr. George Drysdale published his *Elements of Social Science,* a book which dealt more with the arguments for contraception than it did with the techniques. Nonetheless, in the fifty years during which it was in print it went through thirty-five editions in England alone, not to mention those published in other European countries. The few pages that he does devote to techniques are significant because of his recommendation of the use of the condom in conjunction with the sponge and the use of a "safe" period, even though he was aware of the dangers of this method.

Drysdale's *Elements* was to have a significant (though indirect) effect because of his association with Charles Bradlaugh, who was to play a towering role in the nineteenth-century birth control movement. As coeditor of the *National Reformer,* Bradlaugh gave that publication's support to Drysdale's book, much to the chagrin of the coeditor, Joseph Barker. Like Drysdale, Bradlaugh was a neo-Malthusian. He wrote articles in support of Malthus's ideas and during the 1860s founded a Malthusian League. This organization was shortlived, although such efforts were later to meet with more success, largely due to Bradlaugh's activities.

By 1876 the calm before the storm broke, and a bookdealer in Bristol, England was sentenced to two years at hard labor for publishing an edition of Knowlton's *Fruits of Philosophy,* which the court claimed was illustrated with "obscene" drawings. (Fryer feels that the illustrations in question were probably of male and female genitalia.) Actually the edition published was the same one that had been published in Britain for forty-three years. Bradlaugh and Annie Besant, a woman who had worked with him in the Freethought movement, saw this harsh sentence as an attempt to suppress a book which was not only not obscene, but which had considerable merit. In order to create the test case that they felt was necessary, they organized a Freethought Publishing Company for the exclusive purpose of republishing the Knowlton volume. In addition, they defiantly notified the police of where and when they would begin selling the book, having rented a shop for this purpose. Predictably, they were arrested, but in the time that elapsed between their arrest and trial, 125,000 copies of the book were sold—almost three times as many as in the previous forty-two years. The pair, according to the records, appear to have accounted for themselves well during the court proceedings. Mrs. Besant spoke eloquently of the hardship the absence of contraceptive information created in the lives of poor women and their children. While the judge seemed to be impressed, the jury decided that although the defendants were innocent of any wrong motive in publishing it, the book was "calculated to deprave public morals" (Fryer, 1965:164). This was interpreted by the judge as a decision of guilty. At their sentencing a week later, Bradlaugh and Besant indicated that they would not desist from selling the book and were fined £200 and given terms of six months each. The case was successfully appealed a week later on a technicality and the defendants, despite warnings to the contrary, proceeded to sell the book again, but now with a red stamp across the cover that read, "Recovered from the Police" (Fryer, 1965:164).

In addition to giving new impetus to the Malthusian League, the Bradlaugh-Besant trial gave Knowlton's book tremendous publicity. As a result, public interest in contraception grew enormously. Himes seems to feel that the publicity attendant upon the trial played a major role in the dramatic reduction in the English birth rates since the late 1870s. Himes claims that, "In the three and a half years after the trial (up to August 28, 1881) 185,000 copies of the Freethought Publishing Company editions were sold at sixpence each" (1963:243). Other English editions were also published at the time, and Himes estimated that, excluding the Freethought edition, between 50,000 and 100,000 copies were probably sold. Moreover, Annie Besant published a pamphlet entitled *Law of Population* (1879). By 1891, this had sold 175,000 copies. Certainly such widespread dissemination of birth control literature could not help but make an impact, but one must be careful in attributing too great a significance to the impact of the birth control movement. It must be remembered that other sociocultural factors, discussed earlier, such as the new expectations concerning living standards, were also at work.

In our discussion of changes over time in household size it became obvious that one could not talk merely of premodern and modern household size, but that one also had to consider changes within periods, as well as changes in what might be spoken of as the postmodern era. We must now consider the fertility picture in the latter.

POSTMODERN FERTILITY PATTERNS

In the United States the fertility trend between 1800 and 1936 was a downward one, declining from an average of 7.0 births in 1800 to 2.1 in 1936. In the years since 1936, fertility rates began to rise, reaching their apex in 1957 with a figure of 3.8 (Westoff and Westoff, 1971:209). Since 1960, however, the decline has been dramatic. In 1972 fertility fell below the 1936 nadir, and has even fallen to a level of 1.8 in 1976, below the replacement level of 2.1 children (*New York Times,* February 2, 1977:14a). While the presence of a vast pool of potential mothers in the population makes demographers hesitant to make too much of this downward trend, we must not overlook the significance of the fact that for the first time in history, fertility has fallen below the replacement level. (This does not mean that the population is already stable. Only if the current fertility rate maintains itself for about seventy years would population growth in this country stabilize itself.) The United States is not alone in these patterns. Similar trends are also evident in Western European nations.

If we are to understand Western fertility patterns in the twentieth century, we must not only examine the continuation of the trends discussed earlier, but also study the important contraceptive breakthroughs that this century has seen, especially since World War II.

The Contraceptive Revolution

If a contraceptive revolution did occur in the nineteenth century, it was more a result of the diffusion of information concerning birth control and the presentation of the information in a positive light than it was a breakthrough in birth control technology (La Sorte, 1976). This spread of information may have served to bring the idea of family planning to the minds of those who either had not previously entertained the idea or who had viewed it negatively. In the twentieth century, however, technology rather than information was probably a more important factor in the spread of birth control, particularly during the 1960s with the development of the pill and the IUD. In 1965 the National Fertility Study (NFS) discovered that 84 percent of the white married women in the 18–39 age group had at *one time or another* used contraception; a similar study in 1955 found this was true of 70 percent of the women (Westoff and Westoff, 1971:61). (The NFS is based on a random national sample of several thousand American married women carried out at five-year intervals by Norman B. Ryder and Charles Westoff of the Office of Population Research of Princeton University.) By 1970 about 65 percent of all American married couples *were regularly employing* contraception (in 1973 the figure had risen to 70 percent) and of the remaining 35 percent, 12.9 percent were either sterile or unlikely to conceive and 14.5 percent were already pregnant. Only 7.5 percent were nonusers (Westoff, 1976b). Thus contraception has become the virtual norm among the married population.

The types of contraceptives women are using are shown in Table 5-1. Despite the fact that the pill was not introduced until the early 1960s, Table 5-1 shows how quickly it made its presence felt. Data from 1970 indicate that this is becoming the case for the IUD, though not in as dramatic a way.

It is interesting to note that in 1970 the National Fertility Study indicated that contraceptive patterns among Catholics were increasingly coming to resemble those of Protestants. The number of Catholic women using contraceptive means other than rhythm method, the only method approved by the Roman Catholic Church, jumped 51 percent between 1955 and 1970, reaching a figure of 68 percent at that time (Westoff and Bumpass, 1973). Moreover, the demographers who carried out the 1970 study predict that by 1980 Catholics will be unidentifiable from Protestants in

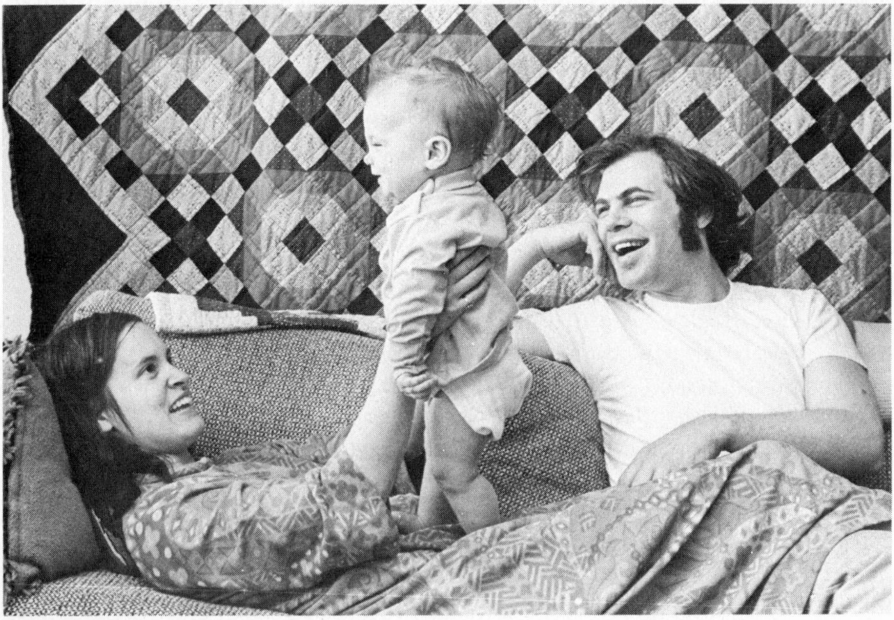

Charles Gatewood

terms of their contraceptive practices. Evidence to support this prediction can be found in a recent study carried out by the National Opinion Research Center, which found that the percentage of Catholics approving of artificial contraception rose from 45 percent in 1963 to 83 percent in 1974 (*Newsweek,* April 5, 1976:57).

As we have already pointed out, the problem with trying to evaluate the role played by contraceptive technology in increasing fertility control is that people have long had a perfectly workable technique at their disposal in the form of withdrawal. We must nonetheless recognize that this technique is frought with problems. It requires considerable self-control to employ and it may interfere with the pleasure of both the male and the female—for the male the totality and continuity of the act is interrupted, for the female withdrawal may impede orgasm as well as hamper pleasure generally. The new contraceptives such as the pill and the IUD separate the act of contraception from the act of sex, place control in the hands of women, and very simply allow a couple to engage in sex with minimal worries of unwanted pregnancy occurring. When we realize how many pregnancies were unplanned in past periods because of forgetfulness, error, or malfunction, even among couples using contraception, the importance of the new improvements in contraception is evident. It might be noted that the mean coital frequency of married women sampled in the NFS increased 14 percent between 1965 and 1970, suggesting that improved contraception may be affecting sexual behavior (Westoff, 1974:14).

Another aspect of the contraceptive revolution evident from Table 5-1 is the growth in recent years of voluntary sterilization, stemming from new surgical techniques and altered hospital policy. Looking again at data taken from National Fertility studies, we see that in 1965, 12 percent of the couples at risk (that is, couples who are biologically capable of having children but who do not plan to have any more) had been sterilized, while in 1970 the figure had gone up to 18 percent—a rather impressive 50-percent increase (Presser and Bumpass, 1972). In general, the proportion of married couples who were sterilized for nonmedical reasons rose from 16.3 percent in 1970 to 23.5 percent in 1973 (Westoff, 1976b). Some indication of the importance of this trend is made evident by the findings of the 1973 National Survey of Family Growth (Westoff, 1976b). Contraceptive sterilization, largely by means of vasectomy and tubal ligation, was *the* most popular form of contraception among contracepting couples where the wife was in the 30–44 age group; 33.7 percent of this group used this form of contraception, while only 21.4 percent used the pill (Westoff, 1976b:55). There is also evidence of growing acceptance of sterilization among women between the ages of 15 and 24 years, for whom the figures went from 2.3 percent in 1970 to 5.9 percent in 1973 (Westoff, 1976b:55). Given this staggering growth of sterilization in the late 1960s and its continuation in the early 1970s, in addition to the positive attitude shown towards it by many young couples, there is reason to believe that this

Table 5-1. **PERCENT DISTRIBUTION OF CURRENTLY MARRIED U.S. WOMEN AGED 15–44[a] (by current contraceptive practice, according to race and age, 1973[b], 1970[c], and 1965[d])**

Race and Contraceptive Practice	Age 15–44 1973	15–44 1970	15–44 1965	15–24 1973	15–24 1970	15–24 1965	25–34 1973	25–34 1970	25–34 1965	35–44 1973	35–44 1970	35–44 1965
All races												
U.S. total (in 000s)[e]	26,646	25,577	24,710	5,977	6,212	5,324	11,311	10,484	9,316	9,358	8,881	10,070
No. in sample[f]	7,566	5,884	4,810	1,776	1,429	1,067	3,202	2,412	1,815	2,588	2,043	1,928
Percent not using contraception	30.3	34.9	36.1	31.2	36.7	40.0	27.0	31.3	31.7	33.6	38.1	38.1
Percent using contraception[g]	69.7	65.0	63.9	68.8	63.4	59.8	73.0	68.6	68.3	66.4	61.9	61.9
Wife sterilized	8.6	5.5	4.5	2.6	0.6	0.8	8.3	5.4	4.7	12.9	9.1	6.3
Husband sterilized	7.8	5.1	3.3	1.5	0.8	0.9	8.2	5.0	3.7	11.3	8.1	4.1
Pill	25.1	22.3	15.3	44.9	37.1	29.2	25.7	23.8	17.2	11.8	10.0	6.1
IUD	6.7	4.8	0.7	7.2	5.6	1.1	9.0	6.6	0.9	3.5	2.2	0.4
Diaphragm	2.4	3.7	6.3	1.1	1.6	2.6	2.3	3.8	6.0	3.4	5.0	8.6
Condom	9.4	9.2	14.0	5.7	5.7	9.4	9.7	9.2	15.9	11.5	11.7	14.7
Withdrawal	1.5	1.4	2.6	0.8	1.0	1.4	1.3	1.4	2.2	2.1	1.6	3.5
Foam	3.5	3.9	2.1	2.7	4.8	3.0	4.4	4.8	2.8	2.9	2.4	1.0
Rhythm	2.8	4.1	6.9	1.3	2.1	4.6	2.3	3.9	6.8	4.3	5.8	8.3
Douche	0.6	2.1	3.3	0.2	1.6	3.6	0.5	1.5	2.8	0.9	3.2	3.7
Other	1.3	2.9	4.9	1.0	2.5	3.2	1.1	3.2	5.3	1.8	2.8	5.2
Percent total	100.0	100.0	100.0	100.0	100.0	100.0	100.0	100.0	100.0	100.0	100.0	100.0
White												
U.S. total (in 000s)	24,249	23,220	22,382	5,384	5,595	4,724	10,347	9,578	8,387	8,518	8,047	9,271
No. in sample	5,301	4,972	3,771	1,174	1,198	796	2,302	2,051	1,413	1,825	1,723	1,562
Percent not using contraception	29.3	34.3	35.2	30.8	36.1	40.3	26.3	31.2	30.7	32.1	36.4	36.8
Percent using contraception	70.7	65.7	64.9	69.2	63.8	59.6	73.7	69.0	69.4	67.9	63.5	63.2
Wife sterilized	8.2	4.9	4.1	2.4	0.4	0.6	8.2	4.9	4.3	11.9	8.2	5.6
Husband sterilized	8.4	5.5	3.5	1.7	0.8	1.0	8.6	5.4	4.0	12.3	8.9	4.4
Pill	25.1	22.4	15.6	44.5	37.6	30.7	25.8	23.7	17.3	12.0	10.2	6.3
IUD	6.6	4.8	0.7	7.2	5.3	0.9	8.9	6.6	0.8	3.5	2.3	0.4
Diaphragm	2.5	3.8	6.8	1.2	1.7	2.6	2.4	3.9	6.5	3.6	5.2	9.1
Condom	10.0	9.7	14.5	6.1	5.9	9.2	10.1	9.7	16.3	12.3	12.4	15.6

Withdrawal	1.6	1.5	2.7	0.8	1.1	1.5	1.4	1.5	2.3	2.3	1.7	3.6
Foam	3.5	4.0	2.0	2.8	4.8	2.6	4.5	4.9	2.8	2.8	2.4	1.0
Rhythm	2.9	4.4	7.5	1.3	2.3	4.9	2.3	4.1	7.4	4.6	6.3	9.0
Douche	0.5	1.9	2.7	0.1	1.5	2.6	0.4	1.1	2.3	0.8	3.1	3.1
Other	1.4	2.8	4.8	1.1	2.4	3.0	1.2	3.2	5.4	1.8	2.8	5.1
Percent total	100.0	100.0	100.0	100.0	100.0	100.0	100.0	100.0	100.0	100.0	100.0	100.0
Black												
U.S. total (in 000s)	2,081	2,031	2,091	547	506	555	819	787	794	715	738	742
No. in sample	2,197	782	969	592	195	257	869	303	368	736	284	344
Percent not using contraception	39.7	40.8	42.9	33.8	39.5	38.5	36.2	32.7	37.2	48.1	50.7	52.0
Percent using contraception	60.3	59.2	57.2	66.2	60.5	61.5	63.8	67.3	62.8	51.9	49.4	47.9
Wife sterilized	14.0	11.4	8.3	4.3	1.0	1.9	11.4	11.2	7.9	24.3	18.7	13.4
Husband sterilized	1.0	0.6	0.3	0.1	0.0	0.4	1.8	0.7	0.3	0.9	1.1	0.3
Pill	26.3	22.1	12.4	48.6	35.9	17.1	27.1	26.4	17.1	8.2	8.1	3.8
IUD	7.6	4.5	1.7	7.9	6.2	3.5	10.7	5.6	1.9	4.0	2.1	0.0
Diaphragm	1.2	3.1	2.9	0.1	1.5	1.9	1.8	3.6	2.7	1.4	3.5	3.8
Condom	3.2	4.0	9.7	1.4	4.1	10.9	3.1	3.6	12.8	4.7	4.2	5.5
Withdrawal	0.4	0.4	1.2	0.2	0.0	1.2	0.2	0.7	0.5	0.8	0.4	2.0
Foam	3.0	3.6	3.5	1.7	4.1	5.8	4.2	4.3	3.5	2.7	2.5	1.7
Rhythm	0.8	1.0	1.4	1.0	0.5	1.6	0.7	1.3	2.2	0.6	1.1	0.6
Douche	1.8	4.7	10.0	1.0	2.6	12.1	2.0	5.9	7.6	2.3	4.9	11.0
Other	1.0	3.7	5.8	0.0	4.6	5.1	0.8	4.0	6.3	2.0	2.8	5.8
Percent total	100.0	100.0	100.0	100.0	100.0	100.0	100.0	100.0	100.0	100.0	100.0	100.0

SOURCE: Charles F. Westoff, "Trends in Contraceptive Practice: 1965–1973," *Family Planning Perspectives*, vol. 8, March/April 1976.

[a] In 1970, includes 3 women under 15.

[b] Preliminary data from the NSFG Cycle I, 1973, of the NCHS.

[c] Data from the 1970 NFS.

[d] Data from the 1965 NFS.

[e] Population estimates for 1970 and 1965 were derived by interpolation from the 1970 and 1971 Bureau of the Census Current Population Surveys (CPS) of the population by marital status. Estimates for 1965 were similarly derived from 1965 and 1966 CPS data. Estimates for 1973 were projected from the 1970–1973 CPS.

[f] These are unweighted numbers.

[g] Multiple methods were assigned hierarchically to the pill, IUD, diaphragm, or condom if one of these methods was involved in the multiple usage. Other multiple method use was classified in the "other" category. The contraceptive practice of a very small number of couples in 1973 has been recoded in order to increase comparability with procedures followed in the 1965 and 1970 studies.

NOTE: Percents may not add to totals because of rounding.

trend will continue. As more and more people become disabused of the alleged dangers of such practices, for example the idea that vasectomy leads to impotence, this trend seems inevitable.

The two operations that have figured importantly in this explosion of surgical sterilization are the vasectomy for men and the tubal ligation for women, though more recently a variation of the latter has gained popularity. The vasectomy is typically done in a doctor's office and involves an incision being made into the scrotum which permits the severing of the vas deferens, thus eliminating sperm from the male ejaculate, about 10 percent of the total volume. The whole operation takes about twenty minutes. At present the reversal rate is not high enough to make this procedure advisable for those who might change their minds at a future date.

Tubal ligation is a surgical procedure that begins with an abdominal incision permitting a surgeon to gain access to the Fallopian tubes, which are then tied off or cauterized, making it impossible for the egg to travel to the uterus or the sperm to travel to the egg. While this is a more major piece of surgery than the vasectomy and involves general anesthesia for most patients, the reversal rates are as unpredictable as are those for the vasectomy. More recently surgeons have begun to use the laparoscope technique, which involves a small incision being made into the abdomen through which a tube containing mirrors and lights is passed. When the Fallopian tubes are located they are cauterized, thus producing the same result as the tubal ligation. The important difference between the two is that the tubal ligation is a major surgical procedure involving general anesthesia and several days in the hospital, while the laparoscope technique can be done with local anesthesia and only requires a one-day stay in the hospital. In contrast to a hysterectomy, neither technique has any effect on the reproductive system, apart from making pregnancy impossible. Women who have either the tubal ligation or the laparoscope technique done continue to produce eggs and menstruate until change of life.

A factor in the growth of these new surgical procedures since 1969 is a change in the policy of many American hospitals. Prior to 1969 the official manuals of the American College of Obstetricians and Gynecologists had a policy which advised that a woman had to have five children and be at least twenty-five years old to warrant sterilization (with the number dropping to three children by age thirty-five). In 1969 both age and number of children were no longer mentioned in the section of the manual dealing with sterilization. Still, many hospitals and physicians continue to have their own rules in these matters, which together probably keep down the number of sterilizations done on the younger group. As Presser and Bumpass (1972) note, this may explain why there is such a large group of couples who have no more desire for children and have given sterilization serious thought, but who have not as yet gone through with it—or, to put it more accurately, have not been allowed to go through with it. However, hospitals and physicians will probably continue to become more liberal in these matters. For many obstetricians and gynecologists these operations have provided a financial windfall at a time when the obstetrical aspect of their practice is constricting along with the declining birth rate.

At the same time that people have been increasingly able to insulate themselves from the risk of unwanted pregnancy through more reliable contraceptives and sterilization, they have also had more and more access to abortion, should an unplanned conception take place (Sarvis and Rodman, 1974; Tietze, 1975). Thus as a result of new attitudes (Sauer, 1974), new contraceptive technology, new surgical sterilization techniques, and the growing availability of abortion, we are approaching a situation in the United States where unwanted births have almost disappeared (Westoff, 1976a).

Not everyone is convinced that the breakthroughs in contraceptive technology we have been discussing will lead to a continuation of fertility rates below or at the replacement level. Easterlin (1976b), whose work on nineteenth-century fertility patterns we discussed earlier, sees the potential of a baby boom in the 1980s. He feels that the key concept in the understanding of swings in fertility patterns is "relative economic status." People form their consumption aspirations as adolescents living in their family of orientation. When they enter the labor market their assessment of their ability to maintain or exceed parental consumption levels affects their fertility behavior in terms of both when they marry and the speed with which they proceed to have children. The post-war baby boom, then, is interpreted as a result of a cohort coming to maturity that had been raised with modest tastes during the trying economic times of the Depression but who themselves entered the labor market during a growth period having high fertility rates. However, when their children, a large cohort, began to look for work in the 1960s the employment situation was tighter and thus they had fewer children. Easterlin sees the 1980s as a period when fertility may increase because the cohort that will then be seeking employment will be in a strong competitive position due to their small numbers. Easterlin's theory, while an interesting one, is perhaps overly simplistic and not surprisingly it has been the subject of criticism. For example, Oppenheimer (1976) has pointed out it does not adequately consider new patterns of female employment which clearly affect family earnings.

THE "CHILD-FREE" COUPLE

In any discussion of fertility we must also consider if the meaning of parenthood has undergone change, and how this may have affected fertility. J. E. Veevers, a sociologist, has written extensively on this topic and in what follows we borrow heavily from her work (1974, 1975). To begin with, we must examine what might be called the "human nature" question. Do people feel any innate or "instinctual" push to have children? The nature of human beings is such as to make what we feel and do virtually inextricably tied to our social experience. While there may be some physiological and hormonal constraints on our behavior, it appears that the strength of socialization is such as to insure great variability in virtually every aspect of human behavior, and child bearing is no exception. Not all societies present their members with as positive an attitude toward parenthood as we do. Margaret Mead in her classic study *Male and Female* (1949) reports that among the Mundugumor of New Guinea, women are scornful and rejecting of motherhood; men are similarly contemptuous of their pregnant wives.

In the West, religious institutions have put considerable pressure on people to obey the biblical injunction "be fruitful and multiply." Roman Catholic doctrine holds that if people enter marriage with the agreement to remain childless the marriage is invalid before God. Similar views are found in Jewish and Protestant theological law as well, where there is the implicit expectation that a couple entering marriage will, barring infertility, become parents.

If an essential or fundamental element of modernization is the growth of secularization and thus the declining importance of religion in people's everyday lives, then we might expect the force of religion as a factor in child bearing to decline. Previous research on the influence of religion on fertility rates has indicated that a positive relationship between religion and fertility existed only for Catholics, not for Protestants or Jews (Westoff, et al., 1963:93). But it is clear, as we have noted, that the overall patterns for non-Catholics and Catholics alike since the nineteenth century have been toward fertility control. In the case of Catholics, this trend is increasing despite the continued contraceptive conservatism of the Church.

Apart from the religious considerations, there are often more subtle, though by no means less compelling, forces at work which both motivate and pressure people to have children. Just stop and think about the assumptions most people make about childless couples. More often than not, they are seen as objects of pity. Most of us look at childlessness as something which befalls a couple because of fertility problems, rather than something opted for as a result of considerations of life style. The pervasiveness of this view is indicated by Charles Westoff and Raymond Potvin's study (1967) of 15,000 college women. They found that 57 percent agreed or agreed strongly with the statement, "Having children is the most important function of marriage." If the question had been phrased to read "Having children is among the most important functions of marriage," the percent agreeing probably would have been even greater. When confronted with the statement, "If people do not intend to have children, they ought not to get married," 27 percent agreed, though there were religious differences, with the Catholics showing much more agreement than either Jews or Protestants. Some evidence of change in such attitudes is offered by Edward Pohlman (1974:276), who found that among students at a "traditional" college the percent indicating they wanted no children rose from "0" in 1965 to 6 in 1970; among students at a more "avant garde" college, the figures rose from 10 percent to 18 percent. Looking at data drawn from national samples we see that while a 1973 Gallup Poll (quoted in Silka and Kiesler, 1977:16) revealed that only 1 percent of Americans saw a childless couple as an ideal, about 5 percent of married women, aged 25–29, interviewed in 1975 indicated that they expected to have no children—up from 2.2 percent in 1967 (U.S. Bureau of the Census, quoted in Mary Jo Bane, 1976:161). It is worth noting that Donald Hastings and J. Gregory Robinson (1974) estimate that double this amount (10 percent) will actually remain childless.

Another factor at work in how we view childlessness is the association in our culture between parenthood and normality, both in terms of mental illness and in terms of social maturity. Veevers notes that statistically speaking childless couples are in the minority (about 12 percent of the total), and to this extent they are atypical. But can one necessarily infer that they are therefore psychologically unbalanced or disturbed as well? Given the evidence currently available to us, this does not appear to be a wise conclusion to draw. There is little data available that indicates that childlessness, whether brought on by choice or infertility, is associated in a significant manner with any clinically recognizable symptoms of mental illness. What we have instead are a lot of unfounded claims, such as the one by a psychiatrist quoted by Margaret Mead who said, "I have never seen a woman who was socially and physically able to have children, and who refused to have children, who did not suffer, psychologically, from that refusal." Apart from the obvious impressionistic character of such a claim, there is also the question of whether the symptoms observed by the psychiatrist were a product of these women choosing not to have children or of the pressures that were brought to bear upon them as a result of the decision and the tensions produced by having to continually explain and make excuses for their behavior.

While it is incorrect to assume that voluntary childlessness is a manifestation of some sort of psychological illness, we cannot make the assumption either that such childless couples are in no way special. They have chosen to follow a pattern of marriage that is atypical. This atypical behavior makes them of particular interest to the family sociologist. But the fact is that we still know little about this group, since the majority of childless couples are so because of fertility problems rather than because they voluntarily choose to be "child-free." The few studies that have been made of couples who have decided against parenthood tend to be compromised by sampling problems (for example, that of Gustavus and Henley, 1974).

The problem confronting family sociologists is that there appears to have been a change in the attitude people have about bringing children into the world, but given the measures available to us, it is difficult to go beyond fertility behavior to get at the motivation for this new attitude. There are data to show that desired family size has declined, but this does not give us data on the altered meaning of parenthood. Still it does seem that for some people marriage and parenthood are no longer synonymous.

Let us look at one final factor—women's work—before we go on to summarize our discussion of fertility.

WOMEN'S WORK AND FERTILITY

It is difficult, if not impossible, to pick up a popular magazine today without seeing an article about (or at least some mention of) the women's movement and its implication for various aspects of American society. We are interested here in the effect the women's movement *may* be having on fertility, but we are particularly concerned with the relationship between female employment and fertility, a phenomenon that goes beyond the women's movement per se, and which has to be understood in terms of changes brought about in the shift from an agrarian to an industrial economy. From the early stages of industrialization, women began to work outside the home, but not all women did so, and not many women worked throughout their lifetimes. That is to say, female employment patterns have been, and continue to be, different from those of men. This is because women continue to give primacy to their roles as wives and mothers. The current feminist movement seems to be having an effect in changing this attitude. In Chapter 4 we carefully investigated changes in the role and status of women during the past 200 years; our attention here will be limited to what relationship, if any, has been observed between female employment and fertility (see Shorter, 1973; Tilly et al., 1976).

The employment patterns of married women are important to our discussion here. The working wife in America is largely a twentieth-century phenomenon. In 1890, 4.6 percent of married women were in the work force, and in 1940 it was 15.6 percent, but by 1976 it had risen to roughly 47 percent (U.S. Bureau of the Census, 1975b:133; *New York Times,* March 8, 1977:21). In general, looking at cross-national data, we see a negative correlation between female involvement in the labor force and fertility. Kasarda finds a negative correlation of –.69 for 60 nations during the 1960s in fertility and the nonagricultural wage earning of females. Linda Waite and Ross Stolzenberg (1976), employing a national sample of American women in their midtwenties, found a strong negative relationship between a woman expecting that she will be in the labor force when she is thirty-five and the number of children she plans to have during her lifetime. In a somewhat similar vein, John Scanzoni (1975) found that couples with "modern" marriages (i.e., those which manifest, among other things, a career orientation toward woman's work) reveal low fertility expectations. Both of these studies are, however, concerned with expected rather than actual fertility. The point to keep in mind here is that when we talk about a "negative" relationship between female employment and fertility, the implication is not that married women who work will have no children, but rather that they will have fewer children than their nonworking counterparts, though we might predict a concentration of the small minority of child-free couples in this group as well. However, this relationship is a complicated one (see Groat et al., 1976). Quoting Smith again:

> The American historical record, however, does not provide much support for this theory. During the 1830–1890 period, there was probably only a slight increase in the labor-force participation of married women and yet marital fertility continuously declined. During both the post-World-War II baby boom and the fertility decline since 1957, labor-force activity of married women increased. *For lower fertility, what is important is the meaning women assign to themselves and their work, either in or out of the home* [emphasis added, 1973a:48].

What Smith is getting at here is that work and fertility are not necessarily antithetical, especially if support mechanisms are present which enable women to work and at the same time be mothers. Thus the context of the work is extremely important. This is evident in Third World nations where we find economically active women often manifesting higher fertility rates than housewives (Birdsall, 1976). In these societies, agricultural activity can be coordinated with childrearing. It is in the modern urban societies where home and work are separated that fertility and labor force participation come into conflict, but even here the conflict can be reduced by means of such things as maternity leaves and adequate daycare facilities.

A factor which is, to some extent, related to the impact of female employment patterns on fertility is the increase in median age at first marriage for females, which rose from 20.3 in 1961 to 21.1 in 1975 (Gibson, 1976:250). While a number of factors must be considered in explaining this increase (for example, the growth in nonmarital cohabitation which we will be discussing in Chapter 7), the changing roles and vocational aspirations of women are among those that most readily come to mind. Since, as we pointed out earlier in this chapter, age at first marriage can affect fertility, we should look into what contribution if any this elevation in median age at first marriage has had on fertility. Campbell Gibson (1976) has noted that a drop in fertility as sizable as that which occurred since the beginning of the 1960s could hardly be accounted for totally by an increase of one year in the median age of first marriage for women. He does, however, argue that the interval between marriage and first birth is a factor of some significance in the 1970 to 1975 period, and it accounted for a portion of the fertility decline during those years.

The reasons a couple may postpone becoming parents are many, but the educational and professional goals of the wife are certainly possible explanatory variables. If a couple's career commitments result in their continued postponement of parenthood, they may reach a point where they become socially if not biologically too old to have children (Rindfuss and Bumpass, 1976:230). Their friends and relatives may consider it inappropriate if the couple remain fecund. At present it is not clear if this is what is happening, but this is something that future research should be able to clarify.

The point of this brief excursion into the question of the working mother is to further show how complicated the issue of the general relationship between modernization and reduced fertility is. Each of the factors we have considered is a piece of a puzzle, but each piece, because of its irregularities, is difficult to fit with the others to finish the puzzle and form a total and coherent picture.

SUMMARY

In general, it seems clear that modernization is associated with declining fertility. The aspects of the process of modernization that are associated with this trend include the triumph of rationality over fatalism, the decline in mortality, better and more effective contraceptives, the general rise in the standard of living, female employment patterns, and the changing meaning of marriage and parenthood. In the United States we have currently reached a point at which fertility has fallen below the replacement level, though as we have pointed out this does not mean that we have reached zero population growth. This will not occur unless the same fertility rates hold for about seventy years. Demographers have been hesitant to predict that this will occur, remembering that their prediction on the post-World War II baby boom did not hold—that is, the accelerated rates continued long after the experts felt that they would have and should have tapered off. Yet, there are factors now present that make the predictions of a continued low fertility rate a much safer bet than previous predictions.

We are moving toward what the Westoffs have described as the "contraceptive society," that is, a society in which inexpensive, effective, and reliable contraception is increasingly becoming available to all those who desire it. In the first half of the 1960s, about 20 percent of the children born were unwanted; in the second half about 14 percent were unwanted. In general, it has been estimated that virtually all of the decline in marital fertility during the 1960s was the result of the reduction in unplanned and unwanted pregnancies (Westoff, 1976a). As a result of the spread of the pill, the IUD, voluntary surgical sterilization, and abortion on demand, women now find themselves, for the first time in history, in a position to exercise almost complete control over their reproductive behavior. Moreover, there is every reason to believe that contraceptives, sterilization, and abortion will increasingly become available as the restrictions on their dissemination and use fall by the wayside. At the same time, sex education programs are making more and more young people aware of the options that are open to them. The implications of greater fertility control go beyond merely reducing the number of unwanted children that will be born into any society. The Westoffs neatly spell out what the unanticipated effects might be:

> Couples would be completely successful in avoiding births before they were wanted. Since control over timing would increase the intervals between births the average age of childbearing would increase. This lengthening of the generation means that the rate of growth would decline even if the ultimate number of births per couple remained the same [1971:327–8].
>
> . . .
>
> The postponement of births may however affect the number of births that ultimately occur. The longer a couple postpones fertility the greater the chance that sterility may develop, that other events will interfere, or that changes in plans will occur. Such postponement of motherhood, especially in the early years of marriage, means that women will have a longer time to develop interests competing with child rearing [1971:328].
>
> . . .
>
> The elimination of unwanted fertility would also probably produce an increase in the age at which couples marry. Without these accidental pregnancies which often force young people into marriage sooner than they wish or are ready for, they could afford to wait until the time was right [1971:331].
>
> . . .
>
> Illegitimacy would also be sharply reduced in the perfect contraceptive society. There would probably be few, if any, children born to unmarried mothers unless marriage and the family as we know it now change in such a radical way as to invalidate the very concept of illegitimacy [1971:331].

It should be pointed out that the authors are not dealing with abortion in their discussion of the "contraceptive society." Nevertheless, their remarks give some sense of how wide-ranging and important are the effects of fertility control.

The decline in fertility that we have seen and continue to see in modernizing nations is part of a broader picture of family change, parts of which we have already touched upon and parts of which we will go on to consider.

NYPL Picture Collection

SOCIALIZATION: The Emergence of Modern Personality

6

We have discussed changes in fertility and the way in which the meaning of parenthood has been modified over time. The decision to have a child rather than remain childless, or the decision to push one's fertility to the limit rather than employ contraception, is obviously only part of the total picture of parenthood. We must also consider the way in which children are socialized and the way in which socialization practices have been and continue to be altered.

An infant begins life as an unformed and highly malleable entity, with the potential for becoming a member of virtually any society. However, within a few years, the same child is easily recognizable as a member of his or her society, with its distinguishing traits, dispositions, and values. The process through which a particular culture is imparted to its members is referred to as *socialization*, a phenomenon which begins at birth and ceases only after a person has died.

SOCIALIZATION

Every society faces the problem of replacement, not merely replacement in numbers, but also replacement in the sense of cultural continuity. Parsons has somewhat facetiously likened the coming of each new generation to the invasion of a barbaric horde. Children must not only be taught the skills associated with adult roles, but they must also be motivated to play these roles. That is to say, it is not sufficient for a young person to be familiar with societal expectations; that child must also see those expectations as meaningful and right. Yet however successful a society's socialization practices, a certain amount of tension always exists between the generations. Listen to Ezekiel Rogers complain to a minister in Charlestown, Massachusetts in 1657:

> I find greatest trouble and grief about the *rising generation*. Young people are little stirred here; but they strengthen one another in evil, by example, by counsel. Much ado I have with my own family; hard to get a servant that is glad of catechising, or family duties: I had a rare blessing of servants in Yorkshire; and those that I brought over were a blessing: but the young brood doth much afflict me. Even the children of the godly here, and elsewhere, make a woful proof. So that, I tremble to think what will become of this glorious work that we have begun . . . [quoted in Bremner, 1970:36].

The complaints of today's parents sound trivial by comparison with the earthly and spiritual concerns of Ezekiel Rogers.

Later in this chapter the argument will be made that we may be currently witnessing some important intergenerational differences, differences which have their roots in widespread societal changes and which are crucial for our understanding of developments occurring in both patterns of courtship and marriage. Before we discuss these differences, however, it is necessary for us to gain some perspective on change over time in socialization practices so as to allow us to place the present situation in perspective.

THE EMERGENCE OF CHILDHOOD

In his very influential book, *Centuries of Childhood* (1962), Philippe Ariès argued that childhood, as a stage in life, is a relatively recent phenomenon which did not assume the currently recognizable form until the seventeenth century.

> In medieval society the idea of childhood did not exist; this is not to suggest that children were neglected, forsaken or despised. The idea of childhood is not to be confused with affection for children: it corresponds to an awareness of the particular nature of childhood, that particular nature which distinguishes the child from the adult, even the young adult. In medieval society this awareness was lacking. That is why, as soon as the child could live without the constant solicitude of his mother, his nanny or his cradle-rocker, he belonged to adult society [Ariès, 1962:128].

This concept is hard to grasp today. We tend to assume that something as basic as the concept of childhood must easily go back to prehistoric time. Ariès instead claims that it first emerged between the thirteenth and seventeenth centuries. However, the evidence he offers for this assertion is not unassailable; it is based on such things as the appearance of children in portraits, the development of distinctions in dress between children and adults, and new terms for children in the language. Yet the total picture Ariès offers us ultimately rings true, and articulates with what others have written about childhood in earlier centuries.

For Ariès, the emergence of childhood as a recognizable stage of life is inextricably tied to the emergence of the modern family. The same forces are apparently responsible for both, forces which we would describe as modernization and its prime mover, social differentiation. Ariès, however, focuses on the school as the agency which played a key role in this process, at least with regard to the development of childhood.

Certainly, the development of schools and schooling is of great relevance to a social-historical understanding of the emergence of childhood as a stage of life. And recognizing this development gives us an appreciation of how much the family has receded in importance in the transmission of various skills and knowledge. Children in the medieval world learned what they needed to know at their parents' side, or, if not there, then as apprentices or servants in the houses of others in the community. Medieval schools were essentially clerical institutions in which age-grading figured insignificantly, if at all. A classroom might contain boys of ten and young men of twenty. Primary education in the modern sense of the three Rs was unknown in the medieval world, though such skills may have been acquired from one's parents or pastor or, in the case of the nobility, from one's tutor. With the growth of the secular school as an institution the importance of age-grading distinctions increased.

Ariès seems to speak of the development of education as though it existed apart from the broader processes that were taking place. But we must recognize that the need for literacy and other skills would not have been so strongly felt, if at all, were it not for modernization, or more precisely, capitalism and later on industrialization. In all fairness to Ariès, he does make the point that the emergent middle class was most directly involved in these changes, and that among the aristocracy and the poor traditional patterns remained in force much longer. This in itself indicates that Ariès is fully aware of the economic infrastructure of which the changes in education are merely one manifestation.

While our focus is on the American family in this text, developments in the European family were significant to the degree that they affected the family here. By the time this country began to be settled in the seventeenth century, many of the processes Ariès speaks of had already been at work for several centuries in Europe. As we shall see, in certain respects the handling of children resembled the medieval model as much as it resembled the modern one, and thus it will be useful to trace the development of childrearing practices.

CHILDREARING IN SEVENTEENTH-CENTURY AMERICA

Relatively little scholarly work has been done on the history of childhood and childrearing in the United States. The problem here is one of reconstructing informal patterns, which, like much of everyday life, go unrecorded, apart from very unusual events that warrant comment. We do know that child naming reveals the medieval pattern of giving children the same names as their deceased siblings (Smith, 1972b). This suggests that children were not as individualized as they are today. Legal documents also tell us something about the status of children.

> If any child[ren] above sixteen years old and of sufficient understanding shall curse or smite their natural father or mother, they shall be put to death, unless it can be sufficiently testified that the parents have been very unchristianly negligent in the education of such children, or so provoked them by extreme and cruel correction that they have been forced thereunto to preserve themselves from death or maiming . . . [Bremner, 1970:38].

A law such as this gives us some sense of the importance placed upon parental obedience. But we are probably safe in assuming that few children, if any, were put to death as a result of transgressions such as those described above. Hence laws can be of only limited value to our discussion. However, there have been a few scholarly attempts to set forth the character of early childhood in colonial America. These studies provide the basis for the discussion that follows.

As in the medieval world, children in seventeenth-century America were treated solicitously and with tenderness during the first year of life (Joseph Illick, 1974). They were breast fed and mother's milk provided the primary source of nourishment during this period. Moreover, there appears to have been little concern with scheduling. Children were fed when they indicated the desire for the breast. After the first year, however, an important theme becomes that of controlling the child's assertiveness and aggressive impulses. Listen to John Robinson, the first minister of Plymouth:

> And surely there is in all children . . . a stubbornness, and stoutness of mind arising from natural pride, which must, in the first place, be broken and beaten down; that so the foundation of their education being laid in humility and tractableness, other virtues may, in time, be built thereon. . . . Children should not know, if it could be kept from them, that they have a will in their own, but in their parents' keeping; neither should these words be heard from them, save by way of consent, "I will" or "I will not" [quoted in Demos, 1970:134–135].

It is this emphasis on breaking the child's self-assertiveness that has caused many critics of Puritan culture to see the Puritans as unduly harsh and demanding parents. Calhoun has written:

> Home discipline was relentless. Stern and arbitrary command compelled obedience, submissive and generally complete. Reverence and respect for older people were seldom withheld [1945:112].

Yet this image of the stern, foreboding and omnipotent Puritan parent requires some tempering. Edmund Morgan, perhaps more so than any other commentator on Puritan culture, seems sensitive to the balancing elements in Puritan culture. To be sure, Puritan parents were strict and austere by modern standards, yet Morgan notes, "Nevertheless, there is no proof that seventeenth century parents employed the rod more freely than twentieth century parents" (1966:103). Puritan parents were deeply concerned with questions of salvation, and to the extent that the early assertive behavior of the child could be interpreted as an indication of original sin, it had to be extirpated (Stannard, 1974). Children, therefore, were frequently confronted with their own depravity and mortality (Zuckerman, 1970:72–84). Of course, many of us are shocked to hear that Cotton Mather, thirty years before his death, took his four-year-old daughter into his study, told her he was to die shortly, and "set before her the sinful condition of her nature and charged her to pray in secret places every day" (quoted in Calhoun, 1945:108). To view this morbidity as perverse would be to misinterpret its basic intent, which was to save the child from a fate far worse than death. Years later, when an epidemic of measles took Mather's wife and three youngest children, this same man could barely cope with his grief, despite his attempts to make sense out of these losses.

Seventeenth-century Puritan children were not exposed to a socialization process that precluded the consideration of personal differences or the expression of warmth and tenderness.

> Children were not subjected to a preconceived discipline without reference to their individual needs and capacities. A parent in order to educate his children properly had to know them well, to understand their particular characters, and to treat them accordingly. Granted its purposes and assumptions, Puritan education was intelligently planned and the relationship between parent and child which it envisaged was not one of harshness and severity but of tenderness and sympathy [Morgan, 1966:108].

Thus, within the boundaries of their religious beliefs, Puritan parents viewed their children with affection and treated them in a manner which reflected this (Stannard, 1974).

Beyond broad generalizations such as these, we know little about the underlying philosophy and treatment of young children, though it does appear that John Locke, who wrote *Thoughts on Education*, may have been the Dr. Spock of his day, as shown by his book's frequent appearance on early library lists (Calhoun, 1960:106). Locke was a firm believer in the hardening of children through their exposure to the elements—to the extent of having them wear thin shoes so that water could get in.

> Most children's constitutions are either spoiled, or at least harmed, by cockering and tenderness.
>
> The first thing to be taken care of is, that children be not too warmly clad or covered, winter or summer. The face, when we are born, is no less tender than any other part of the body: it is use alone hardens it, and makes it more able to endure the cold . . . Our bodies will endure anything, that from the beginning they are accustomed to . . . [quoted in Bremner, 1970:283–284].

Calhoun tells us that such dictums were quite influential and as an example cites the case of Josiah Quincy who was throughout the year taken from his bed to the cellar kitchen where he was "dipped three times in water just from the pump" (1960, vol. 1;107). Locke's concern also extended to diet and bowel movements, and he was as strict and demanding here as with regard to dress (Illick, 1974:319). The good or harm done to children as a result of parents following his advice is difficult to assess, but Locke may have done as much to insure good health as to bring about premature deaths.

Concerning the existence of childhood as a clearly defined stage of life, we must look to the same kinds of evidence that Ariès has employed in his study. The relative permissiveness of the first year was replaced by the harsher discipline of subsequent years, though this may have occurred after more than a year elapsed, perhaps with the birth of another child, since typically there was a two-year period between births. According to Demos, we have little if any information about the toys and games such children had. We do know that apart from the smocks worn by children of both sexes from infancy to about six or seven years, young children were dressed as were their parents, and in other respects lived lives similar to those of the adults.

> There was no idea that each generation required separate spheres of work or recreation. Children learned the behaviour appropriate to their sex and station by sharing in the activities of their parents. Habits of worship provide a further case in point: the whole family went to the same Church service, and the young no less than the old were expected to digest the learned words that flowed from the pulpit [Demos, 1970:139–140].

Of children's lives between infancy and the age of six or seven little is known. We do know that the transformation in dress which occurred at about age seven was also accompanied by a more general entry into the adult world discussed in the above excerpt by Demos. It is at this age that education began in earnest—an education which for some involved leaving the parental home and taking up residence as the apprentice or servant in another family.

The evidence presented by Demos (1970), Zuckerman (1970), and others (e.g., Fleming, 1933) makes a case for the view that the Puritans retained the medieval European practice of not differentiating between children and adults. The truth of this assertion is still being debated by social historians studying the seventeenth century. Both Stannard (1974) and Ross Beales (1975) have argued that a careful reading of the available evidence indicates that the Puritans did have a distinct concept of childhood. Stannard makes an interesting point with regard to customs of dress:

> In the first place, to argue in isolation of other data that the *absence* of a distinctive mode of dress for children is a mark of their being viewed as miniature adults is historical presentism at its very best; one might argue with equal force—in isolation of other facts—that the absence of beards on men in a particular culture, or the presence of short hair as fashion shared by men and

women, is a mark of that culture's failure to fully distinguish between men and women [1974:457].

Beales (1975) points out that Puritan law and religious practice indicate a clear distinction between children and adults. He even suggests that a period of "adolescence" or "youth" may have intervened before the "child" became an "adult." At present, we do not have sufficient data to resolve this controversy.

EDUCATION IN THE COLONIAL PERIOD

Religion was the driving force behind education in colonial New England. Basically children were taught to read so that they might become familiar with the Bible.

> The Puritans sought knowledge . . . not simply as a polite accomplishment, nor as a means of advancing material welfare, but because salvation was impossible without it [Morgan, 1966:89].

If we look at *The New England Primer*, which remained in use as the basic reader from the end of the seventeenth century through the eighteenth century, we see the degree to which religion provided the core of education. Below are some examples of sentences given in the primer to help the child learn reading and spelling, and at the same time give the proper religious instruction:

1. Praying will make thee leave sinning, or sinning will make thee leave praying.
2. Our Weakness and Inabilities break not the bonds of our duties.
3. What we are afraid to speak before Men, we should be afraid to think before God [quoted in Bremner, 1970:83].

By becoming literate and thus familiar with Scripture, children were able to develop the understanding of Christianity necessary for their ultimate salvation (Morgan, 1966:91–92).

Given their belief in original sin, the Puritans saw their children as inherently wicked, but this element in the child's makeup could be suppressed if not eradicated by proper training. Some may see a contradiction here between the Puritans' belief in predestination and their attempts to set their children on the righteous path. But the controversy over the doctrine of salvation through grace versus salvation through works was a recurrent one. Morgan tells us:

> Neither Mather nor any other Puritan saw a contradiction in asserting the inadequacy of education in one breath and the desirability of it in the next. Good habits did not themselves bring saving grace, but they furnished one of the main channels through which grace could flow. God alone would determine whether the channel should be filled but when he saved a man, he often used this means [1966:95].

For the first settlers education did not take place in the context of the schoolhouse. As Bernard Bailyn has argued:

> The forms of education assumed by the first generation of settlers in America were a direct inheritance from the medieval past. Serving the needs of a homogeneous, slowly changing rural society, they were largely instinctive and traditional, little articulated and little formalized. The most important agency in the transfer of culture was not formal institutions of instruction or public instruments of communication, but the family [1972:15].

Thus the family provided the core of a young person's educational experience and, as we have already noted, most of what a person needed to learn to play the adult roles could be gotten either from his or her family or as an apprentice or servant to a nearby family. Yet it is also true that the educational experience during the early years of colonial New England transcended the domestic units. The broader community and the church also played key roles in the educational process. But we must recognize that the boundaries between church, home, and community that for us today are clearly demarcated were not as salient then as now and people easily and unself-consciously moved between these spheres.

According to Bailyn a crisis of sorts occurred within the family in the New World, one which ultimately called forth the need for the legislation of education both within and without the family. Bailyn feels that the laws (such as the one cited earlier in this chapter) containing harsh punishment for parental disobedience are evidence of the kinds of threats to familial integrity and authority that were being faced in New England. Why would the punishments have been so harsh if the fear of imminent collapse were not felt to be so great? But the situation in New England involved more than just breaches of filial authority by children. It also involved basic changes in the nature of community structure and individual relationships to the community. Mobility within New England was so great that it was difficult to speak of any sort of stable community. This created barriers between the individual and his or her town, and a sense of separateness. The community "did not command his automatic involvement" (Bailyn, 1972:26). For Bailyn this change in the structure and meaning of community life had consequences for the socialization experience of the child and ultimately for the picture of the world children would carry with them and their expectations concerning the nature of relationships between people.

In 1642, Massachusetts passed a law which demanded that heads of households see to it that their children and charges were taught to read. Penalties were provided for those who failed to do so. This law, as well as a Virginia law passed in the same year, are seen by Bailyn as recognition of the fact that the family in the New World had grown lax in the exercise of its educational responsibilities. Five years later these laws were followed by others in Connecticut and Massachusetts which required small towns to hire a schoolmaster and larger towns to hire one capable of instructing young men in the Greek and Latin necessary for college entrance. This concern with education goes beyond the importance placed on literacy because of its religious role. Bailyn argues:

> It flowed from the fear of imminent loss of cultural standards, of the possibility that civilization itself would be "buried in the grave of our father" [1972:27].

Measures of literacy are not readily available for the colonial period, but Bremner has noted that, "by 1700 in New England, nineteen out of twenty men could sign their own names to legal documents" (1970:74). This is a measure, although a rough one, of the success of early laws in seeing that basic skills were imparted to a broad segment of the population.

Beyond the transmission of basic literacy, the apprentice system was the key element of the formal educational system of colonial New England. This is made evident when we recognize that the formal schooling of most young persons was very limited and higher education served largely as an entry into the professions, especially the ministry. (Harvard produced more ministers than any other professionals in its early years.) What makes apprenticing of special importance is the extent to which it was tied to a wider practice—that of sending children away to live as servants in the homes of kin, friends, or masters of various trades.

CHILD TRANSFER

The transfer of children from one household to another (discussed earlier on page 57) is a subject that has generated some controversy in historical circles, though not because people have questioned whether or not it in fact existed. Rather, the dispute is over just how widespread child transfer was and what motivated it. To be sure, some children left the parental household to enter formal apprentice relationships with masters of various crafts and trades. Demos has hypothesized that in the early stages of the settlement some children may have gone to other homes to learn the three Rs because their parents lacked these basic skills (1970:72); still others went as servants to wealthier families; and there were also orphans. But there still remains a group who appear to have been "put out" for reasons not explainable in terms of these categories.

> That is, some of the children directly involved came from families that were very much intact, were relatively well-off, and had no lack of educational attainment; moreover, the contractual arrangements made no mention whatsoever of learning a particular trade. The possibility arises, therefore, that some broader social or personal values may have played into this whole pattern [Demos, 1970:73–74].

One explanation for this seemingly anomalous pattern is offered by Edmund Morgan in his classic study, *The Puritan Family*. This practice is seen as a device employed to insure that the children were not "spoiled" as a result of parental overindulgence and excessive displays of affection (1966:78). In his essay on Puritan sexuality, Morgan [1942] makes the point that Puritans were more accepting of the physical aspects of love than many believe, but that they were concerned that love between man and woman did not interfere with or intrude upon the more fundamental relationship between man and God. Morgan saw such concerns also being present in the decision of Puritan parents to separate themselves from their children (1966). Also, as Stannard has suggested, the high rates of mortality among children created a situation in which their placement outside the home became "a means of insulating . . . to some extent against the shock that the death of a child might bring" (1974:466). However, there are those who simply see this practice as a device for shifting labor from large, poor families to richer ones with fewer or no children present (MacFarlane, 1970:209).

What the effects of this experience was on children and parent-child relationships is something that we can only speculate on, but Morgan does offer some interesting possibilities:

> Psychologically this separation of parents and children may have had a sound foundation. The child left home just at the time when parental discipline causes increasing friction, just at the time when a child begins to assert his independence. By allowing a strange master to take over the disciplinary function, the parent could meet the child upon a plane of affection and friendliness. At the same time the child could be taught good behavior by someone who would not forgive him any mischief out of affection for his person [1966:78].

It should also be recognized that this practice, in effect, created a period of life which, while not identical to what we speak of as adolescence today, does represent a stage between the period of childhood dependence and adult independence.

APPRENTICES

The more conventional apprenticeship relationship as practiced by various tradesmen and craftsmen was both an educational and an economic arrangement. From the perspective of the parents concerned about the future of their son or daughter it was a way of seeing to it that the child was equipped with valuable skills; from the point of view of the master, it was a way of obtaining the labor needed for his work and household. Two types of apprenticeship existed: (1) voluntary arrangements between parents and masters; and (2) compulsory arrangements where the town entered into a relationship with a master for an orphaned or indigent child. In the latter case there was little question of choice; the child went where the townfathers sent him or her. In the case of voluntary apprenticeship, some credence was given to the child's preferences, since there was concern about the child's happiness as well as his or her sense of calling, a point to which we will return shortly (Bremner, 1970:104).

The apprentice became more than merely an extra pair of hands in the shop of the master. Apprentices were also integrated into the household and only visited their families with the master's permission. The master's responsibility went beyond imparting trade skills. He was also responsible for seeing that the child became literate, as is evidenced by the Massachusetts law of 1642 cited earlier, and that he or she led a moral life. Certainly there were abuses of the relationship on both sides. Some masters overworked and underfed their apprentices; some apprentices were lazy and carried on immorally, even within the home of the master (Flaherty, 1972). The apprentice relationship usually lasted until a boy reached twenty-one, and until a girl reached eighteen or became a bride. They started as early as seven, though more commonly between the ages of ten and fourteen.

Most children in colonial America typically served their apprenticeships at the side of their fathers or mothers, since America was then a country of agriculturalists; farming was the occupation pursued by most men and carrying out the chores of a farmer's wife was the occupation pursued by most women. The demand for goods and services was sufficiently limited so that even by 1810 it has been estimated that 80 percent

Blacksmith with apprentice. *(NYPL Picture Collection)*

of the work force was still engaged in agriculture (Davis et al., 1972:chapter 1).

We must recognize that the growth of formal schooling in New England was in part at the expense of the apprentice system, and thus indirectly at least supportive of more modern notions of both childhood and family. Bernard Farber notes:

> There were . . . significant differences between the educational and apprenticeship systems. Aries (1962) suggests that the development of a school system oriented toward occupational training permitted the retention of parental authority, since the schoolmasters, unlike the master in charge of an apprentice, did not provide a home and sustenance for his students. Instead, the schoolmaster's tenure and his control over his students remained directly or indirectly (through a school board) at the pleasure of the parents. This development is consistent with the trend noted by Aries of the simultaneous development of secular education and the conjugal unit as a family form. Both represented a decline of the control by extrafamily agencies over the socialization of children [1972:172].

Did this have any directly discernible effect on the manner in which childhood was viewed and the treatment of children? While one is tempted to say that it could not help but have such an effect, the data available is very limited indeed and only allows us to consider the question in the broadest possible terms and over wide intervals in time.

THE BEGINNING OF MODERN CHILDREARING

There is some evidence that even before the founding of the new republic important changes had occurred within the American family, specifically in the area of parent-child relations. Bernard Farber (1972) looks at this question by focusing on the issue of change in Salem, Massachusetts at the turn of the nineteenth century, when this community grew from a town of farmers and fishermen into a major seaport. It is Farber's thesis that if we are to make sense out of the changes that were occurring within the Salem family we must do so in terms of the class distinctions that were becoming more apparent in this community of laborers, artisans, and merchants. Within the artisan classes the continuation of the apprentice system lent support to traditional Puritan views of a stern, authoritarian relationship between parents and children, though an authoritarianism tempered with moderation. Among the merchant classes more change was evident. Merchant families tended to be indulgent and perhaps even permissive in their childrearing. Yet at the same time, their movement out of the apprentice system and their control over the education of their children, whether in the public schools or in the private schools (to which they increasingly sent their sons), resulted in their authority over their children being strengthened, and strengthened within the context of the nuclear family (Farber, 1972:167). The permissiveness evidenced by the elite families of Salem in the rearing of their children is partly seen as a reflection of class differences which date back to the early colonial period, when their apparent state of grace, evidenced by their privileged position, freed the elite from having to manifest some of the outward signs of asceticism demanded of their poorer neighbors.

Given the limits of space here, it is not possible to trace in any detail the course of the changes that occurred during the late colonial and early Federal periods. In brief, what we see during this period is the increasing modernization of the nation, and though some have claimed that the United States was modern virtually from its inception (Brown, 1972), it is nonetheless true that in economic terms it was a nation of small farmers well into the nineteenth century. It can be contended that the whole question of parental authority, and thus relations between parents and children, must be understood in terms of the control parents exerted over the destinies of their children. The picture Philip Greven (1970) paints of the first generation of settlers in Andover, Massachusetts maintaining very direct control over their sons through the device of not allowing land to pass formally to them until their own death (even though the son may have built a house on it and may be farming it with his wife and children) is indicative of how strong was the foundation upon which paternal authority rested.

Such authority patterns notwithstanding, if we look at the nineteenth-century accounts of travelers to this country we see that among the things they found to be most noteworthy was the relationship between parents and children, and the manner and demeanor of the latter. Some were shocked by what they saw; others were favorably impressed. Some sense of the range of response is evidenced by the following two excerpts:

> Their infant lips utter smart sayings, and baby oaths are too often encouraged . . . even by their own parents, whose counsel and restraint they quickly learn wholly to despise. It is not uncommon to see children of ten calling for liquor at the bar, or puffing a cigar in the streets. In the cars we met a youth of respectable and gentlemanly exterior who thought no shame to say that he learned to smoke at eight, got first "tight" at twelve, and by fourteen had run the whole course of debauchery [quoted in Rapson, 1965:521].

At the same time that travelers deplored such "precocity" they applauded this country's growing primary school system, which probably contributed to the situation they found so disturbing. While it is more than likely that the person quoted above was generalizing from a few exaggerated cases, it was probably also true that by English and Continental standards American children were mature for their years and related to adults in a more relaxed and open manner. Yet some travelers did sense that there was a good side as well to the quality of the relations between parents and children they were observing. One commented on how teenage boys and their fathers resembled companions and recounts, with obvious approval, a scene he saw by chance on a train, involving a man and his fourteen-year-old son.

> They had long been talking on a footing of equality. . . . At last, to while away the time, they began to sing together. First they accompanied each other. Then they took alternate lines; at last alternate words. In this of course they tripped frequently, each laughing at the other for his mistakes. There was no attempt at keeping up the dignity of a parent, as might have been considered necessary and proper with us. There was no reserve. They were in a certain sense already on an equal footing of persons of the same age [quoted in Rapson, 1965:530].

Certainly the spirit of the new republic was appropriately expressed here. A country that had put the equality of man at its foundation was not likely to place too much stock in traditional relations in any sphere, even in that of filial piety, but this ideology is really part of something much broader. It reflects the relationship that exists between social organization and the manner in which children are reared. It is a truism to say that societies rear their children differently in terms of the needs, demands, and values of each society. Obviously similarities in childrearing practices also exist between different societies; and it is the root of these similarities that we are most interested in, for it is our contention that the rejection of authoritarian parent-child relations is part and parcel of modernization—a process which crosses cultures and which ultimately has to be seen in terms of personality change as well.

FROM THE LONELY CROWD TO MODERN PERSONALITY

While the so-called "national character" school of anthropological social psychology has fallen out of favor, and many of its assumptions and findings are now seriously questioned, the idea that inspired its adherents' work remains unchallenged, namely, that observable differences in personality types exist between cultures. For us the question is not one of contemporary differences, but rather one of historical changes within the same culture. Students of national character focused on the question of motives shared by members of a particular culture, but they also looked at what they spoke of as habits. Their major concern (not surprising in view of their Freudian leanings) was to relate the motives and habits shared by members of a culture to certain consistencies in their experiences as children. What makes the contribution of these scholars of continued importance is that they sensitized us to the fact that the distinguishing characteristics of a culture that are so striking to an outsider—what the traveler might describe as the odd ways of the French or the Chinese—are not discrete bits but rather are part of an integrated pattern. "The concept of national character refers to the structuring and combination of traits and motives" (Gorer in Kluckhohn and Murray, 1962:257).

Charles Gatewood

Given our interest in modernization and changes in childrearing and personality type, the most relevant study to come out of the national character school is David Riesman, Nathan Glazer, and Reuel Denney's now unfortunately neglected book, *The Lonely Crowd* (1950, paperback 1954). While the focus of the book is on shifts in American national character, it also contains a theory of social organization and personality type which is grounded in socialization theory. In part the book is an answer to the question, "How do societies produce children that are capable of performing the demands placed upon them as adult members?" As the authors indicate, they are as much concerned with "modes of conformity" as they are with "national character." What makes their approach of special importance is that it goes beyond the simple distinction between modern and traditional societies or between preindustrial and industrial societies, and considers change in the context of industrial societies that move, as our own has done, from an emphasis on production to an emphasis on consumption.

In societies where primary economic activity (hunting, fishing, and agriculture) prevails, such as in some Third World countries today or in European societies before the dual revolutions of the nineteenth century, they characterize the mode of conformity as being "tradition directed." Such societies, while hardly static, nonetheless provide a considerable amount of intergenerational stability, and cultural definitions tend to exert strong influence over each individual's behavior. There is "ritual, routine, and religion to occupy and to orient everyone" (1954:26). Moreover, the strength of family and kinship also serves to enforce conforming behavior.

The authors of *The Lonely Crowd* contend that the seeds for the destruction of such traditional societies in the West were sown with the coming of the Renaissance and the Reformation, and were pushed further forward by industrialization. They argue that a new personality type emerges in societies where the rate of social change is greatly accelerated, where personal horizons are widened as the division of labor expands rapidly and the number of people engaged in agricultural activity declines.

> The greater choices this society gives—and the greater initiatives it demands in order to cope with its novel problems—are handled by character types who can manage to live socially without strict and self-evident tradition-direction. These are the inner-directed types [Riesman et al., 1954:30].

The people here described are subject to the pulls and pushes of tradition, but they have a set of internalized controls, described by the metaphor of a gyroscope, which allows them to stay on a course despite the pressures and new demands of a rapidly changing society. Such individuals internalize these controls early in life. Riesman, Glazer, and Denney do not see the controls of the inner-directed person resulting in total rigidity; in their words, "His pilot is not quite automatic" (1954:32). It is merely a matter of working out some reconciliation between internalized controls and external messages.

In perhaps the broadest and crudest sense we might understand American character in the colonial period as being in transition between tradition direction and inner direction. We have people strongly influenced by Biblical notions of proper and improper behavior who at the same time are coping with the adjustment to a new world and in many respects a new life as well. For them, the importance of internalized controls was perhaps of greater significance than for their counterparts who remained in England. Thus, what from today's perspective might be viewed as a harsh and demanding system of childrearing, can from the perspective of differing control mechanisms be looked at as a way a society, undergoing change and beginning to respond to the current of individualism generated by the early stages of modernization in Europe, attempted to maintain personal stability and social control. However, what we see in the Puritan world—and this is a very important point—must be viewed as having elements of traditional society in it as well, since New England in the seventeenth and most of the eighteenth centuries belonged as much to the premodern era as it did to the first stages of the modern one. When Farber (1972) attempts to make sense out of changes in Salem in 1800, what he is doing is looking at the scale being tipped toward inner direction from a society which previously had balanced between tradition and inner directedness. The coming of industrialization in the nineteenth century would bring into bloom the potential for individual action on a scale for which inner direction was eminently suited.

Other direction as the third type of social character is one which Riesman, Glazer, and Denney saw as emerging at the time of their writing, one which was called forth by changes in economic organization associated with a shift in emphasis from production to consumption, but also one which is related to the growth of the large-scale organization of work and virtually all other enterprises.

> [Now] *other people* are the problem, not the material environment. And as people mix more widely and became more sensitive to each other, the surviving traditions from the stage of high growth potential—much disturbed, in any case, during the violent spurt of industrialization—become still further attenuated. Gyroscopic control is no longer sufficiently flexible, and a new psychological mechanism is called for [1954:34].

The replacement is found in a set of controls for which the metaphor of radar is felt to be appropriate, since people are now trained to be sensitive to the response their behavior calls forth from others. The age of the individualistic entrepreneur having passed, the new era of the corporate being is upon us and success here requires that the individual look to others and modify his or her behavior in terms of the response it calls forth from them.

One would be mistaken to assume that other-directed people lack any sort of internalized control mechanisms. It is rather a matter of their having internalized a dependence on others for their guidance. This is seen as being fundamentally related to what they see as the appearance of new small families, small in the sense of few children, with childrearing that is permissive and at the same time places a great deal of the burden for the education of children on extrafamilial agencies, such as the school and the peer group. The end result is a person who looks to others not merely for approval—as did the inner-directed person out of concern for propriety and the maintenance of a life style and personal manner that met with community standards—but also "for guidance in what experiences to seek and in how to interpret them" (1954:40).

The authors of *The Lonely Crowd* are careful to point out that their discussions of three character types are abstractions. Moreover, they recognize that these are not mutually exclusive categories—people may have elements of all three in their makeup. What they are saying is that different personality types predominate in different types of societies, both historically and currently, and that our own society, during the late 1940s, was moving toward the other-directed type. However, we must also recognize that while their book is a study in national character, it is also a critique of the "mass society" they saw America becoming. It was perhaps the first of what was to be a series of such critiques published during the 1950s and which included William H. Whyte's *The Organization Man* (1956) and Vance Packard's *The Status Seekers* (1959), as well as novels such as Sloan Wilson's *The Man in the Gray Flannel Suit* (1955), to name only a few. To the extent that *The Lonely Crowd* is such a critique, it must be read as a reflection of the way intellectuals felt life in America should be rather than how it then was in fact. My own feeling is that the description of the other-directed person is flawed not so much because it is inaccurate, but because of the authors' negative and incomplete interpretation of it. As I shall try to show in what follows, a change in the social organization of American society has indeed brought about change in personality types, but the more empirical evidence we have on the nature of this change, the more positive seem the results. In order to make this clear we shall have to review both the findings on change in childrearing and the assumptions of intellectuals about the nature of life in postindustrial society. Only then will we be in a position to appraise how socialization practices have changed during the twentieth century and what the results of such changes have been.

One of the earliest, most systematic attempts to trace the relationship between changes in social structure, childrearing, and adult personality is the one found in Daniel Miller and Guy Swanson's *The Changing American Parent* (1958). What makes their work of special importance to us is that they draw upon *The Lonely Crowd* as a source of hypotheses. However, the thrust of their work is somewhat different, focusing as it does on the movement from the "entrepreneurial" to the "bureaucratic" organization of work, by which they mean the shift in the United States historically from small farms or businesses, usually individually owned, to large-scale corporations. They argue that four things are involved in this shift:

1. the increase in the size of the organization of production;
2. the growth of specialization in organizations;
3. the great increase in the real incomes of the population; and
4. the enlarged power in the hands of the lower-middle and lower-class workers [1958:43].

Clearly, the authors are zeroing in on major dimensions of modernization.

At the heart of their argument is the notion that work in a bureaucratic setting makes different demands on an individual than in an entrepreneurial one. This should be associated with a different personality type, which in turn can be traced to specific socialization practices. Let us look in depth at what they see as characteristic of the personality and childrearing practices associated with these two settings.

For the entrepreneur the basic personality modes are "self-denial, rationality, and a firm control over his current impulses" (Miller and Swanson, 1958:40). These are supposedly necessitated by the nature of independent economic activity. He must be able to confront the work world and create a place for himself within it. Such a person cannot be loose and freewheeling, but must have a firm sense of who he is and where he is going. Active and independent, he must take an exploitative orientation toward the work, always thinking in terms of long-term prospects. Clearly, such a person would be in many respects similar to the inner-directed man with his gyroscopic controls. Within himself he possesses the necessary guidelines for conduct. The question for us in studying socialization is, how were these internal guidelines installed? Miller and Swanson assert:

> A mother can begin to train her child in self-control and self-denial at a tender age if she will. She can require him to stop nursing before he desires to do so. She can ignore his wails when he is thwarted and upset, leaving him, in crying himself to sleep, to start toward the discovery that all that he wants cannot be had. In feeding him on a schedule which she sets and in putting him on the toilet and rewarding him for having his bowel movements when and as she chooses, she lays a foundation for teaching him that giving up immediate pleasure can lead to future gains. By punishing him when she herself is calm and controlled, she sets an example on which his own conduct can be modeled. By comparing his misconduct to objective standards of goodness, by threatening future punishment for misbehavior that is not amended, by providing deprivations that extend over several hours or days—by any of these instead of through an immediate spanking or slapping, painful at the moment but also something with which she and the child are over in a short time, the mother can underscore the importance of the child's directing himself, counting the costs in the future, and guiding his behavior accordingly [1958:40].

In certain ways this resembles what Demos (1970) and others have described as typical of the Puritans, but we must realize, and this point cannot be emphasized strongly enough, that these are practices which run through American history from the seventeenth century up to the early decades of the twentieth century, and their slow rise to prominence is what we are here concerned with.

Miller and Swanson's emphasis on alterations in the social organization of work places a great deal of weight on the reduced risk taking associated with bureaucratic life. In contrast to the entrepreneurial situation, where speculation and risk are part and parcel of everyday activity, life in the large-scale organization is much less directly competitive and much less fraught with dangers. Income is based on salary, and fringe benefits minimize the sorts of hardships that members of the older middle class were so familiar with. For example, sick leave and sick pay moderate the enormous anxieties associated with illness and loss of income, and pension plans moderate fears of a barren and impoverished old age. Not only are uncertainties reduced, but basic work skills are also modified in the sense that employees must now be skilled socially and able to relate easily and freely with both clients and co-workers.

This picture of organizational life may to many appear to be more benevolent than in fact it is, but we must realize that while large-scale formal organization has brought with it many elements which are problematic, it has, in certain respects, improved the lot of many people in terms of security, pleasantness of work surroundings, and perhaps also in terms of opportunities for creative work. Such changes could not help but have an impact on the way in which children were raised.

> When parents expected that their children would be relatively unsupervised and isolated from others as they moved into adult activities, they needed to train their youngsters by means which would insure that strong consciences were acquired. Armored with a powerful conscience, a man might be expected to obey the social codes even when surrounded by the opportunities and temptations afforded by the anonymity and heterogeneity of an entrepreneurial society. However, when parents can feel that their children will grow up in a closely knit and moral society in which, as members of great organizations, their behavior will be guided and supervised through daily contact with others, there is less need for fathers and mothers to provide the child with a stern, self-propelling conscience [Miller and Swanson, 1958:56].

Therefore the authors expect that two major themes of entrepreneurial society, "self-control and an active manipulative orientation toward the world," would be deemphasized.

Not being able to revivify nineteenth-century entrepreneurs, Miller and Swanson resorted to a research design that permitted some comparisons between families in which the husband was currently employed by a large corporation and those in which the husband owned or was employed by a small firm having three or less employees. They hoped to discover differences in socialization patterns that conformed to their notions about how organizational settings create pressure for particular types of childrearing practices. Their findings, while hardly conclusive, do suggest that their ideas are worth pursuing.

> We find that entrepreneurial mothers among the middle classes are significantly more likely than bureaucratic mothers of similar social status to feed babies on a schedule, to begin urinary training before the baby is eleven months old, and to use symbolic rather than direct punishments. They are also more likely to give a baby who cries when "nothing is wrong with him" some attention only after he sobs for a while or, in some cases, to pay no attention to him at all. Although it is not quite large enough to meet our standard of significance . . . we find that the difference between entrepreneurial and bureaucratic mothers with respect to the age at which bowel training is begun is in the direction we expected. Entrepreneurial mothers are more likely to begin such training with their youngsters before the baby is ten months old [1958:97].

Overall, women whose husbands worked in entrepreneurial settings made greater use of internalization techniques, and in general emphasized "an active, manipulative approach to life" (1958:118).

The data Miller and Swanson offer in support of their thesis is hardly conclusive, and they are aware of this. Still, they have directed our attention to what might be the crucial dimension of social organization as it relates to childrearing practices, namely, the nature of work and the manner in which work is organized in a society. What is also of importance is the bearing that work has upon the research concerning class differences in childrearing practices, a topic which has interested social scientists since at least the 1920s (Robert and Helen Lynd, 1929).

SOCIAL CLASS AND CHILDREARING

In the early 1950s three articles appeared which dealt with childrearing practices advocated in widely distributed periodical literature. Two of these covered the period from the 1890s to the late 1940s, using articles in popular magazines (Stendler, 1950; Vincent, 1951). The last of the three concentrated solely upon the then available editions of the United States Children's Bureau bulletin, *Infant Care* (Wolfenstein, 1953). The findings presented in these articles generated considerable interest among psychologists, sociologists, and others interested in the areas of socialization and parent education. The reason for this interest was twofold: first, as social history they offered a useful picture of change in "expert" opinion on the do's and don'ts of childrearing practices for more than a half century; second, and perhaps more important, these articles were seen by some as shedding light on the apparently contradictory findings of studies of class differences in childrearing practices carried out in the 1940s and 1950s.

Studies of this kind appearing in the 1940s (Davis and Havighurst, 1946) had found that lower-class mothers were more permissive than middle-class mothers with regard to the use of schedules—when they began and finished weaning, toilet training, and so on. The studies carried out in the 1950s found either the opposite to be the case (i.e., middle-class mothers were now more generally permissive in the socialization practices they employed) or no significant differences between the two classes (Sears et al., 1957). A number of hypotheses were put forth to explain this discrepancy, but they can be broken down into two types: (1) those which maintained that no change had occurred and that the differences were due to the studies involved being incomparable in terms of sampling and questionnaire design; and (2) those which claimed that an actual change had occurred.

There are two key articles in this debate, one written by Urie Bronfenbrenner (1958) and the other by William Sewell (1961). Bronfenbrenner reviewed and reanalyzed a sizable group of studies of class-associated childrearing practices, some going back to the 1930s, and concluded that an actual change in class patterns of childrearing practices had occurred and that this change took place around the beginning of the 1940s, with middle-class mothers becoming more permissive at that time. Sewell, in commenting upon this article, only seemed willing to concede that the middle-class mother may have become more permissive in certain areas at the time of the writing of the Bronfenbrenner article. While Bronfenbrenner's study has been attacked by Jay Mechling (1975) on the grounds that the studies he drew upon were based on self-reports of dubious accuracy (see Robbins, 1963), other research does suggest the general trends in class-associated childrearing patterns he described are accurate (McKinley, 1964).

Given these shifts over time in parental behavior, it is not difficult to understand why the studies of childrearing practices advocated in popular periodical literature were greeted with much interest. All of these studies found that, for the most part, in the late 1930s and early 1940s the character of the practices advocated underwent a change in the general direction of what might be called greater permissiveness or indulgence. Stendler analyzed articles published in *Ladies' Home Journal*, *Woman's Home Companion*, and *Good Housekeeping* for the first year of each decade beginning in the 1890s. On the basis of this analysis she concluded:

> Three different schools of thought have prevailed with regard to how children should be raised. The 1890s and 1900s saw a highly sentimental approach to child rearing; 1910 through the 1930s witnessed a rigid, disciplinary approach; the 1940s have emphasized self regulation and understanding of the child. These sixty years have also seen a swing from emphasis on character development to emphasis on personality development [1950:204].

Vincent (1951:204), with a much larger sample of periodical literature for the same period, found little to take issue with in Stendler's findings, and he even used her decade-by-decade percentage figures in his own article.

Of the three studies done in the early 1950s, Wolfenstein's was the one which received the most attention because of the relationship of its findings to those of studies of actual childrearing practices. Her analysis of *Infant Care* dealt with those editions of this bulletin published from its inception in 1914 to 1951. She focused upon four areas of infant development and training: (1) masturbation; (2) thumb sucking; (3) weaning; and (4) bowel training. She presented a picture of changes over time in the practices recommended for dealing with each of these areas.

It is not necessary to review Wolfenstein's findings in detail; nevertheless, a brief summary is in order. The author notes that "in respect to masturbation and thumb sucking, the curve of severity [in method of training suggested] shows a consistently declining direction. In weaning and bowel training we find a U-curve rising in the twenties and subsequently declining" (1953:129). It should also be emphasized, as Wolfenstein herself does, that "in 1942–45 [in *Infant Care*] the handling of the infant in all areas has become very gentle. This tendency is continued and even carried further in 1951" (1953:128).

This correspondence between shifts in the childrearing literature and shifts in actual practices found in the studies mentioned earlier was not long overlooked. Bronfenbrenner, in the article referred to above, had the following to say on this point:

> Our analysis suggests that the mothers not only read these books but take them seriously, and that their treatment of the child is affected, accordingly. Moreover, middle-class mothers not only read more but are also more responsive; they alter their behavior earlier and faster than their working-class counterparts. . . . Taken as a whole the correspondence between Wolfenstein's data and our own suggests a general hypothesis extending beyond the confines of class as such: *child rearing practices are likely to change most quickly in those segments of society which have the closest access and are most receptive to the agencies or agents of change (e.g., public media, clinics, physicians, and counselors)* [1958:411].

Thus, Bronfenbrenner appears to be saying that parent education literature may actually alter patterns of childrearing. There are two elements of his argument which warrant further elaboration.

Bronfenbrenner's argument rests on studies which show that there are class differences in the exposure to the various media of parent education. There is no lack of evidence to support the view that middle- and upper-class women are more likely to be exposed to these media (Anderson, 1936; Blau, 1964). There is also some evidence to show that, in the case of written material, they are more likely to read it once it is given to them (Brooks and Sondag, 1962). There still remains the empirical question of whether exposure to this literature or any other form of parent education actually affects behavior.

There have been a number of studies carried out which attempt to assess the effectiveness of various parent education programs (Mechling, 1975). Orville Brim has reviewed the literature on this subject and on the basis of his review concluded:

> The issue of how effective is parent education in changing parents or children remains, therefore, unresolved at present. . . . On the one hand, there are those who argue that there is no reason to expect any important aspects of adult personality to change as a result of parent education. Protagonists of this position would point out that we do not even know if the adult individual ever undergoes any important changes other than changes in factual knowledge even when exposed to educational experience much more impressive than parent education, such as attending college or doing graduate work in child development over a two- or three-year period. Therefore, it is unreasonable to expect that participating one hour a week in a twelve week seminar, or reading a pamphlet, or being counseled for half an hour during a monthly visit to the pediatrician could influence the parent-child relation.

> On the other hand, an argument presented by many is that the educational programs for parents do produce changes but that for several reasons they will continue to escape detection, given the current measuring procedures. The changes which occur are alleged to be too subtle to be captured by other than clinical techniques, or too small to show up in the sparse samples of parents utilized in most evaluation studies; or are delayed in their occurrence so that they are not discernible except through a longitudinal study [1959:411–412].

Does this mean that Bronfenbrenner's argument is totally invalid? Probably not; rather it appears that he may have placed too great an emphasis upon the childrearing literature as a causal variable and that he has overlooked other possible sources of change.

In view of the emphasis we have placed upon overall societal change, the failure to find the total explanation of this change in childrearing literature should not surprise the reader. When we recognize that the differential availability of such labor-saving devices as washing machines, prepared formulas, and disposable diapers also accounts for only a small part of this change, we must again return to the broader societal consideration we were looking at earlier in this chapter. Even if, as we argued earlier, shifts in childrearing practices—away from the theme of breaking the child's will and parental authoritarianism and toward a more permissive and autonomy-creating model—were the result of changes in the nature of the work situation, as well as other related changes, we must still explain why class differences are present.

WORK, SOCIAL CLASS, AND SOCIALIZATION

The whole issue of work, values, and childrearing has been the subject of an ongoing research project under the direction of Melvin Kohn of the Laboratory of Socio-Environmental Studies of the National Institute of Mental Health, in association with Leonard Pearlin and Carmi Schooler. Since the middle of the 1950s they have been looking at issues that arise in large part from the sort of questions Bronfenbrenner was wrestling with in his attempt to bring order to the literature on apparent changes over time in class-associated childrearing practices.

To date, three studies have been carried out: (1) based on 339 mothers in Washington, D.C. in 1956–1957, all of whom were white and either middle- or working-class women and who had a child in fifth grade (Kohn, 1959); (2) a study in Turin, Italy in 1962–1963 by Leonard Pearlin of 341 fathers and 520 mothers with grade-school children (Pearlin and Kohn, 1966); and (3) a national study in the United States of 3,101 men selected so as to be representative of men in civilian employment—unemployed men and men in the military were excluded (Kohn, 1969). The first study focused almost exclusively on parental values, that is, values parents hold as being important for their children. The second and third studies also collected data on men's work situation, and the third questioned the respondents in depth on their general orientations toward their work situations and experiences.

The Washington study revealed that mothers, irrespective of their class, felt that it was important for their children to be "happy, considerate, obedient and dependable" (Kohn, 1959). Also both middle-class and working-class mothers felt it important for them to respect the rights of others. Where differences do emerge is in regard to two complexes of factors which Kohn labels "self-direction," emphasized by middle-class mothers, and "conformity to external authority," emphasized by working-class mothers:

> The essential difference between the terms, as we use them, is that self-direction focuses on *internal* standards for behavior; conformity focuses on *externally* imposed rules. (One important corollary is that the former is concerned with intent, the latter only with consequences.) Self-direction does not imply rigidity, isolation, or insensitivity to others; on the contrary, it implies that one is attuned to internal dynamics—one's own, and other people's. Conformity does not imply sensitivity to one's peers, but rather obedience to the dictates of authority [Kohn, 1969:35].

Kohn is careful to distinguish his concepts of self-direction and conformity from Riesman's inner-directed versus other-directed personality. Self-direction is not the same as inner direction; the former implies a flexibility and an independence that is antithetical to the idea of the inner-directed person, who has rigidly internalized principles. Similarly, conformity to one's peers, as Kohn uses the term, has less to do with other-direction than it does with plain unadulterated "conforming to authority" (Kohn, 1969:36).

Similar results came out of the Turin and United States studies, but in addition the questions on work yielded some rather provocative results. In general the higher a respondent's class position, the more he or she was likely to value self-direction for his or her children. This relationship held when control variables such as race, religion, region of the country, family size, and so on were introduced.

> Self-direction is a central value for men of higher class position, who see themselves as competent members of an essentially benign society. Conformity is a central value for men of lower class position, who see themselves as less competent members of an essentially indifferent or threatening society. Self-direction, in short, is consonant with an orientational system premised on the possibilities of accomplishing what one sets out to do; conformity, with an orientational system premised on the dangers of stepping out of line [Kohn, 1969:87].

But this very plausible explanation does not contain the whole answer.

Kohn then explored the possibility that what was operating was not class per se, but rather the nature of the work men do, recognizing that different kinds of jobs are differentially distributed in the class hierarchy. Jobs differ in a number of ways relevant to the notion of self-direction.

First, some jobs are more closely supervised than others. Second, Kohn argues, work that involves dealing with people and data offers more opportunity for the exercise of initiative, thought, and judgment. Third, there is the element of job complexity which allows a person to choose between alternative solutions to different problems and tasks which themselves are complex. According to Kohn, jobs that score high on all three of these dimensions are jobs that can be thought of as permitting considerable exercise of self-direction. The Turin and United States national data revealed that when the nature of work that respondents did was introduced, with class held constant, it was discovered that the effects previously attributed to class were to a considerable extent attributable to the exercise of job self-direction. That is to say, a working-class man with a job high in opportunities for self-direction was more likely to hold self-direction as a value for his children than a middle-class man with a job that offered little opportunity for self-direction. Moreover, Kohn maintains that this is not merely a way fathers directly prepare their children for the work force, since in Italy they held this value as strongly for daughters who they are not as likely to feel will have careers as sons, and therefore self-direction is something which they must value in its own right as a result of their work experience (Kohn, 1969:163–164).

Had Kohn stopped here his work would still be filled with much valuable data concerning the relationship between work and childrearing, but fortunately he and his associates pushed their analysis of the United States study even further and in doing so provide us with the most complete study to date of the relationship between social organization, values, and work.

Behind much of the criticism in the 1950s and 1960s of the "mass society" was the assumption that one of the key villains was "bureaucracy." Life in organizations structured along bureaucratic lines was supposedly antithetical to the kinds of work and interpersonal relationships the critics felt were supportive of self-actualization. Those who worked for such organizations would ultimately become little more than faceless automatons. For example, even an attempt at an objective analysis of bureaucracy, such as Robert Presthus's *The Organizational Society* (1962), contained the conventional notions about the alienating effects of organizational life. The astute reader will by now have recognized that there is a seeming contradiction here between Kohn's findings about the value men with high SES place upon autonomy and the fact that most of these men must work directly or indirectly for large-scale organizations.

Perhaps the nature of work in the bureaucracy is not as stultifying as previously thought. This is a question which Kohn has also investigated. In a study published in 1971, he found that:

> Men who work in bureaucratic firms or organizations tend to value, not conformity, but self-direction. They are more open-minded, have more personally responsible standards of morality, and are more receptive to change than men

> who work in nonbureaucratic organizations. They show greater flexibility in dealing both with perceptual and ideational problems. They spend their leisure time in more intellectually demanding activities. In short, the findings belie the critics' assertions [1971:465].

To be sure, other factors are to be found here, most notably education, and one of the reasons Kohn found what he did is, as he recognizes, that bureaucracies employ more educated people. However, there is something about working in bureaucracies per se which is supportive of the kinds of values noted above.

> We conclude, then, that job protections, substantive complexity, and income all contribute to and together largely explain, the social psychological impact of bureaucratization [Kohn, 1971:470–471].

The story is not finished, however. Like all stereotypes, the stereotype of life in the bureaucracy appears to have some validity. The correlations between bureaucratic employment and the holding of values in harmony with autonomy, intellectual flexibility, personal morality, etc., were positive but small. Kohn feels that the reason they were not larger is that because bureaucracies so closely supervise work, they do not give their employees "as much opportunity for occupational self-direction as their educational attainments and the needs of the work allow" (1971:472–473). Remembering the relationship found in his earlier study between self-direction as an aspect of work and the high value placed on autonomy, we can see how this could serve to keep the correlations down.

The question in all Kohn's work remains one of whether particular kinds of jobs attract particular kinds of men or whether the job itself has an effect on the person's psychological functioning. This is an issue to which Kohn and Schooler have addressed themselves (1973). Based on further analysis of the national study, they conclude that the job does shape the man, but their article is especially important because in many ways it spells out the relationship between work and psychological functioning. They reaffirm that class is less significant than work in determining men's psychological functioning, though to be sure jobs are differentially distributed within the class structure.

> In terms of psychological effects, the central fact of occupational life today is not ownership of the means of production; nor is it status, income or interpersonal relationships. Instead, it is the opportunity to use initiative, thought, and independent judgment in one's work—to direct one's occupational activities. . . . Not only the conditions that determine occupational self-direction, but all structural imperatives of the job that elicit effort and flexibility, are conducive to favourable evaluations of self, an open and flexible orientation to others, and effective intellectual functioning. Men thrive in meeting occupational challenges. [1973:116–117].

However, one might still contend that what is really at work here is differential education. James and Sonia Wright (1976), based on partial replication of Kohn's work, have suggested that education is a more important explanatory variable than Kohn realized. Kohn suggests in response (1976:544) that we are still not able to distinguish between education as an occupational prerequisite and as something which conveys self-directive values in its own right. From the perspective of trying to understand changes in socialization, alterations in the nature and meaning of work clearly seem to be of great significance, since they both determine, to some extent, the value that fathers *and* mothers hold to be important for their children. But work takes place in a broader society, and changes in economic organization are associated with changes in other spheres of life. Fortunately, this point has not been neglected by Kohn and his associates. Schooler has directly confronted this issue, again using the data from the national study.

THE WORLD BEYOND WORK

In an article entitled "Social Antecedents of Adult Psychological Functioning" (1972), Schooler attempted to use background factors such as a man's age, his father's education, whether he was raised in a rural or urban environment, religion, and the region of the country in which he was raised, to explore differences in such things as a "high level of intellectual functioning, a rejection of external constraints, and a subjectivism stressing concern for the quality of one's inner life" (1972:299). Essentially what Schooler is doing here is expanding his earlier work with Kohn and Pearlin by looking at societal factors other than employment which result in a particular kind of psychological functioning, though by including father's education as a variable he is also getting at the effects of employment as mediated through the socialization experience. In other words, Schooler was looking to find the effects of modernization on personality formation.

Alex Inkeles, in his essay "The Modernization of Man," includes among the factors he sees as defining modern man:

> The first element in our definition of the modern man is his readiness for new experience and his openness to innovation and change. We consider the traditional man to be less disposed to accept new ideas, new ways of feeling and acting. . . .
>
> We also consider a man to be modern if his orientation to the opinion realm is more democratic. We mean by this that he shows more awareness of the diversity of attitude and opinion around him, rather than closing himself off in the belief that everyone thinks alike and, indeed, just like him. . . .
>
> The modern man is one who believes that man can learn, in substantial degree, to dominate his environment in order to advance his own purposes and goals, rather than being dominated entirely by that environment [1966:141–143].

The similarities between what Schooler is interested in and what Inkeles has set forth should be obvious. Moreover Schooler does find a positive relationship between his independent variables and the modes of psychological functioning he sets forth. The younger men who presumably have been exposed to more permissive childrearing, in urban environments, with educated fathers, in liberal regions of the country, and with nontraditional religious backgrounds show more of the flexible and autonomous psychological functioning than their counterparts whose background is more traditional. Similar findings have also been reported by Harold Grasmich (1973) and Vern Bengston and Mary Lovejoy (1973).

Schooler ends his article on a note which nicely returns us to the central theme of this chapter, namely, the relationship between socialization and the ability of young people to assume adult roles in their society. In considering why there has been so much concern with the concept of alienation on the part of social theorists since the nineteenth century he notes:

> Another cause of concern over alienation, particularly when it is defined in terms of the powerlessness of the individual, may have come about because the processes making for individuation may have increased the general desire for self-direction more than the possibility of its actual attainment, resulting in a greater disparity between aspiration and reality than existed heretofore [1972:321].

The situation is not a hypothetical one. There are data to suggest that a point has been reached where some individuals in our society are finding that they cannot find the opportunities for self-actualization they deem desirable and necessary within the framework of conventional institutions. These people have sought and continue to seek alternative structures.

Richard Flacks (1967, 1970, 1971) has presented findings which suggest some important links between the changes in the socialization processes we have been discussing and the emergence of a youth culture. He points out that the traditional perspective on youth culture and youth movements—that is, the perspective identified with Parsons (Parsons and Bales, 1955) and Eisenstadt (1956)—is that these groups allow young people to bridge the discontinuity between familial and occupational spheres, the family being a structure in which values based on personal relations abound and the work world being one in which impersonal ones flourish. In response, some sort of transitional culture is created to bridge this discontinuity by providing an emotionally supportive atmosphere without sacrificing universalistic criteria. Thus we would expect youth culture to be antagonistic toward the prevailing culture in those nations undergoing dramatic alterations, such as those in the process of modernization. In the United States, on the other hand, a highly technocratic society which has been "modern" for many generations, we would expect intergenerational discontinuity to be minimal and the transition between youth and adulthood an easy one. Yet, as we have had more than enough occasions to observe, youth culture with regard to politics in the 1960s and life style from the 1960s to today appears to stand somewhat differentiated from adult culture. It is this seeming violation of folk wisdom that Flacks's work speaks to most cogently.

Given the fact that traditional theory, with its emphasis on the cultural disorganization created by modernization or other major political or economic upheavals, cannot fully explain the emergence of our youth and student movements, what alternative explanations do we have? Flacks elaborates on some of the themes we have been developing in this chapter. His research into the backgrounds of student radicals during the demonstrations of the 1960s revealed a number of interesting and relevant facts. For one thing, these were not upwardly mobile young people who had brought working-class radicalism with them to the university world. Quite the contrary, the students involved in such demonstrations at the University of Chicago tended to come from affluent families, though families that were in many respects rather special. Their parents, both fathers and mothers, were highly educated people, more often professionals or in social service occupations rather than in business. Even their grandparents tended to show a disproportionately high amount of university training, indicating a heritage of higher education. Moreover, their families tended to be ones in which humanistic values prevailed. As children their lives suffered from no shortage of culture.

> Family interests—as they are expressed in recreation, or in dinner table conversation, or in formal interviews—tend to be intellectual and "cultural" and relatively highbrow; these are families in which books were read, discussed, and taken seriously, in which family outings involved museums and concert-halls rather than ball-parks and movies, etc. [Flacks, 1970:346].

Furthermore, these were families whose humanism was an areligious one. Formal religion was not generally practiced, but moral consistency and social usefulness were still strongly emphasized. Yet, these young people were reared to see education as having intrinsic value apart from the direct purposes to which it could be put. Finally, it also appeared that the relationship between these students and their parents was one in which traditional parental authority was not exercised with great zeal. Instead the activists were more likely than nonactivists to say that their parents would not interfere if they chose to leave school or live with a person of the opposite sex.

This then was a situation in which children were not in rebellion against parental values, but instead were behaving very much in accordance with them. Let's pursue this point further so as to make it clearer. The students who were in the vanguard of the protest movement—we might think of them in certain respects as the leadership cadre—were not young people whose values differed from those of their parents. If any gap existed it was one consisting of behavior versus values. In other words, these students were acting on the values their parents inculcated in them. They were raised to value self-direction, creativity, and in general what

Student demonstrators of the 1960s. *(George W. Gardner)*

could be described as a humanistic perspective, yet they were being educated in institutions which require that they conform to certain regulations, whether in regard to freshman-sophomore requirements or regulations governing where or with whom they could live and what could or could not be consumed in those quarters. If they managed to abide by these regulations long enough to graduate, they came up against a society that offered a dearth of jobs that permitted them to act upon their sense of social responsibility and abhorrence of rigid regulations. Here then we have writ large of discontinuity created by socialization practices which place much stock in an orientation toward life that cannot be realized.

Thus a revolutionary-like development sprang up not from a lack of access to the good things in life or from social turmoil, but instead from a generation of young people reaching adulthood and finding that they had not been prepared for life as it actually is (Reich, 1970). To be sure, such young people have set out to change things. Apart from political protest we have also seen young people successfully fight to alter such things as parietal hours in dormitories, to gain a voice for themselves in curriculum determination, and in general, if only in small ways, begin to alter larger structures and processes in the direction of their values and needs.

The situation, however, is more complicated than one can glean by looking only at the research of Flacks. His work is important, but since it deals almost exclusively with the familial background of those involved *early on* in the student protest movement, we cannot generalize too broadly from it. Moreover, since its focus is on the political dimension of youth culture, or what some used to refer to as the counterculture, it does not tell us that much about those who are now into new life styles, but who remain apolitical. Given the seeming revival of political apathy among youth in the 1970s, this is an especially important point.

One of the few social scientists who has commented in a systematic fashion on the differences between the familial background of young people involved in social protest and those who are apolitical is the Yale psychologist, Kenneth Keniston. Recognizing that both types of dissenters probably represent a minority of the young people in the nation, he proceeds to distinguish the "activists" from the "alienated."

> *The activist*—The defining characteristic of the "new" activist is his participation in a student demonstration or group activity that concerns itself with some matter of general political, social or ethical principle. Characteristically, the activist feels that some injustice has been done, and attempts to "take a stand," "demonstrate" or in some fashion express his conviction [1968:300].
>
> . . .
>
> *The culturally alienated*—In contrast to the politically optimistic, active and social-concerned protester, the culturally alienated student is far too pessimistic and too firmly opposed to "the system" to wish to demonstrate his disapproval in any organized way. His demonstrations of dissent are private: through nonconformity of behavior, ideology and dress, through personal experimentation and above all through efforts to intensify his own subjective experience, he shows his distaste and disinterest in politics and society. The activist attempts to change the world around him, but the alienated student is convinced that meaningful change of the social and political world is impossible; instead, he considers "dropping out" the only real option [1968:301–302].

Keniston maintains that while the activists and the alienated tend to be drawn from the same social strata, there are important differences in their family backgrounds. In contrast to the activist, who is seen as acting on parental values, the alienated reject their parents' values, especially those of their fathers whom they see as having been compromised by "the system."

Flacks' *Youth and Social Change* (1971) provides us with a rather provocative analysis of why some families produce activists and others alienated young people. He feels that in families of the latter there is a considerable amount of "parental value conflict and confusion." Parents in these homes have been exposed to the kinds of pressures we have described, which have made them place a great deal of value on self-direction and creativity. Yet these same middle-class parents have been reared in homes where more conventional and authoritarian values prevailed, and where relations between parent and child lacked the equalitarian character they have tried to create in their own homes. Being part of two worlds, Flacks feels, causes them to react to their own children in an inconsistent fashion, sometimes punishing them for certain acts and at other times allowing the same behavior to pass unpunished. They may also set unclear standards with regard to such things as cleanliness, respect for parental authority, etc. There are other problems in these families as well, problems that hinge upon such things as paternal and maternal ambivalence concerning their work, or in the case of women, lack of extradomestic employment. Added to all of this is the general accelerated rate of social change in our society that we have been talking about. Taken together, all of these factors create young people who are confused about themselves and confused about the society they live in.

The return of relative calm to American campuses during the 1970s and the growing concern with careers on the part of college students has been simultaneously heralded or denounced as a return to the mentality of the silent 1950s and as evidence of how short-lived were the seeming cultural revolutions of the 1960s. In a documentary film the author recently saw a sculptor remark, "The sixties were an intermission and now the show's on again." However insightful this person's art may be, we shall have to take issue with his interpretation of the current state of American culture, at least as it manifests itself among youth. While communalism, costume wearing, political activism, and the wholesale rejection of American society may have waned dramatically in the 1970s, in other equally crucial areas we have seen a continuation of trends that first became evident in the 1960s. Perhaps there is no better place to see the continuity between the 1960s and 1970s than in the work of Daniel Yankelovich. His recent book, *The New Morality: A Profile of American Youth in the 1970s* (1974), presents data taken from cross-sectional national studies of American young people carried out between 1969 and 1973. These data show an impressive growth in attitudes that nicely articulates with the findings of Keniston and Flacks. Table 6-1 indicates two apparently conflicting trends at work—a wish to deemphasize money versus a growing emphasis on careers and earning money.

Yankelovich sees these two sets of values as representing a dilemma for college students:

> What we see, therefore, is the simultaneous growth of two sets of values that are in conflict with each other at many points. For example, the de-emphasis on money grubbing is a cardinal tenet of the New Values. At the same time, however, the opportunity to earn good money is one of the key attractions of a conventional career. The tension created by these two conflicting value systems defines the central problem, or dilemma, that presents itself to today's youth [1974:16].

Being an experienced survey analyst, Yankelovich realizes that such results don't necessarily mean that the same students are holding conflict-

Table 6-1. SELECTED ATTITUDES OF COLLEGE STUDENTS

	1969 (%)	1973 (%)
Would welcome more acceptance of sexual freedom	43	61
Would welcome less emphasis on money	73	80
Religion as a very important value	38	28
	1970	**1973**
Size of "career-minded" group	60	66
Challenge of the job as an important criterion	64	77
Economic security as an important job criterion	33	58
Money you can earn as an important job criterion	36	61

SOURCE: Daniel Yankelovich, *The New Morality* (New York: McGraw-Hill, 1974), chapter 2.

ing values. College youth can apparently be divided into three groups on the basis of their stance on the two value complexes: (1) those who emphasize the new values and are unconcerned with career considerations; (2) those who are not strongly committed to the new values and who are concerned with their careers; and (3) those who indeed appear to be conflicted as evidenced by their favorable disposition to both sets of values. For Yankelovich the last group strikes "what is perhaps the dominant theme of today's college youth" (1974:20), and is the "most interesting" of the three. We would concur, but we would also emphasize that roughly two-thirds of the college youth subscribe to the new values, and half of this group is trying to achieve a synthesis of the two sets of values. This is an important point because it conveys the extent to which these values have spread in the population. Further evidence of this can be seen in Yankelovich's findings among noncollege youth.

Table 6-2 indicates an interesting convergence of views between the college and the noncollege groups. By 1973, the noncollege group shows values very similar to those of the college group as of 1969. In view of the fact that the late 1960s supposedly were the high point for countercultural expression in this country, the fact that the college youth continue to move beyond their positions in 1969 (see Table 6-1) and that the noncollege youth are rapidly closing the gap is most significant. The rapid spread of such attitudes among all the country's young people returns us to Schooler's point about the tensions created when a society raises expectations among its citizenry that only a minority may be able to realize. These data also provide support for what Young and Willmott, borrowing from Toqueville, call "The Principle of Stratified Diffusion," that is, "What the few have today, the many will demand tomorrow" (1973:19). One of the key issues of the next decade may hinge not merely on the expansion of job opportunities per se, but rather on the creation of job opportunities that provide for self-fulfillment.

Table 6-2. COMPARISON OF COLLEGE AND NONCOLLEGE YOUTH ON SELECTED ATTITUDES, 1969 AND 1973

	1969 (coll.) (%)	1969 (noncoll.) (%)	1973 (noncoll.) (%)
Would welcome more acceptance of sexual freedom	43	22	47
Would welcome less emphasis on money	73	54	74
See religion as an important value	38	64	42
See patriotism as an important value	35	64	42

SOURCE: Daniel Yankelovich, *The New Morality* (New York: McGraw-Hill, 1974), chapters 2 and 3.

SUMMARY

In this chapter we have looked at the way in which children have been socialized over the more than 300 years of this country's history. We saw that while the Puritans' conception of childrearing might be considered harsh by current standards, its harshness was rooted in a profound concern for the child's spiritual well being and was certainly tempered by love and affection. In discussing Puritan socialization practices we considered the debate generated by Ariès over the existence of childhood as a demarcated stage of life at that time. Initially, scholars seemed to have found that what Ariès saw as true of seventeenth-century France was also true of seventeenth-century New England, but increasingly evidence is coming to light which suggests that this may not be the case. Perhaps it was a matter of North America having moved further along the path toward modern practices than was the case on the Continent.

While the absence of research made it difficult to discuss the transition between seventeenth- and nineteenth-century practices, by the early stages of the latter we do see evidence of growing flexibility and democratization of parent-child relations. This was interpreted as a reflection of changing structural conditions within the nation. *The Lonely Crowd* was discussed as a book which offered some suggestions for interpreting the direction and meaning of these changes; this began a longer treatment of the way in which changes in the organization of work affect socialization practices. This section culminated in a consideration of the work of Melvin Kohn and his associates. Kohn, more than any other social scientist, has concerned himself with the way in which the jobs men have mold their own values and the values they hold for their children. He has shown that dimensions of work are a more powerful explainer of these values than social class.

In an overall sense, the theme of this chapter has been that modernization produces persons who are self-directed, flexible, open to new experience, and concerned with the subjective quality of their inner lives, to name only a few of the more salient characteristics. But, as was pointed out, the ability of modern societies to provide opportunities for such people to lead lives that are in harmony with their modes of psychological functioning is something which remains to be seen.

"Courting by Proxy," c. 1885, at Cape Breton, Nova Scotia. *(NYPL Picture Collection)*

COURTSHIP: From Arranged Marriage to Unmarried Roommates

7

If, in fact, changes in socialization practices resulting from the broad shifts in social organization have produced many young people who are unhappy with conventional societal structures, then there is no better place to look for indications of this dissatisfaction than in the realm of courtship and mate choice. For here we can see if existing structures are beginning to show signs of rejection or at least modification. Before we study the present period, however, it will be necessary to consider the broader sweep of premarital relations between the sexes from colonial days to the present; only by doing this can we gain the historical perspective necessary for assessing the current scene.

It is important to state at the outset that when we discuss premarital relations between the sexes for most of American history we are talking about courtship, that is, behavior more or less directly related to marriage. Yet, one might safely say that since the colonial period premarital relations have been increasingly separated from marriage. In the early colonial period, most contact between postpubescent males and females was directly oriented to mate selection and marriage. This is in sharp contrast to the situation today, where from the onset of puberty, if not earlier, young men and women engage in a variety of activities together, from dating to cohabitation. These practices have increasingly become separated from and independent of marriage. The nature of this trend will be elaborated on as this chapter progresses.

FROM "PARENT-RUN" TO "PARTICIPANT-RUN" MATE SELECTION

The popular view of the courtship systems of premodern societies, whether historically or cross-culturally, is that they were parent-run; that is, the major role in the choice of a mate for a marriageable young man or woman resided with the parents, and in some instances the son or daughter was not even consulted (Goode, 1963). Such a system was probably never rigidly adhered to in any society. Generally, some device was built into the system to allow the potential spouses to meet briefly or at least view each other prior to marriage and exercise a veto (Arensberg and Kimball, 1940). However, in certain segments of traditional societies, such as among the nobility in Tudor and Stuart England, the system operated with virtually no input from the young people involved, who may have been children at the time of their engagement or marriage (Stone, 1960:61).

In our current participant-run courtship system (Reiss, 1971:60), parental influence is hardly lacking, though to be sure there are some couples who marry free of any parental consultation. For the most part the exercise of the parental veto can be a powerful, if not a certain, deterrent of children's marital plans, and Sussman (1953b) has found that some parents will resort to coercion, if necessary, to prevent a marriage they feel is unsuitable. There is no denying, however, the strikingly positive relationship between modernization and the growth of participant-run courtship.

The explanation usually presented for parent-run mate selection places great emphasis on the consideration for perpetuating family estates, in both financial and symbolic terms, in premodern times. It was felt that a desirable wife should bring a sizable dowry with her and should be capable of bearing children to perpetuate the line, as well as adequately serve in her role as wife and mother (Goode, 1963). A husband, in turn, should come equipped with the requisite skills, property, or means to acquire the latter to insure that a marriage to him would not result in any compromise of the bride's family's status. Furthermore, marriage was also seen as a device for creating new alliances (business, political, or military) between families (Lévi-Strauss, 1969). Thus we would not expect parents to place much stock on the whims and wishes of their children, though one suspects that wise and humane parents probably tried to strike some balance between self-interest and the happiness of the pair.

The situation in this country during the early colonial period was one which by no means conforms to the ideal type of parent-run courtship. Lawrence Stone has noted:

> In the last thousand years ideas about the proper method of arranging marriage have passed through four successive phases. In the first, marriage was arranged by parents with relatively little reference to the wishes of the children; in the second, parents continued to arrange the marriage, but granted the children the right of veto; in the third, the children made the choice, but the parents retained the power of veto; and in the fourth, which was only reached in this

> century, the children arrange their own marriages with little reference to the opinions of the parents. In the late sixteenth and early seventeenth centuries, England passed from the first to the second of these phases [1960–1961:205].

Since those who settled New England were largely of English extraction, it is surprising to find courtship in seventeenth-century New England having elements of Stone's second and third phases. Yet these were Puritans whose creed laid great emphasis on the importance of happy marriages and condemned a double sexual standard (Schnucker, 1975). In this respect they led the way for the movement from the second to third phase in England as well. Moreover, Stone's concern is essentially with the nobility, of which the Puritans were certainly not a part. If we look at the findings of such scholars as John Demos (1970), Philip Greven (1970), Kenneth Lockridge (1970), and Daniel Smith (1973c) for each of their respective Massachusetts communities, we see that during the seventeenth century and into the eighteenth, parents exerted significant influence on the child's choice of mate and their approval was necessary; however, it does not appear that the parents actually chose the spouse. Commenting on the Plymouth Colony during the seventeenth century Demos has noted:

> First of all, and most important: when a courtship had developed to a certain point of intensity, the parents became directly involved. An early order of the General Court directed that "none be allowed to marry that are under the covert of parent but by their consent and approbacon." Later on, the Court came to feel that a stronger statement was necessary and amended the law to read as follows: "If any shall make any motion of marriage to any mans daughter or mayde servant not haveing first obtayned leave and consent of the parents or master so to doe [he] shalbe punished either by fine or corporall punishment or both" [1970:154].

The courts were not the only channel open to parents to insure that their offspring not marry without their consent. Perhaps an even stronger incentive for children to defer to parental wishes was to be found in the transfer of property, which was really at the heart of the matter anyway. For the young man, marriage was out of the question until he had the land and the necessary capital to support a family.

> In effect, marriages of second-generation in seventeenth-century Andover depended upon the willingness of fathers to permit sons to leave the parental homestead and to establish themselves as married adults, usually in houses of their own built on family land designated as the married son's responsibility [Greven, 1970:75].

On the other hand, a young woman's parents could express their disapproval by refusing to provide a dowry. Demos cites a will which provides a daughter with "a handsome gift of household furnishings 'att her marriage and if shee please her mother in her match' " (1970:156). There is no shortage of other instances where parents threatened to withhold an inheritance if a child chose to marry a person who did not meet with their approval.

Smith (1973c) has ingeniously shown us the existence of a measure of parental control over mate choice in colonial New England. Using data taken from his study of Hingham, Massachusetts from 1635 to 1880, he compares sons of men who died before age sixty and who could by law inherit at twenty-one with sons of living fathers in terms of their mean age at first marriage. The assumption was that the former would marry earlier because they were free from the kinds of paternal restraints to which the latter were subject. Smith found that from 1635 to 1740 sons of long-lived men married later, while after 1740, and particularly after 1780, the differences between the two groups are negligible. With regard to daughters, he argues that in a parent-run system daughters should ideally marry in the order of their birth, since "passing over a daughter to allow a younger sister to marry first might advertise some deficiency in the elder and consequently make it more difficult for the parents to find a suitable husband for her" (1973c:425). His data reveal a notable increase in sisters marrying out of birth order after the middle of the eighteenth century. Smith also finds a general trend showing wealth to be a less important consideration in marriage, with the daughters of affluent men marrying later, the closer one approaches 1880, suggesting that marriage was becoming less of an arena for the exchange of property.

Data such as those offered by Smith, based as they are on one town and on an indirect measure, can hardly be seen as conclusive, but they do give us some sense of how parental control over mate choice began to break down before the end of the colonial era—not in the nineteenth century as some may have thought. Here again we see preindustrial indicators of modernization at work, and further evidence in support of the argument that the United States in certain respects was a modern country even before it technically underwent the political economic upheavals generally associated with this process (Brown, 1972).

COURTSHIP IN COLONIAL NEW ENGLAND

Having looked at trends in parental control, let us return to a consideration of courtship itself in colonial New England. Regrettably, the information we have on this topic is limited. Regarding the Plymouth Colony Demos maintains:

> The initial phases of courtship must, unfortunately, be passed over with barely a word said, for they are nearly invisible from this distance in time. Probably they lacked much formal ceremony (no dating, dances and so forth). Probably they showed close connection to other aspects of everyday life, to common patterns of work and leisure. Probably too they developed under the watchful eye of parents and siblings, or indeed of the whole neighborhood. (Sustained

privacy is difficulty to imagine, in *any* part of the Old Colony setting.) But all this is very much in the realm of speculation [Demos, 1970:152].

There is some evidence available which suggests that patterns of strict supervision began to break down in the early eighteenth century. Ray Hiner (1975), in his reassessment of adolescence as a life stage in eighteenth-century New England, cites a number of contemporary commentators whose remarks suggest that young people gained freedom at this time.

When children and young people are suffered to haunt the taverns, get into vile company, rabble up and down in the evening, when they should be at home to attend family worship; in the dark and silent night, when they should be in their beds, when they are let alone to take other sinful courses without check or restraint, they are then on the high road to ruin [Loring, 1718, quoted in Hiner, 1975:264].

One certainly has to take such exhortations with a grain of salt, but given the number of ministers who expressed concern over the keeping of bad company at the time it would be foolish to disregard them entirely. Moreover, when we take up the question of patterns of premarital sexual behavior we will see that this alarm was not without foundation.

Of course, we do know something about age at first marriage in colonial times. In general it was considerably older than traditional historical sources would have us believe. Arthur Calhoun, for example, tells us, "The early Puritans married young. . . . Girls often married at sixteen or younger" (1945:67). However, Smith found in Hingham, Massachusetts that before 1691 the average age at marriage was 27.4 for men and 22.0 for women, rising to 28.4 and 24.7, respectively, in the 1691 to 1715 interval (1972:177). For roughly the same intervals in Ipswich, Massachusetts, Susan Norton found the ages to be 27.2 and 26.5 for men, and 21.7 and 23.6 for women (1971:445). It is relevant to note that a recent study focusing on familial patterns in seventeenth-century Maryland found a mean age at marriage of 16½ for women born in Somerset County before 1670 (Carr and Walsh, forthcoming). This is not only much earlier than the New England figures we have just cited, but is also much earlier than contemporary English figures which resemble those prevailing in Massachusetts. A general trend of an increase in age at first marriage for females and a decrease in age of males at the turn of the eighteenth century is confirmed by a number of studies, though there is some variation, with a town like Andover, Massachusetts not showing the drop in male age until after 1730 (Greven, 1970:208), and Hingham not until 1716 (Smith, 1972:177). As this should make evident, the child bride or even the early adolescent bride was not typical of seventeenth-century New England. When we realize that the current median age at first marriage for males is about 23.5 and 21.5 for females (*New York Times,* January 8, 1976:58), we see just how much control parents in the colonial period exerted over the marital destinies of their offspring, and how reluctant they were to part with the property or wealth necessary to establish a young man, no less lose his services in the family farm or business.

There is some evidence to suggest that the pool from which potential mates were drawn was wider than one might expect. Norton (1973) has looked at marital migration in six Essex County, Massachusetts towns for the sample periods (1701–1720, 1751–1770, and 1801–1820) using records which give the residences of both partners at the time of their marriage. While there is considerable variation between towns at the same time and within a town at different times, what is most striking is that in no town and at no time did endogamous marriages (marriages where both partners were residents of the same community) ever exceed 92 percent. Most communities, even in the early period, fell well below that percentage, ranging from 36.4 to 80.4 percent. The importance of this study is that it shows that even early in the settlement of New England, people went outside of the community to find mates. This should not be surprising, in view of the fact that communities were small and early settlers felt that people should marry social equals (Morgan, 1966). Thus in order to obtain a proper mate one might have to go to a neighboring town or even further. But we don't know how such people met each other and became engaged.

Once a couple had decided to wed and had obtained parental approval, the next step was the "betrothal" or "contract," which, according to Plymouth Colony records quoted by Demos (1970:157), involved the couples promising to marry before two witnesses. Being betrothed was a formal status not taken lightly by the Puritans. If either party reneged, a legal suit might follow and the courts were likely to award a considerable sum in damages (Demos, 1970:157). The next step was the publishing of the banns. That is, an announcement had to be made at three successive public meetings or posted at a public place, such as a meeting house door for two weeks in the towns of both parties, so as to ensure that no impediment to the marriage, such as a previous and still standing marriage, existed. This was often followed by the young man or the young woman having family property or other wealth transferred to his or her possession, either in the form of land or dowry. The marriage itself was performed by a magistrate rather than a clergyman, since marriage was seen as a civil contract. Apparently the marriage was followed by a feast (Morgan, 1966:33–34), but laws prohibited dancing and other "riotous merrymaking" so that they were probably pretty staid affairs. Demos says of the marriage ceremony and feast in Plymouth: "Like so many other things in the Old Colony, weddings were probably short, simple, and very much to the point" (1970:165–166).

A marriage was not truly binding until it had been consummated, and a bride who found herself with an impotent husband could easily have the marriage annulled. There is some evidence to suggest, however, that many young men and women did not wait until the bridal night to test the virility of the future husband. In general it is safe to say that the Puritans were not nearly as puritanical on the subject of sex as some of us have been led to believe. This is not to say that they encouraged or even condoned premarital sex, but merely that they took a rather realistic view of it (Morgan, 1942). The major sources of data on this topic are to be found in studies of bridal pregnancy, based on matching records of dates of marriage and first birth, and civic and church records dealing with "fornication." Daniel Smith and Michael Hindus (1975) have data on New England during the seventeenth century which show that less than 10 percent of the marriages involved an already pregnant bride, though we must of course keep in mind that many others went to the altar not pregnant but still hardly virginal. It is worth noting that during the seventeenth century, bridal pregnancy was especially prominent among the less affluent and less religious (Smith and Hindus, 1975). During the second half of the eighteenth century, the figures for bridal pregnancy rose to roughly 30 percent.

Couples who bore such children were generally fined. The fine was less if the couple was betrothed at the time than if they were not bound in any way. Fornication, which was generally discovered when an unmarried woman bore a child, was treated somewhat more seriously. But even here Demos tells us that in seventeenth-century Plymouth the punishment for fornication was a fine of £10 or a public whipping, with both parties bearing the punishment (1970). Thus, as much as the Puritans may be portrayed as saints, they were earthy people in touch with their own sexuality and willing to forgive but not condone the transgressions of their young people.

While we know little about seventeenth-century courtship, we perhaps know less about eighteenth- and nineteenth-century patterns. The only area for which reliable data exists is that of bridal pregnancy. Nonetheless, by using these statistics and looking at other changes in American society during these centuries we can perhaps sketch some of the trends in courtship.

PREMARITAL SEX AND MODERNIZATION

Both European and American sources indicate an increase in bridal pregnancy and illegitimacy roughly between the middle of the eighteenth and the first half of the nineteenth centuries. Obviously this reflects a growing incidence of premarital sexual intercourse, but there still remain the questions of why and how such changes occurred. Edward Shorter (1971) is one of the few scholars to attempt to systematically interpret these changes in terms of other aspects of societal and cultural change and it is to his work that we must turn if we are to begin to understand how Western courtship patterns were altered during this period.

Shorter feels that a fundamental shift occurred in attitude toward sexuality during this period. Recognizing that this involves much conjecture, he offers the following explanation:

> As a first imprudent step, let us assume that people have intercourse for one of two reasons. They may wish to use their sexuality as a tool for achieving some ulterior external objective, such as obtaining a suitable marriage partner and setting up a home, or avoiding trouble with a superior. If they have such motives in mind as they climb into bed, they are using sex in a *manipulative* fashion. Alternatively, they may be intent upon developing their personalities as fully as possible, upon acquiring self-insight and self-awareness, and, accordingly, think of sex as an integral component of their humanity. For such people, sex is a way of expressing the wish to be free, for the egoism of unconstrained sexuality is a direct assault upon the inhibiting community authority structures about them. I call this *expressive* sexuality. This level of intercourse is higher than that for the manipulative variety because self-expression is an ongoing objective, whereas once the object is attained to which manipulative sexuality was employed, the person may lapse into the unerotic torpor society has ordained as proper. Expressiveness means a lot of sex; manipulativeness means little [Shorter, 1971:241–242].

This growth of "expressive" sexuality on the part of working-class Europeans and a similar phenomenon in this country (we don't really have class-specific data for the United States) is seen by Shorter as being very much tied to the processes of modernization. Yet Shorter recognizes that somewhat of a paradox arises here because the middle classes in Europe, the group most directly involved in the new forms of economic activity and new educational structures, were the most repressed sexually and generally the most traditional. He explains this by pointing out that these families were still in a position to control the destinies of their children in a way not unlike that of the landholding families we described earlier in seventeenth- and eighteenth-century Andover, Massachusetts or in any largely agricultural society. We pointed out that with the coming of industrialization children were to some extent freed from their parental yoke as a result of the appearance of a market for free labor. Yet, among the growing class of merchants, factory owners, and other entrepreneurs, a fair amount of control could still be exercised over children because of the degree to which avenues to economic independence were controlled by parents. Therefore it is not surprising that they were able to supervise the courtship behavior of their children to the extent that there was less opportunity for premarital sexual expression than there was for the working classes.

Not unrelated to the important changes in sexual expression Shorter deals with is the emergence of adolescence as a new stage of life (Kett, 1971; Gillis, 1974). With the prolongation of education and the creation of child labor laws, young people were kept out of industry. At the same time their families were leaving agricultural work, which required that children work beside their parents. Thus, in the growing industrial cities we have a concentration of young people who are not working and not under the constant supervision of their parents. The sorts of ideas Shorter sees at the root of expressive sexuality (self-insight, self-awareness, etc.), would seem to flourish in an environment of extended education, leisure, and the company of like-minded individuals. Therefore it is not surprising that cities showed an upturn in illegitimacy before the rural areas did. Shorter feels that this may have been simply a compositional effect, that is, there were more young women in the cities. We should nonetheless seriously consider the kinds of effects urbanization had on youth, on the creation of a youth culture, and on courtship patterns.

In discussing courtship in Plymouth Colony, Demos pointed out that there was little that went on that was not under the surveillance of either parents or other members of the community, though obviously some young people were able to find enough privacy for an occasional premarital pregnancy to occur. Bernard Farber's description of family life in Salem, Massachusetts in 1800 suggests that there was sufficient diversity by the turn of the century in even this small city for much activity to go on that was not under the constant scrutiny of all the townspeople (1972).

The dancing class (c. 1895) taught children a useful social skill and at the same time gave them some early exposure to members of the opposite sex. (*The Staten Island Historical Society*)

From the middle decades of the eighteenth century and into the nineteenth century young people were achieving autonomy in various spheres of life, and they expressed this new and growing autonomy in their sexual behavior. Thus we might also assume that the same was true with regard to other aspects of courting, though the data we have is very limited.

What makes any attempt to understand courtship in the eighteenth and most of the nineteenth centuries difficult is the virtual absence of any systematic material on how young people managed to meet their mates and, moreover, what kinds of sexual activities they engaged in that were not specifically related to marriage. One of the problems here, of course, is the growing diversity of the nation. In addition to regional differences such as those that set New England apart from the old South, there were also the differences that existed between the frontier and the areas that had been settled for several generations. Added to this were the emergent class differences which became increasingly salient throughout the nineteenth century and which were bound to have an effect on the amount of freedom granted young people. Furthermore, during the second half of the nineteenth century ethnic and religious diversity increasingly became part of the fabric of American society as immigration rapidly accelerated. Taken together, these factors suggest that a great deal was probably happening in the realm of courtship and nonmarriage-related interaction between the sexes during this period, but the specific developments still await scholarly examination.

THE EMERGENCE OF DATING

It is not until the twentieth century that we begin to observe what might be seen as a truly revolutionary change in courting patterns, one which throws into question the very use of the adjective "courting." What we have seen emerge in this century, perhaps as a culmination of processes that have been in the works since the eighteenth century, are formalized patterns of heterosexual interaction that are largely separate from marriage.

Let us look at the phenomenon of dating, what it is, how it took form, and what is currently happening to it. Most readers, at least those born in this country, hardly need to have dating defined for them, having either directly experienced it themselves or at least having been in a position to observe others engaged in it. Yet, a brief definition is in order. For the present purposes I will define dating as that behavior involving heterosexual couples that is geared to amusement and recreation (cf. Burgess and Locke, 1945:382). This definition is not meant to distinguish between those couples who have any sort of commitment to each other (going steady, engaged, etc.) from those who are merely seeing each other for the first time, though some might argue that it is best used to characterize those couples whose relationship is a casual one. Such couples may go to the movies, plays, dances, picnics, bars, and athletic events with each other. More often than not, they also engage in some sort of sexual contact ranging from a timid goodnight kiss to sexual intercourse.

The "Rating and Dating" Complex

Before going on to discuss the various forms dating takes and the purposes it seems to serve, we should consider its history.

The first mention of dating in a scholarly context is Willard Waller's famous article (1937) on the rating-dating complex, which described the situation that existed at Pennsylvania State University in the late 1920s and early 1930s. The attention received by Waller's piece has led some to conclude that the 1920s was the decade when dating first emerged. It is unlikely that dating appeared fully formed at that time, but rather it probably developed over several decades or even over a century. Evidence for this view is found, among other places, in James McGovern's article, "American Woman's Pre-World War I Freedom in Manners and Morals" (1968). McGovern maintained that much of the behavior seen as new to the 1920s was already evident during the Progressive era. This included dating.

> The "home is in peril" became a fact of sociological literature as early as 1904. One of the most serious signs of its peril was the increasing inability of parents to influence their children in the delicate areas of propriety and morals. The car, already numerous enough to affect dating and premarital patterns, the phone coming to be used for purposes of romantic accommodation and the variety of partners at the office or factory, all together assumed unparalleled privacy and permissiveness between the sexes [1968:319].

McGovern presents other evidence as well to suggest that recreative heterosexual pairing began to take shape well before World War I. My own current research on courtship, however, would place the origins of dating in the nineteenth century.

Given the emphasis that McGovern and others have placed upon the role of the automobile, and to a lesser extent the telephone, in dating, we may infer that dating first took form in the urban upper-middle class. Certainly in the nineteenth century the upper-middle class was in the vanguard of dating. McGovern quotes F. Scott Fitzgerald to the effect that "as far back as 1915 the unchaperoned young people of the smaller cities had discovered the mobile privacy of that automobile given to young Bill at sixteen to make him 'self-reliant' " (1968:319). Regrettably, we have little but fictional accounts of dating in the early twentieth century. As was noted earlier, Waller's article is the first scholarly piece on dating, but because of special locale and definite temporal limitations, it may not be as reliable a picture as we might like to have. Still, we can learn a great deal from it.

The image Waller offers of dating at Pennsylvania State during the 1920s and 1930s is one which provides us with not only a glimpse of campus courtship patterns, but also of the campus stratification system. Approximately half of the male students on this campus were members of fraternities and dating was almost exclusively their preserve. The various fraternities stood in a relationship of intense competition. This was reflected in the informal but generally acknowledged ranking system that existed on campus. The more prestigious fraternities had a disproportionate number of football players, honor society members, and in general "big men on campus" in their ranks, while such demigods were hardly to be found in the less desirable fraternities.

Dating on this campus was very much a status-sorting device: the most "desirable" men in the community dated the most "desirable" women. Desirability for the men involved not only membership in a prestigious fraternity, but also such things as good looks, attractive clothes, money to spend on dates, and the use of a car, not to mention such essentials as being a good dancer and having an effective "line." Men having all of these features were in a position to pursue the goddesses of this demimonde—and pursue them they did with a vigor and enthusiasm usually reserved for the football field.

At the heart of this system was the ingredient of scarcity, since desirable men and desirable women had to give the impression of being continually sought after and at the same time only being available to the "right" people. This appears to have been particularly the case for women. Waller reports that some women allowed themselves to be paged several times before answering the phone so as to let their dormmates know of their popularity. Being a rather evanescent thing, popularity had to be carefully husbanded. Among the devices used were never accepting a date late in the week, and more importantly, not being seen too often with the same person. It goes without saying that even being seen in the presence of other than the most desirable men or women could cast doubts upon one's social standing.

According to Waller, dates involved such things as going to the movies, college or fraternity dances, football and basketball games, etc., often winding up with a "necking" session in the fraternity parlor.

Critiques of "Rating and Dating"

Subsequent research on campus dating by William Smith (1952), Robert Blood (1955), Everett Rogers and Eugene Havens (1960), Ira Reiss (1965), and others has raised a number of issues with regard to Waller's findings; however, in reviewing their criticisms we must be careful to separate questions of different interpretations from questions of historical change. Three major criticisms emerge from this research literature: (1) Waller placed too much emphasis on the "exploitative, thrill-centered, and prestige-seeking" elements of dating and did not see the more idealistic and humane elements that can also be present; (2) he failed to appreciate the role dating played in mate selection; and (3) he did not recognize the importance of dating with respect to supporting class homogamy. Let us look at each of these points.

Attempts to replicate Waller's research on such diverse campuses as Purdue (Christensen, 1958), University of Michigan (Blood, 1955), and Penn State itself (Smith, 1952) have found that the rating factors upon which Waller placed such great emphasis were nowhere as significant as personality factors, for example, sense of humor, consideration, etc. This is not to say that the rating factors such as looks, cars, etc., were absent, but rather that they were considerably less important than the personality factors. Does this represent an actual historical change in such values, or did Waller merely ask the wrong questions? The fact that Smith (1952) found similar differences at Penn State two decades later suggests that changes may have occurred over time.

Waller believed that the dating he observed at Penn State simply represented casual dalliances that were largely unrelated to mate selection and marriage. Moreover, he felt that the "exploitative" character of dating prevented the idealization associated with romantic love from developing, and thus further prevented its use as a courtship device. In fairness to Waller, we must say that he did realize that under certain circumstances dating led to more marriage-oriented behavior, but basically he saw these two spheres as separate. The fact that recent studies have found dating not to be totally separate from mate choice and have also found it to be associated with a set of personal criteria different from those spelled out by Waller is probably, in part, a result of the greater possibility now of marriage taking place either during or immediately after college. But certain changes may have also occurred in attitudes and values that govern sexual relations.

Waller also felt that students at Penn State all came from very similar families in terms of their socioeconomic status, and he therefore argued that family background was not an element in the rating scheme. Rogers and Havens, however, in their study of dating at Iowa State found that dating tended to take place within particular social groupings, with fraternity members dating sorority members, dorm residents dating each other, and so on (1966). Moreover, within the Greek system of naming fraternities and sororities a relationship was observed between the prestige of a fraternity or sorority and whom its member dated. This study is important for two reasons: (1) it brings out the role dating plays in supporting homogamy; and (2) since it found the same patterns in dating, going steady, and being pinned, it also seriously questioned Waller's contention that different standards were applied in dating and more serious courtship. Moreover similar patterns have been found by other sociologists. During the same period that the Rogers and Havens study was done, Reiss looked at patterns of casual and serious dating at William and Mary College and found that these reflected social class differences (1965). What obviously was at work here was the relationship between the campus dating system and social class. Since sororities and fraternities serve or have served as vehicles for stratifying student bodies along family-class lines, their formal and informal codes concerning who dates whom serve to reinforce homogamy in the dating system (Scott, 1965).

In summary, it appears that the dating patterns described by Waller as characteristic of Penn State students during the late 1920s and early 1930s were not characteristic of the same and other campuses twenty to thirty years later. However, the inferences that can be drawn from this conclusion are limited. For one thing, we really cannot gauge the accuracy of Waller's impressionistic description of Penn State, much less generalize from it to other American universities at the same time. Thus, we have no truly reliable benchmark for assessing change. Moreover, there is no reason to believe that dating, either in the 1930s or 1960s, was a monolithic entity with no regional or other forms of variation. It does appear safe to say that dating did undergo change in the post-World War II years and change continues to take place today. But before we look at more recent changes in the courtship behavior of college people, some comment is in order with regard to the spread of the dating phenomenon to other segments of the population.

HIGH SCHOOL DATING AND GOING STEADY

Lee Burchinal claims that during the late 1930s and early 1940s dating began to make an appearance on the high school scene (1964:624). The fact that August Hollingshead (1961) was able to find well developed dating patterns among the high school students he studied in Elmtown, a small midwestern city, in 1941 and 1942 suggests that it may have occurred even earlier. The confusion here may stem from the belief that dating among college students first began in the 1920s, when there is evidence to indicate that it began before World War I (McGovern, 1968). In any case, some of Hollingshead's informants reported showing an interest in dating as early as the seventh and eighth grades.

> The more adventurous youngsters begin to date when they are 12 years of age —at picnics and family group get-togethers—and the parents are usually present. A definite dating pattern becomes clear during the fourteenth year; 20 percent of the girls and 15 percent of the boys report that they had their first date when they were 13. A much larger number begins to date in the fifteenth year, and by the end of it approximately 93 percent of both sexes are dating with some regularity. Among the 16-year-olds, dating is the accepted procedure, and the boy or girl who does not date is left out of mixed social affairs [1961:167].

The pattern of dating Hollingshead describes shows either class homogamy or boys dating girls in a class lower than their own. The results also confirm the general picture, though perhaps less well articulated, of the kind of rating considerations described by Waller. However, Hollingshead also discusses the "steady date" which, of course, refers to exclusive relationships. What is notable about steady dating as it existed in Elmtown at the time is that it generally involved lower-class high school girls and older nonstudent boys. This pattern appears to have been a preengagement stage. Furthermore, going steady was seen as a relationship in which premarital sex was much more likely to occur than in the casual dating setting.

Since Elmtown was chosen by Hollingshead because it was supposedly typical of the small cities that dot the "corn belt" of the Midwest—a region of the country that has not traditionally manifested especially liberal patterns—there is no reason to believe that the residents were in the vanguard of social change with respect to courtship. Therefore it seems safe to conclude that similar patterns could have been found in other American cities at the time, and that the pattern of going steady may have been even further developed elsewhere.

The research literature on exclusive dating generally fails to make a distinction between involvement which is marriage-oriented and that which is not. Herein lies some of the confusion over fixing the period when steady dating began to be an important aspect of American premarital behavior. It would seem evident that in any largely participant-run mate selection system, engagement would be preceded by a period of exclusivity (earlier in the century this was described as "keeping company"). Waller recognized that "rating and dating" was followed by more exclusive relationships leading to marriage; in fact, he bemoaned the former interfering with the latter. What we are interested in here is the development of exclusive relationships which are seen by both partners as definitely *not* being a preengagement stage.

Burgess and Paul Wallin (1953) in their important study of engagement and marriage looked at the dating and courtship histories of 984 engaged couples during the 1937–1939 period. The sample was predominantly upper-middle class; they estimated that "probably 90 percent or more" (1953:45) of their questionnaires were administered to college and university students in Chicago. When we recall that college attendance was by no means as common then as now, the class bias of their sample becomes even more evident, but, as we shall see, the skewed character of their sample serves our present interests. There is a problem with their procedures, however. They asked the students about their experiences of "keeping company" prior to marriage. While some of the respondents recognized that they were referring to exclusive dating, others thought that it meant dating a person over an extended period but not exclusively. In any case, they found:

> The majority of the men and women first kept company before they were eighteen. But 76 percent of the women in contrast to 50.8 percent of the men had done so when they were sixteen or younger [Burgess and Wallin, 1953:120].

Why is this so important? For one thing, 24 percent reported having had three or four "keeping company" relationships (the data was reported for couples because no male-female differences were discovered) with people other than their current fiancè, and 45.3 percent reported one or two. Given the age at which these people entered into these relationships, the number of relationships they report, and the fact that they were all college bound and therefore not likely to seriously consider marriage in their high school or even college years, and given the times, it would seem clear that steady dating coexisted with "rating dating" during the 1930s and, more important, in a manner rather different from what was found in the early forties by Hollingshead in a provincial midwestern community. However, we cannot forget the confusion that existed in the respondents' minds concerning the meaning of "keeping company" when considering Burgess and Wallin's data.

The real difficulty we face is a lack of research on dating. There are nonetheless other things we can study. Movie buffs may be familiar with the Andy Hardy movies of the 1940s, in which Mickey Rooney played Judge Hardy's adolescent son. In these movies we see a clearly developed pattern of steady dating. There are other popular sources as well which provide some evidence for the existence of such patterns in the 1930s and 1940s and radio programs and comic books figure importantly among them (for example, Henry Aldrich, Corliss Archer, and Archie).

If in fact steady dating coexisted with rating and dating as far back as the 1930s or even earlier, what has been the direction and importance of change over time? What seems to have happened and what has continued to happen is that there has been a progressive shift in the predominant patterns. From the 1920s through the 1940s rating and dating was the reigning pattern, though a minority did engage in steady dating. Since World War II fewer and fewer people have been involved in rating and dating—so much so that there is evidence to suggest that it is virtually disappearing from the American scene.

One of the few sociologists to comment on this shift in an enlightening way is David Riesman.

> There can be no doubt that what many educated young men and women today are looking for in each other is not the rating-dating game of twenty years ago. To be sure, there are still fraternities and sororities on the campus and still an interest in good looks, popularity, good grooming, and smoothness. But all this is more subdued and the relationships increasingly sought for are more searching, more profound, more sincere. There is more desire to share; less desire to impress. There is less desire to dazzle members of one's own sex and more to come to some sort of humane terms with the opposite sex. Moreover, it seems to me that young people are increasingly preoccupied with their capacity to love as well as to be loved [1959:213].

Yet, this is not the total picture. There is another dimension to the movement from rating and dating to more exclusive relationships. There is some evidence that young people also see exclusive relationships as having a dimension of convenience to them, without concern for a more profound relationship. A *Newsweek* poll and feature story in 1966 spoke of a distinction between "going steady" and "going steadily" with the latter lacking the deep commitment we find in the former, though that commitment is not necessarily to marriage (March 21, 1966:60).

Pursuing the idea of convenience in exclusive dating a bit further, we realize that rating and dating was a rather competitive business, bringing with it many stresses and strains. One was essentially putting oneself and one's self-image on the auction block and continually being fed messages concerning self-worth. For those who did not rate high, the psychic costs of such a system must have been very high indeed, and the retreat or advance to a relationship which provided the amenities of rating dating without its costs must have been seen as very desirable indeed.

There are sociologists who take a more global view and see the growth of steady dating in the years following World War II as a reflection of national and international doubts and anxieties. During the cold war years

Boys on one side, girls on the other—a high school dance in the early 1960s. *(George W. Gardner)*

of the 1950s, the dread of atomic holocaust hung heavy over the heads of Americans, young and old, as bomb shelters began to dot the landscape and the schools began to drill their children in preparation for "the bomb." Some feel that in such an atmosphere young people may well have wanted to grasp something which offered permanence in a world that could cease to exist tomorrow.

There are others who bemoan steady dating as a form of premature closure—they worry that young people are blocking themselves off from the kind of varied learning experiences to be gained from nonexclusive dating. What these critics do not seem to realize is that steady dating, which generally begins in high school, is really a form of what we might call serial monogamy. During the course of the four years a girl spends in high school she may go steady with four or five boys, and to the extent that she really gets to know these boys, she is probably learning more about herself in relation to heterosexual relationships than she would from more casual dating. Of course, the same holds for the boys involved. Thus there is really little reason to believe that going steady does much to stifle social-emotional growth and development.

THE DECLINE OF DATING

Our discussion to this point may have exaggerated the extent to which patterns of exclusive dating have replaced the more open previous forms. In fact, until recently casual dating has been the form of heterosexual interaction that preceded going steady. What may be on the horizon, if it has not already occurred in certain segments of the society, is the total disappearance of casual dating and its replacement by group activity as a prelude to exclusive dating. The evidence we have for this development is sketchy. In part the evidence was gathered by the author in discussions with his students, and in discussions of my impressions with others in a position to observe such patterns. Yet, there is also some data which give empirical support to the conclusion that dating is on the decline.

Rebecca Vreeland has done a very important study of changes in dating patterns of Harvard students during the 1960s and early 1970s, and her findings provide us with some insights into the changes that seem to be taking place.

> In just 30 years, then, dating has become less formal, less exploitative and, to a certain extent, less *heterosexual.* Students, in search of their own humanity, have begun to treat their dates as persons and potential friends rather *than as competitors or candidates for marriage.* But just how extensive are these changes, and do they significantly alter earlier interpretation of the function of dating [emphasis added, 1972:66]?

In order to answer her own question, Dr. Vreeland looked at several groups of Harvard undergraduates from the classes of 1964, 1965, 1970, and 1973. Her findings seem to indicate that there has indeed been a shift during the last decade in the things sought for in the dating situation.

> The recreation role of dating seems best to describe the behavior of the Harvard freshmen in the '60s sample. For the seniors of the '60s and for freshmen *and* seniors in 1970, learning about another individual's personality and securing one's own identity were the most important functions of dating. For today's student, the most important dating motive is *finding a friend who is female.* The most essential characteristic in a good date is her ability to make conversation and the primary dating activity is sitting around the room talking. At the same time, the sexual component of dating should not be ignored. Sex was one of the most important dating activities to more than a fifth of the Harvard seniors in 1970. Although possibly the Harvard men date some girls for sex and different ones for companionship, it seems that both sex and companionship are part of the function of dating [1972:68].

The students tend to meet each other not on arranged blind dates or in formal mixers and dances, but rather in more informal settings where the barriers between the sexes have broken down. Today coed dorms, film clubs, and hiking and skiing groups are the places where people meet those with whom they may ultimately form an exclusive, though hardly permanent, relationship. While Vreeland does not make mention of this, there is also evidence to suggest a blurring of sexual role stereotyping in such relationships. For example, instead of the male always paying expenses, the new rule seems to be whoever has the money pays, or each pays his or her own way.

In looking at dating over the course of this century, we have seen the development of techniques of mate selection that grant young people a considerable amount of autonomy and freedom, and which also allow them freedom to interact across sex lines without any courtship commitments, though we are hardly a society which gives its children carte blanche in these matters. The most recent developments suggest that further change is definitely coming—change which can already be seen in delayed age at marriage, the growth of postcollege courtship institutions, and the emergence of large-scale nonmarital cohabitation, topics to which we will turn in the next section of this chapter.

As important as Vreeland's work is, it does not deal with a recent development that seems very much related to the trends in undergraduate dating patterns she has described. The phenomenon I refer to is that of nonmarried heterosexual cohabitation or unmarried liaisons, as Robert Whitehurst (1969) refers to them. Of course, I am not suggesting that the 1960s were the first time this country saw unmarried young people living together, but it is my impression as well as that of people who have done research in this area that during the 1960s there was a marked increase in such activity.

COHABITATION: WAVE OF THE FUTURE?

Research done at Cornell by Eleanor Macklin deals directly with the issue of the growth or opening up of positive attitudes toward cohabitation. She refers to several excerpts from the Cornell student newspaper published during the early 1960s.

> In 1962, a graduate student was indefinitely suspended from the University for living with a woman in his apartment, and in 1964, a male student was reprimanded for staying overnight at a local hotel with a non-University female. Sexual morality was considered a legitimate concern of the University faculty and "overnight unchaperoned mixed company" was considered by the Faculty Council on Student Conduct to be a violation of sexual morality [1972:465].

This quote gives us a good sense of the official posture toward cohabitation in the early 1960s, when *in loco parentis* was the model at colleges and sign-out regulations with curfews were the rule.

During the 1960s a number of changes did occur which, if nothing else, facilitated the growth of cohabitation. These took three forms. First, there was a trend toward the abolition of undergraduate curfews, which existed at most coed institutions, if only for women. Second, there was a liberalization of rules governing the entertainment of guests of the opposite sex in dorm rooms. It is now possible for student couples at most universities to set up housekeeping in a dormitory, be it a coed dorm or not, and accordingly there has been an increase in the requests for single rooms. Third, rules governing off-campus living have also been liberalized. At one time some universities and colleges required that all students live in university-controlled dormitories or supervised fraternity and sorority houses. Others allowed male upper classmen to obtain off-campus housing. At present, more and more schools are easing their rules so as to make it easier and easier for students to live off campus.

These changes have certainly created greater opportunities than previously existed for cohabitation. Yet, changes in housing rules do not contain the whole explanation for the apparent growth of nonmarital cohabitation. The other component is one which we have already touched upon in our discussion of the work of Vreeland and Riesman. It appears that young people are looking for something different from these relationships. Listen to Macklin discuss this question:

> When students were asked to hypothesize why cohabitation has become more common and more open, [they mention]: youth's search for more meaningful relations . . . and their consequent rejection of the superficial "dating game"; the loneliness of a large university and the emotional satisfaction that comes from having someone to sleep with who cares about you; the widespread questioning of the institution of marriage and the desire to try out a relationship before there is any, if ever, consideration of permanency . . . the fact that young people mature earlier and yet must wait so long until marriage is feasible; and the fact that the University community provides both sanction and feasibility for such a relationship to develop. Given peer group support, ample opportunity, a hu-

> man need to love and be loved, and a disposition to question the traditional way, it seems only natural that couples should wish to live together if they enjoy being together. One might almost better ask: Why do students choose *not* to live together [1972:466].

Support for some of Macklin's arguments are to be found not only in her research findings but in those of Judith Lyness et al. (1972). In their comparison of student couples who were going steady with those who were cohabiting, Lyness and her colleagues discovered that while the two types of couples could not be distinguished from each other in terms of their involvement with their partners, or in terms of their happiness with the relationship (see also, Lewis et al., 1975, and Cole, 1977). They were, however, clearly distinguishable in terms of their commitment to marriage with the couples who were going steady showing the most commitment to marriage. Macklin herself offers evidence to suggest that at the college stage, cohabitation is often not seen as a premarital liaison.

> Not only did they not consider themselves married, they rarely considered marriage as a viable alternative to their present cohabitation. When asked, "did you consider the possibility of getting married instead?", a frequent response was "Heavens, no!" Marriage often might be seen as a possibility for the future, the distant future [1972:467].

Just how widespread is the practice of cohabitation? The Census Bureau recently reported that between 1970 and the end of 1976 the number of unmarried Americans sharing their residence with a member of the opposite sex rose from 654,000 to 1,320,000 (*New York Times,* February 10, 1977:69). This may be a conservative figure.

The question now raised is, will cohabitation ultimately come to replace marriage? Trost notes:

> In 1966 there were 61,101 marriages in Sweden. The number of marriages decreased steadily during the following years and in 1973 there were only 38,251—a decrease of 37 per cent during seven years [1975:679].

Drawing upon several studies, Trost estimates that between 1970 and 1974 the percent of lasting cohabitative relationships that did not involve marriage increased from 6.5 percent to 12 percent (1975:678). Some of these people will ultimately marry and others will be classified as married because of common law definitions of marriage, but it does seem that cohabitation in Sweden is becoming a viable, if temporary, alternative to marriage.

What of the United States? We do not have the same sort of figures available that Trost has for Sweden, but we do know that people are postponing marriage. A recent census bureau study revealed:

> Six out of every 10 men between 20 and 24 were unmarried in 1975 as against 5.5 of every ten in 1970. The percentage of unmarried women aged 20 to 24 increased from 28 to 40 in the five years [quoted in the *New York Times,* January 8, 1976:58].

But such figures can be deceptive, as Table 7-1 reveals. What is most striking about the figures in Table 7-1 is how clearly they show that women are not rejecting marriage but rather are delaying it. At age 21 there is almost a 10 percent difference between the number of women single in 1960 and in 1970, but by age 30 this is down to less than a percentage point. Whether the pattern will hold in the 1980 census remains to be seen.

Other evidence for this trend is to be found in the emergence of places where older "young people" can meet potential friends and mates. Joyce Star and Donald Carns have written:

> In increasing numbers the young college graduate has come to expect more from life than immediate security. For many, social and financial independence and career mobility have replaced early marriage as immediate post-graduation goals. . . . Most cities [now] appear to have an abundance of singles bars; some have co-ed singles apartment houses. Ads for singles weekends and excursions pad out the travel sections of big city newspapers. All of this would seem to suggest an unprecedented institutionalization of this new life style in the cities [1972:43].

The authors go on to argue that these new "singles" institutions do not provide much of what their glowing ads seem to promise. Many find the bars dreary and disappointing, and the singles apartment complexes offer more in the way of anonymity than they do in opportunities for contacts. Others (Stein, 1976) offer a more positive image of "singlehood" and hold that for some being single is becoming an alternative to marriage.

PREMARITAL SEX: REVOLUTION OR EVOLUTION?

Earlier in the chapter we discussed premarital sex in the Puritan era and the later shift from what Edward Shorter called manipulative sexuality to expressive sexuality. Having dropped this theme to discuss more mundane aspects of courtship, we now return to it, hopefully to shed some light on how and why the new courtship practices have emerged.

In our previous discussion we noted that the Puritans were not as Puritanical as some would have us believe, and that there was hardly an absence of premarital sex in the colonial era. In fact, there is some evidence available to suggest that there was a rise in rates of premarital sex during the eighteenth century and a subsequent downturn in part of the nineteenth, giving credence to what some have characterized as the cyclical character of American sexuality (Smith, 1973b).

This cyclical view of American sexuality calls into question what has, until recently, been the prevailing view among sociologists concerning the history of sexual relations in America—namely, that the twentieth century saw a great revolution in American sexual manners, mores, and behavior, and that these radical alterations took place during the 1920s in

Table 7-1. PERCENTAGE OF SINGLE WOMEN BY AGE, 1960 AND 1970

Age	1960	1970
19	59.6	70.5
20	45.8	56.7
21	35.1	44.4
22	25.8	32.2
23	19.4	24.6
24	15.6	19.9
25	13.1	16.2
26	11.5	13.2
27	9.9	11.4
28	9.3	10.3
29	8.7	9.3
30	7.9	8.6
31	7.2	7.6

SOURCES: U.S. Census of the Population, 1960, Final Report PC (2)-4E; and U.S. Census of the Population, 1970, Subject Reports Marital Status PC (2)-4C.

particular (Robert Bell, 1966). This prevailing view was partly based on the commonly encountered notion that World War I marked the end of America's period of innocence, ushering in the era of the flapper, the hip flask, and generally a new way of life. In addition, the studies of Alfred Kinsey bolstered this view of the sexual revolution.

The Kinsey study revealed a seemingly important difference in the incidence of premarital coitus among women born before 1900 as compared with those born after that time (1953:339). Not only did women born after the turn of the century engage in more premarital sex, but also, as measured by the incidence of orgasm, they seemed to derive more pleasure from it. This fact alone would seem to indicate that the World War I period did indeed mark a watershed in American sexual customs. However, there are a number of problems with these data that make generalization somewhat hazardous. Referring to the Kinsey (1953) study and to the Terman (1938) and Davis (1929) studies as well, the historian Daniel Smith has pointed out:

> Between two-thirds and three-fourths of the women in the three most important historical studies of premarital coitus had some college experience while only 10.2 percent and 13.1 percent of native-born women, respectively, between 1891 and 1900 and 1901 and 1910 went beyond high school [1973b:328].

Thus the women included in this study may have had *their* revolution in the 1920s but their background was rather different from that of most other American women. Furthermore, there is still some question as to just how representative these women were of the larger population of college-educated groups.

Smith goes on to elaborate on class differences in the timing of the sexual revolution by directing our attention to discrepancies which existed between the findings of the three major early studies of premarital coitus and the results of various studies of bridal pregnancy.

> While 7 percent of the Davis Sample, 13 percent of the pre-1890 and 26 percent of the 1890–99 birth cohorts in the Terman study, and 27 percent of the pre-1900 Kinsey birth cohort had premarital intercourse, 16 percent of the first births were conceived before marriage in Hingham, Mass. (1861–1880), 19 percent in Lexington, Mass. (1885–1895), 20 percent (1905–1907) and 29 percent (1913–1915) in Utah County, Utah, and 20 percent in Tippicanoe County, Indiana (1919–1921) [1973:328–329].

These discrepancies suggest to Smith that growth in the incidence of premarital intercourse during the course of this century was differentially distributed among various segments of the population, with college women maintaining conservative standards longer.

Thus Smith concludes that the decade of the 1920s was not the watershed it was made out to be. Rates of premarital intercourse had been rising since about the middle of the nineteenth century—one of the troughs in the country's cyclical sexual history—but rising at a different rate for different segments of the population. Concomitant with such changes are found not only the growth of women's economic power and feminism, but

The public display of affection appears to have become less inhibited in recent years as shown by this preoccupied couple in a city park. *(Marion Bernstein)*

also other indicators, such as divorce and an increasingly positive orientation toward sex in literature such as marriage manuals. Furthermore, the growth of hysterical prudery in the form of Anthony Comstock and his followers' attempts to legislate morality (Broun and Leech, 1927) can be seen, as Smith (1973) so aptly notes, as a response to what was feared to be a weakening of the sexual morals. Why the need for a crusading reformer if all were behaving themselves?

More recently, sociologists and poets have discovered another "sexual revolution," this one occurring in the late 1960s. Supposedly between the first revolution of the 1920s and the beginning of the 1960s no change took place with regard to rates of premarital intercourse, but in more recent years an acceleration has again occurred. In the words of a poet (Philip Larkin, 1974:34):

> Sexual Intercourse began
> In nineteen sixty-three
> (Which was rather late for me)
> Between the end of the Chatterley
> ban
> And the Beatles' first LP.

This new "revolution" is discussed in several studies, including those by Robert Bell and Jay Chaskes (1970), Harold Christensen and Christina Gregg (1970), Karl Bauman and Robert Wilson (1974), and most notably Zelnik and Kantner (1977).

The Bell and Chaskes study is a replication of an earlier study done by Bell at Temple University in 1958. The second study again took a classroom sample of coeds at Temple University, this time in 1968, and compared them with their 1958 counterparts. While the authors do not offer findings regarding total incidence of sexual intercourse, they do offer data on the context in which first intercourse occurred and feelings of guilt concerning it. The most dramatic finding was the rise in incidence of first intercourse in the dating and going steady situations. In 1958, 10 percent of the respondents had intercourse while dating, 15 percent while going steady, and 31 percent while engaged; in contrast, in 1968 these figures were 23 percent, 28 percent, and 39 percent, respectively. At each level in the 1968 study, about 50 percent fewer women reported feeling guilty as evidenced by their responses to the question if they thought they "went too far." As the authors note:

> The most important finding of this study appears to be that the commitment of engagement has become a less important condition for many coeds engaging in premarital coitus as well as whether or not they will have guilt feelings about that experience. If these findings are reasonably accurate, they could indicate that first significant change in premarital sexual behavior patterns since the 1920's [Bell and Chaskes, 1970:84].

Whether the findings of Bell and Chaskes prove that the new behavior represents the first significant change since the 1920s, however, is still questionable.

Christensen and Gregg's research (1970) is also a replication of an earlier study. In this case, the 1958 and 1968 samples were drawn from college students in Denmark and in two areas of the United States: the Midwest and the western intermountain region. Both attitudes and behavior had become more liberal during the ten-year period. Twenty-one percent of the midwestern coeds admitted having premarital sex in 1958 while the figure was 34 percent in 1968. In Denmark the figures for female premarital sex rose from 60 percent in 1958 to 97 percent in 1968; these figures actually exceed those reported by males.

Bauman and Wilson (1974), using a random sample from one university, found that more male and female students were nonvirginal in 1972 than in 1968. The rate for men went from 56 percent in 1968 to 73 percent in 1972; that for women, from 46 percent in 1968 to 73 percent in 1972. As these figures reveal there were no sex differences in the 1972 rates. Similar findings appeared in a campus study done by *Playboy* (October 1976:159–160). Not only were the rates of virginity identical at 26 percent for both men and women but the number of partners each had showed relatively little difference. The latter finding may be especially important because it suggests that the premarital sexual behavior of male and female college students may be converging both quantitatively and qualitatively.

The problem with all of the recent studies of premarital intercourse we have been discussing is that they are based on samples of college students. Since a majority of American high-school graduates do not go on to four-year institutions of higher education, this is a significant shortcoming. Thus we are fortunate in having the research of Melvin Zelnik and John Kantner (1972, 1977) which is based on two comparable national samples of unmarried female American teenagers aged 14–19 interviewed in 1971 and 1976. While Zelnik and Kantner have no data on males and the females they have sampled are young, their work, nonetheless, gives us an important and statistically representative picture of premarital sexual behavior among half of the adolescent population at two points in time. Looking at Figure 7-1 we see that in 1971 just about 27 percent of the 15- to 19-year-olds in the sample had already had intercourse and by 1976 this figure had risen to just under 35 percent—an increase of slightly more than 30 percent. Not only has the incidence of sexual intercourse increased but as Figure 7-2 shows the number of partners reported has also grown. In 1971 61 percent had intercourse with only one partner; in 1976 this was the case for about 51 percent (Zelnik and Kantner, 1977:61). But interestingly enough, the median age at first intercourse dropped only by roughly four months (16.5 to 16.2 years) in this five year period. Zelnik and Kantner do not feel that this drop explains the increase in number of partners and speculate that it may in part have grown out of a tendency to postpone marriage (1977:61).

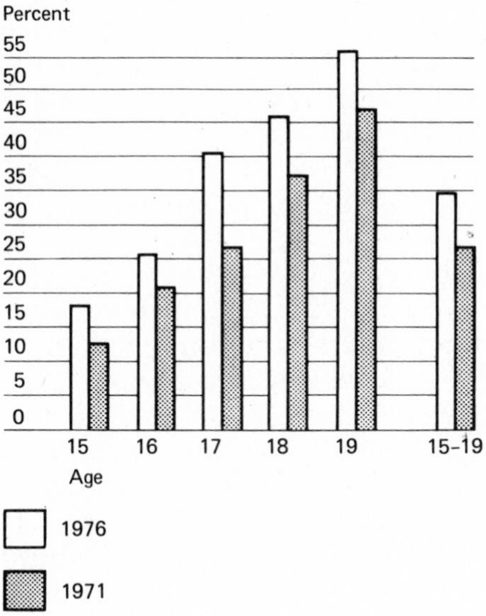

Figure 7-1. Percentage of never-married women aged 15–19 who have ever had intercourse, by age, 1976 and 1971

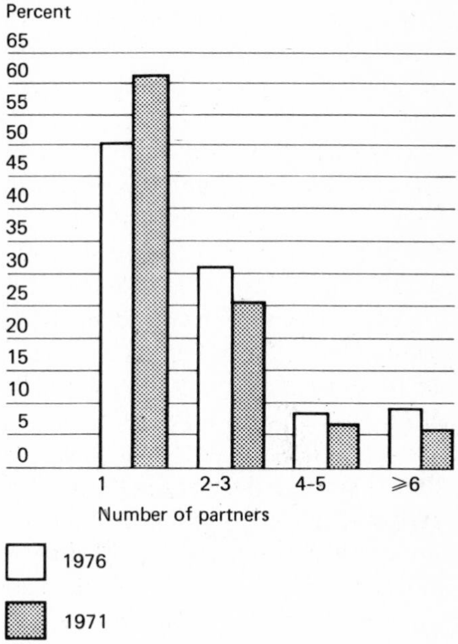

Figure 7-2. Percentage of sexually experienced never-married women aged 15–19, by number of partners ever, 1976 and 1971

SOURCE: Melvin Zelnik and John F. Kantner, "Sexual and Contraceptive Experience of Young Unmarried Women in the United States, 1976 and 1971." *Family Planning Perspective,* vol. 9 (March/April 1977): p. 56 and p. 61.

One problem, of course, with Zelnik and Kantner's data is that it is limited to unmarried women. These women have not, so to speak, completed their premarital sexual experience, and some who were virginal at nineteen will be unmarried but no longer inexperienced at twenty. Therefore, making comparisons with earlier studies is problematic. Hunt, however, does have data that give us some sense of change in "completed" premarital sexual experience that can be usefully compared with the earlier figures of Kinsey. While between 42 and 47 percent of the Kinsey women who were married by or before 25 were no longer virgins, in 1970 the figure for a comparable group had risen to 80 percent (Hunt, 1974:33–34). The findings of both Zelnik and Kantner and Hunt make it clear that we are rapidly moving toward a situation in which premarital sexual experience is the norm, and only a minority of men and women will enter marriage with their virginity intact. This would certainly seem to suggest that we have witnessed the passing of the "double standard."

Several of the studies we have looked at reveal a convergence in the rates of premarital intercourse among young men and women (Christensen and Gregg, 1970; Bauman and Wilson, 1974; *Playboy*, October 1976), but does this mean that the double standard has disappeared and a wave of promiscuity is upon us? The double standard refers to the belief that it was right and proper for a young man to have sexual relations before marriage, but not for a woman. As a result of the double standard, women were frequently categorized into "good" and "bad girls"—"good girls" being those who did not have premarital sexual intercourse and were thus eligible mates, and "bad girls" being those who did and were therefore disqualified as mates (Whyte, 1943). Studies focusing on the alleged decline of such attitudes in the period between the 1930s and the 1950s show mixed results. Some have argued that there has been a decline (Smigel and Seiden, 1968) and others that there has been no change (Ehrman, 1960). More recently Christensen and Gregg (1970:619) found that a greater number of Midwestern college students approved of premarital sex in 1968 than they had in 1958, but women were more conservative than men. Robert Sorensen, in his national study of American adolescents, found that only 27 percent of the girls and 42 percent of the boys said it would be "abnormal or unnatural for a girl to remain virginal until marriage," while more than half of both said the same for boys. Moreover, 30 percent of the boys indicated a desire to marry a virgin (1973:358–359). Many of these teenage boys may change their minds before they are ready to marry.

The *Playboy* study, as we have already noted, found that 74 percent of the college men and women they sampled were no longer virgins, but there were differences in the attitudes they brought to the experiences and this may have had an effect on their behavior. More specifically, more women than men had had only one partner (28 percent versus 21 percent), and more men than women had had six or more partners (38 percent versus 29 percent); these rates were almost identical for two to five partners (October 1976:160). When asked how close a sexual partner should be, 27 percent of the men but only 7 percent of the women said a "casual acquaintance," and 14 percent of the females and 8 percent of the males said a "spouse." We see then that college women remain somewhat more conservative than men in their sexual attitudes and behavior, but the great majority of both felt that sex should occur within the context of some sort of emotional relationship. This would seem to support Ira Reiss's (1967) argument that what is taking place among young people today is not the growth of totally casual sex, but rather "permissiveness with affection." Sex is acceptable when it takes place between two people who have some degree of emotional involvement, even if they have no intention of marriage. The fact that age at first marriage is increasing will probably result in people marrying with more varied experience than ever before, but it would be wrong to characterize current premarital sexual patterns as promiscuous.

In the final analysis, our delineation of premarital sex and especially male-female differences has to be interpreted in terms of widespread factors in our society, factors such as those we considered earlier when we discussed Edward Shorter's explanation of shifts in illegitimacy patterns in Europe during the eighteenth and nineteenth centuries. Simply put, women now have less need to subject themselves to a separate standard of sexual behavior, since their emerging economic position provides them with sources of identity separate from those derived from marriage. As an illustration of this, one study of college students' attitudes found that while 56 percent of the career-oriented women did not feel that intercourse among people in their twenties should be limited to marriage, only 40 percent of the non-career-oriented women felt this way (Packard: 1968:507).

SUMMARY

In this chapter we have looked at changes in courtship and premarital sexual behavior between colonial times and the present. In the process we have observed, among other things, that this country has never had a predominantly parent-run courtship system, though increasingly the veto power of parents has been weakened. However, it would be a mistake to assume that parents currently have no input into marriage decisions. Sussman (1953b) has shown how some parents will employ both persuasion and downright coercion—for example, the withdrawal of economic support—when faced with a potential son- or daughter-in-law of whom they disapprove. Moreover, they appear to meet with success through the use of both methods. To be sure, as economic enterprise has become more free of parental control, their say in mate choice has necessarily declined; however, we should not for a moment overlook the important role parents continue to play in providing access to the educational opportunities that are prerequisites for maintaining middle- and upper-class status. Readers should ask themselves if they would currently be in college were it not for the financial support provided by their parents, and at the same time ponder the question of what sort of job opportunities would be open to them if they had only a high school degree or less. Therefore, we cannot speak of our current system as being truly participant run, though it comes as close to this as any we know of.

We have also discussed important changes in relations between the sexes prior to marriage, perhaps most notably in the growth of structured patterns of interaction separate from the actual process of mate selection. Just how the practice of dating began is something which remains to be explored by social historians, but it does appear that it is associated with the separation of work and home, the prolongation of education, the concentration of young people in urban environments, and in general the appearance of adolescence as a new stage of life.

More recently, we have seen dating alter its character and increasingly move away from the competitive rating and dating system described by Waller, to the point where currently very little dating of a nonexclusive variety appears to be going on; most young people move from groups to exclusive relationships without passing through the kind of open dating that was characteristic of earlier decades. Moreover, within the context of the current patterns, there appears to be considerably less sex role stereotyping to the degree that each person in a couple is now more apt to either pay his or her own way or else the partner having more money at the moment shoulders the cost.

The past few years have seen the growth of nonmarital cohabitation on and off the college campus. We also know that in the past decade people appear to have delayed rather than avoided marriage; some of these people, though certainly a minority, are choosing to cohabit while they wait. The fact that many people involved in nonmarital cohabitative relationships do not see them as trial marriages, especially among college students, is not without significance, for some of these relationships have apparently become truly alternative structures.

Regarding premarital sex, we have observed a somewhat cyclical pattern with troughs in the seventeenth and nineteenth centuries and high points in the eighteenth and twentieth centuries. The fact that pretwentieth-century estimates are virtually all based on bridal pregnancy and illegitimacy figures means that we cannot get any truly accurate estimate of the extent of premarital sex. Nevertheless, such figures do allow us to note variation and can provide a needed corrective to studies of premarital sex based on problematic samples.

In the twentieth century, there has been a continuation of the upturn in premarital sex that probably began some time after the middle of the nineteenth century. There also appears to have been some acceleration since the 1960s. However, what is most notable about current rates is that much premarital sex is occurring within the context of affective relationships, raising questions about the views of those who see a wave of "promiscuity" descending rapidly upon us. Nonetheless, the fact that young people are starting to have sex earlier and at the same time marrying later makes it inevitable that they will marry with more varied sexual experience than their parents' generation.

What do such changes mean? We have already commented on a number of the factors at work here—factors such as the decline in parental control over courtship and the growth of adolescence as a stage of life. We have perhaps not given sufficient consideration to the changes in the economic position of women and how these have affected the courtship system. Women can now drive a better "role bargain" and define their relationships with men in such a way as to be less subject to traditional conceptions of morality.

The Shipload of Wives. *(NYPL Picture Collection)*

MARRIAGE: From Partnership to Companionship to Symmetry

8

In Chapter 4 we looked at how modernization affected the economic position of women in the West. In the process we indirectly touched upon the concomitant changes brought about in the structure and meaning of marriage. We shall now directly consider this topic by looking at marriage as it existed 200 years ago and as it exists today. Our perspective will continue to be that the economic position of women is the key determinant of the relations between husbands and wives, as it is the key determinant of relations between men and women in the society at large.

FROM ECONOMIC PARTNERSHIP TO COMPANIONATE MARRIAGE

In Chapter 2 we discussed the topics of kinship and household size and noted that until recently a dominant view in sociological circles had been that modernization was associated with the growth of the "isolated nuclear family" and the decline of the extended family. This notion could not withstand empirical research, however, which raised serious questions about its validity. In talking about marriage we must also consider some sociological catchwords whose accuracy have really not been put to the test—for example, Ernest Burgess, Harvey Locke, and Evelyn Thomes's (1971) discussion of marriage moving from "institution to companionship."

> A basic thesis of this book is that the family has been in transition from a traditional family system, based on family members playing traditional roles, to a companionship family based on mutual affection, intimate communication,

> and mutual acceptance of division of labor and procedures of decision-making. The companionship form of the family is not to be conceived as having been realized but as emerging. . . .
>
> The American family is moving toward the companionship family system, which may be described as follows: (1) affection is the basis for its existence; (2) husband and wife have mutual acceptance of procedures in decision-making; (3) major decisions are by consensus; and (4) common interests and activities coexist with mutual acceptance of division of labor within the family and individuality of interests. In most families the control is still moderately patriarchal; in some it is more or less matriarchal; and in only a small proportion it is by consensus of husbands, wives, and children. The proportion that includes participation of children is extremely small [Burgess et al., 1971: 7–9].

While the authors speak of "the family," their focus is generally upon the conjugal dyad, and family sociologists who cite this work generally do so when discussing marriage. Essentially, what Burgess and Locke have presented us with is a broad picture of marriage changing as a result of the family losing its economically productive function. Marriage, they are saying, has become an end in itself rather than a means for perpetuating the family line or acquiring an economic partner. While broadly speaking there is probably much that is valid in this conceptualization, it is seriously compromised, as we shall see, by its oversimplification of marriage before and after. Increasingly we are learning that bipolar distinctions are hard to reconcile with the more evolutionary nature of social reality.

In order to consider the question of how marriage has changed we must develop a comparative baseline. We have already established that in the preindustrial West, marriages were marked by a strong element of economic partnership. In contrast to today's situation, women participated more directly in the productive process and therefore much of the responsibility for domestic chores and childrearing was often assumed by servants (Clark, 1968). Despite the important contribution made by wives to the family's economic activities, it would be wrong to assume that marriages during this era were equalitarian. Quite the contrary. The authority and dominance of the male partner were established in both law and custom. By marrying, a woman lost many of the legal rights she held as a single person; most notably her husband gained virtual control of the property she brought with her to the marriage. Outside of the legal realm, a woman who exceeded the boundaries of acceptable wifely behavior might find herself and her husband the objects of scorn and derision in the local community, and few men would tolerate such a situation for long. However, the fact that women did play a crucial role in the family economy kept men from abusing their authority. But self-interest was not the only factor that motivated this restraint. Bonds of affection between husband and wife were probably also a factor here.

Romantic Love

Mention of conjugal affection brings us to what should be the beginning of our discussion of marriage in the preindustrial era, namely, the role of romantic love in the choice of mate. In Chapter 7, which deals with courtship, we pointed out that parents had a much greater say in their child's choice of mate when they directly controlled access to economic opportunity than is currently the case, but did this preclude considerations of romantic love? Frank Furstenberg has argued that:

> Free mate selection and the "romantic-love complex" are often linked to the demands of the economic system or to the weakened control by family elders in an industrialized society. In fact, however, the same system of mate selection and emphasis on romantic love appear to have existed here [the U.S.] prior to industrialization [1966:326–327].

Yet, the data Furstenberg offers in support of his contention are drawn from the second quarter of the nineteenth century, a period during which industrialization was already taking place. A somewhat more balanced and perhaps more accurate view is provided by Herman Lantz and his associates.

> The data certainly indicate that the romantic love complex was known in colonial America and that, indeed, it may have been a common pattern among large sections of the upper status groups. Thus, with regard to the impact of industrialization, it may well be that industrialization *facilitated* the development of a romantic love complex already in *existence.* Finally, presence of the romantic love complex must be seen in the broader context of the emergence of individualism and the role of personal wishes as an important basis in mate choice [1968:420].

It certainly does not seem that the Puritans placed much stock in romantic love as a criterion for the choice of a mate. Edmund Morgan (1966:55) in his history of the Puritan family speaks of love being seen more as an outgrowth of marriage than as a criterion for selecting a mate. The main consideration, he tells us, was the "social rank of the persons involved," clearly reflecting the kind of traditional criteria we might expect in a system where parental input was great. Morgan claims that the existing evidence shows that considerable financial bargaining took place between the parents of proposed spouses, and thoughts of emotional compatibility did not seem to enter into the bargain. In his words, "The latter process, however, was usually supposed to follow rather than precede the financial arrangement" [1966:57]. Morgan may be overplaying the role of parents in the actual selection process. From what we can glean from his research and that of others it appears that while parents did play a crucial role in negotiating the contractual arrangements, more often than not, the young people expressed their inclinations before parental action took place.

The Puritans obviously did not represent the totality of our colonial experience. What Lantz and his associates are getting at when they say a romantic love complex may have been in existence among upper status groups during the colonial era is that the children of eighteenth-century merchants and professionals probably were the first to have the time and education to allow such notions to flourish. But it would be wrong to assume that within this group children were simply allowed to follow their whims when it came to matters of mate choice. Levin Schücking, in his study of Puritan literary sources, notes:

> The truth is that where marriage is concerned a whole host of considerations must be taken into account and only one of these is mutual affection [1970:26, first published 1929].

Then, as now, people tended to choose their mates so that rich people married rich people, Protestants married Protestants, whites married whites. However, the existence of homogamy is not antithetical to the existence of romantic love; it merely sets the boundaries in which that love may operate.

In arguing that romantic love was probably not widespread in the preindustrial West as a criterion for mate choice we are not arguing that once married the bonds of affection, often deep affection, did not spring up, but family sociologists have been careful to separate their discussions of marital love from their discussions of romantic love. The former is presented as less intense and all-encompassing, though no less genuine or profound. In contrast to romantic love, which, because of its intensity and extreme idealization, has been sarcastically described as "cardio-respiratory," marital love is more tranquil and arises out of the sharing of experiences and the growth of knowledge about the other person. Whether the ties of marital love were as deep in the preindustrial world as they sometimes are today is difficult to say. A poem written in the seventeenth century by Ann Bradstreet (quoted in Calhoun, 1945, vol. I:91) suggests that for some the answer may have been yes.

TO MY DEAR AND LOVING HUSBAND

If ever two were one, then surely we.
If ever man were loved by wife, then thee;
If ever wife was happy in a man,
Compare with me ye women if you can.

I prize thy love more than whole mines of gold,
Or all the riches that the East doth hold.
My love is such that Rivers cannot quench,
No ought but love from thee, give recompence.

Thy love is such I can no way repay,
The heavens reward thee manifold I pray.
Then while we live, in love lets so persever,
That when we live no more, we may live ever.

We would be hard pressed to find a contemporary expression of marital love greater in intensity than this one written three centuries ago. Such feelings were probably not characteristic of most marriages in colonial America, but for that matter, they may not be characteristic of most marriages today. Still, the Puritans appear to have appreciated the emotional aspects of marriage (Schnucker, 1975).

Marital Sex in Traditional Societies

From the perspective of a person living in the last quarter of the twentieth century, sex is one of the crucial elements of marriage. Certainly the sex drive is nothing new, and marriage has long been seen as the most appropriate arena for its expression. Nevertheless there are those who argue that sex has not always been as important a criterion of marital adjustment for both husband and wife as it is today.

> First, it is likely that women in traditional society did not enjoy intercourse, that they attempted to evade their husbands' sexual demands, although women probably were willing to make themselves available simply as a matter of wifely duty. Just as men held the political and economic power in traditional society, they possessed sexual controls as well. And if Helmut Möller is right, husbands exercised their sexual prerequisites so peremptorily and brutally as to leave women little erotic pleasure [Shorter, 1973:326].

This image of marital sex in premodern Western societies is one which sits comfortably with many contemporary scholars because it fits in so nicely with cherished beliefs concerning modernization and the appearance of affectionate conjugal regulations. But how well does it withstand scholarly scrutiny? Unfortunately, the qualitative aspects of marriage are not readily accessible to historical investigation, but there are sources that allow us to indirectly gain some insight into this topic.

David Flaherty, in *Privacy in Colonial New England* (1972), indicates that married couples were concerned with privacy.

> Such physical factors as the crowding of beds and bedchambers and the lack of insulation in the home inevitably challenged the availability of sexual privacy for husband and wife. . . . Presumably married couples learned to accommodate themselves to these limitations on their privacy and took preventive measures. They expected privacy for sexual relations and could achieve it more successfully than unmarried persons [1972:79–80].

While such a statement does not directly contradict Shorter's thesis, it does raise questions about it. Why would a couple desire privacy if their sex lives were in fact as "short, nasty, and brutal" (an expression borrowed from Daniel Smith) as Shorter would have us believe. We also have statements like one by Jeremy Taylor, the Anglican divine, who writing in 1650 spelled out what he saw as legitimate grounds for marital copulation.

> *A Desire of children, or to avoid fornication, or to lighten and ease the cares and sadnesses of household affairs, or to endear each other* [quoted in Schücking, 1970:39].

This certainly seems to indicate an appreciation of sex as a means of expressing affection. John and Robin Haller have noted that seventeenth- and eighteenth-century marriage manuals differed importantly from the conservative crop that turned up in the middle of the nineteenth century.

> The most obvious difference lay in their emphasis on "pleasure." . . .Another popular manual encouraged sexual pleasure by demanding that both sexes meet "with equal vigor" in the conjugal act. The woman's interest in sex as well as her ability to conceive depended entirely upon pleasurable reciprocity [1974:92–93].

To be sure, we cannot assume that these books present us with an accurate picture of the practices and beliefs of those living at that time, but they do raise questions about the view which denies female sexuality altogether. It should also be noted that there may have been considerable variation by social class. What held for the middle class need not necessarily have held for the peasantry.

These brief remarks are not meant to topple Shorter's analysis, but rather are offered to counterbalance it. There is not enough information currently available to say which interpretation of marital sex is valid and for whom. Having said this, it should be pointed out that while mutually pleasurable sex for the married pair might have been more common in the premodern period than Shorter would have us believe, it still may not have been held to be as important an aspect of marital adjustment as it is today. This is possible if only because the whole issue of marital adjustment was not a salient one at a time when marriage rested more on economic ties and procreation than on ties of affection and mutual interests.

While marital adjustment, sexual or otherwise, might not have been of paramount concern in the premodern world, a couple whose life together was continually punctuated by quarrels and bickering might find themselves hauled up in court, as were George and Anna Barlow of the Plymouth Colony who were "severely reproved for their most ungodly living in contension one with the other, and admonished to live otherwise" (quoted in Demos, 1970:93). The records of the Colony are filled with other cases, more often than not with one or the other of a married pair being called before the court, and in the case of recalcitrance, punished by whipping. This reflected more the high valuation placed on domestic tranquility than it did a concern with marital adjustment per se. Adjustment emphasizes the relationship as a relationship; what the courts were concerned with was a standard of appropriate conduct. This emphasis on propriety notwithstanding, the Puritans did see "mutual solace and comfort" as important aspects of marriage (Robert Schnucker, 1975:660).

Winds of Change

While the preceding picture of marital relations is far from complete, it should nonetheless give the reader some sense of marriage as it existed in colonial America, and as it exists in many premodern countries today. The questions we must now answer are why and how marriage changed. Much of the answer to the former is found in Chapter 4. That is, the prime factor was the change in the economic position of women, which was potentially improved but initially compromised by the coming of industrialism. In a very fundamental sense it sowed the seeds for the emancipation of women.

> The woman, like the child, no longer needed to depend on her family elders or males when she wanted to work. Consequently, she achieved an independent basis for her own existence, so that she could, in the larger society as well as within the family, drive a better "role bargain." That is, she could achieve a better set of rights and obligations with respect to other statuses [Goode, 1963:56].

Obviously, women have yet to achieve the full benefits from the new economic opportunities offered to them by the changes in the organization of work brought about by industrialism. Part of the reason for this is to be found in what Barbara Welter (1966) has described as "The Cult of True Womanhood" and Gerda Lerner (1969) as the transformation of the "mill girl" into "the lady." The point both historians make is that during the first half of the nineteenth century women were presented with a saintly and highly domestic conception of themselves which was hardly supportive of an aggressive participation in the economic realm or the driving of a hard role bargain in marriage. This idealized and ultimately repressive image of womanhood went hand in hand with the departure of the woman from the work force and the appearance of the housewife as a new social category (Oakley, 1975).

To an extent, economic growth during the nineteenth century made it possible for more and more middle-class women to strive for an ideal that had previously been the exclusive property of a wealthy few, though Branca (1975a) has issued a needed warning about exaggerating the affluence of the nineteenth-century middle-class household. Nevertheless, as the middle classes grew, the wife became a billboard for her husband's achievement and the manner in which she dressed, the activities she engaged in, and the kind of home she managed all served to tell the world of her husband's success. Associated with this image was the image of the woman as a vessel of the virtues that were absent in the harsh and often cruel work world outside the home.

Given such a perspective, the appearance of negative attitudes toward the external employment of married women becomes more comprehensible. Since she was supposed to be the guardian and symbol of domestic virtues, her venturing out into the work world would expose her to its corrupting influence and drain her energy from the sphere where it should be exercised (Haller and Haller, 1974:80).

> The great current of society is created by those thousand little streams, which are pure or impure according to the character of their homes. To purify them, or to keep them pure, is chiefly woman's work; and if truly done, the current would roll on pure as a mountain stream, to the eternal ocean [Eliot, 1854:42].

According to this image, a woman's time was to be spent in making the home a comfortable retreat (Jeffrey, 1972). Women's magazines during the nineteenth century progressively offered more in the way of advice on all aspects of home management—cooking, decorating, childcare, gardening, and so on. We have come to take periodicals such as *Good Housekeeping, Ladies' Home Journal,* and *Woman's Home Companion* for granted without realizing that the proliferation of their nineteenth-century counterparts, for example, *Godey's Book,* reflected the increasingly high standards of homemaking to which women have been subject since that time. Goode (1963) has argued that the appearance of so-called labor-saving devices in the last century has done less to "save" women's labor than it has done to raise the standards of housekeeping to which women are subject, and data are available that support Goode's point (Vanek, 1974). It is not too farfetched to consider these magazines professional journals, read in the same way that other professional groups read their specialty journals, that is, as a way of keeping abreast of new developments and a device for evaluating one's own performance. This "professionalization" of housework and mothering became even stronger toward the end of the nineteenth century (Filene, 1976:chapter 2) and culminated at the end of the nineteenth century in the Domestic Science movement, with homemaking finally becoming an area for classroom instruction (Laslett, 1973).

Thus, by the end of the nineteenth century the image demanded that a good wife have a tastefully furnished home, prepare varied and imaginative meals, and know how to entertain. This is not to say that in an earlier age such matters were of no concern, but rather that the growth of real income permitted more of the population to consume in a way that was undreamed of previously. Many families could maintain a life style that would have been considered ducal by medieval standards. The burden for the implementation of this standard of living falls upon the wives (Page Smith, 1970.) Only a loving mother is seen capable of catering to the special needs of children (Branca, 1975a:108–109). These same women are also subject to standards of childrearing which demand considerable study and effort. A good mother increasingly must be responsible not merely for seeing to it that a child survives physically, but she must also see to it that the child has the proper environment for psychological growth and development (Wishy, 1968).

Marriage manuals of the midnineteenth century, the "how-to" books written specifically to instruct people about marital pitfalls, also provide us with some interesting insights into the new expectations surrounding

Proud that it is a Frigidaire!
THE hostess whose home is equipped with Frigidaire Electric Refrigeration takes real pride in showing it to her guests—in serving delicious, wholesome desserts, taken from Frigidaire's freezing compartment—in telling them how it keeps all foods fresh and delicious for surprising lengths of time.
She takes pride in the fact that it is a genuine Frigidaire—the finest electric refrigerator built—with its beautiful exterior finish of lustrous white Duco, its clean, smooth, gleaming porcelain-enamel lining, its quiet, dependable, automatic operation. And she does not hesitate to say that the cost of operation is surprisingly little.
The new low-priced metal cabinet Frigidaires offer outstanding values and can be bought on deferred payments.
We should like you to have copies of two Frigidaire books; recipes for delightful frozen desserts, and a book of prize-winning kitchens equipped with Frigidaire. Send to us, or ask for them at any Frigidaire display room.
This modern "ice man" calls once—with Frigidaire—and the ice stays always
DELCO-LIGHT COMPANY, Dept. Y-33, DAYTON, OHIO
Subsidiary of General Motors Corporation
The World's Largest Builder of Electric Refrigerators
More than 150,000 satisfied users are now enjoying the convenience and economy of Frigidaire Electric Refrigeration.
Frigidaire
ELECTRIC REFRIGERATION
THERE IS ONLY ONE ELECTRIC REFRIGERATOR NAMED FRIGIDAIRE

An advertisement depicting the wife's role as homemaker and hostess, c. 1920. *(Courtesy, Frigidaire)*

husband-wife relations. What is most readily observable in the authors, who are largely clergymen and physicians, is a commitment to a basically patriarchal view of marriage and the family. I have described this (Gordon and Bernstein, 1970) as the wife's "obedience-reverence-submission" complex, since these words so nicely reflect the wife's role vis-à-vis her husband. He is master of the home and the focal point of its organization. While the husband's authority is unquestioned, marital experts of the period recommended that he exercise it with kindness and consideration.

> Husbands should remember that in order to have the submission of their wives they must temper their authority with love, prudence and wisdom [Brandt, 1892:121].

The wife in turn must realize that:

> Of all these social, domestic, and personal obligations, her husband is the centre: when they are properly discharged, his welfare and happiness are certainly promoted; and his esteem, affection and confidence established on a permanent basis. In neglecting them he is neglected, his respectability diminished, and his domestic peace and comfort destroyed [Anonymous, 1836:19].

What is notable in the nineteenth-century marital literature is how little space is devoted to the husband's role as father. While to some extent this may be a result of the fact that the literature studied was focused more on marriage than on parenthood, it may also indicate that parenthood was seen largely as the mother's responsibility.

The role that sex played in the marriage of the midnineteenth century is a most interesting topic. My own research (Gordon, 1971) and that of the Hallers (1974) and Charles Rosenberg (1973) reveal that the dangers of marital sexuality became an important theme during this period.

> Such warnings applied, moreover, to both sexes: only the need for propagating the species, some authors contended, could justify such an indulgence. Even if the female did not suffer the physical "drain" that ejaculation constituted for the male, she suffered an inevitable loss of nervous energy [Rosenberg, 1973:135].

While both partners might share the risk attendant upon such indulgence, it was believed that they were not both equally susceptible to the desire to do so. Women were thought to be creatures who lacked sexual desire, and if they had such a desire, it was expressed in a much less clamant form than in men.

> There can be no doubt that sexual feeling in the female is, in a majority of cases, in abeyance, and that it requires positive and considerable excitement to be roused at all; and, even if roused (which in many instances it never can be), is very moderate, compared with that of the male [Hayes, 1869:226].

The aggressive, dominant male and the submissive, docile female—both in the world and in the bedroom—this is the mid-Victorian ideal (G. J. Barker-Benfield, 1975).

Interestingly enough, one of the first indications of change in the conception of marital roles took place with regard to sex. During the last quarter of the nineteenth century we find a growing acknowledgment both of female sexuality and the propriety of nonprocreative marital sex as a way of expressing affection within marriage and simultaneously strengthening the relationship (Gordon, 1971). Henry Guernsey argued:

> The sexual relationship is among the most important uses of married life: it vivifies the affection for each other, as nothing else in the world can, and is a powerful reminder of their [the married couple's] mutual obligation to each other and to the community in which they live [1882:103].

In certain respects this "new" evaluation of marital sexuality should be seen as a delayed reaction; it may reflect the fact that the experts were slowly catching up with their audience. Alfred Kinsey's data (1953) and Carl Degler's (1974) discovery of a group of medical histories kept by a Stanford physician indicate that the sex lives of American women in the second half of the nineteenth century were not all that "Victorian." Given the emphasis on marriage as companionship and its emotionally supportive functions, it would be surprising if sex did not assume an important expressive role. Perhaps it was the sanctification of women and the idealization of the home as bulwark against the "urban wilderness" that retarded the open acceptance of marital sexuality.

At the same time that we observe the rejection of Victorian prudery regarding the role of sex within marriage, we also observe the increasing use of contraception and abortion. This is evidenced not only by the obvious decline in marital fertility (see Chapter 5), but also by the literature of the time, which reveals the new interest in and use of birth control. Carroll Smith-Rosenberg and Charles Rosenberg remark on the concern this caused in the medical community.

> Particularly alarming was the casualness, doctors charged, with which seemingly respectable wives and mothers contemplated and undertook abortions, and how routinely they practiced birth control. One prominent New York gynecologist complained in 1874 that well-dressed women walked into his consultation room and asked for abortions as casually as they would for a cut of beefsteak at their butcher. In 1857, the American Medical Association nominated a special committee to report on the problem, then appointed another in the 1870s; between these dates and especially in the late 1860s, medical societies throughout the country passed resolutions attacking the prevalence of abortion and birth control and condemning physicians who performed and condoned such illicit practices. Nevertheless, abortions could in the 1870s be obtained in Boston and New York for as little as ten dollars, while abortificients could be purchased more cheaply or through the mail [1973:343–344].

In the chapter on fertility we drew attention to the argument that interpreted the declining fertility of the nineteenth century as a symptom of the pressures on middle-class families to maintain even grander life styles, involving among other things, servants and private education for children. The Rosenbergs, while not disregarding this motivating element, feel that another factor may have been the growing awareness on the part of women that the seemingly endless cycle of pregnancies and births, with their attendant strains and threats to health and well being, were not inevitable. They recognize that such awareness certainly may have existed at an earlier time, but "that economic and technological changes in society added new parameters to the age-old experience" (1973:346). One can infer from this that the debates over contraception and the publicity called forth by the Bradlaugh-Besant trial in England and their American counterparts, the Comstock trials, made more people aware of the possibility and propriety of birth control. Technological developments such as the vulcanization of rubber during the mid-1840s made the condom sufficiently inexpensive to be within the reach of a wide section of the population, but it probably did not gain wide acceptance until the end of the century. In general, however, the spread of the use of contraception was more a matter of how people came to define the role of sex and childbirth in marriage than a matter of the means of contraception at their disposal. While cervical caps, douching, condoms, and other "mechanical" means were used throughout the nineteenth century (Branca, 1975a), withdrawal was probably still the primary form of contraception employed by married people (Himes, 1963).

While there was still a good deal of ambivalence regarding marital sexuality as the nineteenth century drew to a close, the fact is that during the nineteenth century we do see a growth of marriage where affection and companionship played an important role. Just how important a role is paradoxically enough revealed by the growth of divorce during the second half of the century.

While late-nineteenth-century divorce rates are low by modern standards, it is nonetheless true that the rate per 1,000 marriages jumped by almost 100 percent between the 1860–1864 and 1880–1884 periods, and the rate continued to rise, though at a slower pace, until recently when divorces have again begun to spurt (Davis, 1972). In view of the fact that the liberalization of nineteenth-century divorce laws took place in most jurisdictions before the middle of the century, we cannot attribute the post-Civil War rise in divorce to legislative change. More likely, what was at work was the new conception of marriage with its emphasis on love, affection, and compatibility. The fact that this created marital expectations which some couples found difficult to achieve was, to some extent, reflected in the divorce courts, but given the expense and stigma associated with divorce at that time, the divorce rate was probably only the tip of the iceberg of discontent.

The Impact of the Feminist Movement

In our discussion of changing marital patterns during the nineteenth century, we have not yet considered the influence of the Feminist movement. This movement is important both in terms of the substantive changes it brought about in the position of women, through its efforts to alter discriminatory legislation, as well as in terms of its effects on women's sense of themselves and their place in marriage and society.

The legal status of married women at the beginning of the nineteenth century was a strikingly compromised one. By marrying, a woman essentially renounced many of the rights she held as a single person. Her husband, for all intents and purposes, gained control of the property she brought with her to the marriage. While there were certain restrictions on his ability to dispose of some of this property (real estate versus chattel) and there was an element of accountability built into the system, essentially the husband had enormous powers over the wife's premarital property. Thus not only was the nineteenth-century woman compromised economically by having lost her function in the marketplace, but even the privileged few who came from families that provided them with some financial leverage lost this as soon as they married.

The legal principle behind the compromised position of married women is the feudal doctrine of coverture, which according to Blackstone holds that:

> By marriage, the husband and wife are one person in law; that is, the very being or legal existence of the woman is suspended during the marriage, or at least is incorporated and consolidated [quoted in Kanowitz, 1969:35].

During the nineteenth century, we see this principle being challenged and new legislation instituted which alters the position of women. In 1839, Mississippi enacted a Married Woman's Property Act, and by 1850 most other states had passed similar laws. Kanowitz neatly summarizes the thrust of these laws:

> Responding in great part to the rising tide of individual and organizational protest against the married woman's status of legal subjugation to her husband, these laws generally granted married women the right to contract, to sue and be sued without joining their husbands, to manage and control the property they brought with them to the marriage, to engage in gainful employment without their husbands' permission, and to retain the earnings derived from the employment [1969:40].

While it is true that feminist agitation was a factor in bringing about such legal reform, elements of masculine self-interest were hardly absent (Ditzion, 1953:244). A man who declared himself bankrupt under the new laws did not lose whatever capital his wife might have in her own name, and thus the family might be afforded some protection from his bad judgment or misfortune. Correspondingly, wealthy fathers would not inevitably see their daughter's inheritance slipping into the husband's coffers. With the high rates of marital dissolution through death at this time, this was no small consideration. Still, all things considered, women benefited most from such legislative change, though they have only gradually moved toward a position of equality with men in the eyes of the law (Griffiths, 1970). Remember that it was not until 1920 that women gained the vote!

The Feminist movement of the nineteenth century involved more than lobbying for change in the legal status of women, though such change represented an important fruit of their efforts. While William O'Neill (1969) is probably correct in his assertions that radical feminism lost out to the more polite and politic variety, the attacks of the radicals on the institution of marriage and the relations between men and women in the larger society echoed and reechoed throughout the century and into the next. Feminists like Elizabeth Cady Stanton, Charlotte Perkins Gilman, and Susan B. Anthony exposed the problems inherent in a system which had the subservience of women as a foundation stone. Writing in 1870 Ms. Stanton noted that her supporters were not opposed to marriage per se but "only against the present form that makes man master, woman slave" (quoted in O'Neill, 1969:21). Radical feminists were also in favor of contraception and divorce legislation that would make marital dissolution less problematic. Some feminists, such as Victoria Woodhull, questioned the virtues of monogamy and advocated free love, but they represented the extreme fringe. While it is difficult to assess the impact of the speeches and writings of these women, it is certainly safe to say that the views they expressed were widely disseminated in the mass media and lecture halls, and thus surely came to the attention of middle-class women.

TOWARD SYMMETRICAL MARRIAGE

Until very recently a reading of most family sociology texts would have left one with the impression that companionate marriage had continued unchanged from the nineteenth century to the present. More recently we have begun to see an appreciation of the change that has taken place during the twentieth century, but before we discuss the character and direction of this change, a few points about the diffusion of companionate marriage should be made. While companionate marriage first took form among the growing urban middle classes during the early decades of the nineteenth century, it did not remain their preserve. Slowly but definitely we see indications of similar patterns appearing in the poorer segments of the population. Since working married women with children have always come disproportionately from the working class, it is not surprising that the authority of the husband was kept at least slightly in check by the economic contribution of the wife. But by the end of the century very few married women from any economic group were in the work force, and the agricultural population was rapidly declining. Most married women were housewives (Oakley, 1974). Still, into the twentieth century and even today we can detect important class differences in marriage, with the lower-class groups showing more segregation by sex in socializing, greater rigidity in division of labor along sex lines, and less shared leisure (Komarovsky, 1962; Rubin, 1976). Still, when we compare marriages as they existed in working-class districts of London or New York 100 years ago and those of today, change in the direction of the companionate form is obvious (Young and Willmott, 1973).

Bipolar models always pose problems for the sociologist, though as a group sociologists seem to have a propensity for them. If we look at the traditional-companionate dichotomy in light of current data we see that it is most problematic. The wife who devotes most of her married life solely to housework and childcare is a dying breed, as is the husband who refuses to assume any responsibility for the domestic sphere. Of course, we have a long way to go before we see both husband and wife work at careers and assume equal responsibility for cleaning, cooking, and child-rearing. We are, nonetheless, beginning to find discussions of the "symmetrical" family and "androgynous" marriage in the literature (Bernard, 1972; Young and Willmott, 1973). This phenomenon is not something totally different from the companionate marriage we have been discussing. It is, rather, an extension of this pattern, with important modifications.

The movement toward symmetry or androgyny does not represent a rejection of the companionate mode of marriage, but rather an alteration of it. There are no sociologists who argue that marriage today is marked by a decreasing emphasis on emotional support, physical affection, and shared leisure—these are all things that people still avidly seek within marriage. What sociologists feel has *begun* to change are attitudes toward the external employment of married women and the way in which work is divided in the home. While women still undoubtedly bear the major burden of housekeeping and childcare, men may be *beginning* to assume responsibility for these spheres at the same time that they are growing less critical of having a working wife. Still, data from the 1970 National Fertility Study, which was analyzed by Mason and Bumpass (1975), reveal a considerable degree of conservatism remaining. For example, 76 percent of the white people sampled and 77 percent of the blacks agreed with the statement:

> It is much better for everyone involved if the man is the achiever outside the home and the woman takes care of the home and family [Mason and Bumpass, 1975:1219].

Only 52 percent of the whites and 71 percent of the blacks said "yes" to the statement: "Men should share the work around the house with women such as doing dishes, cleaning, and so forth" (ibid.). Thus we see a majority of both samples agreeing with the traditional conception of the male's breadwinner role, but the white sample split about evenly on the desirability of husband and wife sharing domestic work. It is unfortunate that similar data from an earlier period are not available. It is relevant to point out that one study of a Washington State sample felt that the trend toward women working outside the home was a good thing. Among the respondents younger males and females (that is, under thirty-five) were more favorably disposed to this than were older people, suggesting a potential growth of positive attitudes (Hoffman and Nye, 1975:12).

THE WORKING WIFE

Rosabeth Kanter has penetratingly observed that the traditional view in the United States of the work of men and women can be summed up as follows:

> It is the *unemployed* man who is seen a social problem, likely to have disturbed marital relations and likely to produce delinquent children. For women, it was the *employed woman* who was seen in *virtually the same ways.* [1977:61].

If this is the stereotype, what is the reality of the situation faced by families in which both husband and wife work outside the home (about 47 percent of the total [*New York Times,* March 8, 1977:21])? Unfortunately, the research in this area is far from definitive. Many questions remain unanswered and some of the answers we have occasionally exist in conflicting form. For example, while it does appear that the number of hours spent on family-related tasks does decrease for working women, the picture is somewhat more ambiguous with regard to their husbands. Kathryn Walker, for example, found that the number of hours spent daily

While few of today's marriages are truly egalitarian, men do seem to be helping out more with the housework than they once did. *(Charles Gatewood)*

on family-related tasks was 8.1 for unemployed women and 4.8 for those working 30 or more hours weekly, yet husbands' daily time maintained itself at 1.6 hours irrespective of their wives' work (Walker, 1969, 1970). Robert Blood and Robert Hamblin (1958), however, found that in homes with working wives, husbands did 10 percent more of the housework than in those where the women did not have jobs; others have come up with similar findings (Blood and Wolfe, 1960; Nolan, 1963; Lamouse, 1969).

These seeming contradictions may, according to Joseph Pleck (1975), be because these studies have used measures which are not quite comparable. For example, Blood and Wolfe (1960) look at a couple's housework in ways that assume complementarity and the husband's and wife's scores are the inverse of each other, but Walker, using a time-budget approach where people keep records of how every waking hour is spent, have a measure where spouses' scores are independent of each other. Moreover, Blood and Wolfe did not include childcare in their measures. Childcare, however, turns out to offer no solution to the contradiction because some comparable studies have found it to be divided more evenly when the wife is employed (Lein et al., 1974) while others have found just the opposite to be true (Dahlström and Liljeström, 1971). To make matters even more complicated, George Farkas (1976), in one of the more sophisticated of the studies done to date, found the number of children accounted for more variation in the division of labor of married dual-employed couples than any other variable, but unfortunately his measure does not include childcare. Thus, what we see here is a confused picture which only allows us to say with certainty that externally employed wives do less home-related work, but it is not clear if their husbands do more.

Many readers are probably asking themselves what effect does the wife's employment have on marital conflict? As it happens, such marriages appear to show more conflict, suggesting that such transitions are not all that easily carried out. But Nye's research (1958–1959), comparing working and nonworking couples, found that the most frequent conflicts between dual-employed couples dealt with the "house and furniture," suggesting that this conflict is not generalized, but is limited to those roles tied to the home. Artie Gianopoulos and Howard Mitchell (1957) report findings similar to Nye's in their Philadelphia study. The conflict they discovered focused largely on the "domestic-economic" sphere. An interesting qualification or refinement of these findings are found in Blood and Wolfe's (1960) Detroit study. They find that dual-employed families that report conflict over the handling of money tend to be concentrated in the working-class group. Among the higher-income groups, disagreement over marital roles are more often at issue.

There are several important observations to be garnered from this discussion. Perhaps the most notable one (and the one to which we will have to later return) is that the entry of a wife into the labor force does create some degree of domestic disorganization, which leads to the reassignment and sharpening of certain marital roles. While such couples hardly become truly equalitarian in their domestic division of labor, they do show more sharing of responsibilities than those families in which the husband alone is working. This shift is also accompanied by an elevation in the level of marital conflict. Blood suggests that this is the case because:

> Dual-income couples quarrel over money not because of the extra income but in spite of it. Indeed, it is because they have financial difficulties that the wife goes to work. Longitudinal research is needed to show how much financial conflicts are resolved by the extra income and how much they persist due to the working wife's greater involvement in financial decision-making [1963:290].

On the other hand, the less financial need there is for the wife to work, the more conflict families manifest over marital roles, with the husband apparently showing an unwillingness to "unnecessarily" have to expand his share of domestic responsibilities. The picture here is obviously a complex one and one whose ramifications we do not completely understand.

Are marriages in which both man and wife work happier than those in which only the husband works? The findings in this area are not clear cut. Some studies suggest that there are important class differences here, with working-class couples benefiting most in terms of expressed satisfaction with the wife's employment (Blood, 1963). But other studies (e.g., Nye, 1975) come up with the opposite results. The matter is further complicated by more recent studies (Gendell, 1963; Fogarty et al., 1971; Scanzoni, 1975) which find no clear-cut relationship between a wife's working and marital satisfaction. It is possible that the earlier studies found differences because of the critical attitude taken toward a wife leaving the home to work. Since this pattern has become increasingly common, it may no longer cause problems, and hence the decline in its impact on marital satisfaction. Hoffman and Nye provide a useful summary of the literature on this subject.

> We could sum up the research of almost three decades by concluding that the early studies, in general, showed slightly more marital problems among couples in which the mother was employed; but even in those studies, the differences in tensions and satisfactions occurred mostly at the lower-class levels. Recent studies suggest that the small, sometimes nonsignificant, differences in middle-class families found in earlier studies no longer exist; if the wife enjoys her work, the marital satisfactions of this sub-group of wives may average higher than for housewives in general. However, in lower-class families, research supports the conclusion of continuing differences, favoring couples in which the wife is not employed [1975:206].

Having explored the effects of female employment on the division of labor within the home and on marital satisfaction, we now turn to family power structure, which in some ways gets to the heart of dominance relations within marriage. The research on this area of family life offers less clear-cut findings than was the case with regard to the division of labor, but nonetheless we can discern some important trends. It is generally believed, at least as popular folklore would have it, that a working wife is able, because of her economic power, to exert considerably more power in family relations than her nonworking counterpart. As it happens, the outcome of female employment appears to be less clear cut and therefore perhaps a bit more interesting as well. We noted earlier that one of the effects of a wife entering the labor force was that her husband began to assume greater responsibility for household tasks, both in the traditionally masculine sphere, such as shovelling snow, and also in the traditionally feminine spheres, such as house cleaning. Therefore, it is not surprising to find that in the area of household tasks a wife's power decreases as a result of her becoming externally employed. She becomes less autonomous in this sphere and shares decisions with her husband. At the same time that her autonomy is decreasing in this sphere, she is gaining an important say in such areas as the decision to buy a house, a car, insurance, etc. (Blood, 1963:192). As Blood has pointed out, these are major economic decisions which involve a considerable investment of the family's resources, and which are only made after considerable thought. Similar findings appear in David Heer's (1958) Boston study, where working wives reported having a greater influence on "important decisions" than nonworking wives (see also Kligler, 1954; Bahr, 1972; and Rubin, 1976). European studies have also yielded comparable results (Kandel and Lesser, 1972; Michel, 1967).

Blood concludes that a wife's employment has an impact on family power structure, but a selective one, and therefore any approach that chooses to view this problem "globally" would inevitably come up with mixed findings. The fact that going out to work for a woman results in her losing some control over household decisions at the same time that she gains control over larger economic decisions suggests to Blood that this change is based on enlarging competences. That is to say, the increasing role played by the husband in domestic decisions reflects his growing awareness of them resulting from his new participation in this area; on the other hand, his wife's new economic experience results in her having more competence and awareness with regard to the larger economic issues. In Blood's words:

> The fact that this is not a question of economic bargaining is suggested by Blood and Wolfe's report that the wife's voice in the same eight decisions also increases when she is an unpaid participant in church activities and other formal organizations [1963:294].

Other researchers point out that while the working wife may have more say in various decisions, in terms of broader measures of power, she cannot be differentiated from her nonworking counterpart (Hoffman, 1963; Safilios-Rothschild, 1969).

Scanzoni has made a rather important and interesting point regarding the impact of a wife's employment on family power structure.

> Furthermore, several studies have indicated that while working increases the wife's power to some extent, even the working wife has less power than her husband. In most cases, the working wife becomes merely a *junior partner* to her husband.... The husband remains the unique provider—the woman remains ultimately dependent on him for material benefits and for social status. Up to this time, most working women have not possessed the same degree of commitment to their work as do men, neither had individualistic occupational achievement been central to their work behavior. There is almost unanimous agreement with Degler's observation that the chief concern of most women has heretofore been with "jobs" rather than with "careers" [1972:70].

Scanzoni's point is well taken and leads us to what must be our next consideration, namely, the division of labor and power relations in those families where the wife does pursue a career. Such families have been referred to as dual-professional families.

Dual-Professional Families

Dual-professional families are of great interest to sociologists because they provide us with a glimpse into emerging family dynamics. In dual-professional or dual-career families, the wife has been able to overcome the difficult obstacles that stand in the way of high-level vocational achievement for a woman, and at the same time is involved in a domestic relationship with husband and children. These are women who view their work—or at least we would expect them to view their work—not merely as "an extension of their roles of wives and mothers but as an intrinsic part of their destinies" (Goode, 1963). This is what Degler speaks of as a career orientation (1964). By looking at these families we may be able to get a sense of what the impact will be of the greater employment of women in careers rather than just jobs.

Perhaps the most interesting thing to emerge from the research literature is the degree to which even professional women showed what has been described as "female tolerance of domestication." That is to say, many of these women did not really see their work as a career and did not rebel against a lack of equalitarianism in their homes (see also Holmstrom, 1972). These two interrelated phenomena have to be looked at in greater depth. To begin with, *only one* of the fifty-three families studied by Margaret Poloma and T. Neal Garland (1971) could be described as truly equalitarian in the sense that domestic responsibilities including child-care were truly divided equally. Only in this one family were both the career of the wife and that of the husband seen as being equally important. In most of the other families, evidence of male dominance was found in all spheres, with the responsibilities for the children falling on the wife and the husband's career being viewed as the basis on which family decisions were made. Furthermore, the husband was generally seen as the head of the household in such families. Even where the family employs outside help to clean and look after the children, the residual tasks, such as taking children to the doctor and cooking for guests, fall to the wife. In most respects these were very traditional families with the wife being seen principally as a mother and homemaker, despite her outside professional work. Another group of families, which Poloma and Garland describe as "neotraditional," evidenced a break from the traditional family mode to the extent that the wife's income was needed to maintain the family's style of life, and where the work of the wife was given consideration in terms of important decisions such as moving and taking vacations. But keep in mind that these two types of families still do not differ with regard to marital role expectations:

> As with the traditional families, the wife is expected and expects to see that the house is run smoothly, that her husband's needs are met, and that the children are cared for. The husband is expected and expects to be the *main* provider and status giver. He does not expect his wife to work if she does not want to. The career is *her choice.* By the same token, he will *assist* his wife with her domestic tasks if there is little or no domestic help and if he has no strong personal objections to performing such tasks [Poloma and Garland, 1971:535].

The great majority of women in the Poloma study who were mothers (thirty-six out of forty-five) interrupted their careers to stay at home completely or work part-time while their children were little. (By way of a relevant aside, Rhona and Robert Rappoport (1971) found this was a strategy employed by the married career women they studied, but a number of the sample delayed childbearing until they were established in their jobs and thus had the means and prerequisites to reduce the burdens of childcare.) For many this meant the definite compromises that go with not pursuing a career on a fulltime basis. Obviously, certain avenues were closed to these professional women who could only give part of their time to their work. Those who did work found it necessary to engage in what Poloma describes as "compartmentalization," that is, very definitely and clearly separate the worlds of work and home. How does one account for this seemingly odd and unjust situation in which professional women must become truly superhuman characters maintaining responsibilities for both work and home?

There are a number of factors at work here: social, psychological, and structural. Women as a result of the kind of socialization experience to which they have traditionally been subject probably bear an unnecessary load of conflict and guilt over leaving the home to work (Rossi, 1965; Rubin, 1976) and also may think it more natural for themselves to assume parenting responsibilities. While this may be changing, structural factors are more resistant. Hanna Papanek (1973) has insightfully pointed out that many middle-class men occupy what she speaks of as "two person careers." More specifically, the job of college president, minister, diplomat, to name only a few, are predicated on the presence of a wife who assumes responsibilities for the provision of important but ancillary services. For example, a boarding school teacher's wife would provide "tea and sympathy," and a small town executive's wife would play an active role in community volunteer work. But the problem may go even further than this.

Janet and Larry Hunt (1977) have argued recently that it may be very difficult to reconcile the nuclear family as we know it and the pursuit of a career by both husband and wife, a point which the present author has also made (1972:10–14). Taking off in part from Papanek's work mentioned above, they try to show that if women are to pursue careers, someone else must provide the supportive and auxiliary services they have traditionally provided. Since the working woman cannot delegate responsibilities the way the husband of a nonworking wife can, this means that she and her husband must rely more and more on hired help, and the Hunts feel that this perpetuates a class of workers who receive low wages to provide the domestic services such a family needs. Moreover, they feel that children may suffer in the process as one more area of childrearing is delegated to nonfamily members.

SUMMARY

What we have seen during the twentieth century is a trend in the direction of increasing female participation in the labor force. In 1900, 20.6 percent of this country's women were in the labor force; in 1974 the figure was up to 45.2 percent, and it has continued to rise. Moreover, most of this change has come since 1940, when the rate was 25.8 percent. As we have repeatedly pointed out, what is more significant is the change in the composition of the female work force. The participation of married women went up by 300 percent between 1900 and 1940, more than 250 percent between 1940 and 1960, and has continued to rise. Concomitantly, though not really beginning until the 1950s, we have seen a growth in the rate of work force participation by married women with children under six, almost tripling between 1950 and 1970. Clearly, work is increasingly becoming something which women do not relegate to the years before marriage and after the children are grown.

The significance of this change is that it may result, if it has not already done so, in a reorientation to and reorganization of female life cycles, to the degree that work will now figure much more importantly and for a much longer period in the lives of women. The kinds of employment in which women have traditionally been concentrated, low-paying service jobs, are readily seen by women today as jobs rather than as careers. But as more women begin to take a career orientation toward their work, and as their work makes such a definition more appropriate, it would seem that some sort of adjustment in family relations will be forthcoming. Adjustments are already becoming evident in some families, such as the dual-professional families we spoke of earlier. However, men assuming an increasing responsibility for what has traditionally been women's work is a very slow process, though perhaps men now do such tasks as dish-washing, changing diapers, and so on, somewhat less reluctantly than did their fathers. The implications of the growth in female employment go beyond the question of who does what in the home; women's work also has important implications for the future of marriage as we know it.

Since we do not have a crystal ball, it is risky to make predictions concerning the future of conjugal relations. Nevertheless, it is probably safe to say that we will continue to observe some growth of equalitarian-symmetrical marriages at the expense of patriarchal sex role stereotyped ones *if* opportunities for female employment continue to grow, but as we have tried to show it may be difficult to reconcile the nuclear family with the pursuit of a career by both husband and wife. In the face of a contracting economy, the situation becomes somewhat more problematic (Valerie Oppenheimer, 1973). It is possible that the result of fewer job opportunities for women will be greater marital conflict, as more and more women, traditionally among the last hired and first fired, find themselves locked into the home. Even were this to happen, it would not preclude the experimentation with alternative forms of marriage. In the next chapter we shall consider the ways in which some couples are going beyond the boundaries of conventional marriage.

Photograph by Byron. The Byron Collection, Museum of the City of New York

BEYOND THE CONJUGAL FAMILY: Open Marriage and Other Alternatives 9

The current preoccupation in the mass media with the family has been expressed largely in terms of the kinds of changes that are taking place within this institution. Generally the media have emphasized the more dramatic manifestations of familial change. Are the media accounts of family change accurate or sensational? In Chapter 7 we looked at the way in which courtship has changed over the last three centuries; in this chapter we will emphasize those changes that have occurred within the boundaries of the nuclear family, or which articulate with the nuclear family. Virtually all of these developments are expressions of the same theme: a broadening of the boundaries of marriage, that is, a general trend toward making marriage a more *permeable* structure in terms of entry, exit, and personal freedom once in the relationship. Many of the trends we have so far discussed, such as changes in the functions of the family and the economic position of women, are at the heart of the developments we will discuss below.

Perhaps the most important marital trend to be observed in recent years is the concern with and appearance of something which has been variously described as "open" or "free" marriage. For many, these adjectives evoke sordid scenes of seething adultery, but while some sexual freedom is implied by these terms, this is hardly an accurate image of open marriage (though we will also discuss swinging, which perhaps fits the image better). In point of fact, advocates of open or free marriage call for a relationship in which each person can continue to grow and develop as a person and where each partner has the freedom on which such personal growth depends. Interestingly enough, this is not as new an idea as some would think. In fact, this concept made its appearance relatively early in the twentieth century. However, the reception such an idea received at that time was hardly as hospitable as that being received today by similar ideas.

In 1927, Judge Ben B. Lindsey, who played an important role in legal reform at the turn of the century, published a book in collaboration with Wainwright Evans entitled *The Companionate Marriage,* in which he advocated, "legal marriage with legalized Birth Control and with the right to divorce by mutual consent for childless couples usually without payment of alimony" (1927:v). While today this hardly seems like a very radical idea, it was greeted with considerable outrage in 1927 by defenders of conventional morality, who saw it as representing a clear and present danger to the integrity of American family life.

Lindsey developed the concept of "companionate marriage" because of his obvious concern about the plight of American marriages. He felt that both divorce and marital unhappiness were spreading because the laws then covering both divorce and the dissemination of contraceptive information were so prohibitive as to make it difficult for young people to establish relationships which had any chance of enduring. They were pushed into marriage by the heat of romantic love and sexual desire and soon found themselves disillusioned with the marriage but often burdened with children. Lindsey felt that had birth control information been more readily available, and had couples had the opportunity to divorce without going through a tremendous legal and financial maze, much unhappiness and sorrow could have been avoided. Lindsey separated "companionate marriage" from "procreative marriage," advocating that the latter should be more difficult to enter into than the former, since it involves children. Companionate marriage, Lindsey felt, would represent a legalization of a practice that people already engaged in. It was distinct from trial marriage which, he felt, had a tentative and noncommittal quality; companionate marriage represented a deep commitment, but one which had an escape clause both in terms of avoiding the inevitability of children and the provision for divorce without penalty.

> The Companionate is a firmly established, perfectly respectable institution among us right now. Childless couples are socially respectable, and they are as much married as any one else. There is no "trial marriage" about it. It is simply that they are forced to practice bootleg contraception instead of legal contraception, and that if they want a divorce by mutual consent, it is a bootleg affair, since they can and do get it by collusion and perjury instead of under the law. Also the woman has a hold on the man for alimony which she would not have under the Companionate if the Companionate were regulated under law [1927:141].

Lindsey was hardly a prophet of anarchy; he was deeply impressed by how much unnecessary unhappiness was created by norms and laws that forced people into almost inextricable relationships before they were ready to make such a commitment.

However, Lindsey's book goes beyond the mere discussion of companionate marriage, and this is one of the reasons why his book may have called forth such a hostile response. While he hardly advocated adultery, under certain circumstances he did condone it. Essentially he said that whether or not one or both partners enter into extramarital sex outside of procreative marriage is a matter "for individual decision, based on culture, fineness of feeling, good sensitiveness and good taste" (1927:278). While he recognized that such behavior may have had very detrimental effects on a marriage, he pointed out that this need not always be the case, that many people were able to handle such relationships and more would increasingly be able to do so.

The fact that *The Companionate Marriage* was written half a century ago seems at first to be truly amazing. But if we stop for a moment to put it in the historical context of the 1920s, we see that it is not at all surprising. Certainly by the 1920s many of the sexual trends that were to become evident by the 1960s were already developed in more than an incipient form. There was a growing acceptance of sex as a natural and proper part of marriage, and an acceptance of female sexual desire along with the idea that women had a right to be satisfied (Gordon, 1971). At the same time, the middle-class marriage had become essentially a matter of companionship. Therefore, in the context of all these developments, we should expect that the question of divorce and extramarital liaisons certainly would be raised. Being a judge in the juvenile and family court of a large city, Lindsey was more likely than most to encounter cases of out-of-wedlock birth and divorce. Still, the fact that his ideas were greeted with such alarm is indicative that, while they spoke to a segment of the population, most people were not yet ready to have such blasphemy publicly discussed, much less condoned. When Margaret Mead advocated essentially the same thing in 1966 in *Redbook,* a widely circulated women's magazine, under the name of "marriage in two steps," no hue and cry was raised. Obviously, companionate marriage was an idea whose time had come.

DIMENSIONS OF MARITAL CHANGE

The success of Nena and George O'Neill's book *Open Marriage* (1972), which was on the bestseller list for almost a year and sold over 200,000 copies in the hardbound edition alone, is evidence of the wide interest in new concepts of marriage. Since this book was written in the beginning of the 1970s, it takes for granted much that Judge Lindsey so strongly advocated, for example, easy access to birth control information and divorce. However, the book is not concerned with marriage in two stages. Rather it is written for couples who have established a viable relationship, but which for some reason is not satisfying the needs of both partners. The book is strongly informed with the Maslowian idea of self-actualization (See Maslow, 1962), and the importance of entering into and developing relationships that facilitate this process. For the O'Neills a marriage which foists conventional notions of companionship and togetherness on a couple, and at the same time forces them into stereotypical roles, is one which is detrimental to the socioemotional health and growth of both partners. Thus the book is a "how to" manual of sorts, which leads the soon-to-be-enlightened couple down the path of what promises to be a new and more satisfying marital life style.

Simply put, they recommend ways in which each partner can maintain some existence independent of the marriage without evoking jealousy from the other or guilt from oneself, even if this involves an extramarital sexual relationship. To be sure, the authors believe that in order for a couple to do this they must have first established a fundamentally sound relationship. Nevertheless, a considerable distance must be traversed before the state of open marriage is reached. Once having arrived at this state, a couple can allow their own interests rather than their conception of mutual interests to dictate their actions. Thus, if one partner wants to go to a film and the other wants to stay home and read, neither should feel that they have to accommodate to the other's plans. Instead, they should feel free to do what they want to do, and not have to worry about what this means to their relationship. Again, we must remember that the O'Neills assume that people in basically stable relationships do share much in common and their interests will overlap much of the time.

Open Marriage was not a book whose ideas were completely novel. In the 1960s a number of books appeared which focused on similar themes, among them John Cuber and Peggy Harroff's *The Significant Americans* (1965), and Rostum and Della Roy's *Honest Sex* (1968). In the same year that *Open Marriage* was published, two similar books appeared—one by Carl Rogers, the dean of American clinical psychology, entitled *Becoming Partners: Marriage and Its Alternatives* (1972), the other by John and Mimi Lobel, *John and Mimi: A Free Marriage* (1972). The Rogers book, not surprisingly, places a tremendous amount of emphasis on the psychological aspect of desirable change in marital relations, but as in the O'Neill book, a key point is the opening up and broadening of marriage so as to permit relationships outside of it and growth within it. The Lobel book focuses on the sexual side of what the authors call "free marriage." Often it appears to be more a vehicle for the explicit description of sexual acts than an attempt to explore new relationships, but partly hidden by the sighs and moans is a book that does tell us something about a young couple's efforts to alter the character of their relationship so as to permit them some freedom to move beyond it while remaining within it. More recently Gordon Clanton and Chris Downing (1975) have published an account of a married couple who, after nine years of marriage, decide to expand their relationship by including another woman in it. We also find considerable attention being focused on such phenomena in the professional literature. For example, the entire issue of *The Family Coordinator*

(October 1975) was recently devoted to the subject of "Variant Family Forms and Life Styles," and one of the authors of an article in that issue has written a book in which he discusses the ways in which people have been trying to alter monogamous relationships (James Ramey, 1976).

There have also been a number of fictional books recently published which deal with the opening up of monogamous relationships, most notably the novels of Robert Rimmer—*The Rebellion of Yale Marrott* (1964), *The Harrad Experiment* (1966), *Proposition 31* (1968), and *Thursday My Love* (1972). Virtually all of these have been bestsellers. *The Harrad Experiment* was even made into a motion picture. All these books deal with multiple relationships, sometimes two-couple group marriage, other times three-person relationships. While from a literary point of view these novels are hardly memorable, they appear to have had great didactic value for many readers. Larry and Joan Constantine (1973), for example, report that many of the members of the group marriages they studied got the idea for such relationships initially from reading *Proposition 31.*

The growth of interest in such new relationships suggests to sociologists the appearance of a new stage in the evolution of marriage, one which seems to have become conspicuous in the postwar years. This suggests that, as with changes in household size, one must also consider whether there has been a postindustrial pattern of marriage. We indicated earlier that the initial changes brought about by the economic aspects of modernization placed new emphasis on the relational and affective aspects of marriage at the expense of the economic and partnership qualities so characteristic of many premodern societies, especially in the West. What we are seeing now is a continuation and elaboration of this trend. As women have less need for marriage as a means of placing themselves in adult roles and maintaining an identity, and as men no longer need a wife as a "helpmate," the relational aspects of marriage become even more important. The question of "why marry" is now answered in terms of the desire for a relationship which is fulfilling and rewarding. But given this new emphasis, the amount of flexibility that exists should be maximal; therefore couples now have room to experiment with and choose different kinds of marriages or no marriage at all (Rappoport and Rappoport, 1975).

Let us look at some of the developments in marital and nonmarital life styles that have become part of the fabric of American society during the 1970s. We have already commented (see Chapter 7) on the postponing of first marriages, which appears to have begun to occur during the 1960s. While this does not indicate any wholesale disillusionment with marriage, it does seem to show that people are willing to delay marriage while they either live in nonmarital cohabitative relationships or by themselves (Glick, 1975). To be sure, the fact that many people live alone is a simple reflection of this country's affluence. When we discussed the boarding and lodging phenomenon in Chapter 3, we pointed out that this was a result of the shortage of housing and the inability of young migrants to maintain single-person households. Today, however, the starting salaries of young college graduates are such as to permit many of them the option of their own apartments.

Housing developers have not allowed this turn of events to pass them by. In recent years we have seen the appearance of apartment complexes created specifically for single people. Often containing pools and facilities for various court games, such apartments bring like-minded young people together at a time in their lives when they are either looking for a mate or for the freedom to pursue relationships free from the scrutiny of people not wholly sympathetic to their life styles and values (Proulx, 1973). Such apartment complexes have received their share of bad press, being described as scenes of debauchery. While these stories probably contain a fair amount of hyperbole, it is probably true that the behavior of residents would shock some of our more conventional citizens. But from the point of view of the family sociologist, the presence or absence of abundant premarital sex is less important than the fact that such apartment complexes exist and reflect a new development.

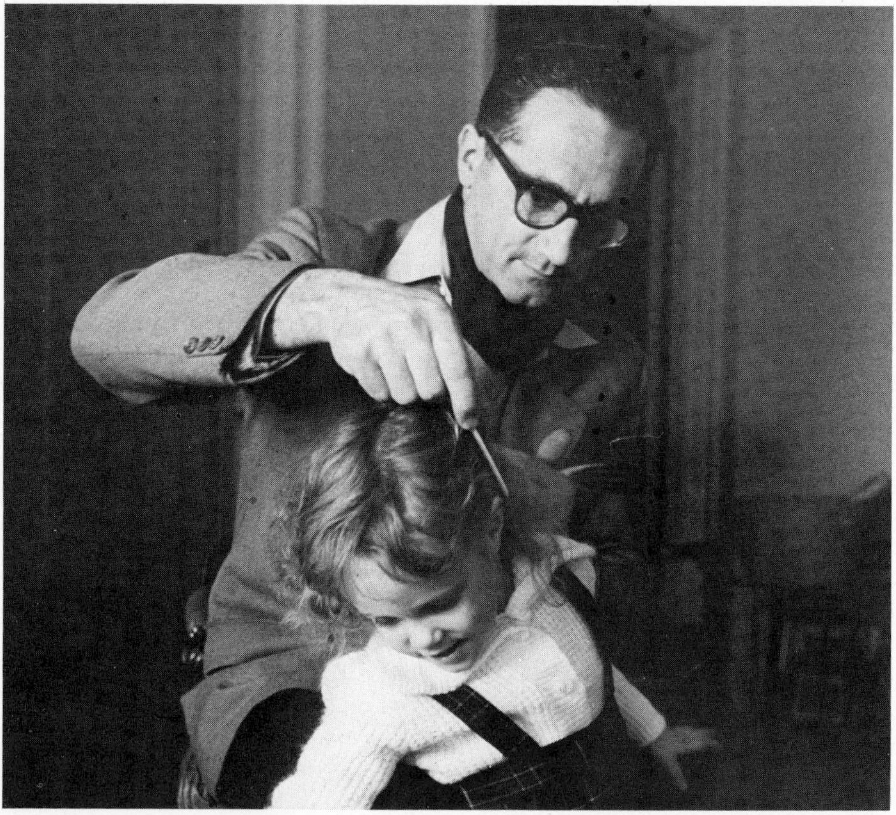

Being a single parent isn't easy, but it is a common phenomenon in contemporary America. *(George W. Gardner)*

It does seem clear that during the time that many of today's young people live alone they go through periods of living with persons of the opposite sex; though from the little we know it seems that even when they are cohabiting many maintain their own apartments, either out of a desire for independence or to mollify parents who would disapprove of their new arrangements.

The fact that these young people do not appear to be abandoning marriage, as evidenced by the fact that most of them do ultimately marry, is of prime importance to us, suggesting that marriage is still seen as an important and potentially fulfilling relationship. Still, young people are aware that this relationship no longer need have the permanency it previously did, given the growth of liberal divorce legislation, nor the inevitable presence of children, given the availability of efficient and reliable contraception (Veevers, 1975; Lorber, 1975; Weitzman, 1975). Thus the conditions for Judge Lindsey's companionate marriage have been fulfilled.

Our task here is to try to explore the meaning of the types of alternative structures people have been creating within the conjugal family. It should be emphasized that we are not concerned here with alternatives to the conjugal family; we are interested in the ways in which the conjugal family has been adapted to the pressures for change resulting from larger societal developments.

EXTRAMARITAL SEX

It is often said that one of the most important and persistent pressures impinging on today's marriages is that of the movement away from exclusivity. Marriages in our society have traditionally been described as monogamous, indicating that the relationship is to be limited to one male-female pair. To be sure, there are instances of adultery reported in colonial New England (Howard, 1904: vol.2), but given the degree to which the behavior of individuals was under community scrutiny and the strength and influence of religion, adultery (apart from those who had left a wife in England and conveniently forgot that they had been married upon landing in the New World) was a rather uncommon occurrence. With the emergence of large cities during the nineteenth century we saw the appearance of widespread prostitution. The second half of the nineteenth century also saw such developments as the "social purity movement" (Pivar, 1973), a movement whose primary goal was the eradication of prostitution. Certainly, many of the clients of nineteenth-century prostitutes were single men, but married men probably figured importantly as well. It is not until the twentieth century, however, that we have any systematic data on the extent of extramarital sex in this country. We are of course referring to the Kinsey studies which, while problematic with respect to the representativeness of their samples, still are, in most respects, the most comprehensive and reliable studies of American sexual behavior available to us. Kinsey found that by age 40, about 50 percent of the men in the sample, and 26 percent of the women, had had at least one experience with extramarital sex (1953:437), and Kinsey and his associates feel that these may be the most underestimated of their figures because people were likely to dissemble about this behavior. Of special interest are their figures on cohort differences:

> The accumulative incidence of extramarital coitus among the females in the sample who were born before 1900 had reached 22 per cent by forty years of age. The incidences among the females who were born in the first decade after 1900 reached 30 per cent by that same age. The later generations seem to be maintaining that level of incidence [1953:422].

Yet, they did not feel that more recent figures reflected an increase in the amount of individual experience, but rather that more women were involved in such activity. Regrettably, similar data are not available for the men in the sample.

A rather interesting sidelight to this issue is provided by the question relating to the spouses' knowledge of extramarital relations and their response to this knowledge. Of the women who had had extramarital sexual experience, 40 percent thought that their husbands were aware of it and another 9 percent believed that they suspected it. Of even greater interest is that of these 49 percent, 42 percent reported no problem as a result of their husbands' knowledge or supposed knowledge; this figure, of course, excluded the women whose husbands were unaware of their activities (1953:434).

The amount of information available on the character and meaning of these adulterous relationships is narrow and again limited to females. Of all adulterous women in the Kinsey sample, 40 percent reported having had extramarital intercourse with between two and five partners and another 40 percent with only one partner (1953:444). Forty-two percent reported being involved for one year or less and 10 percent for over ten years (1953:438). Such data really tell us little about the role such behavior played in the lives of the women involved. Was this symptomatic of sexual dissatisfaction or general marital unhappiness, or was it motivated by the feeling that monogamy is too restrictive and that one should be able to explore other relationships while remaining within what was generally seen as a satisfactory relationship? Answers to such questions are not forthcoming from the Kinsey data. However, they do have some divorced respondents' assessments of how importantly their extramarital sex contributed to their divorces.

> Some 14 per cent of the females and 18 per cent of the males believed that their extra-marital experience had been prime factors in the disruption of the marriage, and something between 21 and 25 per cent more believed that it had been a contributing factor. It is noted, however, that these were the subjects' own

> estimates of the significance and, as clinicians well know, it is not unlikely that the extra-marital experience had contributed to the divorces in more ways and to a greater extent than the subjects themselves realized [1953:435].

When we turn to the subjects' evaluation of how their spouses' extramarital sexual relations figured in their divorces we find a very interesting difference by sex. Almost twice as many men as women (51 percent versus 27 percent) felt that this was a prime factor in their divorce. This can perhaps be seen as a comment on the degree to which men and women alike have accepted the double standard both in and outside of marriage (1953:436). We might note here that a recent study found that extramarital sexual experience was indirectly associated with marital strain (Edwards and Booth, 1976). More specifically, as marital tension grew, coital frequency declined and as the latter declined the likelihood of adultery grew. Robert Bell, Stanley Turner, and Lawrence Rosen (1975) also find that low evaluation of a marriage was a factor in the adultery of a large sample of women.

Having established that adultery was by no means uncommon during the first half of this century, what can we say about change since that time? One thing seems clear; for some people, extramarital sex is moving out of the realm of deviant behavior and becoming, if not normative, certainly not the highly charged subject it once was (if nothing else, we don't see people walking around these days with scarlet letters on their clothing). Until recently professional and lay-people alike generally felt that extramarital sex represented a symptom of marital problems, if not downright failure. For example, Clifford Kirkpatrick, a noted family sociologist writing in 1955 remarked: "Doubtless married persons would be more faithful if they enjoyed more complete sex harmony in marriage" (1955:439). According to this reasoning, people look for sex outside of marriage only when marital sex leaves something to be desired. Furthermore, it assumes that people should be satisfied with one relationship.

There are also those who see adultery as symptomatic of some sort of psychological problem. Extramarital sex is seen as a way of proving something, compensating for some sort of deficiency, or getting back at a partner for a hurt, real or imagined. Christensen, for example, sees emotional immaturity as a factor in the philandering of some men, a symptom of some emotional need being unfulfilled (1958:433–434). This "evil causes evil" type of explanation, while having a certain currency during the heyday of psychoanalytic thinking in American social science, is now under attack as researchers question traditional assumptions about the ways in which certain behaviors are defined. Furthermore, as the emphasis has shifted from a value judgment of the kinds of people involved, focusing on the characteristics of specific deviants, to a concern for understanding why certain types of behavior come to be defined as deviant, there has been an attempt to consider the nonpathological aspects of extramarital sex (Becker, 1963; Erikson, 1966).

Among those who have been working in this new tradition are Gerhard Neubeck, Robert Whitehurst, and John Cuber, all of whose work is represented in Neubeck's collection, *Extra-Marital Relations* (1969), as well as Ronald Mazur (1973) and James Ramey (1975). While not necessarily advocating extramarital sex, these people feel that many of us are capable of maintaining other relationships while married, which may or may not include sex. Thus their concern is not with the legitimation of sex outside of the marital relationship per se, but rather with the expansion of the opportunity for relationships that allow personal growth and sexual expression. Why, they ask, should the sexual-emotional life of a person be restricted to one pair-bonded relationship? Moreover, they maintain that people, even after marriage, should have the opportunity to try other relationships that will not only permit them to learn more about themselves, but also provide them with satisfactions that may not be obtainable in their marriage, however satisfactory and valued this primary relationship may be. Perhaps these scholars are merely facing up to and confronting the difficulty of achieving an ideal that is so pervasive in our culture, namely, that one can find *complete* fulfillment and happiness in one monogamous relationship for the whole of one's adult life.

It is striking that such opinions can be presented in widely circulated books and not call out the fury of the guardians of American morality. However, this clearly indicates that some changes have taken place in attitudes regarding extramarital sex. While no longitudinal or follow-up studies of public opinion on this matter are available, there was one survey conducted by a national television network in 1970 on a national sample, which found that nearly 90 percent of the respondents reported that adultery was wrong for both men and women (quoted in Neubeck, 1969:29). In addition, a National Opinion Research Center study in 1974, also based on a national sample, found that 74.11 percent of the respondents said that adultery was "always wrong," 2.47 percent, "not wrong at all," and the rest fell somewhere in the middle (Singh, Walton, and Williams, 1976:706). While the blanket statements contained in both these polls would probably have many qualifications, it does give lie to the argument that there has been a complete revolution of values. Yet behind this wall of disapproval there are indications of changing attitudes. As evidence of this, only 34 percent of the adolescents in a recent national study said they would divorce their spouse if they discovered that he or she was having sexual intercourse with another person (Sorensen, 1973:359).

The statements of religious leaders are of particular interest here. William Graham Cole in his "Religious Attitudes toward Extramarital Intercourse" (in Neubeck, 1969:54–64) talks about the impact that "situational ethics" have had upon this area of behavior. Situational ethics holds that moral absolutes can be tempered by the exigencies of particular contexts. For example, Dietrich Bonhoeffer, a German minister, became involved in the plot to assassinate Hitler because he felt that traditional prescriptions against murder could not hold in the face of the greater evil represented by the German dictator. Imprisoned as a result of his activities, he proceeded to work through a system of Christian ethics with the basic principle being:

> The question of the good is posed and is decided in the midst of each definite, yet unconcluded, unique and transient situation of our lives, and in the midsts of our living relationships with men, things, institutions, and powers—in other words, in the midst of our historical experience [quoted in Cole, 1969:62].

Thus sometimes we must violate what are thought to be basic religious principles as acts of Christian conscience.

Current theologians, both Christians and Jews, have not interpreted situational ethics to mean that people now have license to go wherever their impulses may lead them.

> All of them would agree that mere erotic arousal and mutual attraction are insufficient grounds for tumbling into bed with someone other than one's marriage partner. There must be, first of all, genuine Christian love, an outgoing, sacrificial concern for the other's welfare. There must be an absence of any selfish exploitation or abuse of another person, and the act must be totally mutual, expressing in the flesh a union of two personalities [Cole, 1969:63].

Even within such confines as these, most clergymen today would hardly be willing to condone, much less advocate, the violation of marital sexual exclusivity. For example, an essay issued by an English Quaker study group in 1964 was withdrawn and a revised edition issued because it was seen as being too radical in its treatment of extramarital sex (see Mazur, 1973:5). Still, the growing interest in situational ethics indicates that conventional wisdom regarding extramarital sex is under reconsideration, if not under fire.

There are several studies available which allow us to look at current attitudes toward adultery and changes in behavior since the Kinsey study. In 1974 *Redbook* magazine carried out a study on its readership. Since this study involved readers returning questionnaires that had been enclosed in the magazine, we do not know if the respondents were even representative of the readership, much less the society at large. In 1972 the Playboy Foundation underwrote a study based on a sample of 982 men and 1,044 women that was ultimately reported by Morton Hunt. While the Playboy study used a sample that was far from perfect, it was probably more representative than the *Redbook* study. Let us look at the results of these research efforts.

The *Redbook* study, which dealt only with female respondents, suggests that there has been an increase in the incidence of extramarital sex.

> A rough comparison with Kinsey reveals a sharp change in just 21 years. Among 25-year old women, Kinsey found, 9 per cent had had extramarital intercourse; in the Redbook survey, among 20-to-24 year old wives, extramarital sex was reported by 25 per cent. Among the 40 year old women Kinsey found

> that 26 per cent had had extramarital sex; among Redbook's 35-39-year old wives—the group with the highest percentage of extramarital activity—it is 38 percent [*Redbook,* October 1975:42].

Hunt, who did the survey for the Playboy Foundation, engaged in some more sophisticated analysis. Arguing that the Kinsey study exaggerated the incidence of extramarital sex among women by lumping together women who were married at the time of their interview with those who were divorced, separated, and widowed, he introduces corrections which make the comparisons with his own data more meaningful. He finds that only among the age group under 25 had a change of any magnitude taken place. Hunt calculated that in the Kinsey study, by age 25, 8 percent of the respondents reported having had extramarital experience (the period was 1938 to 1948), but among Hunt's 18- to 24-year-old group the rate was 24 percent. A recent study (Maykovich, 1976), based on a small and poorly selected sample of American middle-class women aged 35–40, found rates of extramarital sex (32 percent) between those of the *Redbook* and Playboy studies. No really comparable changes were discovered for the males in the sample, leading Hunt to conclude:

> A generation ago, only a third as many young wives as young husbands ventured outside of marriage; today, three-quarters as many young wives as young husbands do so. The change is not a radical break with the ideal of sexual fidelity, but a radical break with the double standard [1974:263].

This may be somewhat of an overstatement in view of the magnitude of the change revealed among young married women not only in the *Redbook* study but also in a well executed Canadian study which revealed considerably higher rates of extramarital sex among younger women (Edwards and Booth, 1976). If the rates continue to grow at this magnitude, we might see a truly radical change by the end of the century, that is, some extramarital experience could become the rule rather than the exception.

Less tangible evidence of change in attitudes is found in the media. The *New York Times* published an article in its section on family, food, fashions, and furnishings entitled "Fidelity: Is it Nothing More Than an Old Fashioned Concept?" (March 26, 1973:50). A few months earlier, the *New York* magazine published an article called "Can Adultery Save Your Marriage?" (July 3, 1972:36–39), which was subsequently turned into a book (Wolfe, 1975). As early as May of 1971, the *Times* in the same section had an article dealing with extramarital sex headlined "Group Sex: Is it 'Life Art' or a Sign That Something Is Wrong?" (May 10, 1971:38). While none of the writers of these articles (and comparable ones can be found in other magazines and newspapers published in the early 1970s) ardently advocate extramarital sex, they do present the views of those who engage in such relationships or who feel they would be unwilling to enter a restrictive marriage. Listen to one 21-year-old coed:

> It's important for people to love other people. . . . If sex happens to be one way they want to communicate their love, I think that's alright . . . to me, the important thing is the freedom not to put regulations on relationships.
>
> If I were married, I wouldn't mind my husband having another relationship as long as it didn't jeopardize ours. Intellectually, I think I could handle it and I would hope he would apply the same standards to me [*New York Times,* March 26, 1973:50].

Most of the other people quoted in the *Times* article are similarly candid about their rejection of possessiveness and exclusivity, but recognize that they might have pangs of jealousy nonetheless. Interestingly enough the *Times* article on group sex ends with a series of statements by clergymen, most of whom are critical of the favorable descriptions of those involved in such activities.

> "It is a breakdown of the capacity to live within limits and frustrations," said Rabbi Greenberg, who is a teacher at Yeshiva University. "It begins to destroy the reality.
>
> "The ultimate fulfillment is to know one person totally," he added. "I admit it is difficult to do, but you cannot do it running from one to the other" [*New York Times,* May 10, 1971:38].

The rabbi's statement, like those of his Christian colleagues, neatly illustrates the differences between generations; the younger people see no value to living "within limits and frustrations," while those older see something to be gained from the self-discipline of restraint.

In many ways the *New York* magazine article is the most interesting of the three, since it discusses adultery as a way of "saving" a marriage. The author, Linda Wolfe, readily admits that the women whom she knows and upon whose experiences she based the article are not the typical "Mrs. American Homemaker." They are New Yorkers, middle class, college educated, and in their thirties (some work, some do not). "The only trait they seem to share is energy, lots of it, the one thing all adulterous mothers have in common" (1972:36). While the major portion of the article describes how various friends of Ms. Wolfe's have worked out arrangements whereby they are able to have an affair without their husband catching on, for us the important point is her interpretation of the growth of this phenomenon. Polemicizing with the sociologist, Cynthia Epstein, Ms. Wolfe asserts that the increase in female extramarital relations does not reflect the fact that women have more economic resources at their disposal and therefore fear the consequences of being found out less.

> I don't agree. Whatever the various reasons for starting an affair, the one I heard most frequently expressed for maintaining one . . . was: "It's the only way to keep my marriage together." One woman, boasting how well she was coping, actually said to me, "I'm doing things absolutely right. I've found someone who couldn't threaten or even rock my marriage, a lover I couldn't possibly fall in love with" [1972:39].

To be sure the women Wolfe describes have not opened up their marriages to the extent that they and their husbands have agreed to allow themselves freedom to explore other relationships; these affairs still smack very much of old-fashioned "cheating"; nonetheless, there is the essential recognition here of the limited satisfaction that monogamy provides and that "adultery" may be one way of having one's proverbial cake and eating it.

In 1971, Gordon Clanton wrote an article in which he attempted to set forth a typology of contemporary adultery. His typology is not based on the nature of the acts involved, but rather on the attitudes toward adultery manifested by those engaged in it.

> I. CLANDESTINE ADULTERY. Old-style adultery. The spouse does not know about the extramarital relationship and would disapprove if he/she knew.
>
> II. ADAPTATIONAL ADULTERY. The spouse knows about the extramarital relationship and may even be willing to tolerate it *but* he/she does not approve.
>
> III. CONSENSUAL ADULTERY: The spouse knows and approves of the extramarital relationship. [1971:7].

According to Clanton, there are four types of consensual adultery. He defines them as follows:

> 1. *Group marriage.* An agreement which links three or more adults in a common projection of a future together, a future marked by special propinquity, emotional interdependence, economic sharing, and sexual access to persons in addition to one's spouse or prime lover.
> 2. *Open-ended marriage.* A relationship between marriage partners in which each grants the other the freedom to involve himself/herself in important emotional relationships with others—even relationships marked by sexual sharing.
> 3. *Swinging.* Recreational extramarital sexual experiences marked by a relatively low level of commitment and the expectation of relative impermanence.
> 4. *Promiscuity.* Each party to the marriage grants the others freedom to engage in sexual experiences with other persons toward whom there is little or no feeling of commitment and little or no expectation of permanence [1971:7].

This typology provides us with a useful starting point for exploring change in attitudes toward the meaning of marriage within our culture. However, we will look at the various kinds of consensual adultery listed by Clanton in reverse order, since in this way we will see the most dramatic kinds of change last. What Clanton speaks of as "promiscuity" is sometimes difficult to separate from "open-ended" marriage, since the distinction is not hard and fast. For example, John and Mimi Lobel's *John and Mimi: A Free Marriage* (1972) describes a situation in which a young couple has agreed to allow each other freedom to explore sexual relationships outside of their own marital relationship. Some of these relationships appear to be most casual, but others involve emotional as well as sexual commitments. Of course, there are relationships which seem to fall more clearly into the category of "promiscuity." We find them described in books such as Morton Hunt's *The Affair* (1969) or John Cuber and Peggy Harroff's *Sex and the Significant Americans* (1966), but the problem for us is not so much to distinguish between open marriages and promiscuity but rather to distinguish between "consensual" and "adaptational" adultery.

SWINGING

For the family sociologist, one of the most interesting developments in American society after World War II is the emergence of mate swapping, or as it is usually referred to, swinging. But this behavior did not spring full grown onto the American scene, like Athena from the head of Zeus. In fact, there is evidence of "party behavior" in the 1938 edition of Willard Waller's text, *The Family.*

> In the early years of the twenties a group of married people in Elizabeth Heights, a residential suburb, began to engage in their famous "Elizabeth Heights parties." The married couples of the group were all of the upper middle class . . . all . . . owned their own homes or were buying them. All had young children. At the time when the parties began, all had been married long enough to begin to tire of the sexual monotony and the routine of family life. Somehow there arose an increasing intimacy in the group which culminated in trading wives and husbands for the purposes of the party. . . . The party always began with a few rounds of drinks. Then one of the men took one of the women out of the group for a necking party. The woman always responded vigorously to his advances. Another man took one of the other women; pretty soon all began dancing, drinking, petting, telling stories, and making love, pausing once in a while to exchange partners. . . . There were certain unspoken rules. No husband should show the slightest jealousy. . . . The petting itself was limited to what college students would probably call "light necking"; there were distinct limits beyond which it could not go [1938:444–445].

So it began. It was not until the 1960s, however, that such behavior made another appearance, either in the mass media or in the professional literature, but this time the behavior moved from "light petting" to sexual intercourse. Everett Myers, editor of *Mr.* magazine (a "man's magazine") claims that an article he published in 1957 initiated the whole swinger movement. Other magazines soon followed with articles of their own, and *Mr.* launched a regular feature column of letters from readers describing their mate-swapping activities.

At about the same time, ads from couples seeking other couples to swing with began to appear in weekly tabloids. Many were designed simply to titillate readers and others were downright fraudulent. Nonetheless, among the phony ads were serious solicitations, and not long afterward the economic potential of such publications became evident. One of the first publications restricted to ads from swingers was *La Plume,* established in 1955 and claimed by its editor to be the "daddy of them all," which if true suggests that by 1955 swinger networks were already beginning to form.

Through the 1960s such publications bloomed, particularly in the latter part of the decade when there were about forty in existence. At present only a few remain—suggesting not so much that swinging has declined, but rather that in certain circles it has been so widely accepted as to enable people to rely on personal networks rather than magazines. Many of the swingers' bars that came into existence during the late 1960s have met a similar fate.

Duane Denfeld and Michael Gordon (1970) have pointed out that the emergence of the swinging phenomenon was especially significant because of the kinds of people who were initially involved and the motives they revealed for entering into it. However, before we go on to discuss these, some elaboration and description of swinging behavior is in order.

Swinging means that couples engage in extramarital sex with each other's foreknowledge and approval. This differs from what is generally thought of as adultery in that extramarital coitus takes place not only with the consent of one's wife or husband, but also may take place within their view or in the same house or apartment. Typically, a pair of couples may get together for an evening in one or the other's home and after pleasantries are exchanged, some drinks consumed, and other elemental courtesies observed, they exchange mates. The couples may go off to separate bedrooms to engage in sex or use the same room, either for group sex or some voyeuristic activity, that is, one couple watches while another couple indulges. The importance of the presence of one's mate is that it serves to keep jealousy under control, for not only does one have direct knowledge of one's mate's extramarital sexual activity, but it takes place in a setting that reduces the possibility to a minimum of the act leading to a relationship which may pose a threat to the marriage. People may turn to swinging as a way of engaging in extramarital sex without endangering their marriage; thus this is an example of deviance as a "safety valve"—functioning in much the same way that Kingsley Davis (1937) felt prostitution functioned for men. Herein lies the significance of swinging as a form of institutionalized extramarital sex for both men and women. It is not irrelevant to point out here that there is some evidence to suggest that the number of brothels has declined (Winick and Kinsie, 1971) and since one of the prostitute's primary customers has traditionally been the married man, this is possibly an indication both of more marital sexual satisfaction and alternative avenues for extramarital sexual expression—one of which may be swinging.

Probably a very small minority of married couples have direct experience with this phenomenon. Hunt's (1974) study puts it at roughly 2 percent; yet, as we pointed out earlier, its significance resides not so much in numbers as in what this means, if only incipiently, for conceptions of marital rights and prerogatives. Swingers, by extending the carefully guarded male privilege of extramarital sex to women, are symbolizing the strides that have been made in freeing women from the traditional strictures on their behavior. It is true that reports indicate that swinging is not without its sexism, and women appear to a much greater extent than men to be pressured into swinging, but the degree to which this reflects residues of feminine socialization is open to question (Henshel, 1973).

On the face of it, swinging appears to be a rather narrow and limited form of consensual adultery, involving as it does relationships limited largely to sexual encounter with little if any emphasis placed upon the nonsexual aspects of the relationship. A number of researchers in this area have, however, questioned this view of swinging, most notably Carol Symonds (1968), Charles and Rebecca Palson (1972) and James Ramey (1972). Symonds has distinguished between "recreational" and "utopian" swingers. The recreational swingers are those who do not see swinging as a vehicle for building more enduring relationships which allow the transcendence of exclusive monogamous relationships. They resemble those we have discussed earlier who are essentially satisfied with monogamy apart from its sexual restrictiveness. Swinging here provides relief from the sexual monotony they find frustrating without endangering the marriage they generally find satisfying. Most studies have seemed to concentrate on recreational swingers and perhaps the reason for this is provided by the Palsons:

> We had no difficulty finding couples who either wanted to have or had succeeded in having some degree of emotional involvement and long-term friendship within a swinging context. In fact, many of them explained to us that depersonalization simply brought them no satisfaction. In observing such couples with their friends it was evident that they had formed close and enduring relationships. . . . It should be noted that there is no way of ascertaining the number of couples who have actually succeeded in finding close friends through swinging. In fact, they may be underrepresented because they tend to retreat into their own small circle of friends and dislike using swinger magazines to find other couples. Thus they are more difficult to contact [1972:30].

Their point is well taken, and makes sense out of the emphasis on recreational swinging which has been so characteristic of the research literature to date. Swinging, like most social phenomena, defies easy categorization and we must be careful not to readily overlook the diversity that exists here.

Ramey (1972) offers a novel interpretation of the relationship between recreational and utopian swinging. He begins by pointing out that Symonds's categories are hardly mutually exclusive and that some so-called utopian swingers show characteristics of recreational swingers and vice versa.

> We believe Symonds may have failed to differentiate between those beginners who constitute the extremist fringe at the lower end of the spectrum and those swingers who are in the academic, professional and managerial strata and tend to exhibit more the attributes of her utopians than of her recreationals. . . . Also there is the possibility that she failed to distinguish between this latter group and the beginners who are still overwhelmed with the idea of swinging, and even more overwhelmed with relating to people on a more complex level. . . . This could be especially important in California [Symonds's research site] where knowledge of swinging has permeated many layers of society that are not usually involved in complex pair-bond relationships [1972:17–18].

What Ramey is suggesting is that for some, swinging becomes a step on the path from monogamy to either open-ended or group marriage. He actually prefers the term "intimate friendship" to characterize relationships in which friendships between couples also include sex (1975). For some, swinging represents a continued way of life, for others an interlude from which they return to monogamy. But the group that goes on to truly alter their relationships is the most interesting to the sociologist because such people really represent the most significant departure from monogamous marriage.

For those who move from swinging to other more radical kinds of relationships, the two most common paths are those of open-ended marriage and group marriage. Since both of these represent important developments we shall discuss them separately.

OPEN MARRIAGE

"Open-ended" or "open" marriage is something social scientists know relatively little about, since it is only now beginning to become an object of systematic study (Knapp, 1974; Ramey, 1975, 1976; Clanton and Downing, 1975). However, we can sketch some picture of the nature of such relationships by drawing upon the case studies that have been presented in various books which in one way or another touch upon the topic of open marriage. It is difficult, if not impossible, to establish how many couples have been able to reach a point in their relationship where both partners are able to independently explore relationships outside of their marriage that are more than simple sexual encounters. There are such couples, but they are probably a small minority. Why?

Most of us have been raised to expect our marriages, when and if we do marry, to be exclusive relationships; we have had feelings of possessiveness instilled in us that make it difficult to accept someone we love becoming involved with another person (Mazur, 1973). Hence, while we might be able to tolerate our partner having casual sexual encounters, a more serious involvement may threaten our own sense of self, evoking feelings of inadequacy and even personal failure. There is also the issue of time and energy. Relations that move beyond the stage of casual encounter to the stage of profound emotional involvement do make certain demands upon us. The movie, "A Touch of Class" with Glenda Jackson and George Segal (1973), amusingly illustrates the difficulties encountered by a married man (admittedly not in an open marriage) trying to keep his marriage intact at the same time that he is deeply involved in an affair. The various ruses he employs and the amount of energy he expends become the source of much of the movie's humor, but from our point of view, they neatly illustrate the problems of trying to keep two relationships going and still having time left over to pursue a demanding career. While some may see this as a crass example that looks at relationships in terms of temporal economics rather than in terms of emotions, the point still remains, and cannot be overlooked.

Problems of time, in concert with problems of jealousy and possessiveness, create a situation which at present makes open-ended marriage more of an ideal to which couples can aspire than a reality; nonetheless, associated with open-ended marriage are other changes in the marriage relationship. The O'Neills in their *Open Marriage* (1972) and Rogers in his *Becoming Partners* (1972) devote considerably more space to the primary marriage itself than they do to the relationships outside of marriage, despite the fact that they consider the latter no small part of the changes they are concerned with. Mazur (1973) speaks of a "vibrant monogamy" that permits, but does not necessarily require, outside relationships.

The key to all discussions of altered marriage relationships seems to be the movement away from the sex-role stereotyping that characterizes so many marriage relationships—where the husband works and tends to the masculine side of homemaking (home repairs, the car, etc.), and the wife to the feminine chores (cooking, cleaning, and childcare). The O'Neills speak of "role flexibility" (1972: chapters 10 and 11), Rogers refers to "the dissolution of roles" (1972:205–10), Jessie Bernard to "the shared-role pattern" (1972), and Joy and Howard Osofsky to "androgyny" (1972). Each of them advocates moving away from rigid sex roles. Their motives are not only to eradicate the sexist stereotyping that has kept women in their place and thus remove an obvious injustice, but also to break down the rigidity in the allocation of work and domestic tasks that inhibits individual growth, freedom, and options. Listen to the O'Neills:

> The categorization of "masculinity" and "femininity" is needlessly arbitrary and restrictive in a psychological as well as a purely practical sense. Just as men and women are capable of doing one another's tasks, so they could benefit enormously if they shared and openly displayed the admirable qualities that each sex is supposed to have separately. Fortunately, the process is already underway. Our young are refusing to be herded into rigid categories, and are accepting a broader emotional definition of masculinity and femininity [1973:146].

The O'Neills are not simply saying that women should feel free to work outside the home and men should feel free to do diapers, but also that women should not look upon assertiveness as unfeminine and men should not look upon crying as unmasculine. They are questioning the very essence of these stereotypes.

The reader might do well to recall our earlier discussion of dual-professional families and how conventional the vast majority of those studied were when it came to such matters as childcare and housekeeping. Even those women who had achieved a great deal in the professional world found it very difficult to reallocate the work load in their homes so that they were not thrust into the position of being superwomen who carried the responsibilities and burdens of both a job and a home. One explanation for this difficulty may be that many of the couples were over forty, and thus they had gone through the major portion of their marriages free from the pressures created by the ideology of the Women's Liberation movement. In addition, they had probably not experienced the sort of socialization (see Chapter 6) that is supportive of flexibility. Younger people seem to find it less difficult to move away from conventional sex-role definitions. If nothing else, the messages they are getting are different. Men are no longer teased or chided for cleaning, cooking, and taking care of the children; in fact, in some circles expertise in these areas is greeted with respect, even if the respect is more mute than vocal. Thus changes have occurred which bode well for the future of this kind of open marriage, with or without extramarital relations.

Another aspect of open marriage is the attempt to move away from what the O'Neills call "the couples game," or the feeling that everything must be experienced and done as a couple, and that activities done as an individual, other than work, somehow compromise the marriage. Clearly, this aspect of open marriage is an attack on the whole notion of the wife or husband as companion that held sway in the 1950s. For the O'Neills this can involve having relationships with other people that may or may not lead to sex, but for the moment let us simply consider the idea that married people should be free to have a life independent from their spouses.

This notion is hardly revolutionary; men have traditionally gone fishing and to ballgames with their friends, and women have played tennis and bridge with their friends. But such activity has often involved some element of guilt because of the sense that the time really should have been spent with one's spouse. The O'Neills argue that not only is this guilt unnecessary, but also that having a separate existence *is* necessary, since no one can be or should be all things to his or her mate; both members of a pair benefit from being able to do some things with other people. Of course, the trick is to strike the right balance of being together and being with others—a formula for continued personal growth and development.

GROUP MARRIAGE—ON THE FRONTIERS

There are some adventurous souls who choose more dramatic alternatives than open-ended marriage, who opt for relationships that are more encompassing than monogamy with the possibility of outside affairs (Ramey, 1975). For those who see group marriage as a viable option, the goal seems to be the expansion of the conjugal relationship to include several people who see themselves as married not to one woman or man, but rather to all of those members of the opposite sex that make up their group marriage. Group marriages should not be confused with communes.

> The individual in a community either makes no commitment or commits himself to the community, its purpose, or its philosophy. Marriage is a fairly long-term commitment to other *individuals* [Constantine and Constantine, 1972:211].

In other words, people enter group marriages because they want to have certain relationships with *specific* people, while people enter communes more often because they are committed to certain aspects of the commune's structure or ideology. To be sure, people are a factor in entering a commune as well, but not to as great an extent as in group marriage.

Almost all we know of a systematic nature about group marriage is a result of the work of Larry and Joan Constantine (1971, 1972, 1973). Since 1969 the Constantines have been involved in a study of what they speak of as "multilateral relations," what we have called group marriage (see also Houriet, 1971; and Clanton and Downing, 1975). They were able to identify 101 such marriages, but because many (60) had dissolved before contact could be made, and because others posed different problems, they wound up studying 26 marriages, 11 of them in depth (1973). Most relationships involved 4 people, with triads following in popularity; no group had more than 6 people (1973). The age range of those involved was 23–59 and the median age was 31 at the time they entered the group marriage (1973). The vast majority had been to college, and the sample was generally middle class.

In view of what we said earlier of the possible progression for some people from swinging to group marriage, it is worth noting that half of the Constantines' sample had had experience with swinging prior to entering a group marriage, though most of them felt that it was not a good way to move toward a multilateral marriage, since most swingers are mainly interested in casual encounters (Constantine and Constantine, 1971:208).

When the respondents were asked by the Constantines to set forth their motives for entering a group marriage, they appeared to play down the desire for sexual variety.

> The marked deemphasis of sex is probably a reasonably protective mechanism . . . considering the horror often unleashed by talk of open multiperson sexual involvement as an integral part of a family structure. The disparity between the public level disclosures of motivation and what soon became accessible to us as researchers and confidants suggested a multilevel structure of motivation for entry. At the private level personal growth opportunities emerge as the most important. While sexual interest is acknowledged at the private level, it could hardly be said to be emphasized [1971:210].

As with other aspects of human behavior, motivation is complex, though in the case of those involved in group marriage it does appear that current emphasis in intellectual circles on personal growth and fulfillment, and rejection of conventional institutional structures, does play a role.

Once having entered into such a relationship, how do these people fare and what adjustments do they make? The Constantines tell us that the models of group marriage that the participants bring with them from their reading of Robert Rimmer and Robert Heinlein often do not prepare them for the realities they encounter (1972:206). Problems range from simple things, such as deciding which brand of toothpaste to purchase, to much more complicated matters, such as how and by whom children will be disciplined and what system will be employed to rotate sleeping arrangements. Some group marriages arrive at solutions to these and endure, others fail to tackle them and quickly flounder. Almost half the groups they studied survived the first year (49 percent) and 7 percent had been in existence for 5 years or more at the time of the study.

Yet one should not judge these experiments by how long they endure. If a group marriage only lasts one year, the lives involved may be profoundly changed as a result of the experience. Even if a couple returns to a more or less monogamous relationship, they may do so with new insights and new self-awareness, with the result being that the relationship is very different from what it was before they entered group marriage.

One might expect that jealousy would be a big problem for those involved in group marriages, especially for couples who enter such a relationship after having been monogamously married for some time. While jealousy was mentioned as a problem by 80 percent of the Constantines' respondents, among the more long-lived of the groups none listed it as a major problem; more than half of those in the newer groups did (1971:216). Also, older respondents, those over thirty, were less likely to report jealousy as a problem than those under thirty. The Constantines, while realizing that such results are interpretable in a number of ways, suggest that they may indicate that jealousy is something people in group marriages "do learn with time to cope with . . . or even overcome it altogether" (1971:217).

Perhaps the most interesting aspect of life within group marriages revolves around the issue of cohesion. In principle a group marriage is a multiperson relationship in which the individuals involved love all members equally; moreover, the group should be seen as the locus of their emotional and sexual involvement. In reality, however, it was found that members of group marriages have both extramarital relationships and particular pair-bond preferences within the group, without creating problems. While the role of extra-group sexual relations in group cohesion is hardly clear, specific pair primacy does emerge as a factor in group cohesion.

> We are beginning to find support for the view that a prior dyadic relationship which is not only sound but has clear-cut precedence over other relationships is a prerequisite for "successful" participation in a multilateral marriage. Such a prior marriage would constitute a truly *primary* bond. By all indications, some form of primary bond with the prior spouse holds for nearly every couple among respondents [1971:221].

In part, the reason for their success is probably that couples with established relationships have had experience with the fundamentals of day-to-day problem solving and generalize this experience to the group setting.

One important element in explaining why some groups endure and others do not is the simple issue of compatibility. Once the bloom of romantic love fades from a hasty marriage, boredom and conflict often set in. The same may be the case for group marriages. Robert Houriet, in his book *Getting Back Together,* insightfully comments on why the one group marriage he studied did not survive.

> Harrad West had failed, not for lack of sexual allure [the reason Robert Rimmer offers him in an interview as an explanation] or sexual jealousy, but because they had nothing but sex to hold them together—no common culture, no nonsexual forms of communicating and expressing love [1971:276].

Most people entering monogamy have a period during which they have gotten to know one another; most group marriage members first get to know one another after they are sharing the same roof. This is not meant as a criticism of group marriage, but rather as a comment on one of the problems they face.

Given such problems, it makes sense that the Constantines have advocated a trial period during which each primary couple (assuming for argument's sake that it will be a two-couple marriage) live for two weeks with their new partner of the opposite sex and follow this with a couple of weeks with their future partner of the same sex, with periods of evaluation following each episode. Only then should a decision be made as to whether or not to commit themselves to a trial period of six months or a year, and in this way hopefully avoid some of the problems that arise from couples hastily flinging themselves together.

Understandably, a great deal of attention has focused on the sexual aspects of group marriage, if only because this aspect of multilateral relationships touches a note of interest even among those who are far from the fringes of the counterculture. Which of us, male and female alike, has not thought at one time or another of what it would be like to be involved in a relationship that offered a variety of sexual partners? But like many daydreams, the realities of working out the mechanics of such an arrangement can be difficult. Since many of those involved in group marriages are programmatically committed to psychological growth and development in the Maslow-Perls tradition, they place a certain value on doing things in a spontaneous and noncontrived manner; however, it is often difficult to have everyone's spontaneous choice for a particular evening's sleeping arrangements mesh, and thus most group marriages seem, at least initially, to move toward some sort of scheduling arrangements whereby each pair spends a certain number of nights together each week. One should realize that those involved in group marriages, like those involved in dyadic arrangements, do not have coitus every night they sleep together; here too, various rhythms and patterns develop between couples. By way of a final comment on the sexual side of multilateral marriage, it should be noted that group sex is something most have shied away from.

Some readers may be wondering about how children fare in such relationships. Since many of the groups which the Constantines studied did have children, this is hardly a peripheral aspect of group family life. The ideal of most groups, and here they are not unlike communes, is that children, irrespective of biological parentage, should be viewed as children of the group. As it happens, the children seem better at adapting to such a relationship than their parents, despite the children's continued recognition of who their "real" parents are.

> In watching groups form, we find it takes very little for children of any age to adjust and to accept new adults in parental roles, even if differentiated from those of their actual parents. Indeed, we have been impressed by the manner in which children have responded to an expanded family situation. The effects include behavioral manifestations such as increased self-confidence and, in one case, improved performance in school [Constantine and Constantine, 1972:218–219].

With regard to the disciplining of children, the Constantines report that biological parents are generally deferred to, often resulting in a situation where the children of two different primary couples are subject to different behavioral expectations, with friction resulting. By the same token, it is worth noting that at least one group studied by the Constantines tried to overcome the issue of biological paternity by having both males in the group engage in intercourse with the woman during her fertile period (1972:219).

Like many experiments, group marriages are clearly fraught with pitfalls and problems, but at the same time they also offer an extraordinary opportunity for experimentation with new roles and relationships. The fact that these experiments are generally short lived should not be seen as clear evidence of their untenability, but rather we can see this reflecting the same sort of emotional limitations that make open marriage a problem. Most of us just do not have the emotional repertoires necessary for the kinds of demands such complex relationships make; moreover (and again this was mentioned with regard to open-ended marriage), some of us just don't have the time. It is not without significance that two of the men in the group marriage that Houriet visited found it necessary, or at least desirable, to change jobs after moving into the group marriage.

> Herb got home at about nine. He worked as a messenger for a data processing plant and spent most of his working hours driving a Volkswagen around the Bay area. Though he has a master's in social work, Herb found that, like Bud [who gave up his job as manager of a photographic laboratory to develop a free-lance art business and work as an entertainer at children's parties] he lacked the emotional stamina for both the group marriage and a demanding profession. "I need a job that will charge up my batteries." Energies that might have gone into a profession Herb devotes to the marriage, which he views as a "showcase and model of a sexually liberated community" [Houriet, 1971:250].

But even for those who ultimately find that life in the group marriage is not for them—either because of incompatibility with the people or because of the problems it evoked—it is still probably true that the experience of having lived in a group marriage leaves them different people, whose experiences may very well benefit their future relationships.

OTHER DIRECTIONS OF CHANGE

We have so far been considering alternative relationships with a particular emphasis on those that make marriage a more permeable structure. We will now consider some other changes that give evidence of a movement away from sex-role stereotyping.

One-Parent Adoption

Most of us assume that parenthood is something which should and does take place within the context of a legally sanctified union. Yet lately a new form of parenthood has emerged where a single person adopts a child, often with no future plans of getting married. Like many such seemingly innovative developments, this practice may be rooted as much in change of administrative policy as in attitude change on the part of those who are adopting. Certainly it is easy to see that for many years single people may have wanted to adopt children, but both because of the pressures of others ("It really isn't done" or "A child should have *two* parents") and legal obstacles (it is hard enough for a couple to adopt a child) they have refrained.

Oddly enough, we have seen single-parent adoptions emerge at a time when the general adoption picture is, in certain respects, tighter than ever. The "tight market" in adoption is explained by the decline in the

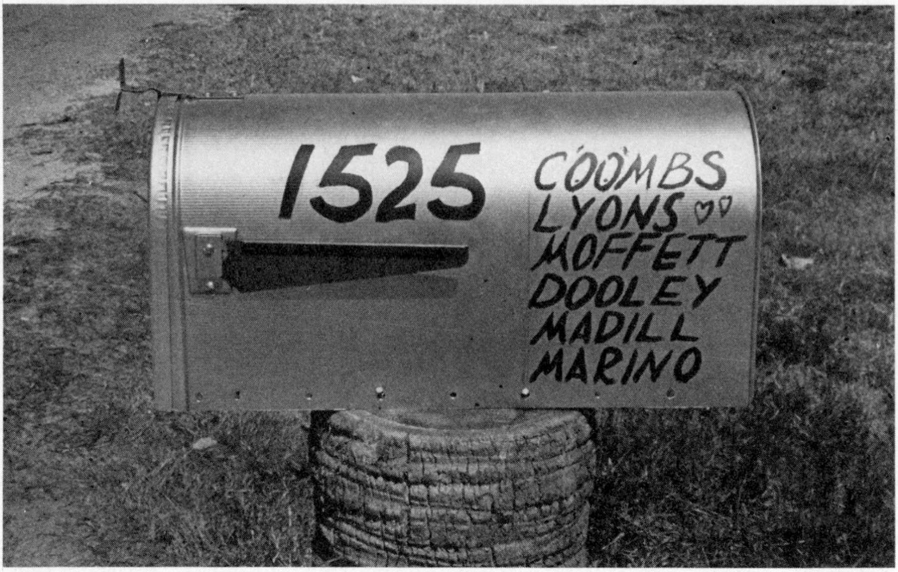

Singles living together. *(Chris Reeberg/DPI)*

number of healthy white babies available, as new and better contraceptive and abortion methods have become increasingly accessible to a broader segment of the population, not to mention more liberal attitudes toward unwed motherhood. Thus the children who remain available for adoption tend to represent "problem" placements in one respect or another: they are either too old (since most people prefer infants), have an emotional or physical problem, or are members of racial minorities. Even though adoption agencies no longer try to carefully match parents and adopted children in terms of everything from appearance to religion, a shortage exists which has resulted in the growth of illegal or semilegal adoptions (*New York Times,* February 20, 1973:1, 40). It is the children who are difficult to place who have become the source for one-parent adoptions. Since the law does not prohibit a single person from adopting a child, adoption agencies are now in a position to allow children who previously would have spent their lives bouncing between foster homes and institutions to be adopted by single people who feel that being unmarried is not incompatible with motherhood or fatherhood. (At present men face more problems than women in trying to adopt a child, and to the best of our knowledge the overwhelming majority of single-person adopters have been women.) The single people who adopt children have been described in the following manner:

> Generally, the single parent is female, in her late thirties, has several brothers and sisters, and is a professional earning at least $12,000 a year. She adopts not out of loneliness but, as a male professor said "out of a sense of fullness," a desire

to love. She sometimes rejects male suitors who feel put out that she chose a child rather than them [*New York Times,* March 28, 1973:42].

Once the child is adopted, such women and men do have problems which couples do not. Their children go through life without having a father or mother, and their parent does not have the partner with whom to share the emotional and physical burdens of childrearing. In many ways, the situation faced by single-parent adopters is not all that different from that encountered by widowed or divorced parents.

There are other examples of changes within marriage that are easily discerned by the astute observer. Some professional couples decide to live in separate cities and spend occasional weekends together so as to be able to pursue their own careers (*Time,* July 9, 1973). There are homosexual couples who have "come out of the closet" and who openly live together in cohabitative relationships, no longer attempting to cover up with the "roommate" story (Weinberg and Williams, 1974). Similar developments are occurring among the elderly in retirement communities, who for reasons of pensions and other benefits, choose not to enter into legal marriages, but instead simply live with a person of the opposite sex, often despite serious protestation and intervention on the part of their children. Other variations exist as well (Kassel, 1966; McKain, 1969).

The meaning of such change is something we have tried to analyze throughout the book, both generally and specifically, as we have looked at change in the preindustrial, industrial, and postindustrial marriage and family. From the perspective of change in the postindustrial family, which has been the subject of this chapter, it should be apparent that what we have seen is an increasing openness to alternatives which remain basically rooted in the nuclear family. Still, the family is different from what it was at the beginning of the century, much less before this country underwent industrialization. This difference is not simply manifested in the fact that adults have more options open to them in forming relationships of various kinds. Children are increasingly being socialized by external agencies; women are more likely to work through their childbearing period; widows and widowers are more likely to live alone, and so on. For some, such changes are a threat to the integrity of the family, if not a fatal blow. But for many sociologists, the author included, all of these changes represent a further adaptation of the family to postindustrial society. To be sure, family life will continue to change, but there is little evidence of dramatic revolutionary alteration in this structure in the foreseeable future.

SUMMARY

In this chapter we have looked at some of the ways in which marriage has changed in the twentieth century. The main point has been that marriage has become a more permeable institution, one into which people can enter relatively free of the familial considerations that weighed so heavily on them in the past, and one from which people can depart relatively free from the social stigma and financial burdens of the past. More importantly, while in marriage, couples are experiencing less rigid sex-role stereotyping and greater freedom to pursue outside interests and relationships. To be sure, many of these developments are still incipient, but all indicators suggest that they will continue to develop further.

While we have argued that the freedom to have relationships, sexual and otherwise, with persons other than one's spouse is only a part of what people have described as open or open-ended marriage, it is one area where empirical data are available, at least for the twentieth century. Comparing the findings of the Kinsey studies with those of several studies carried out in the 1970s, we see that the incidence of extramarital sex has risen dramatically among young married people, so much so that if current trends continue, complete fidelity over the course of marriage will be the exception rather than the rule. Still, it is difficult to interpret these data because they do not tell us much about the quality of the experience —an isolated encounter at a convention hotel is not comparable to an intense affair of several years' duration. Such problems notwithstanding, Ramey's (1975) research among married people engaged in "intimate friendships" suggests that many such relationships currently are not brief encounters, but rather are based on friendships as well as sexual interest.

Group marriage represents an extreme, though hardly fanatical, extension of the ideas that lead some people to explore the casual sexual exchange of spouses and other "intimate friendships." The Constantines' research indicates that while such marriages seldom endure for any great length of time, people leave them with a new appreciation of the possibilities of human relationships and find their lives altered as a result of the experience. While there is little reason to expect such relationships to become the wave of the future, they are, nonetheless, a significant social experiment that warrants careful study by students of the family.

Finally, we briefly touched upon some other developments indicative of the new freedom and flexibility that surrounds marriage, among them one-parent adoption, dual-career separate-residence marriages, and gay marriage. While none of these has any great statistical significance in itself, still these developments are important as evidence of the kinds of changes that have occurred within and around marriage in the twentieth century.

A nineteenth-century satiric drawing depicting then popular misconceptions of the nature of complex marriage in the Oneida community. *(Library of Congress)*

CELIBATES AND FREELOVERS: Marriage and Family in the Commune

10

It is a thesis of this book that while the American family is changing and has changed, there is little reason to believe that we will soon see any dramatic shift away from the nuclear family as the most common household unit, or any decrease in monogamy as the most common form of permanent relationship. This is not to deny that there has been a growing interest in and experimentation with alternative family forms. Just because the basic structure of most people's households and marriages may not undergo change in the foreseeable future does not mean that they will remain untouched by the ideas of those who have rejected conventional forms and sought alternatives—whether in the commune, group marriage, or some other alternative form. In this chapter we will look at the communal family and consider its forms, history, structure, and the broader implications of communal living generally.

Before we look at the commune itself we might do well to consider the factors that have caused some people in our society to reject the family forms they were raised in, or even lived in as adults, and to seek a different experience. A number of distinct but interrelated themes can be discerned in the motivation to live communally, but above all else, the one theme that echoes and re-echoes throughout the literature on communal family forms is the search for "self-actualization" or psychological growth.

THE SOURCES OF THE SEARCH FOR COMMUNITY

While the term "self-actualization" is associated with the name of the psychologist Abraham Maslow (1962), its origins can be found earlier in the century in the writings of people such as Carl Jung, Kurt Goldstein, and Karen Horney. While the term used by these people may have been different—Jung, for example, spoke of self-realization—the basic idea was the same: the realization of a person's capacities for living, loving, thinking, feeling, and so on. The above psychologists were not concerned with mental health in the conventional sense of the term, that is, freedom from psychopathology, whether in the form referred to as psychosis or in the less serious form known as neurosis. Behind most notions of self-actualization is the attempt to overcome the basic life- and love-negating features of our society, the conditions that do not necessarily produce clinical symptoms but which nonetheless take their toll of people's lives.

A good example of the more recent expression of this thread in psychological and psychiatric thinking is to be found in the work of David Cooper, an associate of R. D. Laing, the famous and iconoclastic English psychotherapist and author. Cooper in his *The Death of the Family* (1970) has looked at aspects of family life that he feels are both love- and life-negating. For him one of the great victims of the nuclear family is the child.

> There are numerous taboos in the family system that reach much further than the incest taboo and the taboo against greed and messiness. One of these taboos is the implicit prohibition against experiencing one's aloneness in the world. There seem to be very few mothers indeed who can keep their hands off their child long enough to allow the capacity to be alone to develop [1970:13].

Cooper sees being alone at the heart of human autonomy; without learning this basic lesson of human existence one confronts the possibility of madness.

The child is not the only person to be denied the lesson of his or her aloneness. There is also a broader issue which Cooper sees as having significance for young and old alike, and which he refers to as "the illusion of the quantifiability of love."

> One has (one is led to believe and then further leads oneself to believe) only so much love to offer. If one gives almost all one's love to one other person, one has proportionately very little to parcel out to others. If one operates with this naive algebra, a corollary must be that any act of loving is experienced as a loss of a certain inner quality of love [1970:52–53].

For adults this means that their capacities to love should be exhausted in a two-person monogamous marriage, for children (though Cooper does not deal with them here), we assume it means being limited to one's biological parents for emotional support and love. According to Cooper the commune is a place where much of the oppression associated with the nuclear family can be overcome.

> A commune is a microsocial structure that achieves a viable dialect between solitude and being-with-others; it implies either a common residence for mem-

> bers, or at least a common work and experience area, around which residential situations may be spread out peripherally; it means that love relationships become diffused between members of the commune network far more than is the case with the family system, and this means, of course, that sexual relationships are not restricted to some socially approved two person, man-woman arrangement; above all, because this strikes most centrally at repression, it means that children should have totally free access to adults beyond their biological parental couple. These definitional elements point to an ideological *prise de position* that one may state thus: *making love is good in itself, and the more it happens in any way possible or conceivable between as many people as possible, the better* [1970:44–45].

Not all advocates of self-actualization express this kind of critique of the nuclear family, nor this kind of praise of the commune, but in one form or another they have all come out against the nuclear family. Their major theme is—life as we know it in the intensity of the nuclear family has cut us off from ourselves and others.

Many sociologists have also echoed this theme in critiques of the nuclear family, perhaps none more eloquently than Richard Sennett (1970a) and Philip Slater (1970). Sennett's focus is somewhat different from Slater's, echoing the themes of Philippe Ariès (1962). For Sennett, as for Ariès, the modern family is in retreat from society, and while Ariès compares the medieval and modern worlds to make his point about the current importance and isolation of the family, Sennett looks at comparisons between life among immigrant groups in this country at the turn of the century and their upwardly mobile grandchildren and children who populate today's suburbias. He sees the lives led by immigrants in the ghettos of our large cities as indeed being hard, with poverty, disease, and crowding all too familiar. But still he feels that their existence had a certain civility and urbanity that the lives of their more affluent children and grandchildren lack. The older generation came into contact with people whose backgrounds were different from their own. The very nature of their lives precluded the insulation that characterizes current suburban living. Children were more apt to find their entertainment on the street instead of in front of the television set, for their parents' stoops and sidewalks provided a place where they could relax and talk to friends. The basic point Sennett makes is a simple one, whether we agree with it or not; he holds that living in suburbia means that one can go from day to day with minimal contact with people different from oneself, and that the family has become an entity unto itself, as the house takes on the form of a self-amusement center for an increasing number of people who have high-fi equipment, television, ping-pong tables, and even swimming pools.

At the same time that this isolation is increasing, Sennett feels that certain internal family dynamics are at work to compound the problem. Conflict has become a taboo and therefore there is a playing down of differences between the generations. "A good family of this sort is a family whose members talk to each other as equals, where the children presume to the lessons of experience and parents try to forget them" (Sennett, 1970a:33). Conflict within the family is looked upon as a sign that the family has somehow failed. The emphasis on homogeneity and the guilt-over-conflict syndrome, in concert with insularity, produce a situation in which the family becomes a "microcosm" of the world for its members, and as one of Sennett's informants remarked, nothing "really important" in human relationships takes place outside of the family. For Sennett all of these factors have given modern family life a "brutal" quality.

In many respects the most critical picture of American society and the problems it creates for its members is found in Phillip Slater's *The Pursuit of Loneliness* (1970). He believes that three basic human desires are deeply and uniquely frustrated by American culture:

1. The desire for *community*—the wish to live in trust and fraternal cooperation with one's fellows in a total and visible collective entity.

2. The desire for *engagement*—the wish to come directly to grips with social and interpersonal problems and to confront on equal terms an environment which is not composed of ego extensions.

3. The desire for *dependence*—the wish to share responsibility for the control of one's impulses and the direction of one's life [1970:5].

Slater does not feel we are so much victims of the system as we are participants in it: ourselves working, if only indirectly, to produce the frustrations and limitations that plague us. For the most part, much of what Slater discusses can be subsumed under the rubric of individualism. It is this individualism that has created the frustrations he describes which make some of us feel like one member of a commune who said, "The U.S. is a crummy place but I don't have to go there very often" (quoted by Kanter, 1972:21). For such people resolving the dilemmas and frustrations of day-to-day living has become impossible in the context of the mainstream of American society. As a result some have been led to look for alternative structures, one of which is the commune.

It seems clear that the communal movement is just one facet of the broader response on the part of young people to American society that a few years ago was labeled as the counterculture (Roszak, 1969). Some young people who have not been exposed to the scarcity and restrictiveness that was part of their parents' lives have rejected conventional structures and conventional feelings and attitudes. They have seen the commune as a place that facilitates this rejection and, more importantly, also facilitates the realization of the kinds of relations between people that run counter to what they see as the alienating pressures of the larger American society.

What may come as a surprise to some readers is that this communal movement is not new in our history. This country has a long tradition of utopian communalism, and it is not difficult to find interesting parallels between the motivations of eighteenth- and nineteenth-century communards and those of today, though there are also important differences. Kanter has commented very insightfully on this point:

> The initial impetus for the building of American communes has tended to stem from one of three major themes: a desire to live according to religious and spiritual values, rejecting the sinfulness of the established order; a desire to reform society by curing its economic and political ills, rejecting the injustice and inhumanity of the establishment; or a desire to promote the psychosocial growth of the individual by putting him in closer touch with his fellows, rejecting the isolation and alienation of the surrounding society. These three threads vaguely correspond to the three historical waves of American utopian communities: the first lasted from the early days to about 1845, when religious themes were prominent; the second, stressing economic and political issues, ran from 1820 to 1930, flourishing especially in the 1840s; and the third, psychosocial period emerged after World War Two and became especially important in the 1960s. Nevertheless there are many groups today growing out of all three traditions [1972:8].

Yet, it is not easy to make hard and fast distinctions between various types of communes, either past or present, because there is much that unites them apart from specific emphasis on the religious, economic, or psychosocial dimensions. If nothing else, they all agree that the "good life" cannot be led in the mainstream of society and that a retreat from the world is necessary to establish utopia, however different these utopias might be.

COMMUNE AND FAMILY IN CONFLICT

Neither this book nor this chapter is concerned with the communal movement per se. What we are concerned with is how the commune may modify the family and where certain possibilities for growth and experimentation with family forms exist. As we shall see, some communes have come into existence because of a strongly felt need to eradicate the family, which its members see as repressive and anti-utopian. But the communities that have cleaved to the nuclear family have had to make some compromises with it, if the commune as a commune was to survive.

It is the central argument of this chapter that the utopian commune and the family, whether we are talking about exclusive pair-bond units, nuclear families, or extended kin groups (separate from the commune as a kin group), are basically antagonistic elements. This is so because the primary goal of the commune is to create a sense of brotherhood and sisterhood that transcends any ties which the individual may have felt before entering the community. To be sure not all communes are equally committed to this ideal. Yet, it is significant that Kanter, in her attempt to understand the "commitment mechanisms" that result in some communities enduring and thriving for extended periods while others quickly flounder and die, found that all of the 9 successful communes she studied had either free love or celibacy. (This was true of only 6 out of the 21 unsuccessful ones.) Moreover, 48 percent of the successful versus 15 percent of the unsuccessful communes separated parents and children. This is not to say that the family was the foundation stone upon which community failure or success rested, but the absence of the family in the conventional sense appears to be a very important ingredient for enduring communal life.

SOME HISTORICAL PERSPECTIVE ON COMMUNALISM

Instead of beginning by considering the current communal movement as a context for family change, let us look back into history to see how long humans have sought cooperative life in the commune and also how fundamental is the antagonism that has existed between the family and the commune. The Essenes were a Hebrew sect who lived around the time of Jesus, and who are believed to have had at their high point as many as 4,000 members. They held their property as a group, ate as a group, and shared clothing and living quarters. Individual members had little if anything in the way of private assets. Interestingly enough, they appear to have been less concerned about joint economic activity than they were about joint consumption; however H. Darin-Drabkin (1962) feels that this may reflect a level of technology which for centuries had been geared to the individual and which did not lend itself to communal effort. In any case what is most significant about the Essenes, from our point of view, is their attitude toward the family, which was so negative that celibacy was the rule.

> Some scholars (among them Karl Kautzki) see in the continence of the Essenes and their celibacy the consequence of their communal organization. These scholars maintain that the family formed a danger to the very existence of the collective, because the family brought pressure to bear for the replacement of joint and communal consumption by individual households [Darin-Drabkin, 1962:23].

This statement illustrates how early in the history of communalism the theme of the family in conflict with communal ideals emerged. We do not know enough about the Essenes to say to what degree there were recurrent attempts, if any, to reinstitute some sort of marriage and/or sexual relations. The destruction of the Second Temple in 70 A.D., during the war with the Romans, marked the end of the Essenes as a communitarian group; however, they were to continue to exert an influence on subsequent communal movements, especially those of the early Christians.

Since we do not intend to set forth the world history of communalism here, it is sufficient to say that this is a phenomenon which has periodically recurred in various societies in response to diverse pressures and in order to fulfill a variety of needs. Our interest in communalism is limited to understanding the role of the family in the commune and examining the basic tension that exists between the commune and the family unit. Therefore, in what follows we will concentrate on those aspects of communalism, past and present, which best portray this tension, and the manner in which various communities have dealt with it.

Many of us tend to think that developments in our own time represent phenomena which are historically unique. To the uninitiated it is almost unthinkable that during what was supposedly the most sexually repressive period in our history—the midnineteenth century—a radical attempt would be made to modify the family. We are referring here to the community founded by John Humphrey Noyes and his Perfectionists at Oneida, New York. In order to gain a perspective on the Oneida community, let us stop for a moment and consider the more general character of nineteenth-century American communalism.

The communalism of nineteenth-century America is as varied as the communalism we see today, perhaps in certain respects more so, though most communities had a definite economic or religious ideology at their center as well as a charismatic figure (Holloway, 1966; Noyes, 1966; and Nordhoff, 1965). In comparing nineteenth- and twentieth-century communes it is best not to look for periodic repetition of patterns, but instead to look for a constant thread which becomes more conspicuous in the fabric from time to time. For if we look at the history of communalism in the United States, we see that there was never a time when intentional communities were nonexistent. The landscape has always been dotted with at least a handful of communities struggling to maintain an "alternative" existence. Rather there have been periods of effloresence and periods of dormancy in communalism. It is true that during the 1960s and 1970s as well as during a large part of the nineteenth century interest in communal alternatives was particularly high. But we cannot conclude that the root causes of these movements were essentially similar given the diversity of experiments and the long period during which the nineteenth century experiments took place. If nineteenth-century communalism had been limited only to the second half of the century we could hypothesize that it was a response to the rapid growth of urban industrialism, but communalism was present earlier in the century, before this growth of industrialism. Similarly it is difficult to pinpoint what it is about social conditions in the 1960s that called forth a wave of communalism. To be sure, one could offer glib and facile comparative analyses, but how much would it really tell us about the two movements? Perhaps all we can say is that at various times in our history the pressures that have always led some to look outside of the mainstream of society have intensified. To go beyond this statement would require scholarly work that has yet to be carried out.

Kanter, quoted earlier, believed that there were two important themes in nineteenth-century communalism: a religious one and an economic one. In fact, as she herself acknowledges, the situation was somewhat more complex than this because of the interweaving and overlapping between various themes. There were communities that were basically sectarian, but which nonetheless followed a collective life and sharing of resources, for example, the Rappites and Moravians. In turn, religious concerns were hardly absent in the "economic" communes, such as the Fourierist and Owenite experiments, though here religion was certainly less salient than in the more spiritually oriented communities (Nordhoff, 1965). Some communities combined equal elements of both. Despite Dr. Kanter's claim that "a desire to promote psychosocial growth of the individual by putting him in closer touch with his fellows" (1972:8) is especially characteristic of the wave of communalism after World War II, we must recognize that this desire was by no means absent in the nineteenth century. This is not to say that the same words were used—the term "self-actualization" would have had a very alien ring to the last century's communards—but that the ideas would not have been alien to them. Perhaps this is nowhere more evident than in the Oneida community with its underlying philosophy of Perfectionism.

THE ONEIDA COMMUNITY

Those familiar with the history of America's utopian experiments know that the "free love" community of Oneida stands out as one of the most original and revolutionary of experiments. Like many nineteenth- and twentieth-century utopian communities, Oneida was founded by a truly charismatic figure, John Humphrey Noyes. Noyes was born in Brattleboro, Vermont in 1811, the son of a successful shopkeeper and congressman. He grew up in Putney and at fifteen attended Dartmouth, from which he graduated with high honors in 1830. Later he went on to the Andover Theological Seminary, but found it too conservative and left for Yale Divinity School. While at Yale, Noyes began preaching in New Haven and came under the influence of Nathaniel W. Taylor, a Yale theologian who believed in "the Wesleyan doctrine of holiness, which told man that he could attain a state of perfect love between himself and God" (Carden, 1964:4). Noyes pushed this belief even further than Taylor and ultimately fell into dispute with the Yale Divinity School faculty as an indirect result of which he was forced to give up his parish.

After two years of proselytizing in New York and New England, he returned to Putney, where he began to surround himself with followers and laid the foundation for what would ultimately become the Oneida

Community of Perfectionists. Although he was to continue to go on proselytizing, he became more and more involved with a group of followers in the community. In 1838 he married Harriet A. Holton, who had converted to Perfectionism in 1834 after reading an article by Noyes. Yet before the marriage he had already publicly declared, "When the will of God is done on earth as it is in heaven there will be no marriage" (quoted in Carden, 1969:8). This critical view of monogamy was to create considerable dissension among his followers causing some to fall away, but it was a recurrent theme in future communal movements.

In the nine years following his marriage, Noyes remained in Putney and began to surround himself with a group of people who evolved into a community. He did some traveling in an attempt to attain a position of leadership among the large group of Perfectionists, and to the extent that groups of Perfectionists scattered around the Northeast began to look at him as a spiritual leader, he was successful in this endeavor. In Putney the financial situation among the local followers was improved as a result of an inheritance Noyes received after his father's death. The group was coherent enough, both financially and spiritually, to take on a corporate quality, with almost all of the twenty-eight adults and nine children living in one or another of the three houses owned by Noyes or his brothers and sisters.

During the early 1840s, several members indicated a willingness to act on Noyes's earlier critical preaching on monogamy, but in his capacity as leader—and it was a rather autocratic one at that—Noyes forbade the breakup of monogamy. In 1846, however, he himself undertook to initiate the first experiment with "complex" marriage. At that time, Noyes found himself drawn to Mary E. Cragin, who reciprocated his feelings. Noyes's wife and Mrs. Cragin's husband expressed similar feelings about each other. The four carefully deliberated and agreed that God's will would be served by their exchanging partners, and so they did. The fact that this was going on soon became known to other members of the community and they gossiped about it with Putney residents who were not followers of Noyes. The townspeople became outraged as the news spread and charges of adultery were brought against him. To avoid prosecution, Noyes fled to New York City in November, 1847.

Soon after the debacle at Putney a small group of Perfectionists who had settled in Madison County, New York, near Oneida Creek, invited Noyes to resettle there with his Putney followers. Ultimately thirty-one adults and fourteen children from Putney moved to New York, where they were joined by others of Noyes's followers from northern Vermont. Together with those who settled initially in New York, about a dozen adults and their children, they incorporated themselves to form the Oneida Association. By 1848, there were almost ninety Perfectionists, including children, living in Oneida. It was at Oneida that the Perfectionists developed and elaborated the innovative structures for which they would become so famous.

Complex Marriage at Oneida

We noted earlier that Noyes was critical of monogamy because he saw it as setting certain relationships apart from others and encouraging exclusivity and selfishness. Maren Carden quotes him as saying, "The heart should be free to love all the true and worthy" (1969:49). Therefore, Noyes argued, monogamy should be replaced by complex marriage, which left people to relate to each other without the strictures of exclusivity.

In principle all adult members of the community were married to each other, but in fact certain rules governed the patterns and circumstances of sexual interactions. Perfectionism held that individuals differed in their degrees of perfection, and the members could be ranked in terms of the degree of perfection they had attained. Therefore, Noyes argued that individuals would benefit from interaction with those more spiritually advanced than themselves. Since older people were felt to be more advanced than younger people, association between young and old was encouraged on the basis of the doctrine of "ascending fellowship." This resulted in most sexual contact occurring between older women and younger men and older men and younger women. Just how propitious this was from the point of view of avoiding unwanted pregnancies will be seen when we discuss their contraceptive practices, but I trust that most readers will see the value of this "principle" as a device, whether recognized or not, for preventing undue jealousy.

Within the boundaries of the principle of ascending fellowship, exclusivity was rigorously discouraged, and partners were frequently changed. Carden estimates that, on the average, women often had more than four partners a month, with one report indicating that women had intercourse about every two to four days (1969:53). These encounters, at least in the first year of the Oneida settlement, were arranged through the simple procedure of the man asking the woman with whom he wanted to have relations; however, in the early 1860s the practice of using an intermediary, generally an older woman who was also a central member of the group, was instituted. Obviously, by using an intermediary the possibility of embarrassing refusals was reduced. The couple who had agreed to an "interview" with each other would either retire to one of their rooms or to one of the rooms that was used for "social purposes". At first, couples were permitted to spend the whole night together, but later on this was no longer permitted, ostensibly because so much sexual activity would be too taxing for the male—but perhaps also to discourage the development of any kind of special ties between two people.

Very much in contrast to the prevailing midnineteenth-century view, which saw sex as an unfortunate necessity, the Perfectionists felt that coitus was good and proper in its own right; "sexual communion differs only by its superior intensity and beauty from other acts of love." Sex was "love in its most natural and beautiful form" (Carden, 1969:54).

To a great extent the practice of complex marriage was predicated on a rather special form of contraception which the Perfectionists spoke of as "male continence." Noyes argued that male sexual fulfillment could be achieved without the experience of orgasm, and in its place advocated prolonged intercourse stopping short of orgasm for the male. This technique worked well as a contraceptive, preventing unwanted and often injurious pregnancies. Carden estimated that no more than thirty-one unplanned children were born during the twenty-one years that the experiment was in force. How this was calculated will become more evident when we discuss the Perfectionists' method of selecting people for parenthood.

Noyes was reasonably familiar with the scientific literature of his day. He was conversant with the ideas of Galton and Darwin, and they played a role in the development of his notions concerning what was later described as eugenics, but which he described as "stirpiculture." A committee was selected to decide which couples were to have children. Many members applied to the committee as couples; in fact, only about one-quarter were paired by the committee itself. This experiment in selecting people to be parents who met the committee's standards of spiritual and physical development (they obviously felt that acquired characteristics would be transmitted) worked rather well. Of the fifty-eight children born at Oneida between 1869 and 1879, only thirteen were the result of accidental conceptions. (Noyes and his son Theodore were the fathers of a disproportionate number of the children, twelve between them). The responsibilities of motherhood were more evenly distributed among the women of the community. The children were reared communally, at least after they were weaned, and they spent only a few hours a week with their parents once they moved into the children's house.

Regrettably most of the personal diaries that dealt with the complex marriage and stirpiculture experiments at Oneida were destroyed by the management of Oneida Ltd. (manufacturers of silver plates) during the 1920s because they felt the material contained in them would be embarrassing to surviving relatives (Kephart, 1963). This invaluable record was thus lost. Nonetheless, the little evidence we do have available suggests that these experiments were reasonably successful. To be sure, some heterosexual alliances were formed as couples fell in love with each other. Various sanctions were employed in such cases, such as sending one of the offenders to the branch community at Wallingford, Connecticut or withdrawing their sexual privileges. The fact that it was difficult for clandestine relationships to go unnoticed and that the community placed a great deal of stock in self-criticism and mutual criticism did much to discourage such activities. All told, for the years during which complex marriage was in force, it appeared to function well with a minimum of conflict.

In the Oneida community, the principles of fellowship and religious belief were so tightly intertwined that it is very difficult, if not impossible, to separate the psychosocial from the religious element. However, what is important from our point of view is that the psychosocial element was never neglected, if only because it was at the heart of the Perfectionism that united the group. So strong was this spirit that a European traveler visiting Oneida in 1852 commented:

> The whole family is one marriage circle. The hearts are conscious of one love; consequently all things are common among them—women, goods, ideas, and inventive skill [quoted in Muncy, 1973:167].

If our description of Oneida is not sufficient to convey the weight placed upon primary relations within the community, then perhaps a comment on one further aspect of communalism is in order. Most of us today have some knowledge of or direct experience with T-groups, or encounter groups as they are sometimes called (Back, 1972). These structures are occasionally used in psychotherapy to deal with psychological problems, but increasingly they are being used in a wide variety of settings, ranging from the religious to the business setting, to enable people to better realize their own or their organization goals. Large corporations use such groups as vehicles for internal criticism and suggestions for improvement. For example, publishers may have their sales and editorial people together at "advocacy sessions" where each confronts the other with their problems in an attempt to improve both sales and editorial work.

It will come as no surprise to readers that these mechanisms have been adopted by various contemporary communes, and in some instances, for example, in Synanon houses (therapeutic communes for drug addicts) they are at the center of the community (Yablonsky, 1965). What may come as a surprise to some is that this practice was also a fundamental part of Oneida (Nordhoff, 1965). Spoken of as "mutual criticism," it involved members who violated the rules or principles of the community coming before a group of their peers who discussed their errors. One member described such a session as follows:

> I feel as though I had been washed; felt clean through the advice and criticism given. I would call the truth the soap, and the critics the scrubbers; Christ's spirit the water [quoted in Kephart, 1963, reprinted in Gordon, 1973:63].

Members were generally called before such sessions because of some failure in interpersonal relations rather than a failure of faith, though again the two were almost inseparable at Oneida. But the point for us is that the quality of relations between people was seen as being so important at Oneida that there were formal structures for dealing with them, structures which in many respects resemble those employed by today's communes.

From Oneida we learn that radical experiments in family reorganization and human relations did exist in the nineteenth century. We see how this community resolved the tensions between the family and community by doing away with the family as we know it. To be sure this was a brief experiment from the perspective of the broad sweep of history. Nonetheless it was a very important one, because it showed that possessiveness and jealousy could be dealt with, though not without some struggle and hardship.

Few nineteenth-century communities equaled Oneida in the radical nature of their departure from conventional family forms. There were some other shortlived experiments, such as Josiah Warren's anarchist community, Modern Times, which operated on Long Island in the 1850s, and The Harmonial Vegetarian Society in Benton County, Georgia in 1860 and 1861. Also Frances Wright's Owenite community, Nashoba, was founded in Memphis in 1825 with the hope of enabling freed slaves to adjust to the world outside the plantation by integrating them with whites—this community followed a rocky course and ended in 1831 (Muncy, 1973). There were others, as well, but none of these communities managed to find a way of stabilizing their new "family" relationships as their generally short lives attest to. We must, however, realize that during the nineteenth century a community embarking on a pattern of "free love" faced all sorts of antagonism and hostility from their neighbors, who looked upon the "free lovers" with disdain, fear, and anger. We have already discussed the legal problems that John Humphrey Noyes encountered; similar if not more vitriolic attacks and denunciations were the lot of the other nineteenth-century communities.

THE SHAKERS

But free love was not the only form that communalism took. There were also communities that decided to meet the problem of tension between the nuclear family and the community by doing away with all heterosexual relationships. Ultimately the result was the same—one large family—but the means were different. No better experiment can be found than that of the Shakers, one of the country's most long-lived and creative communal groups (Melcher, 1941).

The Shaker community, or United Society of Believers, was based on celibacy from the very beginning. It has been suggested that Oneida's free love doctrines were in no small part an outgrowth of John Humphrey Noyes's prodigious sexual appetite; similarly, the ascetic character of the Shakers has been attributed to the unhappy marriage of their founder, Mother Ann Lee, the death at birth of all four of her children, and her supposed aversion to sex (Muncy, 1973:17). Such interpretations based on biographical conjectures are interesting, but ultimately tell us little. From our perspective what is significant about the Shakers is that their community, during almost the entire 200 years of its existence, has never departed from the prohibition on marriage.

While different from Oneida in their "family" arrangements, it appears that relations between the Shakers and the Oneida community were cor-

Shaker Meeting House. Note the men entering left, the women right. *(Courtesy, Elmer R. Pearson)*

dial and that they visited each other (Kanter, 1972:232). Both were striving for similar states of fellowship and spirituality, though the means employed were quite different. When one considers other aspects of community life, such as the way in which both groups engaged in industry on a large scale (Oneida with its traps, the Shakers with their chairs, seeds, etc.), similarities are obvious, though parallels in social organization are more relevant to our interests.

While the first Shaker community was founded in New York State in 1787, by 1830 there were 18 communities ranging up as far north as Maine and as far south as Florida, with more than 5,000 members. Within each community, and a community might have several hundred members, members were arranged in smaller groupings of 30 to 90 persons known as families, each of which would have its own dwelling, and in some instances its own industries as well. Men and women lived together in Shaker family residences, which contained cooking and laundry facilities; however, the relations between them were strictly governed. They slept in separate rooms and the hallways were made especially wide so that the sexes could pass without touching each other. In the dining room men and women sat at separate tables, and even among members of the same sex, words were kept to a minimum. As a general rule, men and women could not speak to each other unless another Shaker, older than ten, was present.

Nonetheless, it is interesting and important to note that some safety valves were provided. At religious services, the Shakers engaged in dances for which they grew famous and which visitors came many miles to see. These dances, while permitting no actual contact between the sexes, still provided an outlet for the feelings and desires that they were prevented from achieving through normal outlets.

Ultimately, the Shakers did permit some limited sexual interaction in the form of "union hour." Here a group of "sisters" would enter a room in which a number of "brothers" were present and spend an hour conversing as couples. While the presence of several couples made any sort of impropriety impossible, it appears that such visits did result in affective relations of sorts developing between some couples—for which they were sternly admonished. Occasionally a couple did leave the community ("fleshed out" in the Shakers' words) as a result of ties formed in union hour, but all in all, it does seem to have been a successful device in providing the minimal amount of sexual contact tolerable in an essentially celibate community.

The sense of community created with Oneida and within the various family dwellings in the Shaker communities was in many respects similar. For both, the concern was with "we" as a community rather than "we" as a nuclear family, or "I" as a separate person. Kanter quotes a Shaker hymn that beautifully and dramatically conveys just how deep this sentiment ran among the Shakers:

Of all the relations that ever I see
My old fleshly kindred are furthest from me
So bad and so ugly, so hateful they feel
To see them and hate them increases my zeal
O how ugly they look!
How ugly they look!
How nasty they feel!

My gospel relations *are dearer to me*
Than all the flesh kindred that ever I see . . .
O how pretty they look! . . .
[quoted in Kanter, 1972:90]

Could one possibly ask for a more vivid statement of the antagonism between kinship as it exists in the world outside the commune and the new kinship that must exist if a commune is to move from what Benjamin Zablocki calls "Communion to true community" (1971)?

The Shakers and the Oneida society represent two ways of resolving the tension between family and community, but if we were to examine only these communities we would learn little of the possibilities communes offer for modifying the family without extirpating it. In order to do this, we shall take a look at some present-day situations and how the nuclear family continues to maintain itself in a communal setting.

THE COMMUNAL MOVEMENT IN CONTEMPORARY AMERICA

A discussion of the family and family modifications as they exist in contemporary communes, especially those that might be described as countercultural in contrast to more traditional intentional communities, such as the Hutterites and the Bruderhof, is no easy task. This is true because relatively little in the way of systematic information is available. The 1970s have seen a number of books appear on the current communal movement, among them Roy Ald's *The Youth Communes* (1970), Robert Houriet's *Getting Back Together* (1971), Richard Atcheson's *The Bearded Lady* (1971), and Richard Fairfield's *Communes U.S.A.* (1972). These books are broad surveys of the communal movement, more often than not based on their author's travels throughout the country. In certain respects they resemble Nordhoff's *The Communistic Societies of the United States* (1875), published a century ago. Nordhoff, a journalist and author (like Atcheson and Houriet), visited the Zoarites, the Shakers, the Icarians, and other communes. To some extent his work served as a model for those of his twentieth-century counterparts, but regrettably the results are not quite the same. The fault is not to be found with any less competence or zeal in our contemporaries but rather that today's communes tend to be both small in size and short in duration in comparison with those of the nineteenth-century movement. Even those that have endured, such as Twin Oaks, have had little more than a decade in which to form and flourish or decay. Thus, in most respects, today's books are richer in their discussion of people within communities than in discussion of the structures these communities have generated. While we often get a good deal of detail on the backgrounds of the people making up these communes, the kinds of experiences that led them to "drop out" and try to "get it together" in communes, less space has been devoted to analyzing organizational aspects of these communes.

More recently some sociologists—while lacking the literary gifts of Atcheson or Houriet—have attempted to analyze both the elements in American society from which the current communal movement springs and the structures within communes that serve to produce longevity. Here we are specifically referring to Rosabeth Kanter's *Community and Commitment* (1972), Keith Melville's *Communes in the Counter Culture* (1972), and Ron Roberts's *The New Communes* (1971). Still these general works do not give us the kind of detailed treatment of family life and sex roles that is necessary for the kind of discussion we have in mind. Nonetheless, drawing upon the books we have already mentioned, and others (Hedgepeth, 1970; Kinkade, 1973; and Diamond, 1971), and scattered articles (Smith and Steinfield, 1969; Berger et al., 1972; Kanter et al., 1975; Conover, 1975, etc.), we can construct some image of the contemporary commune and the kinds of experiments with family organization that have been going on, as well as the tensions and strengths these have produced.

What we will try to do in what follows is present a discussion of some broad themes in the current communal movement and then consider developments within this movement that bear upon the family. Berger and his associates at the University of California at Davis have been engaged in a study of childrearing on current communes (1971, 1972). Based on this research they argue that certain very general distinctions can be made between communes. The first is the urban-rural distinction, the second is the creedal-noncreedal one (1972).

Urban and Rural Communes

The urban-rural distinction in many ways goes beyond where a commune is located, because associated with location are certain elements of social organization and self-sufficiency. For Berger et al., the rural commune represents a "more advanced stage" (1972:420) in the communal movement. Let us see why. The roots of today's communalism, like any well-developed social movement, are not monolithic. Rather they spread out widely and go deep down. Since this nation has a long history of communalism, as we have shown, no major innovation was necessary to rekindle the movement in the 1960s. Zablocki (1971) has suggested that the "crash pads" of the 1960s, where many young people had their first taste of communal life, however transient it may have been, represented the beginnings of the renewed communalism of the 1960s. Zablocki feels that this experience with group living motivated some persons to seek a more stable form of communalism, and either the residents of crash pads went out to form communes or crash pads themselves became communes. Those that became urban communes, and this holds today, generally involved less commitment on the part of their members than rural communes because of the degree to which urban communes remained integrated in the larger society. One communard has been quoted as saying:

> My definition of a commune is not just sharing a house and kitchen because it's cheaper. It's sharing work, a common purpose, and a future life together that we're all involved in [Melville, 1972:155].

It is for reasons such as this that Berger sees rural communes as being more advanced, since they are more than a building in which people live together and do cooking, cleaning, and childcare cooperatively (though some do much more—as much as any rural commune). Rural communes tend to be separated from society by the fact of their distance from urban centers and their self-sufficiency, whether it be based on agriculture or individual crafts. Some communes try to grow, raise, or forage as much of what they eat as possible, while others depend more on community industry. For example, Twin Oaks (Kinkade, 1973), a commune in Virginia, makes hammocks, and the Bruderhof in New York makes children's toys (Zablocki, 1971). Associated with this self-sufficiency is often a sense of greater togetherness, if only because their location makes the commune the central part of its members' lives.

Creedal and Noncreedal Communes

Location and the degree of self-sufficiency, however, is not the whole story. There is also the dimension of creedal versus noncreedal communes:

> Creedal communes are those organized around a systematic or otherwise elaborated doctrine or creed to which members are either required or eventually expected to adhere: communes of "Jesus freaks," or ashrams devoted to the teachings of an Indian saint, or crusading communes devoted to the eccentric visions of a self-proclaimed Messiah [Berger et al., 1972:420].

There is also another significant distinction between these two kinds of communities:

> Because creedal communes are sometimes missionary (while non-creedal ones are rarely or never so) their membership tends to be more open so that at any given time there are likely to be several members or incipient members who, fresh from the street or responding to the missionary appeal, do not actually know each other or the older members very well . . . Indeed, non-creedal communes may be said in general to rely upon the history of friendship as a source of solidarity which creedal communes try to find in their commitment to doctrines [Berger et al., 1972:420].

This often results in creedal communes having virtually an open-door policy with regard to membership, though trial periods are by no means rare, while noncreedal communes tend to place some sort of restriction on new members, since they are more concerned with the qualities of relationships than with the obtaining of new believers for the faith. As we shall see, this factor bears on the kinds of relationships that emerge in communes.

In general, creedal communes—whether rural, such as the Bruderhof, or urban, such as the Synanon or Hare Krishna houses—tend to have a much more rigid and clearly defined structure than noncreedal ones. Noncreedal communes often abide by an ethic of everyone doing their own thing as long as it can be done without anyone else being hurt or the commune falling apart. This usually results in a communal crisis and the imposition of some sort of order on the intentional anarchism that characterizes many noncreedal communes.

It is useful to stop for a moment and look at the dimension of anarchism, since it is such an important theme in many of today's communes and bears heavily on questions of social organization in general and on the family in particular. One of the major themes of what has been spoken of as the "counterculture" is antiauthoritarianism. Thus the counterculture rejects authority in its more malignant manifestation in corrupt government and business, but it also rejects authority in its more benign manifestations such as knowledge gained from learning and experience. Zablocki (1971) recounts his experience visiting a commune with a man very knowledgeable about organic farming. This man's advice was resented and disregarded by the communards despite their affection for him as a person. This "learn by doing" attitude has caused many communities much hardship, both in terms of causing disease and unnecessarily wasted effort.

How does one run a community when authority is questioned and emphasis is placed on the maximization of personal freedom? From what we know, it appears that many communes go through a stage of trying to make anarchy work, even a community like Twin Oaks, which takes its inspiration from B. F. Skinner's behaviorist utopian novel, *Walden II* (1948). Twin Oaks started out with people more or less doing what they pleased or what they felt they should do. But feelings of inequity motivated them very shortly to move toward a "labor credit" system whereby people have to earn a specified number of credits per week by doing jobs that are assigned a credit value according to their undesirability, that is, one gets more credit per hour for cleaning toilets than for baking bread (Kinkade, 1973).

This sort of solution is not uncommon. Zablocki feels that it is possible to delineate three types of solutions communes hit upon to deal with the problem of resolving the conflict between giving people the freedom they often joined the community to find and at the same time providing the community with a basis for the degree of social organization necessary for life to go on.

> One is segmentation either of the commune itself into a number of smaller "families" or sub-communes, or of the life into communal, cooperative and individualistic areas. A second type of modification can be called contractual anarchism. The community members make agreements with one another and then expect them to be kept. The third type of modification can be called consensual anarchism. The community actively seeks to find solutions satisfactory to everyone, refusing to override even a one person minority [Zablocki, 1971:311].

Like any broad categorization, exceptions and combinations can be found, but Zablocki has focused our attention on what is perhaps the key issue in modern communalism. To be sure, there were anarchistic communities in nineteenth-century America, perhaps most notably Modern Times on Long Island, but the reader should recall the excerpt from Kanter (1972) quoted earlier, noting that what makes the current wave of communalism somewhat special is the emphasis placed on "psychosocial growth" with particular stress on freedom.

The existence of the family as a definable unit imposes certain limits on personal freedom in terms of adults' sociosexual access to other relationships and children's access to other adults and children; therefore, it

A present-day commune. *(Dennis Stock/Magnum)*

will come as no surprise to discover that the family is a source of controversy in some of America's communes today, especially those of the noncreedal variety.

Based on the limited data currently available it seems safe to say that the majority of creedal communes maintain a fairly conventional or even conservative family structure, especially groups such as the Bruderhof, the Jesus people, and the Hare Krishna followers. All three of these groups are strictly monogamous, and the standards of sexual morality practiced before and during marriage are extremely restrictive. The integrity of the nuclear unit is closely guarded, though aspects of family functioning are taken care of by extrafamilial agencies. In order to better appreciate this phenomenon let us look more closely at family life in one current communal society: a Hare Krishna ashram or community. (Considerably more detailed and systematic information is available on the Bruderhof because of Zablocki's excellent study *The Joyful Community* [1971], but since the Bruderhof is a commune which dates back to early in the present century, it may be best to concentrate on a more recent, though by no means more contemporary, manifestation of the current wave of communalism.)

The Hare Krishna Communes

At present there are a number of communes or ashrams whose members are followers of a particular Indian saint, but in numbers none rivals the devotees of Hare Krishna.

> Of all the Eastern religions and disciplines that spread westward during the sixties, the largest, most organized was Hare Krishna. By 1970 there were fifty centers around the world and in the major cities of the United States. . . . The national membership was estimated at 3,000. Funds and publication of *Back to the Godhead* magazine (circulation 500,000) were controlled by the International Society for Krishna Consciousness, established by a seventy-five year old swami, A. C. Bhaktivedanta, who brought Krishna to the West [Houriet, 1971:331].

Its ashrams, while largely urban, are also beginning to spread to the countryside. Our description of the family in a Hare Krishna ashram is based on one in rural Ohio, and another in New York City.

The lives of the followers of Hare Krishna are informed (or at least this is their goal) with the teachings of the Indian god or saint Krishna as contained in the *Bhagavad-Gita,* the bible of Hinduism. The days are filled with regular periods of religious chanting and meditation and when the spirit catches them members chant the mantra, "*Hare Krishna, hare Krishna, Krishna, Krishna, hare, hare, hare Rama, hare Rama, Rama Rama, hare hare.*" The saffron-robed young men and women you may see in your city or on campus are Hare Krishna followers and the chants you hear them reciting are the one just quoted.

The money for the modest existence in the ashrams is provided by members' independent means, outside work, or community industry (the packaging and selling of incense is the major industry at present). By spiritual prescription women have been assigned the traditional domestic tasks, "all cleaning, darning, sewing, cooking, and churning of butter" (Houriet, 1971:340). We might add to this the serving of food, since women eat separately and only eat after the men have been fed. This traditionalism also extends to the manner in which mates are chosen, at least by those who enter the ashram unmarried. The president of the ashram or temple is approached by an unmarried man who indicates that he feels his spiritual life would benefit from being married. The president considers the available unmarried women and suggests one. In principle the president's choice is the right one and the devotees should not refuse; unfortunately we do not know enough about actual practices to indicate how often in fact this takes place. Once married the couple's life together is supposed to interfere as little as possible with their own spiritual development. While they generally share private quarters, their sexual contacts are limited to the one day when the women are most likely to be fertile, since the purpose of sex is procreation not pleasure. Intercourse does not take place until the couple engages in a purification ritual that might take several hours (Levine, 1971:29). As one might anticipate, a couple is expected not to have had sexual contact prior to marriage. This is not to say that the couple will have entered the marriage without sexual experience. Many members join ashrams after deep involvement in drugs and sex, and often after having been in other more libertarian communes. It is the same search for an answer to life's problems, an answer that they could not find in drugs and sex, that leads people to Jesus or Krishna. Thus one would expect to find important similarities between the members of the Jesus people and the Hare Krishna followers.

Indeed, communities of Jesus people present us with a similar picture of marital and sex-role conservatism (Balswick, 1972). One might speculate on the reasons for this conservatism in terms that go beyond the spiritual dictates of Christianity and Hinduism, since we have seen that the devout Christians at Oneida saw no tension between complex marriage and spirituality. One might note also that India is known for its erotic art. It would seem plausible that for some of today's young people ascetic spirituality represents a retreat from the complexities of the life they have known, with its drugs, sex, and the push to experiment with new relationships. At the same time, they are rejecting the precepts and principles of achievement and consumerism. Their search for community leads them to seek the simplest of relationships as they pursue complex spiritual relationships. While some may see this as a retreat from reality, others will see it as a continuation of one of the oldest threads in human history.

What of the noncreedal communes? The diversity of family forms manifested by this current in today's communal movement is considerably varied. It is probably safe to generalize that in terms of endurance the noncreedal communes show a much higher mortality rate than their creedal counterparts.

This is in part explainable in terms of the importance placed by each on the concept of personal freedom. By their very nature, most creedal communes play down the individual and therefore do not have to wrestle with the dilemmas of anarchy versus community which plague noncreedal communes. When it comes to the family, many people imagine that all current noncreedal communes resemble the Manson family (Bugliosi, 1974)—men with insatiable sexual appetites are confronted by hosts of nubile and willing young women, and life is turned into one endless orgasm. As it happens, few men are like Manson and few women are willing to subject themselves to the sexual whims of the commune's residential guru, however charismatic he may be. To be sure, there are communes that have attempted in their early anarchistic phases to allow people to do their own thing sexually as in other spheres, but for one reason or another things don't work out this way. Sara Davidson cites one communard's response to his "wife" being with another man; he "pulled a knife, and dragged her off, yelling 'Forget this shit. She belongs to me' " (1970:531). While the response of this man is indeed an extreme one, it does illustrate that people have great difficulty in adjusting to "open" relationships, whether in or out of a communal context, because of the possessiveness with which we have been taught to view our relationships with members of the opposite sex. But more on this later.

Some Noncreedal Communal Settings

It is difficult to estimate how many communes there currently are in America. If one includes urban communes where people may do no more than share certain aspects of cooking and cleaning, they probably number in the thousands, (see, for example, Weiss, 1974) but even if one limits it to rural communes the number is still probably a substantial one, though perhaps smaller than during the late 1960s. Therefore it is difficult to speak with assurance about "typical" patterns; nonetheless, from the various journalistic and sociological reports that are currently available, we can make some descriptive statements. For one thing communes show considerably more monogamy than one might expect, given popular notions of communal life. Moreover, it is not helpful to ask whether or not a commune is monogamous. Rather we should ask "at what point in time" (Ramey, 1972;1975) did it become monogamous. That is to say, some communes go through stages of experimentation that may lead them from group marriage to limited sexual freedom to monogamy, or the reverse. Based on what we know so far, communes seem to have been more successful in breaking down conventional parent-child ties, though by no means completely, than they have been in breaking down husband-wife ties or just plain old exclusivity ties. Melville has commented succinctly on this point:

> The habits of the individual system die hard, but none so hard as this one: that two people—paired off—*belong* to one another. Despite the counter culture's commitment to liberation and nonrepressive sexuality, most of the groups practice a familiar form of serial monogamy. This is perhaps the most surprising thing about sex in the communes, that in reaction to a generation that was nearly fanatical in its denial of sex, and in response to the ministrations of the media in which sex is the important incentive in the art of merchandising, the sexual practices of many of the communities should be so thoroughly conventional [1972:188].

This conventionality extends, interestingly enough, to other spheres of relationships between the sexes as well. In a bitter denunciation of male-female relationships in the communes in which she lived, Vivian Estellachild argues that much of the sexism of middle-class American life is evident in the commune, though it may be packaged in leather rather than in plastic (1971). Women, she feels, are made into sexual objects and drudges. Men engage in the more satisfying aspects of communal life, that is, being "studs," farmers, and builders, while the women tacitly accept their men's sexual overtures and the kitchen work. "The major problems of the commune were male chauvinism, insensitivity, and stagnation" (Estellachild, 1971:33). Others have confirmed the existence of a traditional sex-role division in rural communes, but we must not assume that all rural communes of the noncreedal kind were as guilty of these attitudes as were those which Ms. Estellachild lived in (Conover, 1975). Berger and his associates, three of whom are women, offer a somewhat different perspective on this question:

> Communes are not places likely to be praised by serious women's liberationists, since women seem to fall naturally into doing most of the traditional "women's work." But this is less a matter of traditionalism than of natural functionality and available skill. If a woman is in possession of special skills, she will generally not spend a great deal of time in the kitchen or milking goats. If she isn't she's likely to cook rather than haul lumber or do other heavy work which men are better equipped for [1971:517].

There are certainly many women who would see much to criticize in the above statement, as well as the situation it describes. "Natural functionality and available skill" seem like justifications for traditionalism, especially when we realize how little most middle-class men know about farming before they join a commune. Of course, there are communes that are very much committed to overcoming the sex-role stereotyping in the outside world. The work credit system of Twin Oaks (1973) described earlier allocates work not on the basis of sex but on the basis of compensation for how pleasant or unpleasant various tasks are. The rural settings of many communes may be a factor here. Rosabeth Kanter and Marilyn Halter (1976) see urban communes as structures which very much help minimize, though not eliminate, sex-role differences.

The problem with many of today's communes is that they are so ephemeral and have such a high degree of transiency among their members. In the case of noncreedal communes, it is almost impossible to talk about the structure of family and sex roles, since they are in a constant state of flux.

If most noncreedal communes, despite their countercultural roots, seem to cleave to what we might see as fairly conservative sex-role distinctions and relationships between the sexes, this is somewhat less the case with regard to childrearing. In what follows we draw upon the work of Berger and his associates (1971), Smith and Sternfield (1969), and Kanter, Jaffe, and Weisberg (1975). However, the reader should keep in mind that we are dealing with generalizations based on research in communes for the most part located in California and surrounding states, and there is no reason to believe that those studied are a truly representative sample; nonetheless, we can learn something from them about communal themes in childbirth and childrearing.

In the communes studied the question of legitimacy as a legal concept is scorned; children are often conceived and born outside of civilly sanctioned marriages and the births are not formally registered. "The commune people question the entire process of human certification, arguing that such licensing interfered with basic and natural human processes" (Smith and Sternfield, 1969:90). Despite this, the majority of children appear to be born within the context of more or less monogamous relationships, though the male figure in the relationship at the time the child is born may not be the biological father. There are some interesting exceptions, such as one group where in order to blunt biological paternity a number of men had intercourse with a woman during her fertile periods. Thus the infant could more easily be thought of as the child of the commune. Despite the fact that children are seen as having a "special" relationship with a particular couple, many communes attempt to open up the children's relationships to other adults. Berger and his associates (1971) raise an interesting question in this regard. Noting that some communities have more respect for the integrity of the nuclear unit vis-à-vis the child than others, they speculate that this may reflect a stage of communal development rather than overriding ideological differences in types of communes. It does seem evident that even in those communes where nuclear families are more distinct, the commune's structure and ideology do serve to allow the child to have relationships with other adults and children different from those available in noncommunal situations.

The education and disciplining of the children pose some interesting problems for today's communards both because of pressures from external agencies and issues raised by their own ideology. If a major theme of noncreedal communal life is "doing your own thing," then consistency would demand that this right be extended to children as well. In fact, it appears that certain compromises are required, though perhaps more leeway is granted children than adults.

> The communards cope with their problem in *ad hoc* ways every day, sometimes preferring to impale themselves on their dilemma rather than applying severe sanctions to recalcitrant children as a matter of principle, and sometimes making efforts toward creating a model of child rearing which encourages the child's desire to "do his own thing," even if such socialization undermines the sources of recruitment to the commune's next generation. Most communes, it seems at this point, if faced with a choice between training the next generation of communards and training children to be free, would opt for the latter [Berger, et al., 1971:515].

What patterns if any will ultimately emerge for dealing with this issue remains to be seen (Kanter, Jaffe, and Weisberg, 1975).

Since communes are started generally by people who reject the middle-class world they left behind as a dehumanizing one, we would not expect these people to smile on the manner in which they themselves were educated. Thus, not surprisingly, in the communes studied by Smith and Sternfield, public schools were avoided and attempts were made to educate the children on the commune.

> Communal schooling for the young was based upon extensive folk art, music, singing and organic gardening which were, of course, general practices of communal life. There was an almost total absence of television in the psychedelic commune and most members stigmatized the mass media. Although they could not articulate their theories, these young people had intuitively and emotionally interpreted many philosophies that are now so popular with the intelligentsia [Smith and Sternfield, 1969:91].

What the authors are referring to are ideas found in the free schools which derive from such models as Summerhill and the teachings of Maria Montessori. Where schools of this type are available, communards may use them rather than create their own, given the problem of having to conform to state regulations concerning certification and sanitary facilities. One communal school put in toilets to get their school accredited but one member was quoted as saying, "We'll do it their way, but I doubt that anyone will use the toilets even after they're installed" (Houriet, 1971:339). So the communards are willing to placate the authorities when necessary, but such gestures permit them considerable freedom when it comes down to matters of instruction.

By now the reader must have gotten some sense of the tentative state of our knowledge of current communal life. Still it appears that in many ways communalism is an idea whose time has come. For a portion of today's younger generation the values that motivated their parents no longer hold any attraction. Success as it has traditionally been understood must be purchased at too high a price in personal freedom, interpersonal relationships, and general demands on one's life—hence, the "retreat" to or challenge of the commune. We use the word "challenge" here because communal life does represent more of a challenge than a halycon escape from the hardships of urban life. As the Zionist pioneers struggled to create a viable existence in the early days of the Israeli kibbutzim (Melford Spiro, 1954), so today's communards face perhaps greater difficulties in their attempts to create an alternative existence in their communes, whether in a storefront ashram in New York's East Village or on an organic farming commune in rural Oregon. In doing so, they are learning a great deal about the kinds of relationships that are rewarding and satisfying when the honeymoon of utopia has passed and the realities of day-to-day life must be faced. Sociologists of the family who ignore these communities do so only at a great cost to their understanding of the institution which they claim to study.

SUMMARY

In our discussion of the commune and the communal family we have referred to the work of a number of people who have perhaps placed too much emphasis on the degree to which such forms of social organization represent a departure from and an alternative to developments in postindustrial society. Zablocki, for one, has made a great deal of such an interpretation of today's communalism, seeing it as a way of resolving the dilemma between "individualism and freedom" (1971:304). It is not a matter of Zablocki, Melville, and others being wrong so much as perhaps their overemphasizing the degree to which communalism stands apart from the mainstream of American culture in its postindustrial period. In this context, it is important to remember that communalism, as was pointed out repeatedly in this chapter, has a long past in this country, and therefore is not really a departure from the norm.

Earlier in the book we raised the question as to whether or not bureaucracy as a form of social organization is as antithetical to autonomy and creativity as the critics of the 1950s and 1960s thought. We found that in fact there is evidence to suggest that as a work setting bureaucracy seems to be conducive to the development of people who place great stock in autonomy and creativity, and who function well in fulfilling these values. Could it be that there are other aspects of our society that work similarly and that have helped push young people into the commune? Bennett Berger, with his usual acuity, has raised a rather intriguing possibility:

> In our analysis of recruitment to communes, we are currently exploring two interpretive perspectives, one of them, we believe, quite unusual. The first is whether communal development, particularly in its rural manifestations, can be understood as continuous with long existing social trends; for example, the exodus from the cities, the suburbanization of the past 25 years (of which the parents of the communards were presumably a part) which expressed at least partly the ideology of "togetherness" much publicized in the late 1940s and 50s: the suburban family, warm and secure in its domestic enclave full of plenty. Other existing social trends include the increasing diffusion of the encounter movement in middle-class circles, the development of homogeneous communities, represented by retirement communities and apartment developments renting exclusively to young "swingles," groups which come together on the basis of common problems they have by the virtue of age or some other status attribute which they can solve collectively but not singly. In this perspective communes are not nearly so radical a phenomenon as they are commonly thought to be [Berger et al., 1972:422–433].

While highly speculative, Berger's important interpretation helps us to look at the commune as part of more general change, not only in the United States but also all postindustrial societies. New forms of social organization are emerging and have to emerge in many spheres.

NYPL Picture Collection

DIVORCE: The Search for Greater Fulfillment

11

Divorce is a topic of great concern to many people at present. Almost everyone has been touched by it recently if not by going through a divorce personally then in all probability by hearing about the divorce of a friend or relative. Moreover, concern is regularly expressed in the media over "soaring" divorce rates and the dire significance these escalating rates have for the future of the American family. In this chapter we will look at trends in both divorce legislation and divorce rates in order to determine where these trends are leading us in terms of the family and its future viability.

DIVORCE IN COLONIAL AMERICA

It is difficult to speak of divorce in colonial America in a unified way because America at that time was really a series of relatively independent colonies, each having separate jurisdiction over matters such as divorce. Therefore, we must talk about divorce in the Plymouth and New Haven colonies, and divorce in Massachusetts, Connecticut, Pennsylvania, Virginia, etc. Yet beneath this variation some consistency based on cultural continuity is present, especially in such areas as New England, the Middle-Atlantic region, and the South.

In colonial New England, legislation and attitudes toward divorce were in many respects more liberal than those found in England at the same time. In England true divorce, that is divorce which permitted remarriage, was seldom granted. The only exceptions were granted to noblemen who successfully petitioned the House of Lords. This was a very expensive procedure and thus few availed themselves of it (Cott, 1976). In general the best an English person of the seventeenth and eighteenth century could hope for was a legal separation, which did not permit remarriage. In the colonies divorce was clearly preferred to separation and was much more often granted for a variety of reasons, including adultery, desertion and cruelty, and so on. To be sure, members of both sexes were not always treated equally—one should not forget that American society was and still is a patriarchy.

In Massachusetts, as was the case throughout New England, divorce, like marriage, was a civil matter and not a religious one. "Marriage was declared to be, not a sacrament, but a civil contract in which the intervention of a priest was unnecessary and out of place" (Howard, 1904, vol. II:127). Therefore a magistrate or justice of the peace performed the ceremony at most marriages. In view of this secular view of marriage it is not surprising to find a similar disposition toward divorce.

Divorce decisions were in the hands of civil courts, with power in the case of appeals going from the court of assistants up to the general court. Between 1692 and 1786 Massachusetts divorce hearings were held before a court consisting of the governor and his council. For seventeenth-century Massachusetts, Howard was able to find forty cases of either divorce or annulment, though the accuracy of this list is brought into doubt by the absence of the records of the court of assistants for the period from 1644 to 1673. In these early cases we find grounds such as adultery, cruelty, and desertion being cited in divorce proceedings. In some cases true desertion was not present, but rather one person, usually the man, had been gone on a voyage for such a long period that the courts assumed he was dead and granted the wife a divorce.

Bigamy was also often mentioned in early suits for divorce in Massachusetts. Several factors could explain this. (Keep in mind that Massachusetts and Virginia had the majority of the population in the colonial era.) First, many men had migrated from England or other colonies, occasionally leaving a wife behind. Often the best intentions on the part of the husband to send for her were dulled by the length of time necessary to earn passage and the loneliness of the New World. Second, there was considerable room for anonymity as people moved from colony to colony and bigamy was not easily detected. In view of these considerations, it is not surprising that bigamy was so frequently mentioned in the early divorce suits. (By 100 years later conditions had changed so much that bigamy was rarely cited.) In addition to bigamy, the other three factors that figured strongly in divorce cases were adultery, desertion, and cruelty. These grounds indicate that by modern standards the view taken of divorce in colonial Ameria was a rather conservative one, but one which at the same time reflected marital expectancies.

Cott (1976) has done an intensive analysis of Massachusetts divorce proceedings from 1692 to 1786. Her results are most illuminating on a number of counts. In general, those petitioning for divorces during this period came from virtually all strata of Massachusetts society, but most were from the middle ranks. Of the 229 petitions that came before the governor and his council during this period, 128 were brought by women (several petitioned more than once), but they were somewhat less successful than men in getting their petitions acted upon. The grounds given varied. While adultery was cited most (84 percent of the men and 59 percent of the women mentioned it in their suits), bigamy, sexual incapacity, desertion, and cruelty were also important charges. It is interesting to note that despite the fact that the Puritans were critical of the double standard shown toward adultery in English law and practice, only one woman was able to gain a divorce on the *sole ground* of adultery during the seventeenth century, and this decision was subsequently reversed.

Taking a broad perspective, if we compare the success rates of men and women in gaining divorces in the 1692–1774 period with those of the 1775–1786 period we see that in the former, 49 percent of the 75 women and 66 percent of the 68 men gained favorable decrees (which include annulments and separations as well as divorces); while in the latter period the figure was 70 percent (53 women) and 73 percent (33 men), respectively. This increasing success in petitioning for divorce during the second period is commented upon by Cott.

> Sexual fidelity and good conduct were expected of both partners, but fidelity was not regularly enforced upon husbands by the threat of divorce until the mid-1770s, and a husband's abusive conduct never warranted divorce. The husband's characteristic obligation was provision of support; the wife's, obedient service. In this, marriage resembled an indenture between master and servant [Cott, 1976:611].

The fact that in the last quarter of the eighteenth century there was a marked increase in the average number of women per year who petitioned for and received divorces is felt to be reflective of a new set of assumptions regarding marriage.

> Divorce pleas by both sexes increased during the Revolutionary period and efficiency in treating them improved, reflecting modernization of both personal values and bureaucratic procedure. The disproportionate growth in women's petitions suggests that they, even more than men, had rising expectations in marriage; and the changing treatment of their petitions implies that wives' objections were being regarded more seriously—that their status within the family had risen, in the eyes of authorities [Cott, 1976:613].

So we see that while there was a certain consistency in colonial practices, as the new nation began to emerge there was evidence of a movement toward marriage based more on affection than on contract and with this went a concomitant change in granting of divorces.

To get some sense of the variation that existed within New England during the colonial era let us look at another jurisdiction, Connecticut. Connecticut was in the vanguard of early divorce legislation. There is only one recorded instance of a separation being granted; in virtually every other instance divorce (divorce *a vinculo*) was granted so as not to discriminate between husband and wife, and the grounds were liberal by then prevailing standards.

> By the act of 1667 the court of assistants is empowered to grant bills of divorce from the bond of matrimony to either party, with the privilege of remarriage, for adultery, fraudulent contract, three years' willful desertion with total neglect of duty, or for seven years' "providential" absence unheard of [Howard, 1904, vol. II:354].

Until 1843, these grounds stood despite the drafting of new divorce acts (at that time "habitual intemperance" and "intolerable cruelty" were added). Howard tells us that a real appreciation of the sweeping character of the Connecticut laws cannot be arrived at without an understanding of the broad meaning given to adultery in the early Connecticut laws. Somewhat in contrast to Massachusetts, adultery here covered the behavior of both husband and wife and also extramarital relations between the husband and an unmarried woman. Furthermore, fraudulent contract also assumed a much broader meaning than it had in other jurisdictions.

Among the interesting Connecticut cases discussed by Howard is that of Elizabeth Rogers, who in 1675 came before the court of assistants with a plea for divorce on the grounds that her husband was a "free thinker." In granting her custody of the children and alimony, the assembly noted that her husband had, among his other sins, "in open court declared that he did utterly renounce all the visible worship of New England, and professedly declare against the Christian Sabbath as a mere invention" (Howard, 1904, vol. II:357). Another interesting case is found close to a century later when, in 1753, Mary Larkum was granted a divorce from her husband on the grounds of his "barbarous and inhuman cruelty toward her." These two cases show both how traditional and how progressive the Connecticut courts could be.

In the other New England colonies the same enlightened picture was not present. Rhode Island, for example, resembled England in many respects more than it resembled Connecticut or even Massachusetts. In 1650 a bill was passed in Rhode Island which made divorce permissible only in the case of adultery, though in all fairness to our now smallest state it should be said that there was no discrimination between men and women. In 1685 the colony added "five years neglect or absence of either party" as grounds for divorce. But the overall picture is still a very conservative one (Howard, 1904, vol. II:365).

Before going on to discuss nineteenth-century developments, it should be emphasized that divorce in the seventeenth and eighteenth centuries was probably not a widespread phenomenon. In fact, it was probably a rare occurrence. That divorce was permitted in New England while it was generally prohibited in the southern colonies probably reflects the openness of the southern family system and the availability of sexual opportunities outside of marriage. On this point O'Neill has remarked:

> There was no divorce in the South because the loose, easy family system made it unnecessary, while the customs and doctrines of the prevailing Anglicanism forbade it. In the Northern colonies the situation was reversed. Allowing for local exceptions caused by the peculiarities of each colony's historical experience, the patriarchal family made divorces sometimes necessary, while the relatively libertarian ideas stemming from the Reformation made them possible [1967:10–11].

The new republic saw the "patriarchal" family mentioned by O'Neill being replaced by a "conjugal" one which was not only more equalitarian but also placed more emphasis on the qualitative aspects of marriage. This was the case in North and South alike. Divorce legislation in the nineteenth century must be understood in these terms.

NINETEENTH-CENTURY DEVELOPMENTS

During the nineteenth century some of the most liberal and at the same time some of the most conservative episodes in the history of American divorce took place; this century saw both the development of the divorce colony and the birth of the League for the Protection of the Family. One broad trend in the post-revolutionary period was the taking of divorce out of the hands of the many state assemblies and legislatures. In 1785 Pennsylvania gave its supreme court the right to terminate marriage on the grounds of impotence, bigamy, adultery, or desertion (Blake, 1962:49). New Jersey gave its chancery courts similar jurisdiction in 1794, though the grounds were limited to adultery and desertion. Corresponding legislation was carried out in New England during this period as well. The South, on the other hand, persisted well into the nineteenth century with a pattern of legislative divorce, that is, only the legislature could pass bills of absolute divorce. In Virginia, for example, it was not until 1827 that the chancery court was empowered to annul marriages and grant divorces, yet even then the legislature kept for itself the power to grant absolute divorces, not relinquishing this right until 1848. It was not until the Civil War, Blake claims, that the practice of legislative divorces had been abandoned by most states, although Delaware was still using this procedure as late as 1897 (Blake, 1962:56).

Not only do we see abandonment of legislative divorce during the first quarter of the nineteenth century, but we also see a liberalization of the existing grounds for divorce. We have already noted that in 1843 Connecticut broadened its already enlightened law by adding the grounds of "habitual intemperance" and "intolerable cruelty." Even earlier, in 1815, Pennsylvania had cut the period of desertion from four to two years and added "cruel and barbarous treatment by the husband endangering the life of the wife, and such indignities to the wife's person as rendered her condition intolerable, thereby forcing her to leave home" (Blake, 1962:57). In 1811, Massachusetts also loosened its stringent laws to include husband's neglect, cruelty, or desertion of his wife, and in 1835 included criminal conviction for which the sentence was seven years at hard labor. Yet, the real contribution of Massachusetts to innovative divorce legislation was not to come until some time later.

> In 1867 and in 1870, the Massachusetts legislature made two very important changes in the divorce laws. In the first year, the decree *nisi,* borrowed from English legislation, was introduced into American jurisprudence. This meant that a divorce decree became final only after a six months' waiting period—a useful device in discouraging hasty remarriages and uncovering any chicanery that might invalidate the original decree. The statute of 1870 abolished divorce from bed and board and broadened the grounds for absolute divorce to include extreme cruelty, habitual intoxication, and failure of the husband to provide. In rejecting judicial separation—that canonist invention which had survived the Reformation and become rooted in the English common law—the Massachusetts legislature were acting with their eyes wide open [Blake, 1962:61–62].

Yet not all states were so enlightened. New York continued until very recently to consider only adultery as grounds for divorce, thus driving its citizens elsewhere.

A very important development in nineteenth-century divorce legislation was the so-called omnibus clause, enacted by several states beginning with Indiana in 1824. The Indiana statute of 1824, after listing a number of grounds for divorce including adultery, cruelty, one year's abandonment, etc., ended by listing the following clause: "Any other cause for which the court shall deem it proper that a divorce should be granted" (quoted in Barnett, 1939:19). Similar clauses were enacted by Illinois in 1832, Washington in 1860, Utah in 1852, and other states such as Maine, Louisiana, and Arizona (Barnett, 1939:20). Such laws provided the courts with an extraordinary amount of discretion in determining divorce cases and the states that had such statutes often came to be known as divorce colonies because people began to go to these states for divorces. It is not surprising that conservative elements who opposed divorce aimed to eradicate these infamous omnibus clauses, a goal which they successfully achieved during the last half of the century.

THE MIGRATORY DIVORCE AND DIVORCE REFORM

The existence of conservative jurisdictions such as New York led many to seek what have been characterized as migratory divorces. Around the middle of the nineteenth century, a new trend emerged as the then western states started to be recognized as places not adverse to accommodating those looking for divorces. Ohio, in particular, seemed to service a fair number of outstaters, as is evident from the records of various counties within the state which show unusually high ratios of divorce to population size. This did not go unnoticed by influential people in those states, and outcries for more restrictive divorce legislation were soon heard.

Indiana enjoyed a special place in the hearts of those seeking marital dissolution. The absence of a residence requirement, in concert with an omnibus clause enacted in 1824, made Indiana a very attractive place to get a divorce. Even in 1852, when the 1824 statute was revised to require that the plaintiff be a resident, all that was needed was an affidavit. Blake quotes the *Indiana Daily Journal* in 1858:

> We are overrun by a flock of ill-used, and ill-using, petulant, libidinous, extravagant, ill-fitting husbands and wives as a sink is overrun with foul water of the whole house. . . . Nine out of ten have no better cause of divorce than their own depraved appetites [1962:119–120].

Yet, it was not really until 1873 that the state passed a divorce law that had teeth in it; not only did the 1873 law require a residence period of two years, but it also required proof of residence beyond a mere affidavit.

In the late 1860s, Chicago achieved a certain fame (or infamy) as a divorce mill, and stories were told of visitors being greeted at the platforms by young men promising a divorce within hours. Chicago was not alone in this lucrative trade; those states west of Illinois were also involved. As the country moved west, so did the divorce havens. South Dakota and North Dakota, when they were the Dakota territory, had a three-month residence requirement that made them obvious places for people to turn when laws got tough elsewhere, and even after they were admitted to the Union in 1889 they kept a brief residence period. In South Dakota concern was shown not merely with divorce but also with the vice it supposedly brought as a result of the influx of people seeking divorce. Towns began competing with each other for the "tourist" business. While it was not certain that those seeking divorce were actually the major consumers of these tainted or sinful pleasures, nevertheless a hue and cry was raised by some outraged citizens. Despite investigations by the National Divorce Reform League—which found that there had been many fewer divorces granted than was previously believed and which showed that those who came seeking divorces were rarely guilty of debauchery—passions continued at a feverish pitch. The banner of conservative reform was carried in South Dakota by one William H. Hare, an Episcopal bishop. His efforts in the early 1890s resulted in the passage of a bill in 1893 which lengthened the residence requirements to six months and in some cases this was extended to one year. He was not satisfied and the battle was carried further through the decade and into the twentieth century, when Hare's forces were finally able to get a statewide referendum which resulted in the passage of a 1907 law that required a one-year residence (Blake, 1962:124–128).

The story does not end here, however. The Oklahoma territory played a role in the 1890s not unlike that played by the Dakota territory in the

1870s. Wyoming joined into the act as the century drew to a close, and by 1910 only a small handful of states (Texas, Nebraska, Idaho, and Nevada) still had by then a relatively short six-month residency requirement. As we shall see, Nevada was to emerge as the modern center for the "quickie" divorce.

The conservative backlash to the growth of divorce in this country during the second half of the nineteenth century gained impetus during the 1880s. Early in 1881 the New England Divorce Reform League was founded. (In the previous year there had been 20,000 divorces awarded in the whole nation; while this figure may seem a tiny drop in the bucket by current standards, it was seen as a deluge by contemporary moralists.) This organization soon received national recognition and four years after its founding it became the National Divorce Reform League. In 1897 the name of the organization was changed to the National League for the Protection of the Family. The secretary of the New England organization was a Congregationalist clergyman, Samuel W. Dike. Dike refused to wed a couple because the male partner's previous marriage had ended in a divorce. Since this couple came from leading families in Royalton, Vermont, where Dike's parish was located, he soon found himself without a job. With considerable leisure time to devote to divorce, Dike rapidly became an expert in the area of divorce statistics and legislation and was soon chosen as secretary of the newly formed league (O'Neill, 1967:48–49).

Dike ultimately became an important lobbyist and argued in favor of legislation that would require the government to collect national divorce statistics. Such a bill was passed by the Senate in 1884, but a congressional adjournment brought an end to this bill. When it was revived two years later, it again went down because of a congressional adjournment. Finally in January 1887, under pressure from the Episcopal church, Congress appropriated a sum of $10,000 with an additional sum of $7,500 for the following year so that the commissioner of labor could collect statistics on marriage and divorce. We will have more to say on these early statistical studies later in this chapter.

An important development in divorce reform, in which Dike was to play a minor role, was the movement to develop some sort of uniformity in state divorce laws; this was seen by some reformers as a solution to the problem of migratory divorces. New York State was to take the lead in this cause under the governorship of David B. Hill, who finally succeeded in having his state's legislature appoint a body of three persons who were known as the Commissioners for the Promotion of Uniformity of Legislation in the United States. This commission was to deal with other matters as well, but divorce figured heavily in their considerations and deliberations. Other states were to join in this movement and the first annual meeting of the commission to discuss uniformity in state divorce laws was held in Saratoga, New York in 1892. Ultimately the divorce question was to prove too controversial for this commission, and little progress was made in the area of divorce legislation, though some positive action was taken in other areas. Nevertheless, by the end of the decade, thirty-two states were involved in this legislative uniformity movement.

Various religious bodies also entered into the struggle over divorce legislation during the 1890s and early 1900s. In January of 1902 the Interfaith Conference on Marriage and Divorce met, with representatives of twenty-five Protestant denominations in attendance. This body endorsed some of the earlier actions taken by the Commissioners for the Promotion of Uniformity. Under pressure from the Interchurch Conference, President Roosevelt came out in favor of uniform divorce legislation. Blake argues that as a result of this statement Congress created laws which permitted the further collection of national divorce statistics. Moreover, the National Congress on Uniform Divorce Laws (NCUDL) began to take shape under the leadership of Samuel W. Pennypacker who was then governor of Pennsylvania. The first meeting of this body was held in Washington, D.C. in February 1906, and representatives of all the states except five (South Carolina, Mississippi, Kansas, Montana, and Nevada) were present. Considerable controversy was generated at the meeting over matters such as the grounds for divorce, but especially over migratory divorces, which some felt were a result of the extremely conservative laws in New York and California. After much debate, the NCUDL was able to come up with six grounds for divorce on which agreement could be reached: adultery, bigamy, conviction for a felony, intolerable cruelty, willful desertion for two years, and habitual drunkenness (Blake, 1962:142).

But the most difficult matter to resolve remained that of migratory divorce. A motion was made for a proposal that would prevent people from obtaining a divorce in a state other than the one in which they were a permanent resident, unless the grounds for the divorce in the "foreign domicile" were also grounds in their home state. After an attempt by less conservative factions to offer a substitute motion that would have allowed a woman to return to the state in which she lived prior to her marriage in order to obtain a divorce, the more conservative motion was passed. The resolutions of the conference were handed to a committee to draft a law on which nationwide legislation could be modeled. When this was done, another national meeting was called by Governor Pennypacker in November 1906. At this meeting little was done to alter the letter or the principle of what had been decided at the previous meeting, and the nonmigration clause was included.

There was a long way to go, however, between passing a model divorce law and getting the states to accept it. While all the key figures in the divorce reform movement were overjoyed with the model bill, it was greeted with less enthusiasm by many others. As it happened, despite the acclaim it garnered in some quarters, the model statute was made into law by only three states: New Jersey, Delaware, and Wisconsin. Strangely enough, Pennsylvania, the home of the movement, did not get such a law through the state legislature.

MIGRATORY DIVORCE IN THE TWENTIETH CENTURY

During the twentieth century migratory divorce continued to be controversial, especially in states such as New York, New Jersey, and South Carolina, all of which had stringent divorce laws. It was during the first half of the twentieth century that the new divorce colonies arose to meet the needs of those states. In contrast to the divorce havens of the nineteenth century, those of the twentieth century—existing as they did in a less traditionally moralistic climate—endured and even flourished with the help and support of state governments and local business interests.

While a number of states, as well as several other countries, were to play an important role in the traffic in divorces, the state that is associated most readily in the public mind with the quickie divorce is Nevada—hence the title of Blake's excellent book, *The Road to Reno* (1962). It is worthwhile to look at divorce legislation in Nevada to see how it emerged as the major divorce colony in the twentieth century.

At the beginning of the century Nevada was among the few states that still had a six-month residence requirement for obtaining a divorce. This brief period, it is held, had less to do with stimulating a brisk divorce trade than it had to do with the fact that so many early migrants were miners for whom a brief residence regulation was appropriate in matters of voting and divorce. After a number of Nevada divorce cases were widely publicized early in the century, people in other parts of the country (particularly in the East) began to think of Nevada as a good place to get a divorce. To be sure this was helped along by enterprising people, such as the New York lawyer, William H. Schnitzer, who moved to Reno in 1907 from New York and began sending pamphlets to those who responded to his advertisements for quick divorces in newspapers around the country (Blake, 1962:153). While this attorney ran into trouble with the law, his efforts and those of others were not in vain, so much so that a conservative reform movement sprang up in the state.

The conservative forces included in its ranks not only clergymen, who played a pivotal role, but also women's groups and Reno's leading newspaper as well. They were ultimately successful in having the state's residence requirement changed from six months to one year. However, this was to be a pyrrhic victory. In the election of 1914 the state government underwent a shake-up; several legislators who had played a key role in the reform legislation and the governor were voted out of office. Their replacements apparently held different views on these matters, and under pressure from business interests (though the conservative church and women's groups were hardly quiet) the six-month residence period was returned.

Nevada's next step on the road to becoming a divorce capital came in 1927, when through some political chicanery a three-month residence requirement was instituted. In 1931, for fear that Nevada's place as the country's number one divorce spot—no small consideration in terms of

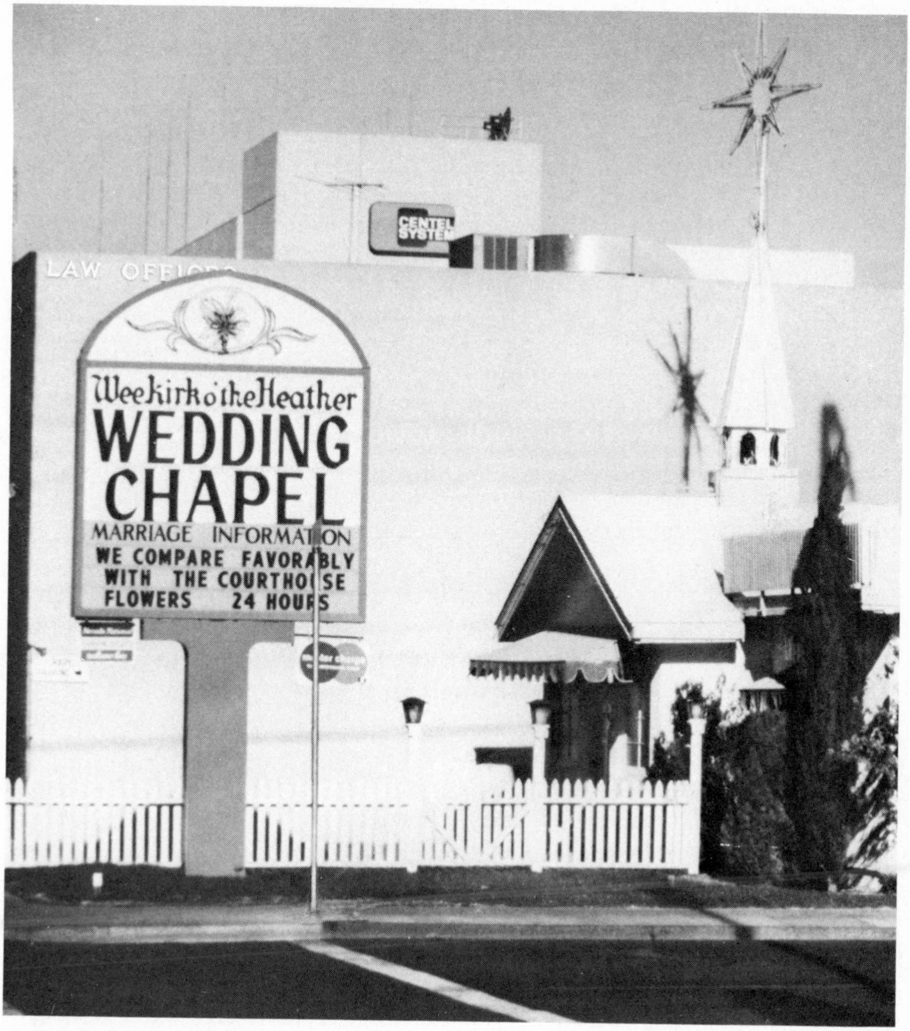

A Las Vegas wedding chapel. *(Lillian N. Bolstad/Peter Arnold Photo Archives)*

the annual revenue for the state—was threatened by other states reducing their one-year requirement to three months, Nevada's politicians went one step further and reduced the period to six weeks thus, temporarily at least, keeping its position secure.

> As streamlined in 1931, Nevada procedure permitted her Courts to grant a final decree of divorce to a plaintiff on the forty-third day of residence in the state, providing the defendant would cooperate by filing an appearance through a Nevada lawyer. If the defendant refused to appear but could be served with a summons, the divorce could be granted after 73 days; if notice had been given by publication, the case required 102 days for completion. The strictest requirement of the law had to do with the initial six weeks of residence. Corroborative

> proof that the plaintiff had actually lived in the state for this period was required, both to protect the interests of Nevada innkeepers and to give the divorce as strong a standing as possible in case it were challenged in the courts of other states. The nine grounds on which a divorce action could be based—adultery, cruelty, desertion, nonsupport, alcoholism, felony, impotency, five years' separation with cohabitation and five years' insanity—were no more liberal than those of many other states, but proof was made easy in uncontested cases by accepting the unsupported testimony of the plaintiff and by not requiring specific instances to support a general charge of cruelty [Blake, 1962: 158].

So Nevada kept its place as divorce capital of the nation.

While Nevada has maintained its special place both in the public mind and in national statistics during this century as the state to go to for a divorce, it has had competition from other states and other countries. For example, France and Mexico, during the 1920s, 1930s, and 1940s, figure importantly as migratory divorce havens for those rich enough to take advantage of them, though policy changes within these nations, especially in the case of France, made this only a temporary haven. The French government in the late 1920s began to investigate American migratory divorces. As a result, the law was not changed, but it was more carefully enforced so that it became increasingly difficult for Americans to obtain divorces in France, so much so that such divorces were down to 25 in 1934 from about 300 in 1926. In Mexico, the situation was different. While policy changes within the country did account for some variation, through the 1940s and 1950s, Mexico proved to be a divorce haven for many Americans, especially those from nearby California. California residents often applied for quick Mexican divorces while they waited for the longer California law to operate (that is, they also applied for a California divorce, but since this took a year, they first got the Mexican divorce so that they could remarry without waiting).

On the domestic front, Nevada had its main competition from Arkansas, Florida, Idaho, and Wyoming, all of which reduced their residency requirements during the depression in a more or less competitive manner. For a number of reasons, however, not all of these states were able to compete effectively against Nevada; as it turned out, Florida was the only state to offer real competition.

Yet when all was said and done, the extent of migratory divorce during the twentieth century appears to be rather exaggerated. It has been estimated that about ten years ago migratory divorces probably accounted for fewer than 5 percent of the divorces in this country. While more recent estimates are not available, the general easing of divorce requirements in many states, especially in New York (a state which contributed disproportionately to migratory divorce), has probably led to a reduction in their number.

LEGISLATIVE REFORM

The present decade has witnessed significant changes in divorce legislation. In 1970, California adopted a statute which allowed that irreconcilable differences were grounds for divorce. Since that time most states have adopted similar statutes or at least ones which are based on a no-fault principle. The no-fault principle, in contrast to traditional divorce law, holds that no one member of the marriage need be specified as the guilty party, either in terms of having committed an act, such as adultery, which is defined as grounds for divorce or being responsible in less specific terms for the marriage having broken down. Thus, "the 'guilt principle' and adversary system that heretofore traditionally characterized divorces are eliminated" (U.S. Department of Labor, 1975:375). Now it is necessary for a couple simply to satisfy the court that the marriage has reached a point of irreconcilability, and this may be tied to an argument of incompatibility in order to obtain a divorce. Moreover, in some jurisdictions, if a couple has legally separated for a specified period, the legal separation may be converted into a divorce. By mid-1974, only five states (Illinois, Mississippi, South Dakota, Pennsylvania, and Massachusetts) did not have a no-fault provision in their divorce statutes (U.S. Department of Labor, 1975:376). One final point with regard to recent divorce legislation warrants comment. In the old days alimony was something which only women received as a result of divorce settlement. Now, thirty states have statutes that permit the courts to award alimony to either party, depending upon need and other circumstances (U.S. Department of Labor, 1975:37).

DIVORCE STATISTICS

There is probably no body of statistical data that poses more problems for the sociologist than that on divorce. This is true not simply because of variations in the recording procedures and definitions, but also because of problems regarding the population sample that should be used as a base to compute such statistics.

Paul Jacobson, in his important study *American Marriage and Divorce* (1959), presents figures on the absolute number of divorces and rates per 1,000 in the population and per 1,000 existing marriages from 1860 to 1956. Figures for this period are not completely comparable since the accuracy of current figures (Jacobson's only go up to 1956) are considerably greater than those for earlier periods, especially those for the nineteenth century. Figures for the Civil War were estimated by Jacobson and those for 1867 and on were based on various sources. For example, we noted earlier that under pressure from the New England Divorce Reform League, the gov-

Table 11-1. ANNUAL MARITAL DISSOLUTIONS BY DEATH AND LEGAL DIVORCE, AND RATES PER 1,000 EXISTING MARRIAGES, 1890–1970

Year	Dissolutions per year		Per 1,000 existing marriages[a]			Divorces as percent of total dissolution
	Deaths[b]	Divorces[c]	Deaths	Divorces	Combined	
1860–64	197,200	7,170	32.1	1.2	33.3	3.5
1865–69	207,000	10,529	31.1	1.6	32.7	4.8
1870–74	226,400	12,417	30.3	1.7	32.0	5.2
1875–79	238,600	15,574	28.7	1.9	30.6	6.1
1880–84	285,400	21,746	30.6	2.3	33.0	7.1
1885–89	290,400	27,466	27.6	2.6	30.2	8.6
1890–94	334,800	36,123	28.3	3.1	31.3	9.7
1895–99	328,800	45,462	24.9	3.4	28.4	12.1
1900–04	390,800	61,868	26.5	4.2	30.6	13.7
1905–09	427,400	74,626	25.4	4.4	29.8	14.9
1910–14	453,600	91,695	23.7	4.8	28.5	16.8
1915–19	551,000	119,529	26.0	5.6	31.6	17.8
1920–24	504,200	164,917	21.9	7.2	29.0	24.6
1925–29	573,200	193,218	22.6	7.6	30.3	25.2
1930–34	590,800	183,441	21.9	6.8	28.7	23.7
1935–39	634,600	239,600	21.9	8.3	30.2	27.4
1940–44	656,400	330,557	20.4	10.3	30.7	33.5
1945–49	681,200	485,641	19.2	13.7	32.8	41.6
1950–54	692,400	385,429	18.2	10.0	28.3	35.9
1955–59	733,600[d]	385,385	18.3	9.2	27.8	34.2
1960–64	n.a.	419,600	n.a.	9.6	n.a.	n.a.
1965–69	n.a.	544,800	n.a.	11.7	n.a.	n.a.
1960	790,400	393,000	18.9	9.4	28.3	33.2
1961	789,200	414,000	18.7	9.8	28.6	34.4
1965	820,800	479,000	18.5	10.8	29.4	36.9
1970	908,200	715,000	19.3	15.2	34.5	44.0

SOURCE: Kingsley Davis, *Demographic and Social Aspects of Population Growth*, vol. 1 (Washington, D.C.: Government Printing Office, 1972), p. 256.

[a] Existing marriages, 1860–1949, from Paul H. Jacobson, *American Marriage and Divorce* (New York: Rinehart, 1969), Tables A6-A9, A22 (number of married *men*); 1950–60, from U.S. Bureau of the Census, *Historical Statistics of the United States;* 1961 and 1965 from *Statistical Abstract of the United States;* 1970 from *U.S. Census of Population: 1970, United States Summary,* p. 311.

[b] Deaths to married persons, 1860–1955 from Jacobson, *op cit.,* p. 178; 1959–61 from National Office of Vital Statistics, Mortality (A) for relevant years; 1965 and 1970 estimated by present writer.

[c] Divorces 1860–1954, from Jacobson, *op. cit.*, Table 42; 1955–69, from NCHS, "Divorce Statistics, 1969," *Monthly Vital Statistics Report*, July 22, 1971, Vol. 20, No. 4, Supplement 2; 1970 from "Annual Summary for the United States, 1970," *ibid.*, September 21, 1971, Vol. 19, No. 13.

[d] Average for 1955 and 1959 only.

ernment authorized the commissioner of labor to collect statistics on marriage and divorce. The first study, which was published in 1889, covered the years 1867–1886, and supposedly contains more reliable figures on divorce than it does on marriage, but since state files varied in completeness and comprehensiveness, these figures are not completely accurate, though they are certainly the best approximation we have to date. The second national study also grew out of the lobbying of Reverend Dike and his associates. This study, which covered the period 1887–1906, together with the first study, resulted in our having at least some picture of the divorce situation in this country from 1867 to 1906. Table 11-1 was put together by Kingsley Davis (1972) for the Commission on Population Growth and the American Future and draws largely upon Jacobson's work with new data added from other sources.

As we have already indicated, it is extremely difficult to come up with accurate estimates of divorce before 1860; however, when we realize that the rate for 1860 is 1.2 and that for 1890 is 3.0, projecting backward 30 years from 1860 would give us a negative rate, so we may assume that during the first half of the nineteenth century rates probably maintained themselves below or around 1.0. In any case the growth in divorce between 1860 and 1970 is dramatic to say the least. While some of the long-term trends in divorce can be partially explained in terms of such compositional effects as proportion of the population married and availability of divorce as well as more accurate reporting in recent years, the short-run changes, such as a growth of nearly 50 percent between 1965 and 1970, are more difficult to explain, though legal changes during this period are possibly at work. Moreover, rates are continuing to rise. The rate for 1974 comparable to that found in Table 11-1 was 19.3, an increase of about 30 percent; in 1972 it was 17.0, and in 1973, 18.2 (U.S. Dept. of Health, Education and Welfare, 1976:2).

A point that has been made over and over again by those attempting to study long-term trends in American divorce is that we must take into account changes in life expectancy (Jacobson, 1959). Divorce, we must realize, is only one form of marital dissolution—separation, desertion, and death are also important factors. We noted earlier in the book that life expectancy in this country has gone up dramatically since the nineteenth century.

> In the 1860's, the annual marital dissolution due to the death of the husband or wife averaged 31.5 per 1,000 existing marriages. With the ensuing reduction in mortality, this rate dropped to 26 per 1,000 in the 1900s and to less than 17.5 during 1954–56 [Jacobson, 1959:141].

Thus it is important to get a total picture of the combined impact of what Walter Willcox, the first demographer to recognize this problem, spoke of as marital dissolutions that occur "naturally" and "civilly" (1891). In the period from 1860 to 1864, according to Table 11-1, the marital dissolution rate by death was 32.1 and by divorce 1.2, giving us a total of 33.3, while in 1970 it was 19.3 and 15.2, respectively, giving us a combined rate of 34.5, which is only slightly higher than what was found 110 years earlier.

> Since that data as far as possible, including annulments, we can say that, except for *de facto* separations and desertions (the changes in which are unknown), *the overall rate of marital dissolution in the United States has not increased during more than a century* [Davis, 1972:255].

Still, as Davis goes on to point out, the differential contribution of death and divorce to dissolution rates has changed significantly, with divorce rising from 3.5 percent to 44.0 percent in the contribution it makes to the total, though as of 1970 it had yet to exceed death as the primary factor in marital dissolution.

The growth of divorce in the 1970s does suggest, however, that we are on the verge of a situation where divorce will play a greater role than death in annual marital dissolution rates for all age groups. A senior demographer recently pointed out that, "Available evidence indicates that about one of every three women who are now 30 years old may expect to have their first marriage end in divorce" (Glick, 1975).

WHY HAS DIVORCE INCREASED IN THE LAST CENTURY?

How does the sociologist make sense out of the increasing divorce rate? There are two explanations that sociologists bring to this phenomenon: one focuses on changes in the meaning of marriage, the other on changes in personality. Both of these changes have been discussed earlier, but not in relation to divorce.

The first explanation directs our attention to the facts discussed earlier concerning the way in which marriage has changed as a result of the impact of modernization. William Goode has noted:

> One may say, with reference to the rise in the divorce rate (in all countries that permit divorce), that it is based upon (1) changes in the *value* system, (2) lessened emphasis by the *circles* of friends and kin on the necessity for marital stability, and (3) new *alternatives* to the existing marriage. For instance, the wife can now support herself, even if poorly, by her own effort. In addition, since there are many other divorcees, both husband and wife can almost certainly remarry. In most adult age groups in the United States, the chances of eventual marriage are higher for divorcees than for single people of the same age [1963:81].

Related to Goode's above remarks is the fact that marriage has now become more of a relationship associated with the pursuit of leisure than one associated with economically productive activity. Elaine May (1975) analyzed a sample of 500 Los Angeles divorce cases from 1890 to 1920 and interpreted these cases as reflecting the failure of many marriages to live up to the new heightened standards of married life. She does not feel that the divorced women she studied were avant-garde libertarians; rather they were housewives committed to a home-centered happy marriage that they were unable to achieve. May argues that in many respects these women were more Victorian than flappers. The premodern chain of economic necessity was apparently much more binding than the thread of interpersonal relationships.

To be sure, a divorce is not something lightly contemplated even in this day of liberal divorce laws. While the role of children in keeping a couple together has often been exaggerated (in point of fact, more children are now affected by divorce than ever before [Davis, 1972]), this is in fact a consideration for many people, as well as more mundane factors such as the ability of the husband to pay child support and/or alimony and still have enough money to remarry or live alone. For others the fear of loneliness is also present. But when all is said and done, many people do take the leap and end their marriages despite the problems created. Couples are increasingly unwilling to bear the burdens of a conflict-filled or empty relationship. Yet this behavior is not proportionately distributed in the population; some people appear more divorce prone than others. Perhaps by exploring the differences among those who seek divorce we can further our understanding of the dynamics of divorce.

One indirect bit of supporting information for our general interpretation of divorce is found in Carter and Glick's data on urban-rural differences (1970). Urban rates of divorce are consistently higher than rural rates for men and women, white and nonwhite. One should not too readily interpret this to mean that rural areas show low rates solely because these are agricultural areas where we are likely to find large numbers of farm couples who have strong economic bonds. However, some data show that farm workers have the lowest divorce rates of any broadly defined occupational group, and farmers and farm managers, those who would be even more likely to have traditional cooperative marriages, show an even lower rate (Winch, 1971:590). What may also be an important factor in low rural rates is the nature of the community.

New values and behavior patterns enter rural areas slowly. Max Rheinstein quotes Plateris discussing variation by community in divorce:

> The main characteristic of communities, underlying variations in permissiveness of divorce laws and in the distribution of marriage disruption, seems to be social stability or, conversely, social anomie [quoted in Rheinstein, 1972:469].

While it is not safe to say that rural communities always manifest less anomie than urban ones, this is generally the case—precisely because of their traditionalism. In these communities religion is apt to be found in its fundamentalist form, kinship ties are likely to be of a functional character, and in general the community looms larger in the life of an individual than in urban areas. It is probably because of this traditionalism, as well as the "economic-bond" character of marriages, that divorce rates are consistently lower.

The persistence of traditional values even within urban-industrial societies is really only part of the picture of divorce differentials in our society. To be sure, they help us understand that as the country has become more urban, and more people abandon farms for the city, as they have done in great numbers during this century, this has affected divorce rates. Yet to some extent we would expect this to be offset by changes in such things as education, type of employment, and socialization.

In Chapter 6 we argued that changes in middle-class socialization practices, which themselves grew out of changes in the nature of work, resulted in more and more young people manifesting what we might describe as a new personality type, one which places great emphasis on such things as intellectualism, creativity, antiauthoritarianism, and a concern with the quality of one's inner life. Carmi Schooler (1972) found such characteristics to be particularly true of young people who came from homes in which the father had higher education, which were located in urban areas, and in which religious training was nonfundamentalist and nonritualistic, if it existed at all. Such people probably manifest the results of exposure to the most modern aspects of society. Therefore we must study these people and their lives if we are to understand whether modern education, employment, and socialization offset the rise in divorce rates created by the disappearance of traditional society. For example, does education as an independent variable show a negative correlation with divorce?

The relationship between education and divorce is a rather complicated one. Carter and Glick (1970) have national data showing that only for white males do we see a more or less directly negative relationship between education and divorce (that is, the more educated the man the less likely he is to divorce). These data are problematic because they show the number of individuals who are divorced at the time of the census, but they do not enumerate those who were divorced but who later remarried. Since highly educated women are somewhat less likely to marry in the first place than their less educated sisters, it would not come as a surprise to find the remarriage rates among divorced women in this group to be lower than for men. Although these figures must be taken with a grain of salt, they do reveal a trend which others have discovered as well. Winch in commenting on Hillman's findings notes:

> Where education is the index and where, therefore, it makes sense to report data on females as well as males, the picture becomes very mixed. If we had only the separation rates on white males, we could be categorical about the negative correlation. If we had only the divorce rates for nonwhite females, we could insist just as categorically on a positive correlation between socioeconomic status and divorce rates. And a curvilinear relationship can be demonstrated on the basis of the divorce rates of nonwhite males, the separation rates of nonwhite females, or the combined divorce plus separation rates for whites, both males and females [1971:590–591].

There is some reason to believe that the reason such disparate findings have been discovered for education and divorce is that the data are being confounded by the effects of income, a variable which, while related to education, has a much greater independent effect on divorce. Evidence for this is found in an excellent article by Phillips Cutright (1971).

INCOME AND DIVORCE

Cutright's article deals with marital stability rather than divorce per se, and focuses on married males aged 45–54 living with their first wives and married only once (1971). In general, his findings support the relationships discussed earlier of negative correlation between education and marital dissolution for white males and a curvilinear one for nonwhite males. What is more significant here, however, and what Cutright rests his case on, is the consistently linear effect of income for both whites and nonwhites. The net mean effects seem to make it clear, as Cutright argues, that "It is earnings, not education, that affects stability of first marriages" (1971:293). Not satisfied to stop here, Cutright goes on to look at occupational prestige and divorce. In general there is a positive relationship between occupational prestige and marital stability, for example, 83 percent of the professional and technical personnel were still living with their first wives in contrast to 75.8 percent of nonfarm laborers (1971:294). But, when income is controlled, the overall relationship is dramatically reduced, so much so that Cutright concludes that "the overall positive association of stability with prestige disappears" (1971:294). He summarizes his findings as follows:

> We conclude that for both whites and non-whites: 1) the majority of men remain with their first wife, regardless of socioeconomic position; 2) when high years of education are not accompanied by high earnings marital stability will usually decrease; 3) stability of marriage among farmers and farm managers is not related to either education or earnings; 4) the prestige of occupations has no positive effect on stability when earnings are controlled; 5) education and occupational status are positively related to stability because they are causes of earnings levels, *but neither education nor occupation has positive effects independent of their association with earnings* [emphasis added, 1971:295].

Given the arguments that have so far been developed in this book, one might legitimately be confused by Cutright's findings. We would certainly expect that education would produce the flexibility in interpersonal relations that would be highly conducive to marital stability. Moreover, we would assume that highly educated couples would have more in common, score higher on those dimensions of domestic life that have been found to be associated with marital happiness, and in general manifest the resources that Winch (1971), among others, has argued are at the heart of marital stability. In order to understand how income acts as it does on marital stability we might do well to turn briefly from the topic of divorce and consider the topic of marital happiness.

In what is perhaps the most carefully conceived and executed study of "happiness" to date, Norman Bradburn found that there was a positive relationship between the percent of married people describing their marriages as "very happy" and socioeconomic status (1969:156). The question for us now becomes what is it that contributes to the greater marital happiness of the high SES group? Partial answers for this question are found in further analysis of the happiness data, specifically in a paper by Susan Orden and Norman Bradburn (1968).

Orden and Bradburn find that those individuals who rate their marriages as "very happy" tend to score high on their indexes of marital companionship, low in sociability, and low on their index of marital tensions. This is to say that these people are likely to visit friends together, go to a movie together (marital sociability), and also spend an evening chatting, taking a drive, or walking for pleasure (marital companionship); they are not likely to have disagreements and arguments about in-laws, being tired, not showing love, etc. (marital tensions). If, then, a happy marriage is one characterized by a fair amount of sociability and companionship and a low amount of tension, why are rich people more likely to have such a marriage? Again, it would seem that education might provide a more conducive culture for such a marriage to grow in than would income per se, yet as we have learned, this is not the case. To be sure, there are other factors at work, such as stage in family cycle, whether or not a wife is working, etc., but when all is said and done, money is still pivotal.

The only sociologist who has directed his attention specifically to this question is John Scanzoni, who in the book *Opportunity and the Family* (1970), sets forth a series of propositional statements which he sees as tying together the questions of economics and marriage. He summarizes his arguments in the following fashion:

> In simplified form, we may suggest that the husband in modern society exchanges his status for conjugal solidarity. If we accept as given that expressive satisfactions are the major manifest goals of modern marriage, and the major latent goal is status and economic well being, then we may say that the latent goal influences the attainment of the manifest goal. . . . Specifically, the greater the degree of the husband's articulation with the economic opportunity system, the more fully and extensively is the interlocking network of conjugal rights and duties performed in a reciprocal fashion. The economic rewards he provides induce motivation in the wife to respond positively to him, and her response in turn gives rise to a continuing cycle of rectitude and gratitude [1970:21].

What Scanzoni is saying may have a very unpleasant ring for many people, suggesting as he does that marital satisfaction rests to a considerable extent on the ability of the husband to adequately provide for the family's needs and desires, yet Scanzoni clearly points out that this model rests on the assumption that the woman is not pursuing a career, though it does not preclude her working. He recognizes that:

> In our society, a theoretically related long-range trend may be toward educated women pursuing individualistic careers to the degree that their status is recognized independently of their husband's. What the actual consequences of this might be for the conjugal family system as we now know it is unclear because the pervasiveness of this trend is speculative at best [1970:22].

It is to Scanzoni's credit that he recognizes this development, because if it does continue and becomes the rule, even in the middle class, it could drastically alter current patterns of marriage and divorce. But for now let us look at what obtains currently in American marriages regarding economic position and marital satisfaction.

The results of Scanzoni's research, based on 900 couples in the Detroit area, for the most part confirm his preconceptions. Based on his findings, he puts forth a series of generalizations about the study and at the same time suggests directions for future research.

> a. Therefore, the greater the degree of marital-status rewards provided by the husband, the greater is the degree of perceived satisfactions with primary relations (valued goals) and with authority relations, and thus:
> (1) The greater is the degree of husband-wife interdependence.
> (2) The greater are the degrees of husband-wife feelings of cohesion and solidarity.
>
> b. The greater is the interdependence, and the greater the feeling of cohesion and solidarity, the greater is the probability of system-maintenance, of stability, or order, and the more is dissolution unlikely.
>
> c. Conversely, the less the degree of material-status rewards provided by the husband, the less the degree of perceived satisfactions with primary relations and with authority relations. Therefore:
> (1) The less is the degree of husband-wife interdependence.
> (2) The less is the degree of feelings of solidarity and cohesion.
> (3) The less is the probability of system maintenance [1970:187].

While by no means providing us with *the* answer—a considerable amount of the variance remains unexplained—Scanzoni nonetheless gives us some sense of why divorce should be associated more with income than with occupation or education. But as Scanzoni has recognized, this could be changing as more and more women not only enter the work force, but begin to think of their work as careers. As this happens we would expect the whole economic linkage of the family to the larger society to undergo change and affect the divorce rate. The direction of this change is not easy to predict; divorce rates could be higher or lower, depending on associated changes in marital expectations.

Before leaving this topic, it should be noted that one recent study of 2,500 families did not find a positive relationship between income and marital stability.

> In fact, high income families, or those in which the husband was highly successful, appeared to be more unstable than those with moderate incomes [Ross and Sawhill, 1975:161].

This could mean that the new expectations Scanzoni was talking about have already begun to make themselves felt, or that previous studies have not included a sufficiently wide range of income groups, that is, they may have merely compared lower- and middle-income groups. Those at the upper end of the income scale may not be constrained by financial worries, since there may be sufficient income for both to live in the style to which they have grown accustomed. Such people quite readily therefore may contemplate divorce. To be sure, such an interpretation is speculative, but still worthy of consideration.

What about the new personality type mentioned earlier? What does that have to do with divorce rates? It would seem clear that the marital patterns of people socialized with the values of intellectualism, creativity, and antiauthoritarianism are difficult to estimate as of yet. We would think that such people would be likely to wind up in dual-career marriages, or at least not wind up in those where sex-role stereotyping and fundamental role allocations in terms of instrumentality and affectivity would be as present as in more conventional families. Therefore, we would expect that financial resources per se would be of less consequence in determining the degree of marital satisfaction and the likelihood of the couple winding up in a divorce court. We might further expect that such couples would be more concerned with the degree to which a relationship permitted personal growth than the degree to which it allowed a couple to consume at a particular level, though one should be careful not to play down material considerations too much. Obviously, we lack the data to say anything with certainty here.

THE DIVORCE PRONE

There is no shortage of evidence to show that those who marry young are more divorce prone than those who marry later. Paul Glick and Arthur Norton (1971) report that the annual probability of divorce for white men under 70 years between 1960 and 1966 was 12 (per 1,000) for those who married at 19 years or under; while it was 6 (per 1,000) for those married between 20 and 24; 4 for those between 25 and 29; and 5 for those who were 30 or over. Using 1960 vital statistics data, P. Krishnan (1971) presents divorce tables from 18 states which show that the probability of ever becoming divorced for white and nonwhite women was .490 for the 14–19 group, .2448 for the 20–24 group, .1745 for the 25–29 group and .1286 for the 30–34 group. Others have reported similar results (Bumpass and Sweet, 1972). It seems clear that however the data is presented, either in terms of actuality or probability, people who marry young show a marked divorce proneness. Why?

One reason that has been put forth to explain the high rate of divorce among young people is the frequency of shotgun weddings among this group. As a group, those who marry before twenty are much more likely to be pressured into marriage by an unplanned pregnancy than their older counterparts. In the middle 1960s, 30 percent of the first-born children of women married under age 20 were premaritally conceived, in contrast to 6 percent of those who married after 25. The situation is compounded here by the fact that not only are young brides more apt to walk to the altar already pregnant, but they are also more likely than their older sisters to suffer from other disadvantages in terms of marital stability (Bumpass and Sweet, 1972). Scanzoni, citing 1970 figures, notes:

> Among married women whose family incomes were under $3,000, 38 percent of first births were conceived prior to marriage. When the income was $3,000 to $4,999 the premarital conception figure was 23 percent; for $5,000 to $6,999 incomes the figure was 18 percent; it was 12 percent for incomes $7,000 to $9,999; and 8 percent for incomes of $10,000 and over. Finally, among all married women with four years or more of college, only 7.5 percent of the first births were premaritally conceived. With one to three years of college, the figure was 18.1 percent; four years of high school, 20.7 percent; one to three years of high school, 31.6 percent; elementary school, 21.2 percent [1972:22].

Thus it may just be that people who marry young lack the finances, the education, and the social-emotional resources necessary for a stable relationship.

Throughout the major portion of this century there has been a decline in age of first marriages. In 1900 it was 25.9 years for men and 21.9 for women, while in 1960 it was 22.8 for men and 20.3 for women. However, since the late 1960s there has been an upturn. The average age in 1970 was 23.2 for men and 20.8 for women; in 1975 it was 23.5 for men and 21.5 for women. If this trend continues it could have an effect on divorce, since as we have just noted age at first marriage is strongly related to divorce.

Another factor affecting divorce proneness that has been investigated by a number of sociologists is the intergenerational transmission of marital instability. The question here is, do the children of divorced parents show a greater likelihood of winding up divorced than their counterparts from more stable families? Jerold Heiss (1972) with a national sample of black Americans found the correlation strongest in the middle-class, especially for females, if the parental break occurred when the woman was young; however, even among this group the explanatory power of parental marital instability was small. Hallowell Pope and Charles Mueller (1976) with several national samples, including both blacks and whites, obtained results which they feel show parental marital instability to be positively related to divorce for males and females black and white alike. But their findings are really not all that different than Heiss's; they just seem to make more of them. The upshot of this research is that it is not possible at present to say with any certainty if divorce proneness is intergenerationally contagious, but it is a subject that does warrant further research.

THE IMPACT OF LIBERALIZED LAWS

The impact of increasingly liberalized divorce legislation is difficult to estimate. Rheinstein (1972) carefully reviews the literature on this topic. He argues that liberalized laws have had a positive effect on divorce rates, not because they precipitate more marriage breakdowns, but rather because people who would previously have had to resort to separations can now obtain divorces. Nonetheless, he feels that the major amount of variation in divorce rates discovered between various jurisdictions is explainable largely in terms of nonlegal variables such as religion, economic position of women, degree of industrialization, etc. (1972:306–307). This interpretation has, however, been called into question by Dorothy Stetson and Gerald Wright's data (1975), which reveals a strong relationship between permissiveness of divorce laws and divorce rates when interstate comparisons are made.

In 1967 New York changed its divorce laws (prior to 1967 adultery was the sole ground for divorce) to a more liberal statute including cruelty. The fruits of this change are readily apparent:

> This law became effective in September 1967, and the number of divorces and annulments doubled from 7,136 in 1967 to 14,861 in 1968 and tripled to 21,184 in 1969. The rate grew accordingly from 0.4 to 0.8 to 1.2 (these are crude figures based on total population rather than on marriages). Thus, in spite of the exceptional increase, the New York rate for 1969 was less than one-half of the national rate [U.S. Department of Health, Education and Welfare (DHEW), 1973:3].

Moreover, there is no evidence that states to which New Yorkers have traditionally gone for divorces, such as Nevada, showed any concomitant decline. Thus one can interpret the rise in the New York rate as an addition to the national rate rather than a substitution of change in place (DHEW, 1973:31). It will not come as a surprise to readers to learn that in 1969 annulments represented 10 percent of the total number of divorces and annulments in New York, while in 1967 and in previous years they represented more than one-third. Thus we see a redistribution in the mode employed by people to dissolve unsatisfactory relationships, but what also may be happening nationally as a result of an increase in "no fault" legislation is "an advancement in timing of divorces that, under previous conditions, would have been spread over a longer number of years" (Arthur Norton and Paul Glick, 1976:13).

Before going on to make a summary statement about the topic of divorce, something should be said about the meaning of escalating divorce rates as a sign of disillusionment with marriage. Some of those who have brooded and moaned in the media over the recent growth in divorce rates have held that this is a threat to marriage and that people are leaving marriage in vast numbers. What these Jeremiahs forget is that many of these people ultimately remarry, most rather quickly. At every age the chances of a divorced person remarrying are greater than those of a person who has not previously been married. That this holds for the young as well as the old is especially significant because it gives the lie to the notion that the reason divorced people marry more readily than previously unmarried persons is that by the time they have reentered the marriage market those who have never been married are in some way unfit, rejected, handicapped, etc. The 1970 census data show that three-quarters of divorced American females remarry after divorce and the same holds for five out of six divorced men (Glick, 1975). Since 1970, however, there has been some decline in remarriage rates but they are still very high (Norton and Glick, 1976:5). Davis neatly summarized the meaning of this trend by writing:

> The significance of the brisk rate of remarriage is plain; it means that the American people do not have a high and rising rate of legal divorce and annulment because they are losing interest in marriage and family. Rather, they have such a high rate because they desire a compatible and satisfactory family. Thus, despite a high legal divorce rate, a high proportion is married—higher than in any other industrial society. Americans expect a great deal out of the state of wedlock, and when a particular marriage proves unsatisfactory, they seek to dissolve it and try again [1972:262].

In many ways, then, the rise in divorce during the twentieth century is indicative of the growing importance we place upon marriage, rather than this institution's demise. To be sure, what we expect from marriage and how we judge it are rather different from what was true years ago. But marriage today shows few signs that it will soon slip into oblivion.

THE FUTURE OF DIVORCE

Demographers have learned the bitter lesson of trying to predict future fertility rates from past behavior, and students of divorce might do well to learn from them. With this in mind the most cautious statements should be made about the future of divorce in this country. We can say that in recent years the probability of marriage ending in divorce has risen. As we have already noted, a census bureau demographer estimated that one-third of the first marriages which in 1975 involved a woman aged 30 would be dissolved by divorce (Glick, 1975). Despite such seemingly clear cut indications of future growth in divorce, we must keep in mind that what we are dealing with here are projections. Any number of things, including the growth in the median age at first marriage, could bring about a deceleration or even a reversal of this trend!

SUMMARY

We have seen in this chapter that divorce is not new to the twentieth century. Quite the contrary, it has been with us virtually from the inception of English settlement here. Certainly, it was not a phenomenon of great consequence in the seventeenth century, but it was nonetheless a reality of Puritan life and one which was dealt with in a rather enlightened manner, compared with the attitudes and laws that prevailed in the mother country at that time. In England divorce with the right to remarry was the exception; here it was generally the rule. Still, up until the last quarter of the eighteenth century, women were subject to a double standard wherein they could be divorced by their husbands on the sole ground of adultery, but their husbands were treated less harshly when similar claims were brought against them. Cott (1976) sees the increase in divorce suits in the 1770s and the more even-handed treatment received by women as evidence of a new attitude toward marriage, one which placed more emphasis on its relational aspects and less on its contractual ones—a trend which May's (1975) research reveals continued throughout the nineteenth and into the twentieth century.

In the nineteenth century we saw the growth of new and liberal divorce laws, most notably the so-called omnibus clauses, which made divorce more readily accessible to a greater portion of the population, especially when they were combined with lenient residence requirements. While early nineteenth-century divorce statistics are not available, it does appear that rates were rising sufficiently to call forth reform movements. These movements, ostensibly concerned with the standardization of divorce laws, were in fact concerned with keeping divorce rates down.

From the Civil War onward, the period for which we first have data, U.S. divorce rates have climbed, and since the 1960s they have climbed at an exceptionally high rate. Currently they are among the highest in the world (Davis, 1972). We have argued that this increase is not an indication of any wholesale disillusionment with marriage per se, but rather is a reflection of the kinds of demands people are placing on marriage. Evidence in support of this interpretation is found in the rapidity with which divorced people remarry.

NYPL Picture Collection

ETHNIC VARIATION: The Black Family

12

In one respect this chapter represents a departure from those that have come before it. Each of them was concerned with an aspect of American family life and the changes it had undergone as a result of modernization. Now we shift our attention to one group of Americans and their experiences in this nation, in an attempt to convey how varied and diverse American family experience has been and continues to be.

ETHNICITY AND THE FAMILY

Ethnicity refers to cultural traits associated with national origins that give a group a sense of identity and a certain distinctiveness. Thus we speak of Italian-Americans, Polish-Americans, Irish-Americans, and so on. Each of these groups is supposedly set apart from the dominant culture by traits that derive from previous direct or indirect contact with another culture. In the case of first-generation ethnics, the contact refers to the primary experience of persons who were born in another country. Second- and third-generation ethnics may still maintain a certain distinctiveness as a result of parental and community interactions. Most Americans are the children, grandchildren, or great-grandchildren of people who were immigrants, and therefore identify with a particular ethnic group.

It may come as a surprise to many to learn that not long ago many people with very definable ethnic heritages had rather ambivalent feelings about acknowledging their heritage, often going to great lengths to conceal it and resorting to such ruses as changing their names, straightening their hair, denying that they could speak the language they were first taught at home, etc. They wanted to be Americans with a capital "A" and this often meant assimilating to a model of white Anglo-Saxon culture. For a variety of reasons—perhaps most importantly because of the black Civil Rights movement of the 1960s—many people now take a different view of their ethnic past, and today pride themselves on the very things their parents tried so hard to hide.

For the family sociologist, the question of ethnic difference is important because it raises doubts about the old theory of the "melting pot." This concept views American society as an amalgam of the cultural heritages of the peoples who have come here during the two centuries of our existence. Supposedly, the people who first came were more Norwegian or Japanese than American, but if not within their own lifetimes then certainly within their children's lifetimes American culture superseded their ethnic culture, and their descendants, at least culturally, become Americans whose only real distinctiveness resided in the fact that they had different last names. In the early 1960s, Nathan Glazer and Daniel Moynihan published an important book called *Beyond the Melting Pot* (1963). They argued that, at least in American cities, the melting pot may not have had a fire under it. Certainly people of various ethnic heritages were thrown together in the big cities, but even after three generations there were still important cultural differences to be observed. Their thesis came as no surprise to the sociologists who were working in the field of ethnic identity, but it did cause the discipline as a whole to take a second look at the melting pot theory.

For the sociologist interested in questions of family and kinship, the topic of ethnic differences was more celebrated in belief and anecdote than in carefully researched publications. At the time that Glazer and Moynihan published their book there were only a handful of studies that focused on ethnic variation in family-related traits and those that existed were far from rigorous, with a few notable exceptions (Campisi, 1948; Rubel, 1966; Padilla, 1958; Kramer and Leventman, 1961). In the next decade the picture changed dramatically, and while all the facts are not in, we are beginning to have some reliable research literature on this topic (Schlesinger, 1971; Grebler et al., 1970; Ianni, 1972; Mindel and Habenstein, 1976). Still, this literature represents a comprehensive treatment of the topic for only one group—Afro-Americans (Willie, 1970; Rainwater, 1970; Ladner, 1971; Heiss, 1975; Stack, 1974).

THE MOYNIHAN REPORT

When one looks back at the 1960s the reason for the preponderance of research on the black family becomes evident. During that decade the Civil Rights movement became a key political issue in the nation, resulting in the passage of much antidiscrimination legislation, as the cry of "black is beautiful" resounded throughout the country. Part of the more recent interest in white ethnics is an offshoot of this, as other groups developed a new pride in their own heritage, but as yet this has not been translated into wide-ranging research on their family structures. Moreover, for the black family a veritable conflagration was started by a report published in 1965, *The Negro Family: The Case for National Action,* by Moynihan, the second author of *Beyond the Melting Pot,* who was then an assistant secretary for labor. The thrust of this report can be summarized in two brief excerpts:

> The United States is approaching a new crisis in race relations. . . .
>
> The fundamental problem, in which this is most clearly the case, is that of family structure. The evidence—not final, but powerfully persuasive—is that the Negro family in the urban ghettos is crumbling. A middle-class group has managed to save itself, but for the vast numbers of the unskilled, poorly educated city working class the fabric of conventional social relationships has all but disintegrated. There are indications that the situation may have been arrested in the past few years, but the general post-war trend is unmistakable. So long as this situation persists, the cycle of poverty and disadvantage will continue to repeat itself [Moynihan, 1965:intro.].

This report had important sociological and political implications. Moynihan was arguing that the economic and social problems faced by black Americans were the products of maladaptive family relations, and that if the family structure could be rendered less "pathological" a long stride would be taken to move black people out of poverty and into the mainstream of American life. Many social scientists and politicians thought that this was a gross misplacement of blame (Billingsley, 1968; Herzog, 1966). They felt that these ills were the results of broad racist structures in the society that went well beyond family structures. For the family sociologist the question was sharply focused by those who raised the question as to whether Moynihan was holding up to black people the ideal of the white middle class and at the same time denying viability and integrity of structures in the black community. It can be argued that nothing published on the black family since 1965 has not in some way been either an explicit or implicit attempt to refute or confirm Moynihan's picture of black family life and analysis of its consequences.

What were the "pathological" features of the black family as Moynihan saw them? He cited three factors: (1) nearly one-quarter of urban black marriages are dissolved; (2) nearly one-quarter of black births are now illegitimate; (3) almost one-fourth of black families are headed by females (1965:Chapter 2).

The reader should notice that none of these figures comes anywhere near a majority and that the first figure refers to urban settings while the other two refer to the whole nation. For the moment quibbles over statistical niceties are not in order, nor is this an attempt to refute Moynihan's data or their consequences. Let us instead look at the black family experience in this country historically in order to come to an appreciation of whatever distinctiveness it may have and to understand the roots of this distinctiveness.

THE HERITAGE OF SLAVERY

At the beginning of this chapter we spoke of ethnicity, national origins, and how the cultural traits associated with particular groups are believed to have their foundation in that group's experience in another culture. What can we learn about the family of black Americans by looking at their ethnic past? Most black Americans are the descendants of African slaves who were brought to this country during the seventeenth, eighteenth, and nineteenth centuries. By 1860, only about 1 percent of American slaves were not American born, and even during the last decades of the eighteenth century only about 20 percent of the black population was African born (Fogel and Engerman, 1974:23–24). The point of such figures is to reveal how far removed any direct contact with African culture was for most black Americans, even during the nineteenth century. Still, we must consider the African experience and see in what ways, if any, it bears on current practices.

Not all of the peoples of sub-Saharan Africa suffered equally under slavery.

> Like many Indians, African hunting, pastoral, and fishing tribesmen were too nomadic or warlike to be captured. As a result, most of the Africans brought to North America were members of agrarian tribes in West Africa, accustomed to hard, continuous labor and a sedentary life. A majority of them belonged to the Ibo, Ewe, Biafada, Bakongo, Wolof, Bambara, Ibibio, Serer, and Arada tribes [Blassingame, 1972:2].

The first question one might ask is, can we discern anything in the family lives of today's Afro-Americans that seems directly or indirectly traceable to African culture? To some extent, this is implicitly a loaded question. For one thing, it assumes a homogeneity within West Africa that simply did not exist. For example, the Ibo people were patrilineal while the Yakos were matrilineal. In general there is a considerable amount of intertribal variation in aspects of kinship and family life among Africans. Still, what we do see in all the tribes from which slaves were taken is that kinship and other family-related activities were a complex and vital part of each society. Marriage, for example, was treated with great seriousness. It involved alliances between definite groups and intricate rules of exogamy and endogamy. In addition, bride price was an important matter in marriage in virtually all of these cultures. It is most important to remember, however, that intertribal variation in family life played a less important role than the fact that these African peoples were violently wrenched from their societies and thrust into a new situation that not only provided little support for the maintenance of African traditions, but also in many respects actually discouraged them, both for reasons of economic expediency and misplaced notions of cultural superiority. Billingsley speaks eloquently on these points.

> Thus the men and women who were taken as slaves to the New World came from societies every bit as civilized and "respectable" as those of the Old World settlers who mastered them. But the two were very different types of society, for the African family was much more closely integrated with the wider levels of kinship and society. The simple transition of millions of persons from Africa to America would in itself have been a major disruption in the lives of the people, even if it had proceeded on a voluntary and humane basis. As we shall see presently, however, this transition was far from simple, voluntary, and humane [1968:48].

In other words, under the best of circumstances it would have been difficult for people of a culture so different from that encountered in the New World to maintain traditional patterns, but in a situation of coercion and subordination this became virtually impossible. Thus E. Franklin Frazier concluded, "As regards the Negro family, there is no reliable evidence that African culture had any influence on its development" (1939:8).

Less removed from the current situation and frequently cited as a source of the present "problems" of the black family is the condition of the black family under slavery. Until recently most historians held the view that conditions under the plantation slavery system in the South made family life impossible. Given the fact that slaves were property, they were denied the legal rights which free men took for granted, a crucial one being the right to marry. "Since slaves, as chattels, could not make contracts, marriage between them was not legally binding" (Kenneth Stampp, 1956:198). This led some scholars to conclude that conjugal ties were not strong and their recognition of little consequence to either slaves or their owners (Bernard, 1966:1). Therefore it was assumed that the masters broke up families as financial need dictated, used slaves for breeding purposes when this was felt to be profitable, and vented their lust on female slaves at whim (Elkins, 1959; Wade, 1964). The alleged result of all this was that marriage came to be held in low regard, illegitimacy was inevitable and widespread, and conventional morality nonexistent. Moreover, slave children never benefited from consistent and prolonged care, since parental ties were attenuated by the structure of slavery and the ever-present fear of separation. The question we must ask now is, how widespread were such practices and to what extent were slaves able to overcome such obstacles to family integrity?

The 1970s have seen the development of a "revisionist" history of American slavery, but in contrast to much revisionist history, this has resulted in a more benign view of the subject matter. The basic thrust of this new historical work is manifested in such books as Blassingame's *The Slave Community* (1972), Rawick's *From Sundown to Sunup* (1972), Fogel and Engerman's *Time on the Cross* (1974), Genovese's *Roll, Jordan, Roll* (1974), and, most recently, Gutman's *The Black Family in Slavery and Freedom* (1976). These authors do not argue that slavery was a laudable institution or that the motives of slave owners were in any way altruistic, but rather that the conditions of life faced by American slaves were not as destructive of family life as earlier historians would have had us believe. While some have interpreted this new scholarship, especially that of Fogel and Engerman, as an apology for slavery, the authors of such works would deny this. Basically, they hold that what motivated slave owners to behave in a way that was supportive of black life and black institutions was enlightened self-interest. This was the best way to take care of their "property" and manage their estates. At the same time they maintain that traditional history of slavery does not give blacks enough credit for creating and maintaining viable institutional structures while they were in bondage. Let us consider some of the points raised by these new historical writings.

While many historians have recognized that stable familial relationships did exist among slaves, they have traditionally tended to emphasize that because marriage had no legal status slaves often had minimal commitments to such relationships and that these ties were further weakened by the ever-present threat of the family being broken up by the sale of one or more members. Moreover, they have pointed to the alleged practice of slave breeding—calling up images of stud farms—to support their contention that marriage ties were weak.

> The demise of the sanctity of marriage had become absolute, and the Negro had lost his moral personality. Legally he was chattel under the law, and in practice an animal to be bred for the market [Tannenbaum, 1946:85].

The revisionist historians place their emphasis somewhat differently. (Gutman, 1976). While they recognize that marital and familial relationships were often tenuous, they also point out that there was in fact a high degree of familial integrity and stability. In doing so they do not applaud the morality of the planters or vaunt their altruism.

> It is obvious that most slaveholders did not care about the sexual customs of their slaves as long as there was no bickering and fighting. As a result, planters were generally more interested in encouraging monogamy because it was conducive to discipline than because of any interest in encouraging morality in the quarters [Blassingame, 1972:81–82].

Blassingame does not mean to suggest that the plantation owners should be given full credit for the fact that nuclear family relationships were more common than previously believed. The slaves themselves obviously placed enormous value on such relationships.

> Almost every study of runaway slaves uncovers the importance of the family motive: thousands of slaves ran away to find children, parents, or wives from whom they had been separated by sale. Next to resentment over punishment,

> the attempt to find relatives was the most prevalent cause of flight [Genovese, 1975:451].

After the Civil War the search for loved ones continued, and large numbers of ex-slaves applied to the Freedman's Bureau offices for marriage certificates (Blassingame, 1972:475).

In what appears to be one of the most controversial books of the decade, *Time on the Cross* (1974), the historians Fogel and Engerman have brought together and carefully analyzed an enormous body of data on the economics of slavery. While the theme of their book is that slavery was, contrary to much traditional scholarly belief, a highly profitable form of

A black family shortly before the Civil War. *(Courtesy, The New-York Historical Society)*

economic endeavor, in the process of documenting this point they provide us with much evidence that bears on the question of the family under slavery. For one thing they argue that "By far the great majority of slave children were born to women who were not only quite mature, but who were already married" (1974:137). The evidence for this assertion comes from probate records they examined which indicated that the average age of slave mothers was 22.5 when they had the eldest child who was still living with them. Also, the records show that the highest number of first births for slaves occurred during the last quarter of the year, something which would be expected if postharvest marriage, customary in agrarian societies, was the norm. In other words, while second and subsequent births were equally distributed throughout all four quarters of the year, the largest number of first births took place in the last quarter of the year. Fogel and Engerman also note that if slave masters indeed controlled marriage decisions, one might expect sizable differences between the ages of husband and wife; yet their data show that by far the largest number of marriages occurred between men and women who were close in age, the average age difference being three years.

The authors also bring evidence to bear on the point that plantation owners respected conjugal unions formed by their slaves:

> To many, the most critical aspect of the slave trade was its corrosive effect on the integrity of the slave family. . . .
>
> That the interregional slave trade resulted in the destruction of *some* slave marriages is beyond dispute. What is at issue is the extent of the phenomenon. Data contained in the sales records in New Orleans, by far the largest market in the interregional trade, sharply contradict the popular view that the destruction of slave marriages was at least a frequent, if not a universal, consequence of the slave trade. These records, which cover thousands of transactions during the years from 1804 to 1862, indicate that more than 84 percent of all sales over the age of fourteen involved unmarried individuals. Of those who were or had been married, 6 percent were sold with their mates; and probably at least one quarter of the remainder were widowed or voluntarily separated. Hence it is likely that 13 percent, or less, of interregional sales resulted in the destruction of marriages. And since sales were only 16 percent of the total interregional movement, it is probable that about 2 percent of the marriages of slaves involved in the westward trek were destroyed by the process of migration. Nor is it by any means clear that the destabilizing effects of the westward migration on marriage was significantly greater among blacks than it was among whites [Fogel and Engerman, 1974:49].

They go on to maintain that sales of preadolescent children (under 13) were infrequent and did not amount to more than 234 per year, a figure which may have been made up largely of orphans (1974:49–50). It is also their contention that when slave families were split up through sale this was done not because planters held such units in low esteem but often because their estates were broken up through death and bankruptcy.

Again it bears repeating that their evidence does not lead Fogel and Engerman to conclude that slave owners were primarily concerned with the moral and personal sensibilities of their slaves. According to the authors, the primary reason for the respect shown for the integrity of slave families was economic—it was good business.

Another aspect of the domestic lives of slaves which Fogel and Engerman discuss is the sexual exploitation of black women by white plantation owners, their sons, and overseers, as well as allegations concerning the existence of breeding farms. A common image in the popular and the older historical literature is that of the unscrupulous slave owner forcing attractive female slaves into concubinage or simply using them sexually and disposing of them at whim. There is no shortage of evidence to confirm the existence of gross sexual exploitation of slave women by white men, but again we must see if the frequent references to such behavior actually reflect the pervasiveness of this practice. The Abolitionists, as Ronald Walters has documented, emphasized the rape of black women to illustrate the decadence of southern life under slavery:

> "Illicit intercourse" was embedded in the very conditions of Southern life, abolitionists believed. For the master "the temptation is always at hand—the legal authority absolute—the actual power complete—the vice a profitable one" if it produced slaves for the market . . . and the custom so universal as to bring no disgrace [1973:182].

The historians who came later were predisposed to see such customs as the rule rather than the exception because of their own sympathies and the frequent references to such behavior in travelers' accounts of the period. Fogel and Engerman, while not quite contradicting this picture, do raise some questions about it. Their major point is as follows:

> To put the issue somewhat differently, it has been presumed that masters and overseers must have ravished black women frequently because their demand for such sexual pleasures was high and because the cost of satisfying that demand was low. Such arguments overlook the real and potentially large costs that confronted masters and overseers who sought sexual pleasures in the slave quarters. The seduction of the daughter or wife of a slave could undermine the discipline that planters so assiduously strove to attain. Not only would it stir anger and discontent in the families affected, but it would undermine the air of mystery and distinction on which so much of the authority of large planters rested [1974:133–134].

The authors go on to cite statistics from the 1860 national census which show that while 20 percent of the city of Nashville was black at this time, only 4.3 percent of the prostitutes were black. If, they argue, the lust of white men was so great for black women, why weren't more of them employed by Nashville brothels? Moreover, the data presented earlier on age at first birth suggests that the sexual exploitation of black adolescents was hardly rampant. So it appears that slaves were not as promiscuous as some would have us believe, nor were slave owners and other white men as sexually exploitative. Still, the fact that such exploitation did occur and that it was an ever-present danger has led another revisionist to conclude:

> Enough violations of black women occurred on the plantations to constitute a scandal and make life hell for a discernible minority of black women and their men [Genovese, 1975:415].

That the integrity of slave unions was recognized and that most slaves were not continually subject to sexual abuse bears crucially on the question of male-female relations within the slave family and parent-child relations. In the past the prevailing view has been that slave families were frequently headed by females and even when a male was present, these families were seen as female dominated. Also, it has been maintained that the care of children by slave parents left much to be desired and that youngsters were neglected, if not ill treated.

Fogel and Engerman contend not only that the nuclear family unit was recognized by slave owners, but also that this unit was patriarchal. Moreover, the position of the male in the household reflected his position in the larger slave society.

> For better or worse, the dominant role in slave society was played by men, not women. It was men who occupied all of the managerial slots available to slaves. There were very few female overseers or drivers. Men occupied nearly all the artisan crafts [1974:141].

Fogel and Engerman also maintain that there were clear sex-role differentiations within the family, beginning at courtship, which was male initiated. Once married, the tasks of childcare, cooking, and cleaning fell to the women, while the men assumed responsibilities for chopping wood and providing supplementary food by hunting. That slaveowners recognized the male's role in the family is evidenced by households being listed in their name, by family allotments being made them, and purchases charged against them. Genovese offers a complementary picture:

> A remarkable number of women did everything possible to strengthen their men's self-esteem and to defer to their leadership. What has usually been viewed as a debilitating female supremacy was in fact a closer approximation to healthy sexual equality than was possible for whites and perhaps even for many postbellum blacks. The men did not play the provider for their families in a full and direct sense, but they did everything they could to approximate it [1975:500].

Thus the slave family appears to be more of a traditional unit than a female-headed, female-dominated unit, as it is often portrayed.

What about childcare in the slave family? Kenneth M. Stampp, in what is perhaps his best known work, *The Peculiar Institution,* wrote, "Still another consequence [of the instability of slave families] was the indifference with which most fathers and even some mothers regarded their children" (1965:346). Similarly, E. Franklin Frazier remarks:

> In Africa tribal customs and taboos tended to fix the mother's attitude toward her child before it was born. In America this traditional element in the shaping of maternal feeling was absent. Consequently, the development of maternal feeling was dependent largely upon the physiological and emotional responses of the mother to her child [1966:37; originally published 1939].

More supportive responses, Frazier feels, were inhibited by plantation work schedules which kept mothers separated from their children for long periods.

> Consequently, where such limitations were placed upon the mother's spontaneous emotional responses to the needs of her children and where even her suckling and fondling of them were restricted, it was not unnatural that she often showed little attachment to her offspring [Frazier, 1966:38].

We often encounter travelers' reports in the literature which seem to confirm such a view—images of sick children neglected by their mothers, parents seemingly indifferent to the death of their offspring, etc. Here again, the revisionists, Blassingame, Fogel and Engerman, and Genovese strike a note of clamorous dissent. While it is recognized that postnatal mortality among slaves was high, it was no higher than among southern whites.

> If he survived infancy, the slave child partook, in bountiful measure for a while, of many of the joys of childhood. . . . Slave parents, in spite of their own sufferings, lavished love on their children [Blassingame, 1972:94].

During the preadolescent years little was expected of slave children in the way of labor. Thus they were able to enjoy a rather carefree existence, which often included playing with the children of their owner (Genovese, 1974:502–519). Certainly, the literature contains examples of abusive and neglectful parents, but we are concerned with the general pattern, and for the most part, parents seemed to be supportive, though we cannot forget the psychological problems that the awareness of oneself as another person's property may have created for a child.

When Fogel and Engerman's book, *Time on the Cross,* was first published, the response it received was quite favorable. Many critics saw the techniques it employed as laying the foundation for a revolution in historiography. But there were also those who felt that it was an apology for slavery. More recently, it has come under substantive attack, most notably from Herbert Gutman (1975b). Gutman has himself been engaged in a massive study of black families in nineteenth-century America (1976), and based on the data he has collected, as well as a critical analysis of Fogel and Engerman's data, he raises some serious questions about a good many of their interpretations.

To begin with, Gutman argues that their estimates of average age of women at birth of their first child are of dubious accuracy because they are based on probate records which list the woman's age at the time she had the oldest child *still living with her*. Children who died in childbirth, and in infancy as well as those who had already left home would not be included in the calculations, thus creating significant distortions in Fogel and Engerman's mean and median figures (1975b:149–152). Gutman also maintains that other data available do not show the concentration of first births occurring in the last quarter of the year (1975b:152). Furthermore, he points out that the reason they may have found so few prostitutes listed in Nashville in the 1860 census was because the occupations of slaves were not enumerated (1975b:157–162). Perhaps most damning are the data and analyses Gutman offers on the breakup of slave families as a result of their members being sold. He rather convincingly argues that Fogel and Engerman's figures greatly minimize this phenomenon (1975b:122–140). Yet, when all is said and done, Gutman does not argue for a return to the old picture of the nonexistent slave family and the promiscuous slave. Quite rightly he points out that more research is needed, but it is also significant that other researchers employing different techniques have come up with results similar to those of Fogel and Engerman (Genovese, 1975; Rawick, 1972; Blassingame, 1972).

THE RECONSTRUCTION ERA

If under slavery black Americans were able to maintain some semblance of family life, the question we must now ask is, what was the impact of the end of slavery on the black family? For many of the elder scholars, the Reconstruction era marked the beginning of modern black family life. W. E. DuBois, for example, held:

> With emancipation the Negro family was first made independent and with the migration to cities we see for the first time the thoroughly independent Negro family [1967:72, first published 1899].

Committed as he was to the view that the black family, as a stable and meaningful unit, was almost nonexistent under slavery, DuBois felt that based on what he saw in Philadelphia during the 1890s, there was room for optimism. But in his book *The Philadelphia Negro* he also maintained:

> The great weakness of the Negro family is still lack of respect for the marriage bond, inconsiderate entrance into it, and bad household economy and family government [1967:72; first published 1899].

E. Franklin Frazier, writing several decades later, saw the situation of the ante-bellum black family as one which derived its fundamental instability from the slave experience, a condition which was aggravated by the conditions blacks encountered in the cities of the North.

> In many cases, of course, the dissolution of the simple family organization has begun before the family reaches the northern city. But, if these families have managed to preserve their integrity until they reach the northern city, poverty, ignorance, and color force them to seek homes in deteriorated slum areas from

> which practically all institutional life has disappeared. Hence, at the same time that these simple rural families are losing their internal cohesion, they are being freed from the controlling force of public opinion and communal institutions. Family desertion among Negroes in cities appears, then, to be one of the inevitable consequences of the impact of urban life on the simple family organization and folk culture the Negro has evolved in the rural south [1966:255; first published, 1939].

Despite the broad explanation Frazier offers, he saw economic conditions as the primary determinant of family stability and argued that the minority of blacks that were able to maintain male-headed, two-parent households were able to do so because of their ability to acquire salable economic skills and property. As we shall see, Frazier may have overestimated the degree of instability in the black family, but he did put his finger on what may be one of its key causes.

In the last few years a number of studies have been published that shed considerable light on the family experience of blacks in the ante-bellum period (Pleck, 1972; Hershberg, 1971–1972; Lammermeier, 1973; Gutman, 1975a and 1976; Furstenberg et al., 1975; Shifflett, 1975). On the whole, these studies reveal a rather high degree of family stability. Table 12-1, based on Gutman's work, shows that in the 1855 to 1880 period no fewer than 70 percent and as many as 90 percent of the black families surveyed had a father present. But while figures like these may seemingly question "the myth" of the female-headed black household, they only take on meaning when they can be contrasted with comparable white families at the same points in time. Such data are provided by Furstenberg et al.

Table 12-1. PERCENTAGE OF MALE-PRESENT BLACK HOUSEHOLDS, 1855–1880

Place and Date	Number of Households	Male-Present Households (%)	Male-Absent Households (%)
Buffalo, N.Y., 1855	145	90	10
Buffalo, N.Y., 1875	159	85	15
Troy, N.Y., 1880	128	85	15
York County, Va., 1865	994	85	15
Montgomery County, Va., 1865	500	78	22
Princess Anne County, Va., 1865	375	84	16
Natchez, Miss., 1880	769	70	30
Beaufort, S.C., 1880	461	70	30
Richmond, Va., 1880	5,670	73	27
Mobile, Ala., 1880	3,235	74	26
Rural Adams County, Miss., 1880	3,093	81	19
St. Helena's Township, S.C., 1880	491	87	13
St. Helena's Island, S.C., 1880	904	86	14

SOURCE: Herbert G. Gutman, "Persistent Myths about the Afro-American Family," *J. Interdisciplinary History*, vol. 6, no. 2 (Autumn 1975), p. 196.

(1975). Comparing black, Irish, German, and native whites in Philadelphia in 1880, Furstenberg and his associates find that the percent with female-headed households are 25.3, 12.7, 8.3, and 18.3, respectively (1975:219). While this is only one data set in comparison to the several used by Gutman, and therefore offers only limited opportunities for generalization, it does suggest that by 1880 there were already racial differences in the number of female-headed households.

Apart from revealing that family instability was relatively high in the last third of the nineteenth century, these studies also show some interesting trends which appear to shed some light on the foundations of current black family patterns. Furstenberg, Hershberg, and Modell find that the percentage of two-parent families in both the ante-bellum and post-bellum periods was higher among ex-slaves than among blacks who had not been in bondage (1975:216). This would seem to raise serious questions about the argument that the "heritage of slavery" figured so importantly in twentieth-century explanations of black family patterns.

Furstenberg et al. (1975), Gutman (1975a), and Shifflett (1975) see family instability as having its roots in the economic discrimination faced by black males in the post-bellum era. This not only put these men in an increasingly compromised position, but also led to a higher mortality rate which in turn resulted in more widowed household heads. These factors seem especially salient in the urban context. The rate of female-headed households is higher in cities than in rural areas and Hershberg finds that even within a city the rates of female-headedness were higher among native-born blacks than among migrants (Hershberg, 1974). Thus, as the nineteenth century came to a close, more and more black people were living in families where one parent, more often than not the father, was absent. Nevertheless, what must be repeated again and again is that the large majority of blacks still live in two-parent households and continue to live in two-parent households today.

It is unrealistic to expect that a complete explanation of current black family patterns can be found in the slavery or Reconstruction periods. Of course, there are some links to the past because conditions that shaped the black family in the post-Civil War period persist today. At the same time, new problems have arisen.

THE BLACK FAMILY TODAY

The proportion of the United States population classified as black has remained relatively stable since 1890 (then it was 11.6 percent; in 1974 it was 11.4 percent), but the actual number of black Americans has increased since that time from roughly 8.8 to 24.0 million (U.S. Bureau of the Census, 1975c:11). Black people still tend to be concentrated in the South where they make up almost 20 percent of the population, while in the North and West they make up less than 10 percent. Nonetheless, during the twentieth century there has been a considerable migration of rural southern blacks to cities in other regions, and today about 75 percent of American blacks live in metropolitan areas. In the cities, black people tend to live in segregated areas, and this tendency has increased over the last thirty years. These areas, in many cases vacated by middle-class whites who have left for the suburbs, are often among the most physically deteriorated sections of the city.

The fact that blacks continue to be set apart from the mainstream of American society is evident from employment and education figures, both of which reveal their disadvantaged position. While 15 percent of the white work force is classified in the high-prestige "professional and technical" category, only 9 percent of the "black and other races" categories are so classified; moreover, 15 percent of the latter are classified in the low-prestige "service workers" category in contrast to 7 percent of the former. The results of this are reflected in the income figures for both groups: in 1974 median income of black families was only 58 percent of the median income for whites (U.S. Bureau of the Census, 1975c:25). As if this were not enough, the unemployment rate of blacks in 1974 was twice as high as that of whites, 10.4 versus 5.1 (U.S. Bureau of the Census, 1975c:69). Similarly we see differences in educational achievement, health, mortality, housing, and virtually every other measure of any social significance. To be sure, there has been improvement, even dramatic improvement in some areas, but black Americans still remain a group apart (U.S. Bureau of the Census, 1975c.)

In attempting to characterize the family life of contemporary blacks we must be careful to specify which blacks we are talking about. Most of the furor that has raged in the professional and popular literature following the publication of the Moynihan report was over the families of poor ghetto blacks, the lower class, and not over the black family per se. Yet there remains the question of whether there are certain characteristics of black families that seem to override socioeconomic status, and which seem more prevalent among blacks, irrespective of their education, income, or occupation.

To investigate this question, there is perhaps no better characteristic to start with than female-headed households, since this is at the heart of the Moynihan report as well as most other discussions of the "pathological" aspects of black family life. Female-headed households are much more common among blacks than among whites. In 1974 the figures were 35.3 percent for blacks and 9 percent for whites; since 1960 the rate of growth of female-headed black households with children has been twice that of whites (U.S. Bureau of the Census, 1975c:107; Ross and Sawhill, 1975:13). When faced with figures such as these the first question a sociologist must ask is whether the differential is merely a matter of variation in socioeconomic status. That is, are the rates higher among blacks because blacks tend, on the whole, to be poorer than whites? When we look at variation within specific income groups we see that even among the lowest-income families, those earning less than $4,000, about half as many black children as white are living with both parents (U.S. Bureau of the Census, 1975c:105).

Illegitimacy, an obviously related phenomenon, is also concentrated more heavily among blacks than among whites (U.S. Bureau of the Census, 1973:62). The percentage of both illegitimacy and female-headed households is higher in the black than in the white community, irrespective of class, though the highest rates tend to be among the poorest people in both communities. These facts pose two questions for us: (1) why the higher rates among black people; and (2) what are the effects of these higher rates? We do not have the final answers to these questions, but they are worth exploring.

Some sociologists, while recognizing the realities of black life in America, feel it is chauvinistic to hold up rates of illegitimacy and female-headedness as measures of social disorganization and as explanations for the economic hardship endured by blacks. Most notable among these are Joyce Ladner and Robert Staples. Ladner maintains:

> The normative patterns that exist in the white middle-class society are considered by its adherents as rational, justifiable and an *ideal* model. If one accepts the legitimacy of this model, any deviation from it would be considered within the realm of aberrant behavior. However, if the model is considered illegitimate, there should be no concern that one is obligated to conform to it because the value and behavioral system which undergirds it would be considered irrelevant. This seems to be the core of the white versus Black culture thesis. It is simply a question of whether or not the values, attitudes, behavior and systems of belief which govern the dominant white middle class should be the criteria by which Black people, most of whom have never been allowed to assimilate into the American mainstream, should be evaluated [1972:267–268].

What Ladner is arguing for is a view of black culture as a somewhat autonomous entity that cannot be scrutinized or judged by comparing it with white models. Similarly, Staples has argued that the sexual behavior and attitudes of black people are different from those of whites and that this difference is reflected in the often cited figures on greater incidence of premarital sex and illegitimacy. Rather than seeing this as cause for alarm or as a symptom of social decay, Staples argues:

> As an example of the positive aspects of black family subculture, we can, briefly, examine the culture linkage between sexual attitudes and behavior and out-of-wedlock children. The greater sexual permissiveness of black people more accurately reflects the absence of a double standard of sexual conduct among that group. It is not that white people have high moral standards, but the fact that white women lack the same sexual freedom as white men that accounts for most sexual chastity that still exists among this group. . . . Among blacks, the lack of a double standard means that members of this group can engage in a meaningful sexual relationship rather than participating in sex role conflicts, or developing neurotic feelings of guilt over the question of premari-

> tal sex. As a result, sex relations—both before and after marriage—have a much more positive meaning in the black community [1971:134].

Such interpretations have also come under criticism. For example, Lee Rainwater feels that the values underlying black sexual and marital behavior are no different than those among whites—both groups generally believe that people should be monogamous, children should be borne in monogamous unions, and that sex outside of marriage is potentially dangerous, though of greater danger to women than to men. Rainwater holds that these values are often not expressed in ghetto behavior because of "economic marginality and racial oppression" (1973:472). An attempt to synthesize such opposing views is found in Carol Stack's (1974) work which sees the familial patterns of poor black Americans as complex and variable structures used by these people to cope with chronic poverty, poverty which, she feels, the federal government does more to contribute to than alleviate. Thus we can see how fundamentally different conclusions sociologists can draw from their observations of similar situations. Nevertheless, the point remains that in the realm of behavior, if not in the realm of values, the family patterns of ghetto blacks are distinctive.

Moynihan was not altogether blind to the question of the viability of a semiautonomous black culture. Rather he has argued that the issue of cultural autonomy is not of concern to him; what interests him is the price that blacks have had to pay for this cultural distinctiveness:

> There is, presumably, no special reason why a society in which males are dominant in family relationships is to be preferred to a matriarchal arrangement. However, it is clearly a disadvantage for a minority group to be operating on one principle, while the great majority of the population, and the one with the most advantages to begin with, is operating on another. This is the present situation of the Negro. Ours is a society which presumes male leadership in private and public affairs. The arrangements of society facilitate such leadership and reward it. A subculture, such as that of the Negro American, in which this is not the pattern, is placed at a distinct disadvantage [Moynihan, 1965:29].

The question remains, however, whether there is evidence to support the view that the distinctive characteristics of the black family are really at the root of the economic hardship they face. The fact that two things are correlated does not mean that they are causally related. Moynihan points to the high rates of broken homes, the high rates of black poverty, and other problems to suggest that the one explains the other. This may not be the case.

In a recently published study entitled *The Case of the Black Family* (1975), Jerold Heiss has attempted to directly assess the question of whether the distinctive features of the black family contribute to the problems faced by blacks in America. More than anyone else to date he has asked the key question and at the same time has presented data taken from a national urban sample to provide answers for them. Let us begin with an excerpt from Heiss's conclusion, because it is so different from much of the previous literature.

> Several things seem particularly clear. An attack upon the "family problems" of blacks in this country would, if successful, alleviate some of the problems they face. At the same time, however, it is apparent that the gain would be small. The family is not the main source of these problems, and a "perfect" family situation in the present reality of America would not change very much. Such a program would not only be relatively ineffective, it could be disastrous if it directed attention away from the real sources of the problem. The problem does not start in the black community, but in the white. The real source is racism with all that it implies: discrimination, derogation, and prejudice [1975:228–229].

How does Heiss come to such a conclusion? He has no argument with the researchers who have claimed that black family structure, irrespective of income, is different from that of whites. He recognizes that blacks have more children, are more apt to live in multigenerational households, and their marriages are more likely to be unstable. Where he does differ is in the conclusions he draws about the results of such differences. Since so much has been made of the fact that blacks are more likely than whites to be brought up in homes that are female headed and that this difference is crucial for understanding many of their economic problems, let us first consider this variable.

The literature on the black family has often failed to distinguish between female-dominated and female-headed homes. A household in which both parents are present is considered female-dominated if most of the important family decisions are made by the mother; a female-headed household is one in which through death, divorce, separation, or desertion the husband is no longer present. A female-dominated home is viewed as problematic for somewhat the same reasons a female-headed home is because it results in problems of identification and difficulties in learning appropriate sex-role behavior for the children. Some argue that it results in a feminization of males while others argue that it results in exaggerated masculinity. Heiss was unable to find much support for either hypothesis, but he feels that his measures may not have been sensitive or direct enough. However, he did find that men from female-dominated, intact homes were somewhat less likely to marry than those from father-dominated homes. More importantly, he was not able to find the damaging outcomes that Moynihan would have us believe are associated with the black matriarchy. The sons of female-dominated homes did not seem to suffer in terms of educational or economic achievement. Interestingly enough, for the low SES men, coming from such a home was positively associated with achievement, but only slightly. In general Heiss's findings suggest that maternal dominance is nowhere near as nefarious as has previously been suggested (1975, chapter 5).

Before and since the Moynihan report, no one issue has received anywhere near the same attention as that of the fatherless family in the black community. For Frazier (1939), for Bernard (1966), for Pettigrew (1964), and others, the fact that the male figure in the black family is relatively often absent is at the heart of many of the problems black Americans face. In view of this, it bears repeating that the majority of blacks have grown up in homes where both parents are present. In Heiss's national sample, even among the low SES group, 80 percent of the respondents lived in two-parent homes until they were sixteen (1975:26). Still, the rates are indeed higher among blacks than among whites, and it thus becomes important for us to consider what the outcome of growing up in such a family is (Ross and Sawhill, 1975). The importance of Heiss's work is that it allows us to move beyond the realm of assertion into the realm of facts.

Heiss did not find either feminine characteristics or exaggerated masculinity to be especially prevalent among men raised in either female-dominated or female-headed households. Even when a home was broken before a boy was ten it did not have the effect the literature suggests it would. There are, however, broader questions of psychological disturb-

A contemporary middle-class black family. *(Bruce Davidson/Magnum)*

ance growing out of female-headed households. Pettigrew feels that fatherless homes are associated with an inability to delay gratification, low social responsibility, low achievement orientation, and a proneness to delinquency (1964:17). While not having measures for all of these traits, Heiss did not find men from female-headed homes to be less capable of delaying gratification, nor did they show a lack of self-control. Furthermore, these men did not display any tendency toward hostility, any proclivity for fighting, or other serious extreme reactions to frustration. Men who came from higher SES female-headed homes were more likely than their counterparts from intact homes to report having been arrested, but traffic violations were included in the figures. Overall, we do not see the Pandora's box of psychological troubles we might expect. However, one might argue that the real test is the question of achievement later in life, since this is the crux of the Moynihan thesis.

Previous research by Beverly and Otis Duncan (1969) has shown that black males from intact homes, when compared with those from female-headed homes, scored higher on occupational and educational achievement, but that the differences were small. Heiss also finds that men from intact homes reported higher earnings (his measure of occupational achievement), but in contrast to the Duncans, not higher educational achievement. When education was held constant, the income differentials between men from intact and broken homes became even greater, but for the lower SES group only (Heiss, 1975:107). Using a number of control variables, which include the attitudinal and behavioral measures discussed earlier, as well as parental SES, age, and education, Heiss was able to reduce income differences between the males from intact and broken homes to an inconsequential level for the low SES group, but not for the higher one. This reveals the complexity of the issue. When all is said and done, then, coming from a broken home does seem to result in impaired economic achievement, but not of great magnitude.

Another alleged result of coming from a broken home is that familial instability is transmitted—that there is a self-perpetuating cycle in which people reared in broken homes are themselves unlikely to remain married. Bernard has argued that, "Men socialized without fathers reveal a marked inability to maintain a marital relationship" (1966:125). Heiss does find that there is an association between marital instability in the parental generation and marital instability in the next generation, but this relationship is of any real magnitude only for the higher SES group, especially for females (Heiss, 1975: chapter 7). Here again, as was the case for income, the results are not as the literature would have had us predict. The group which supposedly suffers the most from the results of family breakup—poor blacks—is the group which shows the least effects (Rainwater, 1970:472).

The results of Heiss's research, as well as that of others working in this area, seem to suggest that certain aspects of black family life do contribute to the economic and more general social plight of this group, but this research also reveals that too much importance has been placed upon the family as an explanatory variable. As we have continually repeated throughout this chapter, the vast majority of black American children live in two-parent households, despite the fact that the incidence of female-headed households is higher in the black than in the white community. What Ross and Sawhill's recent work (1975) suggests about the sources of family instability is that the economic factor is crucial to any understanding of this differential. The compromised situation faced by black males in the economic marketplace is something that had its beginning in the Reconstruction era, and unfortunately has continued to the present. Thus if we look to the family as the source of black people's ills we may soothe the national conscience but we overlook the real villain of the piece, which has been and continues to be social discrimination.

SUMMARY

We began this chapter by considering ethnic identity and the interest that has emerged in this topic since the 1960s. We suggested that the new sense of identity that has recently emerged among many white ethnic groups was inspired by the Civil Rights movement of the 1960s with its attendant affirmation of identity on the part of many black Americans. Since no book on the American family would be complete without some discussion of ethnicity in relation to the family, we chose to concentrate on the black family, both because it has been a topic of considerable interest to family sociologists, and also because giving the chapter a single focus seemed to be more productive for our discussion of the family than giving scattered bits of data on many ethnic groups.

Much of the debate about the black family has been focused on the extent to which the relative prevalence of female-headedness is responsible for the economically disadvantaged position black Americans find themselves in. We attempted to seek out the foundation of this supposedly "pathological" phenomenon.

Recent social historical research has forced many scholars to reconsider the impact that slavery had upon the family life of the Afro-Americans who were its victims. While advocates of the traditional view argued that since marriage between slaves was not recognized by law, families were readily split up when the slave market made this profitable, giving little integrity to the nuclear unit. Also, it was held that slave women were frequently sexually exploited by their owners, contributing to a general atmosphere of promiscuity. While not completely contradicting this image, new research has indicated that despite the lack of legal recognition, slave marriages showed a great deal of durability and that while sexual exploitation of slave women by owners was not rare, it was by no means as widespread or as blatant as previously believed. Moreover, according to the new research, there was a clear-cut division of roles along sex lines in the slave family, with males being recognized as the household head and children being raised with considerable love and care, despite the fundamental blow done to their humanity by slavery.

It is during the Reconstruction era that we begin to see the seeds sown for the patterns that we are currently reaping. While initially ex-slave families showed relatively low rates of female-headedness, as did black families in general, the further we move toward the end of the century the more we see the rates of female-headedness in black families moving beyond those of other groups. What this seems to suggest is that slavery cannot be seen as the key factor responsible for current patterns. Rather, we must look to the discrimination encountered by blacks since the Civil War for the source of the problem.

Moving into the twentieth century, we reviewed the debate over the Moynihan report and brought the chapter to a conclusion by reviewing the findings of a recent national study by Heiss which attempted to directly assess the impact of black family patterns on black Americans, both economically and psychologically. While some small differences were discerned, the author of this study maintains that if the black family were to be remodelled to resemble the modal white family it would not significantly alter the situation faced by black people generally, since racism, rather than "family pathology," is the villain in this continuing drama.

NYPL Picture Collection

OLD AGE: Family Life in the Later Years 13

Textbooks on the family often do not devote a separate chapter to the marriage and family life of the elderly, but we feel this is necessary. If this book has a unifying theme, apart from its focus on long-term change in the American family, it is provided by the concept of modernization and the impact this process has on the structure and function of family-related activity. It should be noted first that only in societies that have undergone modernization has old age become something a sizable portion of the population will experience. Therefore it is of interest to look at the effect the general prolongation of life has had upon family relations.

THE CHANGING FACTS OF OLD AGE

Let us consider some of the statistics on old age so as to better appreciate the magnitude and importance of the changes that have occurred in this realm. In 1850 people 65 and over made up 3 percent of the population; in 1900 they made up 4 percent of the population, and in 1974 almost 10 percent. While the proportional growth of this age group since the middle of the last century is in itself impressive, when we consider the gross numbers involved it is even more so. In 1900 there were 3.1 million people 65 and over; in 1974 there were 21.8 million (U.S. Bureau of the Census, 1975d:3). Another way of looking at this is to consider life expectancy at birth; in 1900 it was 48.2 for men and 51.1 for women; today it is 68.2 for men and 75.9 for women (U.S. Bureau of the Census, 1975a:59; *New York Times,* June 1, 1976:1). The United States Bureau of the Census did not collect annual data on mortality until 1900, so before that we have to rely on data from more limited areas such as Massachusetts, which had a reasonably accurate death registration system at an early date. In 1789 life expectancy at birth for men was 34.5, and for women it was 36.5. By 1850 it was up to 38.3 and 40.5, respectively, and by 1890, 42.5 and 44.5 (Warren Thompson and P. K. Whelpton, 1969:240). What is notable here is that life expectancy does not show much significant change between the founding of the Republic and the Civil War. It was really in the last quarter of the nineteenth century that this country began to see a notable growth in life expectancy, and one which assumed major proportions in the twentieth century with people now living, on the average, more than 20 years longer than they would have had they been born in 1900.

OLD AGE AND MODERNIZATION

What appears to be the relationship between aging and modernization? Leo Simmons (1945), a student of aging in cross-cultural perspective, has specified what he feels to be the universals of aging, that is, goals which characterize this stage of life in both the most primitive of societies and in the most complex:

1. To live as long as possible, or at least until life's satisfactions no longer compensate for its privations.
2. To get some release from the necessity of wearisome exertion at humdrum tasks and to have protection from too great exposure to physical hazards.
3. To safeguard or even strengthen any prerogatives acquired in mid-life such as skills, possessions, rights, authority and prestige.
4. To remain active participants in the affairs of life in either operational or supervisory roles, any sharing in group interests being preferred to idleness and indifference.
5. Finally, to withdraw from life when necessity requires it, as timely, honorably, and comfortably as possible [quoted by Palmore, 1969:35].

These universals provide considerable leeway for intersocietal variation, but we should not fall prey to the traditional assumption that the life situation of the elderly, at least in terms of social position, has always been superior in premodern societies.

In Chapter 1 we discovered that it was unwise to speak of the preindustrial family as though it were a monolithic entity. It will be recalled that Blumberg and Winch (1972) found that family size varied in the preindustrial world in association with such factors as level of agriculture, type of government, community size, etc. Similarly, there is variation both historically and cross-culturally in the position of the elderly in premodern societies. It does, however, appear that their position in terms of status and security probably reached its premodern apex in stable agricultural societies. Erdman Palmore (1969) attributes this to the fact that such societies have surpluses of food and shelter to share with the elderly, have capital and property that are generally in the hands of the elderly, and offer opportunities for the elderly to exercise control through their place in an extended family and use their knowledge and expertise, all of which result in their being in a position of authority and leadership. Palmore also makes the point that the nature of work in such societies is such as to allow a gradual rather than an abrupt movement out of the work force, with many people working in their usual adult roles until death (1969:37–38). Retirement, as we shall see, is a modern notion.

Another factor is that the very notion of being old, elderly, or aged seems to be a variable one, with the onset of "old age" being earlier in less complex societies. While in our society today the middle sixties are generally thought of as the transitional period to old age, in premodern societies this may occur ten or twenty years earlier. This is, of course, related to longevity and the associated ability to control the ravages of aging. But the end result is that modern societies have more older people.

Donald Cowgill (1972:9) argues that the status of old people appears to be inversely related to their numbers in the population, but a related factor in the status of the elderly also appears to be the rate of change in a society, not just change per se. He quotes Simmons to the effect that:

> When social conditions become unstable and the rate of change reaches a galloping pace, the aged are riding for an early fall and the more youthful associates take their seats in the saddles [Cowgill, 1972:9].

Similarly, in highly mobile societies the position of the aged tends to suffer. This is true of hunting and gathering societies as well as urban-industrial ones (Cowgill, 1972:9). In traditional agricultural societies, familial wealth is concentrated in land and this is a form of property over which the elderly generally have great control. But in hunting and gathering societies, little familial property exists in any form and in urban-industrial societies familial property is by necessity fluid and thus is dispersed into a number of forms.

The implications of the above factors in determining the status of the elderly are not a very pleasant commentary on human motives, suggesting as they do that the position of the elderly is a function of their ability to control scarce resources, for example, knowledge and property, and the extent to which their existence poses a problem for younger members of the society. Some readers may be familiar with the horror stories early explorers brought back of Eskimos abandoning their elderly to the elements and the self-righteous indignation such stories aroused. But we must realize that for a hunting society the presence of an incapacitated person who can no longer function productively represents a threat to the survival of the other members of that society. Thus their abandonment is a necessity, not a callous and inhumane decision. In our own society the situation of the elderly has also become difficult, for reasons that appear to be part and parcel of modernization (Cowgill, 1974). The picture is more complex, however, than some may think.

Andrew Achenbaum (1974) is one of the few historians who has looked at old age systematically. He studied the period from 1865 to 1914 when a very fundamental change appears to have taken place in the concept of old age in America.

> In the earlier part of the period, old age was idealized: writers described the elderly as the true survivors of the fittest and emphasized the important societal role they played. In the latter part of the period, writers challenged this idealistic image of old age: they stressed the physical, mental and behavioral deterioration accompanying old age and argued that the elderly contributed very little to the well-being of society [Achenbaum, 1974:48].

According to Achenbaum, there are two sources of this change: (1) medical discoveries about the deteriorative processes associated with aging, for example, arteriosclerosis, led to a deromanticization of aging, as people became increasingly aware of the physical problems that accompany growing old; and (2) within the business community there was a growing ambivalent attitude toward old people. On the one hand, the elderly began to be seen as inefficient and costly to employ. On the other hand, this attitude coincided with the appearance and growth of pension plans, which made the new phenomenon of retirement less economically harrowing. Associated with the second factor is a concomitant development, the new glorification of youth, something which has certainly continued to this day. By World War I, the image of old people in America emphasized their physical handicaps and employment liabilities and downplayed the older romantic notions of the survival of the fittest and the wisdom brought by long years.

One of the most interesting aspects of the position of the elderly in modern industrial societies is what has been spoken of as the "roleless role" of old people. The expectancies governing the behavior of most members of our society are generally pretty clear cut, but this is not the case with the elderly, a point upon which Irving Rosow has eloquently commented:

> But aside from such general bromides as that old people should stay active, there is very little specification of what they should do and what standards to follow. In other words there is no role *content.* Indeed, this is precisely why so many old people are consumed by inactivity and boredom. The culture does not provide them with definitions and meaningful norms as it does in all previous life stages. There are no clear expectations connected with the aged role, so this becomes subject to personal preferences and private definitions which are intrinsically unshared. Thus, with the loss of functions, the role of the older person becomes *unstructured* and there is little incentive to adopt with enthusiasm a basically empty role. Like other unstructured situations, role ambiguity in old age may be an independent source of anxiety [1967:31].

Rosow points out that this situation is aggravated by the fact that old age is generally held in low esteem, an evaluation shared by old people themselves. An important dimension of this lack of role content in the lives of old people is the phenomenon of retirement, a very modern creation.

RETIREMENT: A MIXED BLESSING

While retirement is a modern phenomenon, even in the preindustrial world there were some occupational changes associated with aging. When a man felt he was no longer able to manage the family farm he would step aside and let a son assume the major responsibility for this sphere of life. This form of retirement was associated with the son marrying and becoming head of the household, while the elderly parents remained in the household, but in a position that was secondary in certain respects to that of the inheriting son and his bride (Berkner, 1972). Conrad Arensberg and Solon Kimball describe such a situation as it persisted in rural Ireland well into the twentieth century.

> With the transfer of land at the marriage of the son who remains to work the farm, the relations of the members of the farm family to each other and to the farm they work undergo a drastic change. In the first place, the headship of the old couple under whom the family group worked undergoes change. The old couple relinquish the farm, they enter the age grade of the dying, and direction of the enterprise of the group passes from their hands to those of the younger people. Something of the change has already been indicated in the "writings" [marriage contract]. From the point of view of the father, it means the abandonment of the ownership he has long enjoyed; from the point of view of the old woman it means she is no longer the "woman of the house." Her place is taken by the incoming daughter-in-law. Naturally, this change is accomplished in effect only with difficulty and with considerable reluctance on the part of the old couple. Where the transition goes smoothly, father and son continue to work the farm together, but more often as the father grows older he retires to his seat by the hearth [1940:124].

What sets this type of "retirement" apart from the variety we know today is not merely the fact that so many more people survive to old age, but rather that today's retirement is enforced rather than voluntary. Increasingly, mandatory retirement ages have been instituted, which often push a man or woman out of work before they feel ready to leave.

One way to look at the growth of retirement is to compare labor force participation rates by degree of national industrialization. United Nations data show clear and linear differences in the relationship between these two variables. In agricultural countries 70.1 percent of the men 65 and over are in the labor force; in semi-industrial countries 61.0 percent work; and in industrial countries the figure is 37.7 percent (Kreps, 1971:44). In our own country between 1900 and 1974 the percentage of men 65 and over in the labor force dropped from 68.3 to 22.4 percent (Loether, 1967:67; U.S. Bureau of the Census, 1975d:26). This rather precipitous decline in the

United Nations data and the more general trend revealed in the data for the United States is indicative of policy changes both within government and industry that have enabled people in industrial society to contemplate spending their later years in retirement. However, one side effect of this has been the forced exodus of people from the labor force before they feel they want to retire, either because they are satisfied with their work or because their retirement income is inadequate.

Prior to the existence of formal retirement plans, most people worked until they were no longer physically capable of doing so. The fortunate few who had the means retired from work, for whatever reason, when they found it problematic to continue. While no data is readily available, we can safely assume that considerably more of the older men out of the work force in 1900 were unemployed because of physical infirmity than is currently the case. While modern governmental and private pensions generally do not provide generous incomes to the aged, they have removed the horror of the alms house which loomed so large in the minds of working people in the nineteenth century.

However, it was not until 1884 that the first industrial pension plan was established; by 1925 the Department of Labor estimated that there were 200 such plans in the country, but we have no way of knowing how many workers were covered by them (Millis and Montgomery, 1938:369). One 1929 estimate puts the figure at 3,750,000 covered by such plans, a small minority indeed. The Social Security Act was not passed until 1935. Of course, this law represented a watershed in American retirement legislation, for it required that workers and employers both contribute funds which would ultimately be used to pay workers' retirement benefits. With this act the threat of dire poverty was somewhat alleviated, but many problems lingered. Nonetheless, since the early decades of this century, private pension plans have grown dramatically, largely through the efforts of labor unions. It is this growth, in association with mandatory retirement ages, that led to the decline in work force participation on the part of older workers.

Factors that determine a person's satisfaction or dissatisfaction with retirement are numerous and complex (Streib and Schneider, 1971). A number of studies show that those who attach a meaning to work which transcends its economic functions or see it as being valuable, important, etc., are more reluctant to retire than those who work just to provide their daily bread. Yet, when researchers compared white-collar and blue-collar adjustment to retirement they found the former do better than the latter. Loether seems to feel that:

> The probable explanation for the differential success between white-collar and blue-collar workers in adapting to retirement is that the factors leading to the white collar workers' greater identification with and attachment to his occupation also facilitates his retirement. White-collar occupations generally require a higher educational level and are inherently more interesting than blue-collar occupations. As a by-product of his higher level of education, the white-collar

> worker tends to develop greater role flexibility than the blue-collar worker [1967:76].

Despite such class differences, the evidence we have available indicates that the majority of retired workers responded positively (60 percent) to questions asked by the Louis Harris poll in 1965: "Has retirement fulfilled your expectations for a good life or have you found it less than satisfactory?" Only 22 percent of those who responded negatively cited that they "missed work" as the reason. Other reasons given were poor health and loneliness for deceased spouse (Loether, 1967:70–71). Still, we must realize that we are dealing with a sizable number of people who report that retirement did not fulfill their expectations, and these are predominantly men.

There is more to the situation of the elderly in our society than retirement. There are other more fundamental problems such as poor health and meager finances. Not only are older people more likely to be ill than younger people, see doctors more often, and spend more time in hospitals, but 38 percent of those 65 and older face problems keeping house or working as a result of their illnesses, compared to 7 percent of those under 65 (DHEW, 1975). These circumstances are aggravated by the fact that, regrettable as it is, older people are among those in our society least able to afford medical care, despite the availability of programs such as Medicare. A Senate Special Committee on Aging reported that in 1969 the average health bill for those over 65 was $692. This was two and a half times as great as for people in the age group 19–64 and Medicare only covered half the cost (*New York Times,* January 11, 1971). As we shall see the problem of finances can be a major one, even when not compounded by fixed incomes and spiraling doctor and hospital bills.

Senate hearings have revealed that three out of ten older people, in contrast to one out of nine young persons, were living in conditions definable as poverty in 1967—about half of the single elderly had incomes under $1,500 and incomes of $1,000 or less were reported by one-quarter of these people. The Senate task force was not sanguine in its outlook regarding change. Most recent figures suggest that their pessimism was perhaps misplaced. The proportion of people over 65 who are below what the government defines as the "low income" level declined from 29.5 percent in 1967 to 15.7 percent in 1974 (Bane, 1976:119). No other age group experienced a decline of this magnitude. Most of this decline is attributable to increases in Social Security benefits: average monthly payments rose 98 percent between 1965 and 1973, while the Consumer Price Index rose only 41 percent during those years (Bane 1976:119). Moreover, in 1970 it was discovered that 63 percent of families headed by people over 65 owned the house they lived in (U.S. Bureau of the Census, 1975d:41). Furthermore, older families were less likely to be in debt (Loether, 1967:103). Still, it must be realized that like any other large group of people, the elderly show considerable diversity in income as well as other

One of the pleasures of old age: a grandmother with her grandchild. *(Ginger Chin/Peter Arnold Photo Archives)*

aspects of life, but what makes their situation particularly difficult is that for the most part their income is reduced from what it previously was when they were working, and many are widows without pensions. In addition, the pension income of the elderly, in contrast to Social Security payments, is usually fixed and decreases in real value as a result of inflationary pressure.

OLD AGE AND THE FAMILY

In addition to the economic problems of the elderly, what of the family and kin situations faced by those over sixty-five in our society? The fact that we have included a chapter on the elderly in this book is indicative of the relevance we feel this stage of life has for the family, the focal point of this book. Rural life provided a social security system of sorts both in terms of economics and in terms of integration with family. As we noted earlier in this chapter, the transmission of the family's land in no way meant the end of access to home and hearth. The contract between the heir and his father specified that under no circumstances could the material needs of the retiring parents be neglected. In discussing the situation in eighteenth-century Austria, Berkner remarks:

> Why should a father make such specific demands and insist on their being put into a legal contract when he was dealing with his own son? As an *Ausnehmer* [a retired father], the parent relinquished all legal authority over his farm. The reservations in the contract were all he had left of his former possessions. And the only guarantees he had to these rights and to the payments due him were the good will of his son and a legal contract with very specific details in it. The fact that the peasants invariably chose to include the details of their rights in the contract suggests a common-sense awareness of the frailty of such agreements without any legal guarantees [1972:401].

The fact that such contracts also had stipulations that held that if the parents and the inheriting son and his wife did not get on, the son would pay the parents' rent elsewhere is indicative of the strains inherent in such a situation. It is not easy for a man who has made all the key economic decisions regarding the farm, or the woman who has made domestic as well as economic decisions, to relinquish these privileges and responsibilities overnight to a recently subservient son and his new bride. Recognizing that such problems existed, we must still not forget that these people did not experience the marked drop in income and role content that often accompanies retirement and old age in our society.

Once retired on a farm, a man could still be involved in its day-to-day management, even if he were no longer the boss. However, when a man leaves his job today, whether as a gas station attendant or as a bank vice president, for the most part this is the end of his vocational life, though to be sure some organizations encourage men, particularly at the higher levels of management, to maintain an office after retirement.

Followup studies of the couples involved in the first Burgess and Wallin study, begun in 1939, have indicated that fifteen years later these people (mostly middle-class couples with an average of three years of college) show some decline in marital adjustment.

> To be more precise, over two-thirds of the spouses scored lower on the MAS [Marital Adjustment Scale] in the middle years than they did in the early years of marriage [Jan Dizard, 1968:12].

These were not old people; they were in their late thirties and early forties, for the most part. Is there any evidence of curvilinearity, with the early years and the later years being the most happy ones? On a commonsense basis it would appear that the middle years are those most fraught with problems of childraising, occupational pressures, and financial burdens. In fact this may be the case. Irwin Deutscher based on his own research and a summary of the other studies concludes:

> These data seem to indicate that the postparental phase of the family cycle is not generally defined unfavourably by those involved in it. This finding evidently holds true despite the relative newness of this phase of the family life cycle and the assumption which might be made that little opportunity for role-taking or anticipatory socialization has existed [1968:268].

More recent work seems to confirm Deutscher's assessment (Rollins and Feldman, 1970; Rollins and Cannon, 1974), but the question of just when the upturn starts is still being debated.

For the woman who remained in the home the retirement of the husband has little direct effect on her role behavior in the sense that she continues to cook, clean, and look after other aspects of domestic management. Even in the case of a working woman who retires, there is considerably more continuity between retirement and preretirement roles than is true of her husband, because in all probability she carried the major responsibility for taking care of the house and food preparation even while she was working. For the man, however, a key element of his identity is withdrawn with the coming of retirement, and we would thus expect there to be some adjustment necessary on the part of retired couples.

While the research literature on the topic of marriage and the elderly is far from rich, it still provides us with some insights into what might account for the differential adjustment made by couples to the retirement situation. Aaron Lipman's work on well-to-do retired couples seems to indicate that a man's retirement adjustment is in part dependent on his ability to share in domestic management and successfully engage in affective expression by being a loving and affectionate companion to his wife (1962:483–484). Since the woman must accommodate to this new involvement in the domestic sphere, Lipman questions just how much continuity exists between the pre- and postretirement situation of nonworking wives. While we would agree that wives, like their husbands, have adjustments to make, the degree of adjustment involved hardly seems comparable. Yet, Lipman's point is well taken, since it does make us recognize that adjustment to retirement is a problem for both the husband and wife.

Since Lipman's sample was based on the upper end of the SES ladder, his findings may not hold for couples of different SES. Alan Kerckhoff found that in the lower income strata husbands and wives usually frown on the husband playing a role in household tasks; yet, the retired men in his sample participated as much in these spheres of housework as those from the two higher SES groupings. This seeming conflict between attitudes and behavior may, he feels, explain why more tension is shown among the lower SES group in husband-wife relations (1964, quoted in Nye and Berardo, 1973:567). Another factor which may be operative here is the ability of the husband to assume an affective-expressive role. Since there are believed to be class differences in husband-wife relations before retirement, they should certainly persist and take their toll during the retirement period when the dimensions of affective companionship assume greater importance.

Clearly the retirement adjustment of married couples is a multifaceted phenomenon, one which might best be conceptualized in terms of resources. Low SES couples not only are hindered in their retirement adjustment by being more likely than their higher SES counterparts to be committed to strict domestic division of labor and to less emphasis on the companionship role in their preretirement situation, but also are likely to have a harder time of it financially, and as was noted earlier in the book, financial matters loom large in marital adjustment.

One related, though neglected, aspect of marital adjustment among the elderly is sex. Our society places great emphasis not only on sexuality, but also on youth and youthfulness. Therefore many people, whether they admit it or not, tend to see sex and old age as mutually exclusive. Furthermore, it was and is widely believed that aging is associated with a decline in sexual interest and sexual capacities. According to Kinsey's research, the relationship between age and the frequency of sexual intercourse for men is the most linear of the findings in the study of the sexual behavior of males. Married males aged 16–20 have an average weekly intercourse frequency of 3.8; at 26–30 the frequency drops to 2.7; at 36–40, to 2; at 40–50, to 1.5; and by 55–60, it is down to 0.9 (Kinsey et al., 1948:253). Furthermore the variation within age groups levels considerably as age increases. In the 16–30 group some men reported marital coital frequencies as high as 25 times per week, but by 60 the maximum was down to 3 times a week (Kinsey et al., 1948:253). Kinsey and his associates comment on this linearity as follows:

> Although biologic aging must be the main factor involved, it is still not clear how often the conditions of marriage itself are responsible for this decline in frequency of marital intercourse. Long-time marriage provides the maximum opportunity for repetition of a relatively uniform sort of experience. It is not

> surprising that there should be some loss of interest in the activity among the older males, even if there were no aging process to accelerate it [Kinsey et al., 1948:257].

Until recently our knowledge of the physiological contribution to the decline in marital sexuality was very limited, but thanks to the pioneering work of Masters and Johnson (1966) we now have some idea at least of what effect age per se has upon sexual capacities. Their basic conclusions provide us with much room for optimism:

> There is every reason to believe that maintained regularity of sexual expression coupled with adequate physical well-being and healthy mental orientation to the aging process will combine to provide a sexually stimulative climate within marriage. This climate will, in turn, improve sexual tension and provide a capacity for sexual performance that frequently may extend to and beyond the 80-year level [1966:270].

As rosy as this picture sounds, it requires some qualification. The linear relationship that the Kinsey group found between age and frequency of marital coition in part appears to have its roots in aspects of the aging process. A thirty-year-old man or woman is physiologically rather different in terms of sexual responsiveness than a man or woman of sixty. The vagina of the geriatric female manifests a thinning of the lining, a decline in lubrication, and a shortening in both length and width of the vaginal barrel. Furthermore, age is also associated with decreasing elasticity of the vagina. As a result of such changes, many postmenopausal women experience pain during or after sexual intercourse and an urgent need to urinate, which in itself may be painful because the act of urination may be accompanied by a burning sensation. Even orgasm itself loses some of its pleasure because the uterine contractions associated with it now often are painful; this cramping can continue after intercourse. Similarly, the aging process in the male is associated with certain genital problems. More time is now required to achieve erection, though some may see this compensated for by the ability to maintain the erection for an extended period of time without ejaculation. Orgasm itself loses some of the intensity that it previously had, and the refractory period (time elapsed after orgasm until erection can again be achieved) becomes as long as 12 to 24 hours. There are, of course, more serious problems such as the inability to achieve erection at all (primary impotence) or to maintain an erection once achieved (secondary impotence). The latter shows a marked increase after age fifty and continues to increase after that. Three-quarters of the men treated by Masters and Johnson for secondary impotence were over fifty.

In general, it seems safe to say that the sexual responsiveness of the aging person is diminished both in terms of capacity and interest, though this cannot and should not be construed to mean that the aging or even the very aged, even an eighty-year-old, are returned to a childish state of asexuality. Here we must reconsider the suggestion made by the Kinsey group that some of the decline in sexual behavior on the part of older people may be the result not so much of physiological deterioration as it is of boredom, monotony, and routine. In the case of some women boredom may be counterbalanced by the freedom from fear of pregnancy that menopause provides. To today's generation, which came to sexual maturity with the pill and the IUD, the constant and nagging worries of an unwanted pregnancy may not seem like a major concern; but for an earlier generation this was dreaded reality that may have sexually inhibited many women. The sudden release from concern over pregnancy often results in what has been called a "second honeymoon" for the aging couple. For example, one of the respondents in the Hite Report remarked:

> I enjoy sex more since I no longer fear pregnancy. (I'm post-menopausal.) Also it's more enjoyable since my children are no longer at home—children *can* inhibit sexual activity. Because I enjoy it more, so does my husband [Hite, 1976:351].

Given the fact that physical changes associated with aging may result in a woman becoming less attractive to her husband, and he in turn becoming less attractive to her, this renewed interest on the part of the woman and the desire to stimulate her husband's sexual expression may be desirable and necessary. But given the current availability of efficient contraceptives, young women today are less likely to experience this release later on.

In general, however, the aging couple is likely to have fallen into somewhat of a sexual rut. The excitement and novelty of their early years have passed, and sex may have become a mundane and routine matter. At the same time, both of them are, by conventional standards, becoming less appealing physically. The point should be made, however, that too much emphasis has been placed on the sagging breasts and flabby thighs of women past menopause, and not enough attention paid to the bald pate and bulging belly of her male counterpart. What most people fail to realize (and Masters and Johnson also appear to be guilty here) is that the reason so much stress has been placed on the older female's figure is that physical attributes have traditionally been one of a woman's prime commodities, while men have traded on their economic power and prestige (Moss, 1970). Hopefully, in more equalitarian relationships, the physical deterioration will, out of necessity if not humanity, be viewed less destructively by both parties—or at least both husband and wife will have equal access to physically more attractive partners outside of marriage.

What we want to emphasize here is that a couple in their sixties or seventies need not see sex as something which is behind them. In the absence of chronic illness, it does appear that people who recognize the limitations that age brings with it can have fulfilling sexual relationships, assuming that they make the effort to overcome the problems that both the body and the mind impose.

KINSHIP AND THE ELDERLY

Apart from the marital relationships of the elderly, perhaps the next most important dimension of their lives to the family sociologist is their relations with kin. One initial way to study the relations of the elderly to their kin is to look at the residence patterns of the elderly (see Table 13-1). The most striking thing to emerge from Table 13-1, which refers to all people 65 and over in the United States, is how few old people live alone. The overwhelming majority are either living with a spouse or with other people, most of whom are adult children. There is some evidence, however, to suggest a growth since 1940 in the number of widowed people who live alone (Chevan and Korson, 1972), but several studies indicate little change between the middle of the nineteenth century and 1940 (Anderson, 1971; Glasco, 1975; Katz, 1975). Parenthetically, it should be noted that in 1970 only 2 percent of males and 2 percent of females 65 to 74 were residing in institutions and for those over 75 the figures were 7 percent and 11 percent respectively (Bane, 1976:46). The fact that so many of the elderly live alone does not necessarily indicate that the aged have been rejected by their children. Rather many elderly people see taking up residence with adult children as undesirable. This has been found to be the case in Europe as well as in America (Shanas et al., 1968). Given their choice, it appears that the elderly opt for an independent residence, though as we shall see one which does not place them out of the reach of their children and other kin. As one elderly woman has put it:

Table 13-1. MARITAL STATUS AND LIVING ARRANGEMENTS OF THE AGED, 1971 (Percentage Distributions)

	Male			Female		
	65–74	75+	Total	65–74	75+	Total
Marital Status:						
Single	8	6	7	8	7	7
Married	79	63	73	46	22	36
Spouse Present	76	60	70	45	20	35
Spouse Absent	3	3	3	2	2	2
Widowed	10	30	17	43	70	54
Divorced	3	2	3	3	1	2
Living Arrangement:						
Living Alone	12	18	14	33	38	35
Spouse Present	76	60	70	45	20	35
Living with Someone Else	12	23	16	23	42	31

SOURCE: Ethel Shanas and Philip M. Hauser, "Zero Population Growth and the Family Life of Old People," *J. Social Issues*, vol. 30, no. 4, 1974, p. 85.
NOTE: Data from U.S. Bureau of the Census, 1973.

> Most of the people here feel like I do. I don't want to be living with my kids. I love them. I don't want to have, you know, any misunderstandings. Why, if I were to live there, I couldn't have friends in so easy or cook on my stove. They have their friends and the kids have their friends. It's better all 'round, just visiting and being close [quoted in Hochschild, 1973:91].

This pattern has been described as "intimacy at a distance."

The question remains as to whether in fact the old people who live apart from relatives, whether as couples or alone, are isolated from their kin. Here again the evidence comes out against the stereotypical view of the elderly being cut off from kin contact. Shanas's data for the United States, based on over 2,000 respondents, reveal that among people 65 and over 28 percent live with a child, 33 percent live 10 minutes away or less, 16 percent live 11–30 minutes away, 7 percent, 31–60 minutes away, 11 percent over an hour but less than a day, and 5 percent one day or more (Shanas et al., 1968:193). Not only do most of the elderly live near a child, but they tend to see their children as well. Three related studies of the elderly in Denmark, Great Britain, and the United States (Shanas et al., 1968) revealed that more than 60 percent of the parents interviewed had seen a child on the day of the interview and another 20 percent in the week preceding it. Other studies reveal similar patterns (Hochschild, 1973; Rosenberg, 1970).

Such residential and visiting patterns do show some variation between segments of society. Willmott and Young in the comparative study of a working-class section and a middle-class suburb of London found that the working-class married people were somewhat more likely to be living in the same residence as their parents and considerably more likely to live within a five-minute walk than those residing in the suburb (1960:29). However, the researchers did not stop there; they went on to the same sort of comparison, but this time looking at the proximity of the nearest married child of people of pensionable age. Here they found that both the working-class and middle-class neighborhoods tended to resemble each other in terms of the parents residing in the same residence as a child—23 percent in the suburbs and 21 percent in the working-class area—and the other differences tended to balance themselves out. Willmott and Young indicate surprise with this finding, and note that:

> The contrast between the districts is that in one, the generations are together throughout life; in the other, they separate when the children marry but rejoin each other when the parents grow old. The life cycle of kinship follows a different course in the two places [1960:41].

While no other researchers have looked at this question in the identical manner, there is other evidence of class differences in residential dispersion. Bert Adams, for example, in his study of kinship patterns in Greensboro, North Carolina reported that 66 percent of his blue-collar respondents never lived more than 50 miles from Greensboro, while this

Retired couples playing bocci. *(Shelly Rotner)*

was true of only 46 percent of his white-collar respondents. Adams offers the following interpretation of this difference:

> Since industrial working classes can find semi- or unskilled work in one modern city about as well as in another, their migration tends to be related most directly to social group, especially kin relations. Satisfactory relations make movement unlikely; unsatisfactory relations at times result in movement for the sake of escape, not because of greater opportunity elsewhere. The exception to this is, of course, the movement of ruralities into urban blue-collar opportunities. The modern middle or white-collar class, on the other hand, tend to move primarily in response to career demands with less direct concern for the location of kin [1968:23–24].

To be sure, as Adams points out, what we are dealing with here are modal tendencies, and there is considerable overlap between the two classes. It would be interesting however, to see if these class differences became negligible or at least were significantly reduced when we make the comparison only among people with very old parents.

The availability of kin is only part of the social network of older people; the other important dimension is their involvement with friends and neighbors. Rosow, who has done some of the most important work in this area, has argued that when older people rank their reference groups in order of importance they name children first, then neighbors and friends.

> This expresses their relative attractiveness and general significance to the aging. Furthermore, their respective strength approximates a mean proportion, so that children are to neighbors as neighbors are to friends. In this fashion, neighbors constitute a viable alternative to children, and friends are an alternative to neighbors. But friends are not a significant challenge to children [1970:61].

Moreover, Rosow (1970) and Hochschild (1973) point out that relations between child and friend interaction patterns are more or less independent, that is, as older people tend to see one more they don't see the other less; however, for old people whose life situation is disadvantaged through illness, an absence of children living nearby is compensated for by more contact with neighbors and friends. A relevant point to make here is that Rosow and others have found that while middle-class people make a distinction between neighbors and friends, working-class people, because of their limited and locally oriented friendship networks, do not. In general, however, a high density of older people in a residential area does seem to mean that these people will not only have a richer social life, but, in the absence of children nearby, a better chance of getting care during illness and other forms of mutual aid than those who live in areas of low geriatric density. In fact, Rosow and others have found that the social integration of the elderly "increases disproportionately to concentration" (Rosow, 1970:64), though there are some individuals who, even in the presence of other older people, choose to remain outside of local social groupings (Bultena, 1974).

If one were to stop here it would appear that in social terms the lot of old people is not half bad; at least they seem to have no shortage of contacts. Still, we must keep in mind that what has been presented so far is a very general picture which does not convey the special problems suffered by certain groups of the aged: the impoverished, the widowed, the sick, and so on. As an example of the specific problems faced by such subgroups we will focus upon the problems of elderly widows in American society, since this is a group whose situation gives us some general insights into the situation of the elderly as well as into the position of women.

Relatively little research has been done on the status of widowhood, yet there is enough available for us to get some sense of the problems faced by this group. In 1900 the differential life expectancy of men and women was about three years apart; now it is almost eight years apart, though to be sure both men and women have a considerably longer life expectancy at the present time. Recent figures released by the census bureau indicate that the ratio of older women to men is growing. Three-fifths of the people in this country 65 and over are women (U.S. Bureau of the Census,

1975d:1). Another way of looking at this is to point out that in the mid-1930s, the ratio of men to women in the over-65 category was about even, but in 1974 there were only 69 men over 65 for every 100 women (*New York Times,* June 1, 1976:1,19).

WIDOWHOOD

The differences in mortality rates for men and women are reflected in residence patterns. Figures for 1971 show that 70 percent of the men 65 and over were living with their spouses while this was true for only 35 percent of the women of that age. Therefore it is not surprising to discover that over one-third of the women over 65 live by themselves (see Table 13-1). Clearly, when we deal with widows we are dealing with a much larger segment of the older population, and one which we will argue in some ways is not well equipped to cope with the attendant problems.

The death of a husband or wife has consequences which go considerably beyond the loss of someone who was a primary source of emotional support. In many respects women suffer more than men, because for so many women their whole identity is inextricably tied to their role as wife and mother. In the eyes of the community a woman is Joe Todd's wife or Mrs. Robert Stevens. Not only is a woman's symbolic position in a community compromised by the loss of her husband, but there are also very real and threatening financial realities to be coped with. As Berardo (1968) pointed out, the stereotype of the rich widow has little substance in fact. To be sure, women are the primary beneficiaries of life insurance policies (something on the order of 80 percent). However, in one fairly large national study it was shown that almost 75 percent received less than $5,000 in benefits and another 20 percent less than $2,000, leaving us with a grand total of perhaps 5 percent who might have been left anything resembling a "bundle" (Berardo, 1968:192). Moreover, the small sums insurance provides are often quickly eroded by the payment of overdue hospital and doctor's bills, funeral arrangements, and various taxes. In 1963 a study carried out by the Institute for Life Insurance revealed that among widows 55 and over the median income in the early 1960s was less than $2,000 (1968:193). As Berardo notes, this is very much in harmony with census data for the period which show elderly widows with a median income of $1,200 in contrast to some aged married couples with incomes of almost $3,000. (Only 4 percent of the elderly receive regular payments from children, indicating perhaps nothing more than that those in most need tend to have children who are least equipped to help out.) The financial plight of the widow, young or old, is often compounded by her trained incapacity to deal with financial matters (her husband always took care of those things) and her lack of job skills. To be sure, more and more married women work, and the traditional division of labor within the home is breaking down, but we must realize that many, if not most, of *today's* widows came to maturity in much more traditional times.

The monetary difficulties faced by older women are only part of the story. Stop for a moment and think about just how much of the social activity in our society among adults is couple oriented. The Zimmermans have the Brentanos and the Hodges over for dinner; the Meyers and the Winters spend a day at the beach. A widow is rarely invited along when "the men" are present. The presence of a widow not only creates certain embarrassing moments, but may on a more subtle level serve as a reminder of how vulnerable all of us are, a fact which we generally do not like brought to our attention.

Obviously some widows fare better than others in their adjustment to the realities of the loss of a husband. Helen Lopata maintains that:

> The major factor in the amount of disengagement experienced by a woman upon the death of her husband is the degree to which her various social roles were dependent upon him. Such dependence is, of course, influenced by many characteristics of the couple's background and life, including the husband's occupation and income, the age of the man and wife, their health and education [1970:44].

What Lopata is getting at here is the point we raised earlier—that many women are handicapped not only as widows, but also as wives because their social location is determined by being someone's wife rather than as a person in her own right. A woman who is working and has friends of her own, independent of her husband's friends and "their" friends (she and her husband's mutual friends), will have an easier time than a woman who has never worked or in some other way laid the foundation for an identity apart from marriage. Certainly both types of women experience a sense of bereavement at the sudden loss of the husband, but Lopata is sensitizing us to the issue of long-term adjustment, and whether or not the woman becomes socially isolated or retains meaningful involvement in larger social groupings.

REMARRIAGE AMONG THE ELDERLY

One aspect of life for the elderly which has only recently begun to be seriously investigated is remarriage. When we consider that at the beginning of the present decade there were more than six million widows and a million and a half widowers over sixty-five in this country, the magnitude and the poignancy of the problem becomes evident. Moreover, as a group today widows and widowers have reason to expect longer lives, not to mention generally better health and more income than any previous generation. Yet this is a group which still encounters a fair amount of resistance to their remarrying, both on the part of their children and society at large. McKain has noted that:

> Children are especially likely to resist the remarriage of a parent. In some cases pecuniary self-interest lies behind a child's opposition to remarriage in that he is afraid such a move will reduce his inheritance. In addition, most children have never thought of their parents in the role of husband and wife. Instead they see them only as mother or father—a self-sacrificing, asexual and narrow role. The sudden role reversal in which they are asked to accept a new member in the family is beyond their comprehension and they begin to consider their parent as childish, perverse, and certainly not qualified to select a marriage partner. More important, where the tradition of filial responsibility persists, some children look upon a new mate for their widowed parent as evidence of their own failure to provide a home. In this case a feeling of guilt causes them to resist the marriage of their parent [1972:62–63].

Even if children are accepting of such a marriage there is still the problem of broader societal attitudes which define such marriages as childish and unrealistic. Since stereotypes about the asexuality of older people are widespread and there is a general lack of respect for their emotional needs, such disapproval of marriage among the elderly is at least comprehensible, though it is not condonable. Yet a significant number of the elderly ignore or disregard these stereotypes and do remarry. In fact between 1949 and 1959 marriages of people sixty-five and over increased by one-third, and over 70 percent of those involved were widowed (Nye and Berardo, 1973:608). What became of them and their marriages?

Walter McKain's study of remarriage among the elderly in Connecticut is the only comprehensive study of "retirement" marriage available. It is based on interviews with 100 couples all married at least five years at the time of the study, and in which the groom was at least 65 and the bride at least 60 when the couple first married (1969, 1972). McKain discovered that these couples were by no means free of social pressures. Twenty-five percent indicated that they almost decided not to remarry because of pressure, and even those who did not have such clear second thoughts attempted to reduce their visibility by having unelaborate civic ceremonies and no honeymoons.

Once having overcome public opinion and the criticism of their children, the overwhelming majority of couples went on to have highly successful marriages. While 20 couples reported some problems and 6 appeared to be failures, the remaining 74 percent showed excellent adjustment and satisfaction. McKain feels that success in retirement marriage is associated with a number of factors: (1) Couples who had known each other for an extended period prior to marriage tended to fare better than those who married with a short courtship period. He notes that some had been neighbors and friends, and others relatives by marriage. (2) Those marriages which were not disapproved of by relatives and kin also tended to be more successful. In this respect and the former as well the marriages of older people in no way differ from those of younger people—long engagement and kin approval are both associated with marital adjustment. (3) Those who had adjusted well to growing old were successful in their remarriage though McKain is not sure whether successful remarriage leads to adjustment in old age or vice versa. (4) Couples who chose not to live in the residence maintained by a spouse in previous marriage also did better than those who did not make this change. (5) Couples without financial problems did better than those with inadequate funds (1972:65–67).

While for the majority in this group retirement marriage proved to be a very salubrious answer to the problem of loneliness brought on by loss of a spouse, we must keep in mind that the strong imbalance in the ratio of widows to widowers among the elderly makes this a solution which only a minority of women can ever hope to achieve. In view of this, more than one person has suggested that geriatric polygyny may provide at least a partial answer in that it would allow the limited number of aged males to be made maximum use of in providing elderly women with companionship (Kassel, 1966:137–144). Given prevailing conceptions of propriety, this is not likely to happen. Another perhaps more socially acceptable solution is offered by Sylvia Clavan and Ethel Vatter, which they describe as the "family of affiliation" (1972a, 1972b).

THE AFFILIATED FAMILY

Clavan and Vatter begin their discussion of the "affiliated family" by pointing out that not only do we in this country have a growing population of elderly widows, but that we also have a growing number of young mothers in the labor force. Young mothers are often impeded in obtaining employment because of the burdens of childcare. Some families are meeting this problem by moving toward the kind of equalitarian family discussed earlier in which primacy is given neither to the husband's nor the wife's work, and where both share the responsibilities of housekeeping and childcare. Some couples are unwilling or find it impossible to do this; and of course there are also many female-headed households where either because of death, divorce, or desertion women try by themselves to run a home and earn a living at the same time.

Clavan and Vatter feel that one answer to this situation is to bring together women in need of assistance at home to facilitate their employment with the many older women whose lives are filled with loneliness. They define the resulting family form in the following manner:

> We shall define the affiliative family as any combination of husband/father, wife/mother, and their children, plus one or more older persons, recognized as part of the kin network and called by a designated kin term. They may or may not be part of the residential household. Monetary remuneration may or may not be involved. Voluntary commitment to responsiblity for one another within the unit is the single basic criterion [1972a:409].

From the point of view of the children involved in such arrangements, the presence of an older adult has advantages beyond those of babysitting.

For one thing, it gives them some exposure to people who may seem as exotic to them as a member of another culture. The truth of this was vividly brought home to me by a colleague who was recounting a discussion he and his wife had with their seven-year-old son. The boy had been anxiously inquiring about death and dying and his parents were trying to reassure him that death was typically something that happened to old people. Given the fact that this family lived in a university community with many young people and relatively few visible older people, the parents asked if the boy knew what old people were. He responded, "Yes, I remember old people from when (four years ago) we lived in Chicago." The fact that a child in our society must "remember" old people is indicative of the rigid age stratification of so many of our communities, and reflects the fact that through old-age centers and retirement communities the elderly have increasingly become segregated. Given the desire for diversity and variety we see and hear so often expressed, one wonders if multigenerational families, even when artificially created, are not something to be sought after.

For the elderly woman who has been cut loose from any sort of social moorings as a result of the loss of her husband and the departure of her children, being a contributing member of a second nuclear family might be a very enriching experience. Not only would such a person feel that she was doing something worthwhile and beneficial for someone other than herself, but she would also be able to get the affection and companionship that so many older people in our society seem to be so desperately in need of. As one of the elderly women interviewed by Clavan and Vatter states: "I know I get psychic rewards from the [affiliative] relationship" (1972b:501). Obviously what the authors are suggesting is the creation of a fictive or pseudo-kin category, a grandmother or aunt of sorts, who in many respects would play a role vis-à-vis the family similar to that played by the real grandmother or aunt.

For the working mother the benefits of such a relationship are so obvious as to hardly warrant much comment, but perhaps a few words are in order. At the most basic level, the availability of an older woman who either lives with the family or visits daily would allow the mother to go off to work knowing that the children are being looked after by a person whose relationship to them is one of more than mere employment. It is expected that strong bonds would grow up between the children and the woman who cares for them. While it is currently uncommon to hear the elderly spoken of as having any knowledge that is of use or value to those younger than themselves, we would point out that in terms of domestic and childrearing experience, not to mention emotional support during times of crisis, the presence of an older woman might be very helpful indeed. A number of sociologists, but Parsons in particular, has commented on the burden placed on the nuclear family by making it the emotional focal point of industrial society. According to Parsons, so many of each other's needs must be met by the married pair that the question really is not why divorce rates are high, but rather why they are not much, much higher. The third party rather than creating conflict, as mothers-in-law have been believed to do, might actually in certain respects relieve them, since she has no special kin ties to either of the pair.

Of course, the family of affiliation may not be the panacea for all familial problems. Interpersonal relations, as we all know, can be terribly fragile, and the ties of kinship often provide the buffer that permits us to tolerate the friction that arises out of people living together and depending on each other for vital services. Inviting a stranger into one's house with the implicit expectation that the person will become one of the family is fraught with problems. Clavan and Vatter suggest that the people involved might get to know each other slowly and create an affiliative family only later. Nevertheless, this family form, while seeming to have great potential, is still something that many people will find problematic, for one reason or another.

THE ELDERLY IN A COMMUNAL SOCIETY

A family form no less utopian than the one described by Clavan and Vatter is the communal family, a form which we have already discussed, though in doing so we focused almost exclusively on the benefits provided for younger men and women and their children. What of the elderly? How do they fare in such a setting? We have very little information on the situation of the elderly in nineteenth-century communities, but given the fact that life expectancy at that time was so much shorter, we would expect this to have been less of a problem, if only because there were dramatically fewer old people in the general population. Also, expectancies concerning retirement were nonexistent—people worked until they no longer could. All this notwithstanding, communes did contain older people, and from what the contemporary accounts indicate, they were afforded positions of respect, with their physical comforts in no way being compromised by the increasing incapacity to make a material contribution to the life of the community.

There is some evidence available on the situation of the elderly in an ongoing communal system, one which had existed for many years—the Israeli kibbutzim. Talmon (1961), in her article, "Aging in Israel, A Planned Society," looks at the position of old people on several Israeli kibbutzim and concludes that life for them is not the paradise one might anticipate. When she compared the attitudes of aging kibbutz members with those of members' parents now living on the kibbutz, but who had not spent their mature lives there, she found that, surprising as it may seem, the latter were more satisfied than the former. The answer for this seeming paradox is to be found in general kibbutz ideology. The overriding ethic in kibbutz life is work and productivity. A person's worth in his or her own eyes as well as in the eyes of the community is determined by the measurable contribution made to the welfare and growth of the community. Thus, the man who successfully managed the poultry operation or who ran the dairy herd was someone with greater prestige and supposedly greater self-respect than his counterpart who did the community's bookkeeping. This is not to say that the importance of the latter's work went unrecognized, but rather that greater value was placed on productive work than on service work, however valuable. Given this emphasis on productive work, the elderly are placed in a somewhat compromised position. While their retirement from the work sphere is gradual, and in no way associated with a reduction in standard of living, it is associated with a reduction in self-esteem, because the elderly must out of necessity move out of the most visibly productive spheres into less demanding and less valued spheres.

The kibbutz movement in Israel is not unaware of the problems faced by the elderly, and attempts are being made to alleviate them (Feder, 1972). There is talk of having insurance policies which would offer retirement benefits to the elderly so that they could continue to make a direct financial contribution to the community. If such policies were implemented, then the elderly might feel less apologetic about their existence. Nonetheless, this does not answer the more fundamental problem of offering new foundations for positive self-evaluation in a community that values productivity above all else. Retraining programs that would allow people too old to engage in physically demanding work to occupy important nonmanual positions may provide partial answers, but it is hard to believe that they will serve as truly alternative sources of self-esteem. However, with the growing industrialization of the kibbutz, the situation of the elderly may improve.

We should not conclude from Talmon's research that the lot of the elderly on the kibbutz, or in any other commune, is inferior to that of their noncommunal counterparts. Elderly kibbutz members have no fears concerning where their next meal is coming from, how they are going to pay the rent, or secure enough money for needed surgery. Furthermore, their children are available to them and, perhaps more importantly, so are their grandchildren. One of the clear benefits of kibbutz retirement is that grandparents can spend plenty of time with their grandchildren, and in doing so often assist their own children. Relations between the generations seem to be fairly harmonious and characterized by reciprocal services. Grandparents look after grandchildren when their parents must leave the kibbutz for a vacation, a training period, or when some other demand makes it impossible for them to spend the daily visiting period with their children. In turn, adult children are able to help their aged parents by bringing food to their quarters when they are ill and by caring for them in other little ways. Given the fact that the broader community bears so many of the more onerous responsibilities of intergenerational ties, it is not surprising to find that on the kibbutz relations between adult children and parents are generally good. So, while the elderly on the commune may have problems of self-esteem stemming from their lack of active participation in directly productive work, they nonetheless fare much better in most respects than their counterparts in the noncommunal world.

SUMMARY

We have looked at the family life of old people in modern societies, with a special emphasis on the United States. One of the major themes of this chapter has been the mixed blessing that retirement has become in such societies. People now live longer than ever before and there is reason to believe that we will be able to extend life expectancy even further in the future. Also, old age is, as a result of pension plans and various welfare schemes, less fraught with economic insecurity than it was in the early stages of industrialization, though in certain respects it provides less security than many preindustrial settings, for example, the one described by Berkner (1972). Such "benefits" notwithstanding, the wisdom and strength once seen as residing in old age have become compromised; it is now associated with physical deterioration, medical problems, and perhaps most importantly, exclusion from the work force as a result of forced retirement (Achenbaum, 1974). The latter, tied as it is to a reduction in salaried income, creates a situation of economic hardship to compound what has been spoken of as the "roleless role" of old people.

Having looked at the general picture of old age in modern society, we turned to a consideration of various aspects of family life. The married elderly seem to manifest relatively high levels of marital satisfaction, though problems exist as a result of women having to adjust to the presence of their husbands in the home and the difficulty some men have in assuming an affective-expressive role. In terms of sex, while there is no question but that coital frequency declines as a couple ages, largely as a result of the work of Masters and Johnson (1966) we have come to a new appreciation of the sexual capacities and interests of the elderly.

Regarding kinship, we see relatively little physical isolation of the elderly. The majority of the elderly live either with their spouse or with some other relative, though there has been a trend in the twentieth century for the widowed elderly to maintain a separate residence, but one which is near the children. Friends and neighbors also appear to play an important role in the well-being and life satisfaction of the elderly, especially when children are not available.

The fact that women now live on the average about seven years longer than men has resulted in widowhood becoming a more prevalent phenomenon. Given the traditional role of the male as the primary breadwinner and the fact that a great deal of socializing in our society is couple oriented, widowhood is problematic both financially and socially. While remarriage among the elderly is increasing, there are not enough men to go around, a situation which led at least one social scientist to argue for geriatric polygyny.

Other alternatives that have been offered to deal with the problems old age poses in our society include Vatter and Clavan's (1972) family of affiliation, where an elderly widow is incorporated into a nonrelated nuclear family with young children, providing grandmotherly services in return for a sense of belonging and engaging in meaningful activity. Finally, we looked at the elderly in communal settings and saw that while their situation was in many respects better than that encountered by members of the outside world, it still posed problems.

This brief chapter only skims the surface of the life situation faced by the elderly. Nonetheless, we hope that the reader has gotten some sense of the direction change is taking in this important aspect of family relations.

AFTERWORD: Whither the Family?

Having attempted to show that the American family is not in the crisis situation some of its critics would have us believe, but rather has simply adapted to the changing conditions of American society, we are now faced with an issue that some might argue is better left to fortune tellers than sociologists, namely, where is the American family going? Without running too great a risk of speaking in haste and repenting in leisure, there are a few things that can be said on this topic.

We have tried to show that it is a misconception to think that the modern family is isolated from kin. With the exception of the economic realm, there is little evidence to suggest that relations with nonresidential kin have altered since the Pilgrims first landed. The boundaries of the viable kin group appear to have remained the same; kin continue to interact frequently and are viewed as a source of various supportive services. To be sure, there have been distinctive patterns at various times, such as the intense mother and married daughter relations that characterized working-class families during the early and middle phases of the industrial era. Social class variations in kinship patterns that remain appear to be diminishing if not disappearing. Whether, as some have argued, we will see kin functioning in a more and more specialized sphere remains to be seen, but there is no reason to believe that they will not continue to play an important role in people's lives in terms of both reciprocal services and visiting patterns.

Related to the question of kinship is the composition of the household. While historical evidence does seem to indicate that the nuclear family has been the prevalent residential unit from the days of early settlement to the present, there may in the twentieth century have been a movement toward a stricter nuclearity. More specifically, while the proportions of nuclear families may not have risen, the presence of additional people (servants, boarders, lodgers, widowed parents, or older children) has declined. Therefore, not surprisingly, the residential unit that has shown the greatest growth in recent years has been the single-person household, involving elderly widows as well as young single people. This development appears to be a function both of an affluence that allows people to maintain such a costly form of housing and the values supportive of it (for example, elderly people feeling that it is best to maintain some sort of independence from their children). Short of some drastic economic turnabout we might expect these residential patterns to continue, if not expand.

Related to the question of the changes in household composition is the rather extraordinary explosion of cohabitation. While the lack of anything more than very recent data makes it difficult to actually assess the amount of cohabitation that occurred during the first half of this century, we do know that during the 1960s and even more so in the 1970s the number of people sharing a residence with a member of the opposite sex has accelerated dramatically. Whether this is becoming an alternative rather than a stage along the way to marriage is not clear at present, but many cohabitors ultimately do marry. The fact that this development has met with a surprising degree of tolerance everywhere from the media to rental agents suggests that future growth can be anticipated.

The greatest single factor affecting the size of American households over the last 200 years is the decline in marital fertility. People are having smaller and smaller families, and, recently, a tiny but by no means inconsequential minority are marrying but choosing to have no children at all. This is an area where one is on most treacherous ground in making predictions. There is no shortage of fecund women, but since age at first marriage is increasing, female employment growing, and effective contraception available, some demographers feel that we are not likely to see a return to fertility figures much above, if at all above, the replacement level. Yet, others see the decline in fertility since the 1960s as a short-term phenomenon, brought about by previous high fertility and contractions in the economy, which should be reversed as the smaller cohort of the low-fertility days of the 1960s comes on the job market in a good competitive position because of their limited numbers. Our guess would be that those who are bullish on the baby market are probably going to take their losses if they act on their theories and buy stock in Pampers.

Few married American women have ever been truly idle. During the seventeenth and eighteenth centuries and the portion of the nineteenth century when this country was largely agricultural, wives played a vital role in the running of small-scale agricultural businesses, and without such services their farmer husbands would have been seriously impaired. With the coming of the industrial age married women were, for the most part, excluded from the external work force, though for only a few did this mean days devoted to shopping and bridge. For the rest, the chores of housework and child-care occasionally mixed with home industry (whether piece work, boarding and lodging, or marginal agriculture) kept the day filled. While unmarried women have always played an important role in industry, during the twentieth century we have seen married women enter the work force, first those whose children had grown, then those with school-age children, and since the 1950s those with preschool children. Currently 47 percent of American marriages involves a working wife. This is a trend whose continuation is dependent on not only an ideology supportive of wives working, but also the ability of the economy to provide employment opportunities. Some demographers interpreted the growing presence of married women in the work force during the twentieth century as a response to the expansion of that part of the economy containing sex-role stereotyped jobs, such as secretaries and key punch operators. An economic downturn, they argue, might result in women again being excluded from the labor force. However, in the absence of this and in the face of laws that attempt to restrain sex discrimination, we will probably continue to see more working wives. What remains to be seen is whether this will be associated with a growth of what has been described earlier as a "career" orientation toward work on the part of women —simply put, a conception of work similar to that which men have long had.

Declining fertility and growing work force participation should inevitably make their effect felt on the character of the marriages people are entering into, and there is some evidence to suggest that this is happening. Earlier in this book we suggested that there has been movement in the direction of a greater "symmetry" in marriage, by which we meant a decline in sex-role stereotyping. We were, however, careful to point out that the amount of observable change here has to date been small. While the husbands of working wives do carry a greater responsibility for domestic chores than men whose wives do not work, the major share of housework and child-care still falls on the shoulders of women. Still, the diaper-changing husband is a more common sight than he was a generation ago.

Observable changes in marriage go beyond a greater sharing of domestic work, and involve a redefinition of marriage in terms of what we have described as its "permeability." It has become easier for people to both enter and leave marriage, and once in a stable union to at least experiment with a relationship that allows them more independence and freedom than was true in the past. To the extent that this characterization is accurate, it represents a movement away from the "companionate" model of marriage with its ethic of "togetherness." Furthermore, while one hesitates to make too much of the indications of a growth in extramarital sex because of the lack of data on the nature of the relationships involved, it does appear that sexual exclusivity is being questioned, though certainly not disregarded.

Some couples have opted for alternative family structures of a more dramatic nature, whether in the form of group marriages or communal living. While these are very much minority phenomena, they represent important attempts to go beyond certain assumptions or limitations of monogamous marriage and nuclear family living. In the case of group marriage, what is being questioned is the notion of exclusivity and the limited capacities of the individual for more than one intense, heterosexual relationship. In the case of the commune, most of which involve monogamous couples, the idea is to break down the boundaries of the nuclear family and to deal with aspects of day-to-day living in a cooperative way. While the intense wave of communalism that characterized the second half of the 1960s appears to have subsided somewhat, perhaps especially in its agrarian form, urban communes continue to be common (e.g., several families living in one house and sharing domestic responsibilities), suggesting that the commune has become a more or less permanent, if small, feature of the American landscape. Even for those who only briefly experiment with such life styles, it appears that the experience may have consequences of a positive and continued nature when they return to more conventional residential and familial forms.

What has concerned critics of the family more than alternative forms has been the "alarming" rise in divorce statistics over the last century, especially over the last decade. This has been taken as an indication of spreading disenchantment with marriage, but what those devoted to such an interpretation have generally overlooked is the frequency and rapidity with which divorced people remarry. It has been our argument that the high divorce rates we are currently experiencing are less evidence of a disillusionment with marriage than they are an indication of the great expectations people now have for it, and the reluctance of people to stay in an unfulfilling relationship. When we add to this the previously mentioned consideration of the way in which marriage is changing and the demands this must make on people who were socialized into more traditional patterns, we can better understand why so many are severing relationships and starting again.

All in all, the American family continues to be a viable and flexible institution despite the lamentations of today's Jeremiahs. What is most notable about the direction that change has taken is that it has not been of an exclusive kind. To put it differently, people are now faced with a rather broad range of family and marital options without necessarily being censured for choosing one over another. Thus we have people living out "the American dream" married in their suburban home with children, pets, and station wagons, and others choosing to cohabit, having no children and a minimal commitment to any sort of property. Ultimately, the durability of the American family may be found in the flexibility it has come to offer during the twentieth century.

BIBLIOGRAPHY

Abbott, Edith. *Women in Industry.* New York: D. Appleton, 1910.

Achenbaum, Andrew. "The Obsolescence of Old Age in America." *Journal of Social History,* Fall 1974, pp. 48–62.

Adams, Bert N. *Kinship in an Urban Setting.* Chicago: Markham, 1968.

———. "Isolation, Function and Beyond: American Kinship in the 1960's." *Journal of Marriage and the Family,* vol. 32 (November 1970), pp. 575–597.

Adelman, Irma, and Morris, Cynthia T. *Society, Politics and Economic Development.* Baltimore: Johns Hopkins University Press, 1967.

Ald, Roy. *The Youth Communes.* New York: Tower Books, 1970.

Anderson, John E. *The Young Child in the Home.* New York: D Appleton-Century, 1936.

Anderson, Michael. *Family Structure in Nineteenth Century Lancashire.* Cambridge: Cambridge University Press, 1971.

Anonymous. *The Young Husband Book.* Philadelphia: Carey Lea and Blanchard, 1936.

Arensberg, Conrad M., and Kimball, Solon T. *Family and Community in Ireland.* Cambridge: Harvard University Press, 1940.

Ariès, Philippe. *Centuries of Childhood: A Social History of Family Life.* New York: Vintage Books, 1962.

———. "An Interpretation to be Used for a History of Mentalities." In *Popular Attitudes Toward Birth Control in Pre-Industrial France and England,* edited by Orest and Patricia Ranum, pp. 101–125. New York: Harper and Row, 1972.

Atcheson, Richard. *The Bearded Lady.* New York: John Day, 1971.

Athanasiou, Robert, et al. "Sex." *Psychology Today,* vol. 4 (July 1970), pp. 39–42.

Axelrod, Morris N. "Urban Social Structure and Social Participation." *American Sociological Review,* vol. 21 (February 1956), pp. 13–18.

Back, Kurt W. "The Ambiguity of Retirement." In *Behavior and Adaptation in Later Life,* edited by

Ewald W. Busse and Eric Pfeiffer, pp. 93–114. Boston: Little Brown, 1969.

———. *Beyond Words.* New York: Russell Sage Foundation, 1972.

Bahr, S. J. "A Methodological Study of Conjugal Power: A Replication and Extension of Blood and Wolfe." Unpublished Ph.D. dissertation, Washington State University, 1972.

Bailyn, Bernard. *Education in the Forming of American Society.* New York: Norton, 1972. First published 1960.

Baker, Elizabeth F. *Technology and Woman's Work.* New York: Columbia University Press, 1964.

Balswick, Jack. "The Jesus People Movement: A Sociological Analysis." Paper presented at the American Sociological Association Meetings, New Orleans, 1972.

Bane, Mary Jo. *Here to Stay.* New York: Basic Books, 1976.

Banks, J. A. *Prosperity and Parenthood.* London: Routledge and Kegan Paul, 1954.

Barker, Michael B. *California Retirement Communities.* Berkeley: University of California Center for Real Estate and Urban Economics, 1966.

Barker-Benfield, G. J. *The Horrors of the Half-Known Life.* New York: Harper and Row, 1975.

Barnett, James H. *Divorce and the American Divorce Novel.* New York: Russell and Russell, 1968; first published 1937.

Bauman, Karl E., and Wilson, Robert R. "Sexual Behavior of Unmarried University Students in 1968 and 1972." *Journal of Sex Research,* vol. 10 (November 1974), pp. 327–333.

Beales, Ross W., Jr. "In Search of the Historical Child: Miniature Adulthood and Youth in Colonial New England." *American Quarterly,* vol. 27 (October 1975), pp. 379–398.

Beaver, M. W. "Population, Infant Mortality, and Milk." *Population Studies,* vol. 27 (July 1973), pp. 243–254.

Becker, Howard S. *Outsiders.* New York: Free Press, 1963.

Bell, Robert R. *Premarital Sex in a Changing Society.* Englewood Cliffs, N.J.: Prentice-Hall, 1966.

———, and Chaskes, Jay. "Premarital Sex Among Coeds, 1958 and 1968." *Journal of Marriage and the Family,* vol. 32 (February 1970), pp. 81–84.

———; Turner, Stanley; and Rosen, Lawrence. "A Multivariate Analysis of Female Extramarital Coitus." *Journal of Marriage and the Family,* vol. 37 (May 1975), pp. 375–384.

Bem, Sandra L., and Bem, Daryl J. "Case Study of a Nonconscious Ideology: Training the Woman to Know Her Place." In *Beliefs, Attitudes and Human Affairs,* edited by Daryl J. Bem, pp. 89–99. Belmont, Calif.: Brooks/Cole, 1970.

Bender, Donald R. "A Refinement of the Concept of Household." *American Anthropologist,* vol. 69 (October 1967), pp. 493–504.

Bengston, Vern L., and Lovejoy, Mary C. "Values, Personality, and Social Structure." *American Behavioral Scientist,* vol. 16 (July/August 1973), pp. 880–911.

Berardo, Felix M. "Widowhood Status in the United States." *Family Coordinator,* vol. 17 (July 1968), pp. 191–203.

Berger, Bennett, et al. "Child-Rearing Practices of the Communal Family." In *Family in Transition,* edited by Arlene S. and Jerome H. Skolnick, pp. 509–522. Boston: Little, Brown, 1971.

———. "The Communal Family." *Family Coordinator,* vol. 21 (October 1972), pp. 419–428.

Berkner, Lutz K. "The Stem Family and the Developmental Cycle of the Peasant Household: An Eighteenth-Century Austrian Example." *Amer-*

ican Historical Review, vol. 77 (April 1972), pp. 398–418.

———. "Recent Research on the History of the Family in Western Europe." *Journal of Marriage and the Family,* vol. 35 (August 1973), pp. 395–405.

Bernard, Jessie. *Marriage and Family Among Negroes.* Englewood Cliffs, N.J.: Prentice-Hall, 1966.

———. *The Future of Marriage.* New York: World Publishing, 1972.

Billingsley, Andrew. *Black Families in White America.* Englewood Cliffs, N.J.: Prentice-Hall, 1968.

Birdsall, Nancy. "Women and Population Studies." *Signs,* vol. 1 (Spring 1976), pp. 699–712.

Blake, Nelson M. *The Road to Reno.* New York: Macmillan, 1962.

Blassingame, John W. *The Slave Community.* New York: Oxford University Press, 1972.

Blau, Zena S. "Exposure to Child-Rearing Experts." *American Journal of Sociology,* vol. 69 (May 1964), pp. 595–608.

Blood, Robert O. "A Retest of Waller's Rating Complex." *Marriage and Family Living,* vol. 17 (February 1955), pp. 41–47.

———. "The Husband-Wife Relationship." In *The Employed Mother in America,* edited by F. Ivan Nye and Lois W. Hoffman, pp. 282–308. Chicago: Rand McNally, 1963.

———, and Hamblin, Robert L. "The Effects of Wife's Employment on the Family Power Structure." *Social Forces,* vol. 36 (May 1958), pp. 347–352.

———, and Wolfe, Donald M. *Husbands and Wives.* New York: Free Press, 1960.

Blumberg, Rae L., and Winch, Robert F. "Societal Complexity and Family Complexity: Evidence for the Curvilinear Hypothesis." *American Journal of Sociology,* vol. 77 (March 1972), pp. 898–920.

Bottomore, T. B. *Sociology.* London: Allen and Unwin, 1962.

Bradburn, Norman. *The Structure of Psychological Well-Being.* Chicago: Aldine, 1969.

Branca, Patricia. *Silent Sisterhood.* Pittsburgh: Carnegie-Mellon University Press, 1975a.

———. "A New Perspective on Women's Work: A Comparative Typology." *Journal of Social History,* vol. 9 (Winter 1975b), pp. 129–153.

Brandt, John L. *Marriage and the Home.* Chicago: Laird and Lee, 1892.

Breen, T. H., and Foster, Stephen. "Moving to the New World: The Character of Early Massachusetts Immigration." *William and Mary Quarterly,* vol. 30 (1973), pp. 189–222.

Bremner, Robert H., ed. *Children and Youth in America.* vol. 1. Cambridge: Harvard University Press, 1970.

Brim, Orville G., Jr. *Education for Child Rearing.* New York: Russell Sage Foundation, 1959.

Bronfenbrenner, Urie. "Socialization and Social Class Through Time and Space." In *Readings in Social Psychology,* edited by Eleanor Maccoby et al., pp. 400–425. New York: Holt, Rinehart and Winston, 1958.

Brooks, Melvin S., and Sondag, Rodger F. "Sociological Variables in the Reaction of Parents to Child-Rearing Information." *Merrill-Palmer Quarterly,* vol. 8 (July 1962), pp. 175–182.

Broun, Heywood, and Leech, Margaret. *Anthony Comstock: Roundsman of the Lord.* New York: A & C Boni, 1927.

Brown, Richard D. "Modernization and Modern Personality in America, 1680–1865: A Sketch of a Synthesis." *Journal of Interdisciplinary History,* vol. 6 (Winter 1972), pp. 201–228.

Bugliosi, Vincent, and Bugliosi, Gentry. *Helter Skelter.* New York: Norton, 1974.

Bultena, Gordon L. "Structural Effects on the Morale of the Aged." In *Late Life,* edited by J. F. Gubrium, pp. 18–31. Springfield, Ill.: Charles C. Thomas, 1974.

Bumpass, Larry L., and Sweet, James A. "Differentials in Marital Stability." *American Sociological Review,* vol. 37 (December 1972), pp. 754–766.

Burch, Thomas K. "The Size and Structure of Families: A Comparative Analysis of Census Data." *American Sociological Review,* vol. 32 (June 1967), pp. 347–363.

Burchinal, Lee G. "The Premarital Dyad and Love Involvement." In *Handbook of Marriage and the Family,* edited by Harold T. Christensen, pp. 623–674. Chicago: Rand McNally, 1964.

Burgess, Ernest, and Locke, Harvey S. *The Family.* New York: American Book Co., 1945.

Burgess, Ernest, et al. *The Family.* 4th ed. New York: Van Nostrand Reinhold, 1971; first published 1945.

Burgess, Ernest W., and Wallin, Paul. *Engagement and Marriage.* Philadelphia: Lippincott, 1953.

Burr, Wesley R. *Theory Construction and the Sociology of the Family.* New York: John Wiley, 1973.

Bury, J. B. *The Idea of Progress.* New York: Macmillan, 1932.

Busse, Ewald W., and Pfeiffer, Eric, eds. *Behavior and Adaptation in Later Life.* Boston: Little, Brown, 1969.

Caldwell, John C. "Toward a Restatement of Demographic Transition Theory." *Population and Development Review,* vol. 2 (September/December 1976), pp. 321–365.

Calhoun, Arthur W. *A Social History of the American Family.* New York: Barnes and Noble, 1945; first published 1917.

Campisi, Paul J. "Ethnic Family Patterns: The Italian Family in the United States." *American Journal of Sociology,* vol. 53 (May 1948), pp. 443–449.

Carden, Maren L. *Oneida.* Baltimore: Johns Hopkins University Press, 1969.

Carr, Lois Green, and Walsh, Lorena S. "The Planter's Wife: The Experience of White Women in Seventeenth-Century Maryland." *William and Mary Quarterly,* forthcoming.

Carter, Hugh, and Glick, Paul C. *Marriage and Divorce.* Cambridge: Harvard University Press, 1970.

Chafe, William H. *The American Woman.* New York: Oxford University Press, 1972.

Chapman, R. N. "The Quantitative Analysis of Environmental Factors." *Ecology,* vol. 9 (1928), pp. 111–122.

Chevan, Albert, and Korson, J. Henry. "The Widowed Who Live Alone." *Social Forces,* vol. 51 (September 1972), pp. 45–54.

Christensen, Harold T. *Marriage Analysis.* 2nd ed. New York: Ronald Press, 1958.

———, and Gregg, Christina F. "Changing Sex Norms in America and Scandinavia." *Journal of Marriage and the Family,* vol. 32 (November 1970), pp. 616–627.

Clanton, Gordon. "The Contemporary Experience of Adultery." Unpublished paper, copyrighted 1971.

———, and Downing, Chris. *Face to Face.* New York: Dutton, 1975.

Clark, Alice. *Working Life of Women in the Seventeenth Century.* New York: Augustus Kelley, 1968; first published 1919.

Clark, Clifford E., Jr. "Domestic Architecture as an Index to Social History: The Romantic Revival and the Cult of Domesticity in America, 1840–1870." *Journal of Interdisciplinary History,* vol. 7 (Summer 1976), pp. 33–56.

Clavan, Sylvia, and Vatter, Ethel. "The Affiliated Family: A Continued Analysis." *Family Coordinator,* vol. 21 (October 1972a), pp. 499–504.

——— and ———. "The Affiliated Family: A Device for Integrating Old and Young." *The Gerontologist,* vol. 12 (Winter 1972b), pp. 407–412.

Coale, Ansley J., and Zelnick, Melvin. *New Estimate of Fertility and Population in the United States.* Princeton, N.J.: Princeton University Press, 1963.

Cole, Charles Lee. "Cohabitation in Social Context." In *Marriage and Alternatives,* edited by Roger W. Libby and Robert N. Whitehurst, pp. 62–79. Glenview, Ill.: Scott, Foresman, 1977.

Cole, William Graham. "Religious Attitudes Toward Extramarital Intercourse." In *Extra-Marital Relations,* edited by Gerhard Neubeck, pp. 54–64. Englewood Cliffs, N.J.: Prentice-Hall, 1969.

Conover, Patrick W. "An Analysis of Communes and Intentional Communities with Particular Attention to Sexual and General Relations." *Family Coordinator,* vol. 24 (October 1975), pp. 453–465.

Constantine, Larry L., and Constantine, Joan M. "Sexual Aspects of Multilateral Relations." *Journal of Sex Research,* vol. 7 (August 1971), pp. 204–225.

——— and ———. "The Group Marriage." In *The Nuclear Family in Crisis: The Search for an Alternative,* edited by Michael Gordon, pp. 204–222. New York: Harper and Row, 1972; first published 1969.

——— and ———. *Group Marriage.* New York: Macmillan, 1973.

Cooley, Charles Horton. *Social Organization.* New York: Scribner's 1909.

Cooper, David. *The Death of the Family.* New York: Pantheon, 1970.

Coser, Rose L., ed. *The Family.* 2nd ed. New York: St. Martin's Press, 1974.

Cott, Nancy. "Divorce and the Status of Women in Eighteenth Century Massachusetts." *William and Mary Quarterly,* vol. 33 (October 1976), pp. 586–614.

Cowgill, Donald O., and Holmes, Lowell D., eds. *Aging and Modernization.* New York: Appleton-Century, 1972.

Crafts, N. F. R., and Ireland, N. J. "Family Limitations and the English Demographic Revolution." *Journal of Economic History,* vol. 36 (September 1976), pp. 598–623.

Cuber, John F., and Harroff, Peggy B. *The Significant Americans.* Baltimore: Penguin, 1966.

Cumming, Elaine, and Henry, William E. *Growing Old.* New York: Basic Books, 1961.

Cutright, Phillips. "Income and Family Events: Marital Stability." *Journal of Marriage and the Family,* vol. 33 (May 1971), pp. 291–306.

———. "Illegitimacy in the U.S.: 1920–1968." In United States Commission on Population Growth and the American Future, *Demographic and Social Aspects of Population Growth,* vol. 1, pp. 375–438. Washington, D.C.: Government Printing Office, 1972.

Dahlstrom, Edmund, and Liljestrom, Rita. "The Family and Married Women at Work." In *The Changing Roles of Men and Women,* edited by Edmund Dahlstrom, pp. 19–58. Boston: Beacon Press, 1971.

Darin-Drabkin, H. *The Other Society.* New York: Harcourt, Brace and World, 1962.

Davidoff, Leonore. "Mastered for Life: Servant and Wife in Victorian and Edwardian England." *Journal of Social History,* vol. 7 (Summer 1974), pp. 406–428.

Davidson, Sara. "Open Land: Getting Back to the Communal Garden." *Harper's* (June 1970), pp. 91–102.

Davis, Allison, and Havighurst, Robert J. "Social Class and Color Differences in Child Rearing." *American Sociological Review,* vol. 11 (December 1946), pp. 698–710.

Davis, Katherine B. *Factors in the Sex Life of Twenty-two Hundred American Women.* New York: Harper and Bros., 1929.

Davis, Kingsley. "The Sociology of Prostitution." *American Sociological Review,* vol. 2 (October 1937), pp. 746–755.

———. *Human Society.* New York: Macmillan, 1949.

———. "The American Family in Relation to Demographic Change." In United States Commission on Population Growth and the American Future, *Demographic and Social Aspects of Population Growth,* vol. 1, pp. 235–266. Washington, D.C.: Government Printing Office, 1972.

Davis, Lance E., et al. *American Economic Growth.* New York: Harper and Row, 1972.

Degler, Carl N. "Revolution Without Ideology." In *The Woman in America,* edited by R. J. Lifton. Boston: Beacon Press, 1964.

———. "What Ought to Be and What Was: Women's Sexuality in the Nineteenth Century." *American Historical Review,* vol. 79 (December 1974), pp. 1467–1490.

de Mause, Lloyd, ed. *The History of Childhood.* New York: Harper and Row, 1975; first published 1974.

Demos, John. *A Little Commonwealth.* New York: Oxford University Press, 1970.

Denfeld, Duane, and Gordon, Michael. "The Sociology of Mate Swapping." *Journal of Sex Research,* vol. 6 (May 1970), pp. 85–100.

Deutscher, Irwin. "The Quality of Postparental Life." In *Middle Age and Aging,* edited by Bernice L. Neugarten, pp. 263–268. Chicago: University of Chicago Press, 1968.

Diamond, Stephen. *What the Trees Said.* New York: Delta, 1971.

Ditzion, Sidney. *Marriage, Morals and Sex in America.* New York: Bookman Associates, 1953.

Dizard, Jan. *Social Change in the Family.* Chicago: University of Chicago Community and Family Study Center, 1968.

Dotson, Floyd. "Patterns of Voluntary Associations Among Urban Working Class Families." *American Sociological Review,* vol. 16 (October 1951), pp. 687–693.

———. "Marx and Engels on the Family." *American Sociologist,* vol. 9 (November 1974), pp. 181–186.

Dublin, Thomas. "Women, Work and Protest in the Early Lowell Mills." *Labor History,* vol. 16 (Winter 1975), pp. 99–116.

———. "Women, Work and the Family: Female Operatives in the Lowell Mills, 1830–1860." *Feminist Studies,* vol. 3 (Summer–Fall 1975), pp. 30–39.

DuBois, W. E. B. *The Philadelphia Negro.* New York: Schocken Books, 1967; first published 1899.

Duncan, Beverly, and Duncan, Otis D. "Family Stability and Occupational Success." *Social Problems,* vol. 16 (Winter 1969), pp. 273–285.

Easterlin, Richard A. "Population Change and Farm Settlement in the Northern United States." *Journal of Economic History,* vol. 36 (March 1976a), pp. 45–83.

———. "The Conflict Between Aspiration and Resources." *Population and Development Review,* vol. 2 (September/December 1976b), pp. 417–426.

Edwards, John N., and Booth, Alan. "Sexual Behavior In and Out of Marriage." *Journal of Marriage and the Family,* vol. 38 (February 1976), pp. 73–82.

Ehrmann, Winston. *Premarital Dating Behavior.* New York: Bantam Books, 1960; first published 1959.

Eisenstadt, S. N. *From Generation to Generation.* New York: Free Press, 1956.

Eliot, William G. *Lectures to Young Women.* Bostom: Crosby, Nichols, 1854.

Elkins, Stanley M. *Slavery.* Chicago: University of Chicago Press, 1959.

Engerman, Stanley. "The Study of the European Fertility Decline." *Journal of Family History,* vol. 1 (Winter 1976), pp. 245–251.

Erikson, Kai T. *Wayward Puritans.* New York: John Wiley, 1966.

———. "Sociology and the Historical Perspective." *American Sociologist,* vol. 5 (November 1970), pp. 331–338.

Estellachild, Vivian. "Hippie Communes." *Women: A Journal of Liberation,* vol. 2 (Winter 1971), pp. 40–43.

Eversley, D. E. C. "Exploitation of Anglican Parish Registers by Aggregate Analysis." In *An Introduction to English Historical Demography,* edited by E. A. Wrigley. London: Weidenfeld and Nicolson, 1966.

Fairfield, Richard. *Communes U.S.A.: A Personal Tour.* Baltimore: Penguin, 1972.

Farber, Bernard. *Kinship and Class.* New York: Basic Books, 1971.

———. *Guardians of Virtue.* New York: Basic Books, 1972.

Farkas, George. "Education, Wage Rates, and the Division of Labor Between Husband and Wife." *Journal of Marriage and the Family,* vol. 38 (August 1976), pp. 473–483.

Feder, Sara. "Aging in the Kibbutz in Israel." In *Aging and Modernization,* edited by Donald O. Cowgill and Lowell D. Holmes, pp. 211–226. New York: Appleton-Century, 1972.

Filene, Peter G. *Him, Her, Self: Sex Roles in Modern America.* New York: Mentor, 1976; first published 1974.

Finegan, T. Aldrich. "Participation of Married Women in the Labor Force." In *Sex, Discrimination, and the Division of Labor,* edited by Cynthia B. Lloyd, pp. 27–60. New York: Columbia University Press, 1975.

Firth, Raymond, et al. *Families and Their Relatives.* London: Routledge and Kegan Paul, 1969.

Flacks, Richard. "The Liberated Generation: An Exploration of the Roots of Student Protest." *Journal of Social Issues,* vol. 23 (July 1967), pp. 52–75.

———. "Social and Cultural Meanings of Student Revolt." *Social Problems,* vol. 17 (Winter 1970), pp. 340–357.

———. *Youth and Social Change.* Chicago: Markham, 1971.

Flaherty, David H. *Privacy in Colonial New England.* Charlottesville: University Press of Virginia, 1972.

Fleming, Sanford. *Children and Puritanism.* New Haven: Yale University Press, 1933.

Fogarty, Michael, et al. *Career, Sex and Family.* London: Allen and Unwin, 1971.

Fogel, Robert W., and Engerman, Stanley L. *Time on the Cross.* Boston: Little, Brown, 1974.

Fox, Robin. *Kinship and Marriage.* Baltimore, Penguin, 1967.

Francoeur, Robert T. *Utopian Motherhood.* New York: Doubleday, 1970.

Frazier, E. Franklin. *The Negro Family in the United States.* Chicago: University of Chicago Press, 1966; first published 1939.

Freeman, Jesse D. "On the Concept of Kindred." *Journal of the Royal Anthropological Society,* vol. 91 (March 1961), pp. 192–220.

Friedlander, Dov. "Demographic Response and Population Change." *Demography,* vol. 6 (November 1969), pp. 359–381.

Fryer, Peter. *The Birth Controllers.* London: Secker and Warburg, 1965.

Furstenberg, Frank F., Jr. "Industrialization and the American Family: A Look Backward." *American Sociological Review,* vol. 31 (June 1966), pp. 326–337.

______, Hershberg, Theodore, and Modell, John. "The Origins of the Female-Headed Black Family: The Impact of the Urban Experience." *Journal of Interdisciplinary History,* vol. 6 (Autumn 1975), pp. 211–233.

Gendell, Murray. *Swedish Working Wives.* Totowa, N.J.: Bedminster Press, 1963.

Genovese, Eugene V. *Roll, Jordan, Roll.* New York: Pantheon, 1974.

Gianopoulos, Artie, and Mitchell, Howard E. "Marital Disagreement in Working Wife Marriages as a Function of Husband's Attitude Toward Wife's Employment." *Marriage and Family Living,* vol. 19 (November 1957), pp. 373–378.

Gibson, Campbell. "The U.S. Fertility Decline, 1961–1975: The Contribution of Changes in Marital Status and Marital Fertility." *Family Planning Perspectives,* vol. 8 (September/October 1976), pp. 249–252.

Gillis, John R. *Youth and History.* New York: Academic Press, 1974.

Glasco, Laurence A. "Life Cycles and Household Structure of American Ethnic Groups: Irish, Germans and Native-born Whites in Buffalo, New York, 1855." *Journal of Urban History,* vol. 1 (May 1975), pp. 339–364.

Glazer, Nathan, and Moynihan, Daniel P. *Beyond the Melting Pot.* Cambridge: M.I.T. Press, 1963.

Glick, Paul C. "The Changing American Family Structure." Statement before the U.S. House of Representatives, Subcommittee on Census and Population, November 12, 1975.

______, and Norton, Arthur J. "Frequency, Duration and Probability of Divorce." *Journal of Marriage and the Family,* vol. 33 (May 1971), pp. 307–317.

Goldschneider, Calvin. *Population, Modernization, and Social Structure.* Boston: Little, Brown, 1971.

Goode, William J. *After Divorce.* New York: Free Press, 1956.

______. *World Revolution and Family Patterns.* New York: Free Press, 1963.

______, et al. *Social System and Family Patterns.* Indianapolis, Ind.: Bobbs-Merrill, 1971.

Gordon, Michael. "Infant Care Revisited." *Journal of Marriage and the Family,* vol. 30 (November 1968), pp. 578–583.

______. "From an Unfortunate Necessity to a Cult of Mutual Orgasm: Sex in American Marital Education Literature, 1830–1940." In *Studies in the Sociology of Sex,* edited by

James Henslin, pp. 53–80. New York: Appleton-Century-Crofts, 1971.

———. "Primary Group Differentiation in Urban Ireland." *Social Forces,* vol. 55 (March 1977a), pp. 743–752.

———. "Kinship Boundaries and Kinship Knowledge in Urban Ireland." *International Journal of Sociology of the Family,* vol. 7 (Spring 1977b).

———, ed. *The Nuclear Family in Crisis: The Search for an Alternative.* New York: Harper and Row, 1972; first published 1969.

———, ed. *The American Family in Social-Historical Perspective.* New York: St. Martin's Press, 1973.

———, and Bernstein, Charles. "Mate Choice and Domestic Life in the Nineteenth-Century Marriage Manual." *Journal of Marriage and the Family,* vol. 32 (November 1970), pp. 665–674.

———, and Noll, C. Edward. "Social Class and Interaction with Kin and Friends." *Journal of Comparative Family Studies,* vol. 6 (Autumn 1975), pp. 239–248.

Gough, Kathleen. "Is the Family Universal?" In *A Modern Introduction to the Family,* edited by Norman W. Bell and Ezra F. Vogel, rev. ed., pp. 80–96. New York: Free Press, 1968; first published 1960.

Gouldner, Alvin W. *The Coming Crisis of Western Sociology.* New York: Basic Books, 1970.

Grabill, Wilson H., et al. *The Fertility of American Women.* New York: John Wiley, 1958.

Grasmick, Harold G. "Social Change and Modernization in the American South." *American Behavioral Scientist,* vol. 16 (July/August 1973), pp. 913–931.

Grebler, L., et al. *The Mexican American People.* New York: Free Press, 1970.

Greeley, Andrew. *Catholic Schools in a Declining Church.* Kansas City, Kans.: Sheed and Ward, 1976.

Greven, Philip J., Jr. *Four Generations.* Ithaca, N.Y.: Cornell University Press, 1970.

Griffiths, Martha. "Women and Legislation." In *Voices of the New Feminism,* edited by Mary Lou Thompson, pp. 103–114. Boston: Beacon Press, 1970.

Groat, H. Theodore, et al. "Labor Force Participation and Family Formation: A Study of Working Mothers." *Demography,* vol. 13 (February 1976), pp. 115–123.

Guernsey, Henry. *Plain Talks on Avoided Subjects.* Philadelphia: F. A. Davis, 1882.

Gustavus, Susan O., and Henley, James R., Jr. "Correlates of Voluntary Childlessness in a Select Population." In *Pronatalism,* edited by Ellen Peck and Judith Senderowitz, pp. 284–294. New York: Thomas Y. Crowell, 1974.

Gutman, Herbert G. "Persistent Myths About the Afro-American Family." *Journal of Interdisciplinary History,* vol. 6 (Autumn 1975a), pp. 181–210.

———. *Slavery and the Numbers Game.* Urbana: University of Illinois Press, 1975b.

———. *The Black Family in Slavery and Freedom.* New York: Pantheon, 1976.

Hall, Peter D. "Marital Selection and Business in Massachusetts Merchant Families, 1700–1900." In *The Family,* edited by Rose L. Coser, 2nd ed., pp. 226–240. New York: St. Martin's Press, 1974.

Haller, John S., and Haller, Robin M. *The Physician and Sexuality in Victorian America.* Urbana: University of Illinois Press, 1974.

Hammel, E. A., and Yarbrough, Charles. "Social Mobility and Durability of Family Ties." *Journal of Anthropological Research,* vol. 29 (Autumn 1973), pp. 145–163.

Hastings, Donald W., and Robinson, J. Gregory. "Incidence of Childlessness for United States Women Cohorts Born 1891–1945." *Social Biology,* vol. 21 (Summer 1974), pp. 178–184.

Havighurst, Robert J., and Davis, Allison. "A Comparison of the Chicago and Harvard Studies of Social Class Differences in Child Rearing." *American Sociological Review,* vol. 20 (August 1955), pp. 438–442.

Hayes, Albert H. *Physiology of Woman.* Boston: Peabody Medical Institute, 1869.

Hedgepeth, William. *The Alternative: Communal Life in New America.* New York: Macmillan, 1970.

Hedges, Janice N., and Barnett, Jeanne K. "Working Women and the Division of Household Tasks." *Monthly Labor Review,* vol. 53 (April 1972), pp. 9–14.

Heer, David. "Dominance and the Working Wife." *Social Forces,* vol. 36 (May 1958), pp. 341–347.

Heinlein, Robert A. *Strangers in a Strange Land.* New York: Putnam, 1961.

Heiss, Jerold. "On the Transmission of Marital Instability in Black Families." *American Sociological Review,* vol. 37 (February 1972), pp. 82–92.

———. *The Case of the Black Family.* New York: Columbia University Press, 1975.

Hendrix, Lewellyn. "Nuclear Family Universals." *Journal of Comparative Family Studies,* vol. 6 (Autumn 1975), pp. 125–138.

Henshel, Anne-Marie. "Swinging: A Study in Decision Making in Marriage." *American Journal of Sociology,* vol. 78 (January 1973), pp. 885–891.

Hershberg, Theodore. "Free Blacks in Ante-Bellum Philadelphia." *Journal of Social History,* vol. 5 (Winter 1971–1972), pp. 183–209.

Herzog, Elizabeth. "Is there a 'Breakdown' in the Negro Family?" *Social Work,* vol. 11 (January 1966), pp. 3–10.

Himes, Norman. *Medical History of Contraception.* New York: Gamut Press, 1963; first published 1936.

Hiner, N. Ray. "Adolescence in Eighteenth Century America." *History of Childhood Quarterly,* vol. 3 (Fall 1975), pp. 253–280.

Hite, Shere. *The Hite Report.* New York: Macmillan, 1976.

Hobsbawm, E. J. *The Age of Revolution, 1749–1848.* London: Weidenfeld and Nicolson, 1962.

Hochschild, Arlie R. *The Unexpected Community.* Englewood Cliffs, N.J.: Prentice-Hall, 1973.

Hoffman, Lois W. "Parental Power Relations and the Division of Household Tasks." In *The Employed Mother in America,* edited by F. Ivan Nye and Lois W. Hoffman, pp. 215–230. Chicago: Rand McNally, 1963.

———, and Nye, F. Ivan. *Working Mothers.* San Francisco: Jossey-Bass, 1975.

Hollingshead, August B. *Elmtown's Youth and Elmtown Revisited.* New York: John Wiley, 1975; first published 1949.

Hollingsworth, T. H. *Historical Demography.* London: Hodder and Stoughton, 1969.

Holloway, Mark. *Heavens on Earth.* New York: Dover, 1966; first published 1951.

Holmstrom, Lynda L. "Career Patterns of Married Couples." In *The Professional Woman,* edited by Athena Theodore, pp. 516–524.

Cambridge, Mass.: Schenkman, 1971.

———. *The Two-Career Family.* Cambridge, Mass.: Schenkman, 1972.

Hooks, Janet M. *Women's Occupations Through Seven Decades.* Washington, D.C.: Women's Bureau Bulletin no. 218, 1947.

Houriet, Robert. *Getting Back Together.* New York: Coward, McCann and Geoghegan, 1971.

Howard, George E. *A History of Matrimonial Institutions.* 3 vols. Chicago: University of Chicago Press, 1904.

Hunt, Janet G., and Hunt, Larry L. "Dilemmas and Contradictions of Status: The Case of the Dual-Career Family." *Social Problems,* vol. 24 (April 1977), pp. 407–416.

Hunt, Morton M. *The Affair.* New York: World Publishing, 1969.

———. *Sexual Behavior in the 1970s.* Chicago: Playboy Publishing Co., 1974.

Ianni, Francis A. J. *A Family Business.* New York: Russell Sage Foundation, 1972.

Illick, Joseph E. "Childrearing in Seventeenth-Century England and America." In *The History of Childhood,* edited by Lloyd de Mause, pp. 303–350. New York: Harper and Row, 1975; first published 1974.

Inkeles, Alex. "The Modernization of Man." in *Modernization,* edited by Myron Weiner, pp. 138–150. New York: Basic Books, 1966.

Jacobson, Paul H. *American Marriage and Divorce.* New York: Rinehart and Co., 1959.

Jeffrey, Kirk. "The Family as Utopian Retreat from the City." *Soundings,* vol. 55 (1972), pp. 21–41.

Jones, Douglas. "Population Mobility and Persistence in Old and New England Before 1880: An Overview." Unpublished paper, Brandeis University, 1972.

Kandel, Denise B., and Lesser, Gerald S. "Marital Decision-Making in American and Danish Urban Families." *Journal of Marriage and Family Living,* vol. 34 (February 1972), pp. 134–138.

Kanowitz, Leo. *Woman and the Law.* Albuquerque: University of New Mexico Press, 1969.

Kanter, Rosabeth M. *Commitment and Social Organization.* Cambridge: Harvard University Press, 1972.

———. *Work and Family in the United States.* New York: Russell Sage Foundation, 1977.

———, and Halter, Marilyn. "De-Housewifing Women, Domesticating Men: Changing Sex Roles in Urban Communes." In *Family Roles and Interaction,* edited by Jerold Heiss, pp. 197–216. Chicago: Rand McNally, 1976.

———; Jaffe, Dennis; and Weisberg, D. Kelly. "Coupling, Parenting and the Presence of Others: Intimate Relationships in Communal Households." *Family Coordinator,* vol. 24 (October 1975), pp. 433–452.

Kasarda, John D. "Economic Structure and Fertility: A Comparative Analysis." *Demography,* vol. 8 (August 1971), pp. 307–317.

Kassel, Victor. "Polygyny After 60." *Geriatrics,* vol. 21 (April 1966), pp. 214–218.

Katz, Michael. *The People of Hamilton, Canada West.* Cambridge: Harvard University Press, 1975.

Kellogg, Paul V., ed. *The Pittsburgh Frontage.* New York: Survey Associates, 1914.

Keniston, Kenneth. *Young Radicals.* New York: Harcourt, Brace and World, 1968.

______. "Youth as a Stage of Life." *The American Scholar,* vol. 39 (Autumn 1970), pp. 631–654.

Kephart, William M. "Experimental Family Organization: An Historico-Cultural Report on Oneida." *Journal of Marriage and the Family,* vol. 25 (August 1963), pp. 261–271.

Kerckhoff, Alan C. "Husband-Wife Expectations and Reactions to Retirement." *Journal of Gerontology,* vol. 19 (January 1964), pp. 510–516.

Kett, Joseph F. "Adolescence and Youth in Nineteenth-Century America." *Journal of Interdisciplinary History,* vol. 2 (Autumn 1971), pp. 283–298.

Kinkade, Kathleen. *A Walden Two Experiment.* New York: William Morrow, 1973.

Kinsey, Alfred C., et al. *Sexual Behavior in the Human Male.* Philadelphia: Saunders, 1948.

______. *Sexual Behavior in the Human Female.* Philadelphia: Saunders, 1953.

Kirkpatrick Clifford. *The Family.* New York: Ronald Press, 1955.

Klatzky, Sheila R. *Patterns of Contact with Relatives.* Washington, D.C.: American Sociological Association, n.d.

Kleinberg, Susan J. "Technology and Women's Work: The Lives of Working Class Women in Pittsburgh, 1870–1900." *Labor History,* vol. 17 (Winter 1976), pp. 58–72.

Kligler, Deborah H. "The Effect of the Employment of Married Women on Husband-Wife Roles." Unpublished Ph.D. dissertation, Yale University, 1954.

Kluckhohn, Clyde, and Murray, Henry A., eds. *Personality in Nature, Society and Culture.* New York: Alfred A. Knopf, 1962.

Knapp, Jacquelyn J. "Co-Marital Sex and Marriage Counseling." Unpublished Ph.D. dissertation, University of Florida, Gainesville, 1974.

Knights, Peter R. "Population Turnover, Persistence, and Residential Mobility in Boston, 1830–1860." In *Nineteenth-Century Cities,* edited by Stephen Thernstrom and Richard Sennett, pp. 258–274. New Haven: Yale University Press, 1969.

Kobrin, Frances E. "The Fall in Household Size and the Rise of the Primary Individual in the United States." *Demography,* vol. 13 (February 1976a), pp. 127–138.

______. "The Primary Individual and the Family: Changes in Living Arrangements in the United States Since 1940." *Journal of Marriage and the Family,* vol. 38 (May 1976b), pp. 233–240.

Kohn, Melvin L. "Social Class and Parental Values." *American Journal of Sociology,* vol. 64 (January 1959), pp. 337–351.

______. *Class and Conformity.* Homewood, Ill.: Dorsey Press, 1969.

______. "Bureaucratic Man: A Portrait and an Interpretation." *American Sociological Review,* vol. 36 (June 1971), pp. 461–474.

______. "Social Class and Parental Values: Another Confirmation of the Relationship." *American Sociological Review,* vol. 41 (June 1976), pp. 538–544.

______, and Schooler, Carmi. "Occupational Experience and Psychological Functioning: An Assessment of Reciprocal Effects." *American Sociological Review,* vol. 38 (February 1973), pp. 97–118.

Komarovsky, Mirra. *Blue Collar Marriage.* New York: Random House, 1962.

Kramer, Judith R., and Leventman, Seymour. *Children of the Gilded Ghetto.* New Haven: Yale University Press, 1961.

Kreps, Juanita M. *Lifetime Allocation of Work and Income.* Durham, N.C.: Duke University Press, 1971.

Krishnan, P. "Divorce Tables for Females in the United States, 1960." *Journal of Marriage and the Family,* vol. 33 (May 1971), pp. 318–320.

Ladner, Joyce A. *Tomorrow's Tomorrow.* New York: Anchor Books, 1972.

Lammermeier, Paul J. "The Urban Black Family of the Nineteenth Century: A Study of Black Family Structure in the Ohio Valley, 1850–1880." *Journal of Marriage and the Family,* vol. 35 (August 1973), pp. 440–456.

Lamouse, Annette. "Family Roles of Women: A German Example." *Journal of Marriage and the Family,* vol. 31 (February 1969), pp. 145–152.

Lantz, Herman, et al. "Pre-Industrial Patterns in the Colonial Family in America: A Content Analysis of Colonial Magazines." *American Sociological Review,* vol. 33 (June 1968), pp. 413–426.

Larkin, Philip. "Annus Mirabilis." From his collection *High Windows.* New York: Farrar, Straus and Giroux, 1974, p. 34.

Lasch, Christopher. "The Family and History." *New York Review of Books,* vol. 22 (November 13, 1975), pp. 33–38.

Laslett, Barbara. "The Family as a Public and Private Institution: An Historical Perspective." *Journal of Marriage and the Family,* vol. 35 (August 1973), pp. 480–494.

Laslett, Peter. *The World We Have Lost.* 2nd ed. New York: Scribner's, 1971; first published 1965.

———, ed. *Household and Family in Past Time.* Cambridge: Cambridge University Press, 1972.

———, and Harrison, John. "Clayworth and Cogenhoe." In *Historical Essays 1600–1750 Presented to David Ogg,* edited by H. E. Bell and R. L. Ollard, pp. 157–184. New York: Barnes and Noble, 1963.

La Sorte, Michael A. "Nineteenth Century Family Planning Practices." *Journal of Psychohistory,* vol. 4 (Fall 1976), pp. 163–183.

Leach, Edmund. "Review of Murdock's *Social Structure.*" *Man,* vol. 50 (August 1950), pp. 107–108.

Lerner, Gerda. "The Lady and the Mill Girl: Changes in the Status of Women in the Age of Jackson." *Midcontinent American Studies,* vol. 10 (Spring 1969), pp. 5–14.

Levine, Richard M. "Who Is Hare Krishna and Why Are They Doing All Those Strange Things on Fifth Avenue?" *New York,* vol. 5 (September 6, 1971), pp. 28–34.

Lévi-Strauss, Claude. *The Elementary Structures of Kinship.* Boston: Beacon Press, 1969.

Levy, Marion J., Jr. "Aspects of the Analysis of Family Structure." In *Aspects of the Analysis of Family Structure,* edited by Ansley J. Coale et al., pp. 40–63. Princeton, N.J.: Princeton University Press, 1965.

———, and Fallers, Lloyd A. "The Family: Some Comparative Considerations." *American Anthropologist,* vol. 61 (August 1959), pp. 647–651.

Lewis, Robert A., et al. "Commitment in Married and Unmarried Cohabitation." Paper presented at the American Sociological Association Meetings, San Francisco, 1975.

Lindsey, Ben B., and Evans, Wainwright. *The Companionate Marriage.* New York: Boni and Liveright, 1927.

Lipman, Aaron. "Role Conceptions of Couples in Retirement." In *Social and Psychological Aspects of Aging,* edited by Clark Tibbitts and Wilma Donahue, pp. 475–485. New

York: Columbia University Press, 1962.

Litwak, Eugene. "Occupational Mobility and Extended Family Cohesion." *American Sociological Review,* vol. 25 (February 1960), pp. 9–21.

Lobel, John, and Lobel, Mimi. *John and Mimi: A Free Marriage.* New York: St. Martin's Press, 1972.

Lockridge, Kenneth A. *A New England Town: The First Hundred Years.* New York: Norton, 1970.

Loether, Herman J. *Problems of the Aging.* Belmont, Calif.: Dickenson Publishing Co., 1967.

Lopata, Helen Z. "The Social Involvement of American Widows." *American Behavioral Scientist,* vol. 14 (September/October 1970), pp. 41–58.

______. "Social Relations of Widows in Urbanizing Societies." *Sociological Quarterly,* vol. 13 (Spring 1972), pp. 259–271.

______. *Widowhood in an American City.* Cambridge, Mass.: Schenkman, 1973.

Lorber, Judith. "Beyond Equality of the Sexes: The Question of the Children." *Family Coordinator,* vol. 24 (October 1975), pp. 465–472.

Lynd, Robert S., and Lynd, Helen M. *Middletown.* New York: Harcourt Brace, 1929.

Lyness, Judith L., et al. "Living Together: An Alternative to Marriage." *Journal of Marriage and the Family,* vol. 34 (May 1972), pp. 305–311.

MacFarlane, Alan. *The Family Life of Ralph Josselin.* Cambridge: Cambridge University Press, 1970.

McGovern, James R. "The American Woman's Pre–World War I Freedom in Manners and Morals." *Journal of American History,* vol. 55 (September 1968), pp. 315–333.

McKain, Walter C. *Retirement Marriage.* Storrs, Conn.: Agricultural Experiment Station, 1969.

______. "A New Look at Older Marriages." *Family Coordinator,* vol. 21 (January 1972,) pp. 61–79.

McKinley, D. G. *Social Class and Family Life.* New York: Free Press, 1964.

Macklin, Eleanor. "Heterosexual Cohabitation Among Unmarried College Students." *Family Coordinator,* vol. 21 (October 1972,) pp. 463–472.

McLaughlin, Virginia Yans. "Patterns of Work and Family Organization: Buffalo's Italians." *Journal of Interdisciplinary History,* vol. 2 (Autumn 1971), pp. 299–314.

Malcolmson, Robert W. *Popular Recreations in English Society 1750–1850.* Cambridge: Cambridge University Press, 1973.

Maslow, Abraham H. *Toward a Psychology of Being.* Princeton, N.J.: Van Nostrand, 1962.

Mason, Karen O., and Bumpass, Larry L. "U.S. Women's Sex-Role Ideology, 1970." *American Journal of Sociology,* vol. 80 (March 1975), pp. 1212–1219.

Masters, William H., and Johnson, Virginia E. *Human Sexual Response.* Boston: Little, Brown, 1966.

May, Elaine T. "The Pursuit of Domestic Perfection: Marriage and Divorce in Los Angeles, 1890–1920." Unpublished Ph.D. dissertation, University of California, Los Angeles, 1975.

Maykovich, Minako K. "Attitudes Versus Behavior in Extramarital Sexual Relations." *Journal of Marriage and the Family,* vol. 38 (November 1976), pp. 693–699.

Mazur, Ronald. *The New Intimacy.* Boston: Beacon Press, 1973.

Mead, Margaret. *Male and Female.* New York: William Morrow, 1949.

______. "Marriage in Two Steps." In *The Family in Search of a Future,* edited by Herbert A. Otto, pp. 75–84. New York: Appleton-Century-Crofts, 1970; first published in *Redbook Magazine,* July 1966.

Mechling, Jay. "Advice to Historians on Advice to Mothers." *Journal of Social History,* vol. 9 (Fall 1975), pp. 45–63.

Melcher, Marguerite F. *The Shaker Adventure.* Princeton, N.J.: Princeton University Press, 1941.

Melville, Keith. *Communes in the Counter Culture.* New York: William Morrow, 1972.

Michel, Andree. "Comparative Data Concerning the Interaction in French and American Families." *Journal of Marriage and the Family,* vol. 29 (May 1967), pp. 337–344.

Miller, Daniel R., and Swanson, Guy E. *The Changing American Parent.* New York: John Wiley, 1958.

Millis, Harry A., and Montgomery, Royal E. *Labor's Risks and Social Insurance.* New York: McGraw-Hill, 1938.

Mindel, Charles H. "Kinship, Reference Group and the Symbolic Family Estate." *International Journal of Sociology of the Family,* forthcoming.

———, and Habenstein, Robert W., eds. *Ethnic Families in America.* New York: Elsevier, 1976.

Modell, John, and Hareven, Tamara K. "Urbanization and the Malleable Household: An Examination of Boarding and Lodging in American Families." *Journal of Marriage and the Family,* vol. 35 (August 1973), pp. 467–479.

Morgan, Edmund S. "The Puritans and Sex." *New England Quarterly,* vol. 15 (December 1942), pp. 591–607.

———. *The Puritan Family.* New York: Harper and Row, 1966; first published 1944.

Moss, Zoe. "It Hurts to Be Alive and Obsolete." In *Sisterhood Is Powerful,* edited by Robin Morgan, pp. 170–175. New York: Vintage Books, 1970.

Moynihan, Daniel P. *The Negro Family: The Case for National Action.* Washington, D.C.: Government Printing Office, 1965.

Muncy, Raymond L. *Sex and Marriage in Utopian Communities.* Bloomington: Indiana University Press, 1973.

Murdock, George P. *Social Structure.* New York: Free Press, 1965; first published 1949.

Neff, Wanda F. *Victorian Working Women.* New York: Columbia University Press, 1929.

Neubeck, Gerhard, ed. *Extra-Marital Relations.* Englewood Cliffs, N.J.: Prentice-Hall, 1969.

Neugarten, Bernice L., ed. *Middle Age and Aging.* Chicago: University of Chicago Press, 1968.

Nimkoff, Meyer F., and Middleton, Russell. "Types of Family and Types of Economy." *American Journal of Sociology,* vol. 66 (November 1960), pp. 215–225.

Nisbet, Robert A. *The Sociological Tradition.* New York: Basic Books, 1966.

Nolan, Francena L. "Effects on Rural Children." In *The Employed Mother in America,* edited by F. Ivan Nye and Lois W. Hoffman, pp. 282–305. Chicago: Rand McNally, 1963.

Nordhoff, Charles. *The Communistic Societies of the United States.* New York: Schocken Books, 1965; first published 1875.

Norton, Arthur J., and Glick, Paul C. "Marital Instability: Past, Present, and Future." *Journal of Social Issues,* vol. 32 (Winter 1976), pp. 5–20.

Norton, Susan. "Population Growth in Colonial America: A Study of Ipswich, Massachusetts." *Population*

Studies, vol. 25 (November 1971), pp. 433–452.

———. "Marital Migration in Essex County, Massachusetts, in the Colonial and Early Federal Periods." *Journal of Marriage and the Family,* vol. 35 (August 1973), pp. 406–418.

Notestein, Frank W. "Population: The Long View." In *Food for the World,* edited by T. W. Schultz, pp. 36–57. Chicago: University of Chicago Press, 1945.

Novak, Michael. "The Family out of Favor." *Harper's,* vol. 252 (April 1976), pp. 37–46.

Noyes, John Humphrey. *History of American Socialisms.* New York: Dover, 1966; first published 1870.

Nye, F. Ivan. "Employment Status of Mother and Marital Conflict, Permanence and Happiness." *Social Problems,* vol. 6 (Winter 1958–1959), pp. 260–267.

———, and Berardo, Felix M. *Emerging Conceptual Frameworks in Family Analysis.* New York: Macmillan, 1966.

——— and ———. *The Family.* New York: Macmillan, 1973.

Oakley, Ann. *Woman's Work.* New York: Pantheon, 1974.

Ollman, Bertell. *Alienation.* Cambridge: Cambridge University Press, 1971.

O'Neill, Nena, and O'Neill, George. *Open Marriage.* New York: Avon Books, 1973; first published 1972.

O'Neill, William L. *Divorce in the Progressive Era.* New Haven: Yale University Press, 1969.

Oppenheimer, Valerie K. "Rising Educational Attainment, Declining Fertility and the Inadequacies of the Labor Market." In United States Commission on Population Growth and the American Future, *Demographic and Social Aspects of Population Growth,* vol. 1, pp. 305–330. Washington, D.C.: Government Printing Office, 1972.

———. "Demographic Influence on Female Employment and the Status of Women." *American Journal of Sociology,* vol. 78 (January 1973), pp. 946–961.

———. "The Easterlin Hypothesis: Another Aspect of the Echo to Consider." *Population and Development Review,* vol. 2 (September/December 1976), pp. 433–458.

Oppler, Morris E. "Review of Murdock's *Social Structure.*" *American Anthropologist,* vol. 52 (January 1950), pp. 77–80.

Orden, Susan R., and Bradburn, Norman. "Dimensions of Marriage Happiness." *American Journal of Sociology,* vol. 73 (May 1968), pp. 715–731.

Osofsky, Joy D., and Osofsky, Howard J. "Androgyny as a Life Style." *Family Coordinator,* vol. 21 (October 1972), pp. 411–418.

Packard, Vance O. *The Status Seekers.* New York: David McKay, 1959.

———. *The Sexual Wilderness.* New York: David McKay, 1968.

Padilla, Elena. *Up from Puerto Rico.* New York: Columbia University Press, 1958.

Palmore, Erdman. "Sociological Aspects of Aging." In *Behavior and Adaptation in Later Life,* edited by Ewald W. Busse and Eric Pfeiffer, pp. 33–70. Boston: Little, Brown, 1969.

Palson, Charles, and Palson, Rebecca. "Swinging in Wedlock." *Society.* vol. 9 (February 1972), pp. 28–37.

Papanek, Hanna. "Men, Women, and Work: Reflections on the Two-Person Career." *American Journal of Sociology,* vol. 78 (January 1973), pp. 852–871.

Parish, William L., Jr., and Schwartz, Moshe. "Household Complexity in

Nineteenth Century France." *American Sociological Review,* vol. 37 (April 1972), pp. 154–172.

Parsons, Talcott. "The Kinship System of the Contemporary United States." *American Anthropologist,* vol. 45 (January–March 1943), pp. 22–38.

———, and Bales, Robert F. *Family, Socialization and Interaction Process.* Glencoe, Ill.: Free Press, 1955.

Pearlin, Leonard I., and Kohn, Melvin L. "Social Class, Occupation, and Parental Values: A Cross-National Study." *American Sociological Review,* vol. 36 (June 1971), pp. 466–479.

Peck, Ellen, and Senderowitz, Judith, eds. *Pronatalism.* New York: Thomas Y. Crowell, 1974.

Pettigrew, Thomas F. *A Profile of the Negro American.* New York: Van Nostrand, 1964.

Pfeiffer, Eric. "Sexual Behavior in Old Age." In *Behavior and Adaptation in Later Life,* edited by Ewald W. Busse and Eric Pfeiffer, pp. 151–162. Boston: Little, Brown, 1969.

Pihlblad, C. T., et al. "Socio-Economic Adjustment of Widowhood." *Omega,* vol. 3 (November 1972), pp. 295–305.

Pivar, David. *Purity Crusade.* Westport, Conn.: Greenwood Press, 1973.

Plakans, Andrejs. "Seigneurial Authority and Peasant Family Life: The Baltic Area in the Eighteenth Century." *Journal of Interdisciplinary History,* vol. 4 (Spring 1975), pp. 629–654.

Pleck, Elizabeth H. "The Two-Parent Household: Black Family Structure in Late Nineteenth Century Boston." *Journal of Social History,* vol. 6 (Fall 1972), pp. 1–31.

———. Two Worlds in One: Work and Family." *Journal of Social History,* vol. 10 (Winter 1976), pp. 178–195.

———. "A Mother's Wages: A Comparison of Income-Earning Among Urban Black and Italian Married Women, 1896–1911." In *The American Family in Social-Historical Perspective,* edited by Michael Gordon. 2nd ed. New York: St. Martin's Press, forthcoming.

Pleck, Joseph H. "Work and Family Roles: From Sex-Patterned Segregation to Integration." Paper presented at the American Sociological Association Meetings, San Francisco, 1975.

Pohlman, Edward. "Burgess and Cottrell Data on 'Desire for Children.' " In *Pronatalism,* edited by Ellen Peck and Judith Senderowitz, pp. 127–131. New York: Thomas Y. Crowell, 1974.

Poloma, Margaret M. "Role Conflict and the Married Professional Woman." In *Toward a Sociology of Women,* edited by Constantina Safilios-Rothschild, pp. 187–198. Lexington, Mass.: Xerox, 1972.

———, and Garland, T. Neal. "The Married Professional Woman: A Study in the Tolerance of Domestication." *Journal of Marriage and the Family,* vol. 33 (August 1971), pp. 531–540.

Pope, Hallowell, and Mueller, Charles W. "The Intergenerational Transmission of Marital Instability: Comparisons by Race and Sex." *Journal of Social Issues,* vol. 32 (1976), pp. 49–66.

Powell, Kathryn S. "Maternal Employment in Relation to Family Life." *Marriage and Family Living,* vol. 23 (November 1961), pp. 350–355.

Presser, Harriet B., and Bumpass, Larry L. "The Acceptability of Contraceptive Sterilization Among U.S. Couples." *Family Planning Perspectives,* vol. 4 (October 1972), pp. 18–26.

Prest, W. R. "Stability and Change in Old and New England: Clayworth and Dedham." *Journal of Interdisci-*

plinary History, vol. 6 (Winter 1976), pp. 359–374.

Presthus, Robert. *The Organizational Society.* New York: Alfred A. Knopf, 1962.

Proulx, Cynthia. "Sex as Athletics in the Singles Complex." *Saturday Review* (April 21, 1973), pp. 61–66.

Rainwater, Lee. *Behind Ghetto Walls.* Harmondsworth, Middlesex, Eng.: Penguin, 1973; first published 1970.

Ramey, James W. "Emerging Patterns of Behavior in Marriage." *Journal of Sex Research,* vol. 8 (February 1972), pp. 6–30.

______. "Intimate Groups and Networks: Frequent Consequences of Sexually Open Marriages." *Family Coordinator,* vol. 24 (October 1975), pp. 515–530.

______. *Intimate Friendships.* Englewood Cliffs, N.J.: Prentice-Hall, 1976.

Rapoport, Rhona, and Rapoport, Robert. *Dual-Career Families.* Baltimore: Penguin, 1971.

______ and ______. "Men, Women and Equity." *Family Coordinator,* vol. 24 (October 1975), pp. 421–432.

Rapson, Richard L. "The American Child as Seen by British Travelers, 1845–1935." *American Quarterly,* vol. 17 (Fall 1965), pp. 520–534.

Rawick, George P. *From Sundown to Sunup.* Westport, Conn.: Greenwood Press, 1972.

Reich, Charles A. *The Greening of America.* New York: Random House, 1970.

Reiss, Ira L. "Social Class and Campus Dating." *Social Problems,* vol. 13 (Fall 1965a), pp. 193–205.

______. "The Universality of the Family: A Conceptual Analysis." *Journal of Marriage and the Family,* vol. 27 (November 1965b), pp. 443–453.

______. *The Social Context of Premarital Sexual Permissiveness.* New York: Holt, Rinehart and Winston, 1967.

______. *Family Systems in America.* New York: Holt, Rinehart and Winston, 1971.

Rheinstein, Max. *Marriage Stability, Divorce and the Law.* Chicago: University of Chicago Press, 1972.

Riesman, David. "Permissiveness and Sex Roles." *Marriage and Family Living,* vol. 21 (August 1959), pp. 211–217.

______ et al. *The Lonely Crowd.* New York: Anchor-Doubleday, 1954; first published 1950.

Rimmer, Robert H. *The Rebellion of Yale Marratt.* Boston: Challenge Press, 1964.

______. *The Harrad Experiment.* Los Angeles: Sherbourne Press, 1966.

______. *Proposition 31.* New York: New American Library, 1968.

______. *Thursday My Love.* New York: New American Library, 1972.

Rindfuss, Ronald R., and Bumpass, Larry L. "How Old Is Too Old? Age and the Sociology of Fertility." *Family Planning Perspectives,* vol. 8 (September/October 1976), pp. 226–230.

Rivers, William H. *Social Organization.* New York: Alfred A. Knopf, 1924.

Robbins, Lillian C. "The Accuracy of Parental Recall of Aspects of Child Development and Child Rearing Practices." *Journal of Abnormal and Social Psychology,* vol. 66 (March 1963), pp. 261–270.

Roberts, Ron E. *The New Communes.* Englewood Cliffs, N.J.: Prentice-Hall, 1971.

Rodman, Hyman. "Illegitimacy in the Caribbean Social Structure: A Reconsideration." *American Sociological Review,* vol. 31 (October 1966), pp. 673–683.

Rogers, Carl R. *Becoming Partners: Marriage and Its Alternatives.* New York: Delacorte Press, 1972.

Rogers, Everett M., and Havens, A. Eugene. "Prestige Rating and Mate Selection on a College Campus." *Marriage and Family Living,* vol. 22 (February 1960), pp. 55–59.

Rollins, Boyd D., and Feldman, Harold. "Marital Satisfaction Over the Family Life Cycle." *Journal of Marriage and the Family,* vol. 32 (February 1970), pp. 20–28.

———, and Cannon, Kenneth L. "Marital Satisfaction Over the Family Life Cycle: A Reevaluation." *Journal of Marriage and the Family,* vol. 36 (May 1974), pp. 271–282.

Rosenberg, Charles. "Sexuality, Class and Role in Nineteenth Century America." *American Quarterly,* vol. 25 (May 1973), pp. 131–153.

Rosenberg, George S. *The Worker Grows Older.* San Francisco: Jossey-Bass, 1970.

———, and Anspach, Donald F. *Working Class Kinship.* Lexington, Mass.: D. C. Heath, 1973.

Rosow, Irving. *Social Integration of the Aged.* New York: Free Press, 1967.

———. "Old People: Their Friends and Neighbors." *American Behavioral Scientist,* vol. 14 (September/October 1970), pp. 59–70.

Ross, Heather L., and Sawhill, Isabel V. *Time of Transition.* Washington, D.C.: The Urban Institute, 1975.

Rossi, Alice. "Barriers to the Career Choice of Engineering, Medicine and Science Among American Women." In *Women and the Scientific Professions,* edited by J. A. Mattfield and C. G. van Aken. Cambridge: M.I.T. Press, 1965.

Roszak, Theodore. *The Making of a Counter Culture.* New York: Doubleday, 1969.

Roy, Rustum, and Roy, Della. *Honest Sex.* New York: New American Library, 1968.

Rubel, Arthur J. *Across the Tracks: Mexican Americans in a Texas City.* Austin: University of Texas Press, 1966.

Rubin, Lillian Breslow. *Worlds of Pain: Life in the Working Class Family.* New York: Basic Books, 1976.

Rutman, Darrett B. "People in Process: New Hampshire Towns of the Eighteenth Century." *Journal of Urban History,* vol. 1 (May 1975), pp. 268–292.

Safilios-Rothschild, Constantina. "Family Sociology or Wives' Sociology? A Cross-Cultural Examination of Decision Making." *Journal of Marriage and the Family,* vol. 31 (May 1969), pp. 290–301.

Sarvis, Betty, and Rodman, Hyman. *The Abortion Controversy.* 2nd ed. New York: Columbia University Press, 1974.

Sauer, R. "Attitudes to Abortion in America, 1800–1973." *Population Studies,* vol. 28 (1974), pp. 53–67.

Scanzoni, John. *Opportunity and the Family.* New York: Free Press, 1970.

———. *Sexual Bargaining.* Englewood Cliffs, N.J.: Prentice-Hall, 1972.

———. *Sex Roles, Life Styles, and Childbearing.* New York: Free Press, 1975.

Schlesinger, Benjamin. *The Jewish Family: A Survey and Annotated Bibliography.* Toronto: University of Toronto Press, 1971.

Schneider, David M. *American Kinship: A Cultural Account.* Englewood Cliffs, N.J.: Prentice-Hall, 1968.

———. "The Distinctive Features of Matrilineal Descent Groups." In

Matrilineal Kinship, edited by David M. Schneider and Kathleen Gough, pp. 1–32. Berkeley: University of California Press, 1971.

———, and Smith, Raymond T. *Class Differences and Sex Roles in American Kinship and Family Structure.* Englewood Cliffs, N.J.: Prentice-Hall, 1973.

Schnucker, Robert V. "Elizabethan Birth Control and Puritan Attitudes." *Journal of Interdisciplinary History,* vol. 4 (Spring 1975), pp. 655–667.

Schofield, Roger. "Age Specific Mobility in an Eighteenth Century Rural English Parish." *Annals de Démographie Historique 1970.* Paris, 1971.

Schooler, Carmi. "Social Antecedents of Adult Psychological Functioning." *American Journal of Sociology,* vol. 78 (September 1972), pp. 299–322.

Schücking, Levin L. *The Puritan Family.* New York: Schocken Books, 1970; first published 1929.

Scott, John F. "The American College Sorority: Its Role in Class and Ethnic Endogamy." *American Sociological Review,* vol. 30 (August 1965), pp. 514–527.

Sears, Robert R., et al. *Patterns of Child Rearing.* Evanston, Ill.: Row, Peterson, 1957.

Selltiz, Claire, et al. *Research Methods in Social Relations.* New York: Holt, Rinehart and Winston, 1962.

Sennett, Richard. "The Brutality of Modern Families." *Trans-action,* vol. 7 (September 1970a), pp. 29–37.

———. *Families Against the City.* Cambridge: Harvard University Press, 1970b.

Sewell, William H. "Social Class and Childhood Personality." *Sociometry,* vol. 24 (December 1961), pp. 340–356.

Shanas, Ethel, et al. *Old People in Three Industrial Societies.* New York: Atherton, 1968.

———. "Living Arrangements and Housing of Old People." In *Behavior and Adaptation in Later Life,* edited by Ewald W. Busse and Eric Pfeiffer, pp. 129–150. Boston: Little, Brown, 1969.

Shifflett, Crandall A. "The Household Composition of Rural Black Families: Lousia County, Virginia, 1880." *Journal of Interdisciplinary History,* vol. 6 (Autumn 1975), pp. 235–260.

Shorter, Edward. "Illegitimacy, Sexual Revolution, and Social Change in Modern Europe." *Journal of Interdisciplinary History,* vol. 2 (Autumn 1971), pp. 237–272.

———. "Female Emancipation, Birth Control, and Fertility in European History." *American Historical Review,* vol. 78 (June 1973), pp. 605–635.

———. *The Making of the Modern Family.* New York: Basic Books, 1975.

Silka, Linda, and Kiesler, Sara. "Couples Who Choose to Remain Childless." *Family Planning Perspectives,* vol. 9 (January/February 1977), pp. 16–24.

Simmons, Leo W. *The Role of the Aged in Primitive Societies.* New Haven: Yale University Press, 1945.

Singh, B. Krishna, Walton, Bonnie L., and Williams, J. Sherwood. "Extramarital Sexual Permissiveness: Conditions and Contingencies." *Journal of Marriage and the Family,* vol. 38 (November 1976), pp. 701–712.

Skinner, B. F. *Walden II.* New York: Macmillan, 1948.

Skolnick, Arlene S., and Skolnick, Jerome H., eds. *Family in Transition.* Boston: Little, Brown, 1971.

Slater, Philip. *The Pursuit of Loneliness.* Boston: Beacon Press, 1970.

Smelser, Neil. *Social Change in the Industrial Revolution.* Chicago: University of Chicago Press, 1959.

Smigel, Erwin O., and Siden, Rita. "The Decline and Fall of the Double Standard." *Annals of the American Academy of Political and Social Science,* vol. 376 (1969), pp. 6–17.

Smith, Daniel Scott. "The Demographic History of Colonial New England." *Journal of Economic Research,* vol. 32 (March 1972a), pp. 165–183.

———. "Child-Naming Patterns and Family Structure Change: Hingham, Massachusetts, 1640–1880." Paper read at Clark University Conference on the Family and Social Structure, 1972b.

———. "Family Limitation, Sexual Control and Domestic Feminism in Victorian America." *Feminist Studies,* vol. 1 (Winter–Spring 1973a), pp. 40–57.

———. "The Dating of the American Sexual Revolution." In *The American Family in Social-Historical Perspective,* edited by Michael Gordon, pp. 321–335. New York: St. Martin's Press, 1973b.

———. "Parental Power and Marriage Patterns." *Journal of Marriage and the Family,* vol. 35 (August 1973c), pp. 419–428.

———, and Hindus, Michael. "Premarital Pregnancy in America, 1640–1971: An Overview and Interpretation." *Journal of Interdisciplinary History,* vol. 4 (Spring 1975), pp. 537–570.

Smith, David E., and Sternfield, James L. "Natural Childbirth and Cooperative Child Rearing Practices in Communes." In *The Nuclear Family in Crisis: The Search for an Alternative,* edited by Michael Gordon, pp. 196–203. New York: Harper and Row, 1972; first published 1969.

Smith, Page. *Daughters of the Promised Land.* Boston: Little, Brown, 1970.

Smith, William M., Jr. "Rating and Dating: A Restudy." *Marriage and Family Living,* vol. 14 (November 1952), pp. 312–316.

Smith-Rosenberg, Caroll, and Rosenberg, Charles E. "The Female Animal: Medical and Biological View of Woman's Role in Nineteenth Century America." *Journal of American History,* vol. 60 (September 1973), pp. 332–356.

Smuts, Robert W. *Women and Work in America.* New York: Schocken Books, 1971; first published 1959.

Sorensen, Robert C. *Adolescent Sexuality in Contemporary America.* New York: World Publishing, 1973.

Spiro, Melford E. "Is the Family Universal?" *American Anthropologist,* vol. 56 (October 1954), pp. 839–846.

———. "Addendum, 1958." In *A Modern Introduction to the Family,* edited by Norman W. Bell and Ezra F. Vogel, rev. ed., pp. 76–79. New York: Free Press, 1968; first published 1960.

———. *Kibbutz.* Augmented ed. New York: Schocken Books, 1970.

Spruill, Julia Cherry. *Women's Life and Work in the Southern Colonies.* Chapel Hill: University of North Carolina Press, 1938.

Stack, Carol B. *All Our Kin.* New York: Harper and Row, 1974.

Stampp, Kenneth M. *The Peculiar Institution.* New York: Alfred A. Knopf, 1956.

Stannard, David E. "Death and the Puritan Child." *American Quarterly,* vol. 26 (December 1974), pp. 456–476.

Staples, Robert. "Toward a Sociology of the Black Family." *Journal of*

Marriage and the Family, vol. 33 (February 1971), pp. 119–138.

Star, Joyce R., and Carns, Donald E. "Singles in the City." *Society,* vol. 9 (February 1972), pp. 43–49.

Stein, Peter. *Single.* Englewood Cliffs, N.J.: Prentice-Hall, 1976.

Stendler, Celia B. "Sixty Years of Child Training Practices." *Journal of Pediatrics,* vol. 36 (January 1950), pp. 122–134.

Stephens, William N. *The Family in Cross-Cultural Perspective.* New York: Holt, Rinehart and Winston, 1963.

Stetson, Dorothy M., and Wright, Gerald C., Jr. "The Effects of Laws on Divorce in American States." *Journal of Marriage and the Family,* vol. 37 (August 1975), pp. 537–547.

Stockwell, Edward G. *Population and People.* Chicago: Quadrangle, 1970.

Stone, Lawrence. "Marriage Among the English Nobility." *Comparative Studies in Society and History,* vol. 3 (November/January 1960–1961), pp. 182–206.

Streib, Gordon F., and Schneider, Clement J. *Retirement in American Society: Impact and Process.* Ithaca, N.Y.: Cornell U. Press, 1971.

Stricker, Frank. "Cookbooks and Law Books: The Hidden History of Career Women in Twentieth Century America." *Journal of Social History* vol. 10 (Fall 1976), pp. 1–19.

Sussman, Marvin B. "The Help Pattern in the Middle Class Family." *American Sociological Review,* vol. 18 (January 1953a), pp. 22–28.

———. "Parental Participation in Mate Selection and Its Effects upon Family Continuity." *Social Forces,* vol. 32 (October 1953b), pp. 76–81.

Symonds, Carol. "Pilot Study of the Peripheral Behavior of Sexual Mate Swappers." Unpublished M.A. thesis, University of California, Riverside, 1968.

Syzmanski, Al. "The Socialization of Women's Oppression." *Insurgent Sociologist,* vol. 6 (Winter 1976), pp. 31–58.

Talmon, Yonina. "Aging in Israel: A Planned Society." *American Journal of Sociology,* vol. 67 (November 1961), pp. 284–295.

Tannenbaum, Frank. *Slave and Citizen.* New York: Alfred A. Knopf, 1946.

Terman, Lewis M. *Psychological Factors in Marital Happiness.* New York: McGraw-Hill, 1938.

Thernstrom, Stephen, and Sennett, Richard, eds. *Nineteenth-Century Cities.* New Haven: Yale University Press, 1969.

Thompson, Warren S., and Whelpton, P. K. *Population Trends in the United States.* New York: Gordon and Breach, 1969.

Tietze, Christopher. "Contraceptive Practices in the Context of a Nonrestrictive Abortion Law." *Family Planning Perspectives,* vol. 7 (September/October 1975), pp. 197–202.

Tilly, Louise, et al. "Women's Work and European Fertility Patterns." *Journal of Interdisciplinary History,* vol. 6 (Winter 1976), pp. 447–476.

Tipps, Dean C. "Modernization Theory and the Comparative Study of Societies." *Comparative Studies in Society and History,* vol. 15 (1973), pp. 199–226.

Trost, Jan. "Married and Unmarried Cohabitation: The Case of Sweden, with Some Comparisons." *Journal of Marriage and the Family,* vol. 37 (August 1975), pp. 677–682.

Tryon, Rolla M. *Household Manufacturers in the United States, 1640–1860.* Chicago: University of Chicago Press, 1917.

U.S. Bureau of the Census. *Pocket Data Book USA 1973.* Washington, D.C.: Government Printing Office, 1973.

———. *Statistical Abstracts of the United States.* Washington, D.C.: Government Printing Office, 1975a.

———. *Historical Statistics of the United States.* Washington, D.C.: Government Printing Office, 1975b.

———. "The Social and Economic Status of the Black Population in the United States 1974." *Current Population Reports,* Special Studies Series P-23, no. 54. Washington, D.C.: Government Printing Office, 1975c.

———. "Social and Economic Characteristics of the Older Population 1974." *Current Population Reports,* Special Studies Series P-23, no. 57. Washington, D.C.: Government Printing Office, 1975d.

———. "A Statistical Portrait of Women in the United States." *Current Population Reports,* series P-23, no. 58. Washington, D.C.: Government Printing Office, April 1976.

U.S. Department of Health, Education, and Welfare. *Divorces: Analysis of Change in the United States.* DHEW Publication no. (HSM) 73–1900. Washington, D.C.: Government Printing Office, April 1973.

———. *Facts About Older Americans 1975.* DHEW Publication no. (OHD) 75–20006.

———. "Advance Report Final Divorce Statistics, 1974." *Monthly Vital Statistics Report,* vol. 25 (April 14, 1976).

U.S. Department of Labor. *Dictionary of Occupational Titles,* 3rd ed. Washington, D.C.: Government Printing Office, 1965.

———. *Handbook on Women Workers.* Washington, D.C.: Government Printing Office, 1975.

van de Walle, Etienne. "Marriage and Marital Fertility." *Daedalus,* vol. 97 (Spring 1968), pp. 468–501.

———. *The Female Population of France in the Nineteenth Century.* Princeton, N.J.: Princeton University Press, 1974.

Vanek, Joann. "Time Spent in Housework." *Scientific American,* vol. 231 (November 1974), pp. 116–120.

Veevers, J. E. "Voluntary Childless Wives: An Exploratory Study." In *Pronatalism,* edited by Ellen Peck and Judith Senderowitz. New York: Thomas Y. Crowell, 1974.

———. "The Moral Careers of Voluntarily Childless Wives." *Family Coordinator,* vol. 24 (October 1975), pp. 473–488.

Vincent, Clark E. "Trends in Infant Care Ideas." *Child Development,* vol. 22 (September 1951), pp. 199–209.

Vreeland, Rebecca S. "Is It True What They Say About Harvard Boys?" *Psychology Today,* vol. 5 (January 1972), pp. 65–68.

Wade, Richard C. *Slavery in the Cities: The South, 1820–1860.* New York: Oxford University Press, 1964.

Waite, Linda J., and Stolzenberg, Ross M. "Intended Childbearing and Labor Force Participation of Young Women." *American Sociological Review,* vol. 41 (April 1976), pp. 235–251.

Walker, Kathryn E. "Time Spent in Household Work by Homemakers." *Family Economics Review* (September 1969), pp. 5–6.

———. "Time Spent by Husbands in Household Work." *Family Economics Review* (June 1970), pp. 8–11.

Waller, Willard. "The Rating Dating Complex." *American Sociological*

Review, vol. 2 (October 1937), pp. 727–734.

———. *The Family.* New York: Dryden, 1938.

Walters, Ronald G. "The Erotic South: Civilization and Sexuality in American Abolitionism." *American Quarterly,* vol. 25 (May 1973), pp. 177–201.

Ware, Caroline F. *Early New England Cotton Manufacturers.* New York: Russell and Russell, 1966; first published 1931.

Warner, Sam Bass, Jr. *The Private City.* Philadelphia: University of Pennsylvania Press, 1968.

———. *The Urban Wilderness.* New York: Harper and Row, 1972.

Weinberg, Martin S., and Williams, Colin J. *Male Homosexuals.* New York: Oxford University Press, 1974.

Weiss, Michael. *Living Together: A Year in the Life of a City Commune.* New York: McGraw-Hill, 1974.

Weitzman, Lenore J. "To Love, Honor and Obey? Traditional Legal Marriage and Alternative Family Forms." *Family Coordinator,* vol. 24 (October 1975), pp. 531–548.

Wells, Robert V. *The Population of the British Colonies in America Before 1776.* Princeton, N.J.: Princeton University Press, 1975a.

———. "Family History and the Demographic Transition." *Journal of Social History,* vol. 9 (Fall 1975b), pp. 1–20.

Welter, Barbara. "The Cult of True Womanhood: 1820–1860." *American Quarterly,* vol. 18 (Summer 1966), pp. 151–174.

Westoff, Charles F. "The Modernization of U.S. Contraceptive Practice." *Family Planning Perspectives,* vol. 4 (July 1972), pp. 9–12.

———. "Coital Frequency and Contraception." *Family Planning Perspectives,* vol. 6 (Summer 1974), pp. 136–141.

———. "The Decline of Unplanned Births in the United States." *Science,* vol. 191 (January 9, 1976a), pp. 38–41.

———. "Trends in Contraceptive Practice: 1965–1973." *Family Planning Perspectives,* vol. 8 (March/April 1976b), pp. 54–57.

——— et al. *The Third Child.* Princeton, N.J.: Princeton University Press, 1963.

———, and Bumpass, Larry L. "The Revolution in Birth Control Practices of U.S. Roman Catholics." *Science,* vol. 179 (January 5, 1973), p. 41.

———, and Potvin, Raymond H. *College Women and Fertility Values.* Princeton, N.J.: Princeton University Press, 1963.

Westoff, Leslie A., and Westoff, Charles F. *From Now to Zero.* Boston: Little, Brown, 1971.

Wheaton, Robert. "Family and Kinship in Western Europe: The Problem of the Joint Family Household." *Journal of Interdisciplinary History,* vol. 4 (Spring 1975), pp. 601–628.

Whitehurst, Robert N. "The Unmalias on Campus." Paper presented at the National Council on Family Relations Meetings, Washington, D.C., 1969.

Whyte, William F. "A Slum Sex Code." *American Journal of Sociology,* vol. 49 (July 1943), pp. 24–31.

Whyte, William H., Jr. *The Organization Man.* New York: Anchor-Doubleday, 1956.

Willcox, Walter. "Divorce in the United States." *Columbia University Studies in History, Economics and Public Law,* vol. 1, no. 67 (1891).

Willie, Charles. *The Family Life of Black People.* Columbus, Ohio: Charles E. Merrill, 1970.

Willmott, Peter, and Young, Michael. *Family and Class in a London Sub-*

urb. London: Routledge and Kegan Paul, 1960.

Wilson, Sloan. *The Man in the Gray Flannel Suit.* New York: Simon and Schuster, 1955.

Winch, Robert F. *The Modern Family.* 3rd ed. New York: Holt, Rinehart and Winston, 1971.

______ et al. "Ethnicity and Extended Families in an Upper-Middle-Class Suburb." *American Sociological Review,* vol. 32 (April 1967), pp. 265–272.

______, and Greer, Scott A. "Urbanism, Ethnicity, and Extended Familism." *Journal of Marriage and the Family,* vol. 30 (February 1968), pp. 40–45.

Winick, Charles, and Kinsie, Paul M. *The Lively Commerce.* Chicago: Quadrangle, 1971.

Wirth, Louis. "Urbanism as a Way of Life." *American Journal of Sociology,* vol. 44 (July 1938), pp. 1–24.

Wishy, Bernard. *The Child and the Republic.* Philadelphia: University of Pennsylvania Press, 1968.

Wolfe, Linda. "Can Adultery Save Your Marriage?" *New York,* vol. 5 (May 3, 1972), pp. 36–39.

______. *Playing Around: Women and Extramarital Sex.* New York: William Morrow, 1975.

Wolfenstein, Martha. "Trends in Infant Care." *American Journal of Orthopsychiatry,* vol. 23 (January 1953), pp. 120–130.

Wright, James D., and Wright, Sonia R. "Social Class and Parental Values for Children: A Partial Replication and Extension of the Kohn Thesis." *American Sociological Review,* vol. 41 (June 1976), pp. 527–537.

Wrigley, E. A., ed. *An Introduction to English Historical Demography.* London: Weidenfeld and Nicolson, 1966.

______. *Population and History.* London: Weidenfeld and Nicolson, 1969.

______, ed. *Nineteenth Century Society.* Cambridge: Cambridge University Press, 1972a.

______. "Family Limitation in Pre-Industrial England." In *Popular Attitudes Toward Birth Control in Pre-Industrial France and England,* edited by Orest and Patricia Ranum, pp. 53–99. New York: Harper and Row, 1972b.

______. "The Process of Modernization and the Industrial Revolution in England." *Journal of Interdisciplinary History,* vol. 3 (Autumn 1972c), pp. 225–259.

Yablonsky, Lewis. *Synanon: The Tunnel Back.* New York: Macmillan, 1965.

Yankelovich, Daniel. *The New Morality: A Profile of American Youth in the 1970s.* New York: McGraw-Hill, 1974.

Young, Michael, and Willmott, Peter. *Family and Kinship in East London.* Baltimore: Penguin, 1962; first published 1957.

______ and ______. *The Symmetrical Family.* London: Routledge and Kegan Paul, 1973.

Zablocki, Benjamin. *The Joyful Community.* Baltimore: Penguin, 1971.

Zaretsky, Eli. *Capitalism, the Family and Personal Life.* New York: Harper and Row, 1976.

Zelditch, Morris. "Role Differentiation in the Nuclear Family: A Comparative Study." In *Family, Socialization and Interaction Process,* edited by Talcott Parsons and Robert F. Bales. Glencoe, Ill.: Free Press, 1955.

Zelnik, Melvin, and Kantner, John F. "Sexual and Contraceptive Experience of Young Unmarried Women in the United States, 1976 and 1971." *Family Planning Perspectives,* vol. 9 (March/April 1977), pp. 55–73.

Zetterberg, Hans L. *On Theory and Verification in Sociology.* Rev. ed. Totowa, N.J.: Bedminster Press, 1963.

Zuckerman, Michael. *Peaceable Kingdoms.* New York: Alfred A. Knopf, 1970.

———. "Dr. Spock: The Confidence Man." In *The Family in History,* edited by Charles Rosenberg, pp. 179–208. Philadelphia: University of Pennsylvania Press, 1975.

INDEX

About the Author

Michael Gordon is professor of sociology at the University of Connecticut, where he received his Ph.D. in 1967. He previously taught at Temple University and was a Fulbright-Hays Senior Lecturer at University College in Cork, Ireland. Dr. Gordon has also been a National Endowment for the Humanities fellow and is currently an editor of the *Journal of Marriage and the Family* and of *Sociological Analysis.* His publications include many articles in scholarly journals, a monograph, and three edited volumes. He lives in Storrs, Connecticut with his wife and two daughters.